LOCARNO DIPLOMACY
GERMANY AND THE WEST
1925-1929

LOCARNO DIPLOMACY

Germany and the West

1925-1929

By Jon Jacobson

Princeton University Press

Princeton, New Jersey

1972

This book has been composed in

Linotype Baskerville

Printed in the United States of America

by Princeton University Press

For My Parents

Preface

It has been thirty years since a German journalist, Edgar Stern-Rubarth, memorialized the diplomacy of the Locarno period in his *Three Men Tried*. Since then, a mass of British, German, and American state documents has been opened to research along with the letters, diaries, and papers of many European and American politicians, bankers, and public servants. This evidence, much of it available only recently, as well as the passage of time, has rendered possible an international history of this period. And in this book I explore the personalities, the politics, and the diplomacy of the Locarno era and offer a historical interpretation and synthesis of it.

The available sources for this period have been used only to treat a handful of isolated topics, and in the absence of a full range of monographs the present study rests heavily on primary materials, most of them not yet printed. For assistance in finding and using these unpublished records I am grateful to the staffs of the National Archives, the Library of Congress, the Baker Library at Harvard, the Federal Archives of Coblenz, the Foreign Ministry Archives at Bonn, the Bavarian State Archives at Munich, the British Museum, the Public Record Office, the Scottish Record Office, the Beaverbrook Library, the Library of the University of Birmingham, the Bodleian Library, the British Library of Political and Economic Science, and the Libraries of the University of California at Berkeley and Irvine.

I wish to thank the following persons for special permission to quote from unpublished sources: the Librarian of the University of Birmingham and the Chamberlain Trustees for the Austen Chamberlain papers, The British Library of Political and Economic Science for the Hugh Dalton papers, Dana N. Dawes for the Charles Dawes letters, Lord Lothian for the Philip Kerr papers, John M. Meyer, Jr. for the Thomas Lamont papers, The Beaverbrook Foundation for the Lloyd George papers, Malcolm MacDonald for Ramsay MacDonald's letters, Harold MacMillan for his letters, Arnold Toynbee for the Gilbert Murray papers, Sir Anthony Rumbold and Martin Gilbert for the Horace Rumbold papers, Lord Salisbury for the papers of the Fourth Marquess, Richard Young for the Owen Young papers, and the Controller of Her Majesty's Stationery Office for the records of the

British cabinet and Foreign Office and for the correspondence of various Ministers of the Crown and British public servants.

Various scholars generously aided me in locating unpublished sources and by discussing my work with me. They include D. C. Watt and John Barnes of the London School of Economics, Cameron Hazelhurst of Nuffield College, Martin Gilbert of Merton College, and Robert Rhodes James of the University of Sussex.

My colleagues at the University of California at Irvine—Arthur Marder, Henry Cord Meyer, Keith Nelson, and John Diggins— read all or part of the manuscript and offered helpful suggestions. So did Gerald D. Feldman of the University of California at Berkeley, Henry A. Turner, Jr. of Yale, Robert O. Paxton of Columbia, Gaines Post, Jr. of the University of Texas, David Kieft of the University of Minnesota, James Jordan of California State College at Fullerton, and James Hitchman of Western Washington State College. Raymond J. Sontag of the University of California at Berkeley has been my teacher, adviser, and friend for almost fifteen years. My personal and intellectual debt to him is beyond brief description.

John Walker and Ann Bethel gave me research assistance. The final manuscript was typed by Lisa Munsat and Cathy Smith. Earlier drafts were done by my wife, Sybil, who along with my daughters Kirsten and Margreta, has brought me great joy during the time this project was being completed.

Corona del Mar, California
November 1970

Contents

CONTENTS

xi

PART ONE

THE MAKING OF LOCARNO
1925

ABBREVIATIONS AND DESIGNATIONS

ADAP: *Akten zur deutschen auswärtigen Politik*

DBFP: *Documents on British Foreign Policy*

DDB: *Documents diplomatiques belges*

FRUS: *Papers Relating to the Foreign Relations of the United States*

AC 42/519: Papers of Austen Chamberlain

Cab 2/115: Minutes of the (British) Committee of Imperial Defense

Cab 23/25/6: Minutes of the British cabinet

FO. 371/12345/67: Records of the British Foreign Office

2241/5831/123456: Records of the German Chancellery and Foreign Ministry; the papers of Gustav Stresemann

731. 15/52: Decimal files of the United States Department of State

1. Stresemann and the Practice of German Revisionism

AUSTEN CHAMBERLAIN, the British Foreign Secretary, trembled and wept with joy, as did the French Foreign Minister, Aristide Briand. Benito Mussolini kissed Mrs. Chamberlain's hands. Bands played; members of the assembled crowd danced in the village square; even calloused newspaper reporters applauded and cheered. The next day the headlines in the *New York Times* read "France and Germany Bar War Forever," and those in the London *Times* declared "Peace at Last."[1] The day was October 16, 1925; the place was Locarno, a small lakeside resort in southeastern Switzerland; and what evoked the "orgiastic gush," as Harold Nicolson called it,[2] were the feelings of goodwill, the hopes for the future, and the enthusiasm over what had been accomplished on that day when the representatives of seven European powers initialed five agreements called the Treaties of Locarno.

The provisions of the treaties were less thrilling than the initialing ceremony. Four of them were arbitration conventions between Germany and her neighbors—France, Belgium, Poland, and Czechoslovakia. The other, the Treaty of Mutual Guarantee, was a multilateral regional security agreement. It was, first of all, a reciprocal treaty of nonaggression by which the powers situated on the Rhine—Germany, France, and Belgium—promised not to attack, invade, or resort to war against each other. Secondly, it was a treaty of mutual guarantee and assistance by which the nations of Western Europe—England, France, Germany, Belgium, and Italy—promised to observe the demilitarization of the Rhineland, to defend the existing borders between Germany and France and Germany and Belgium, and to render military assistance to any signatory who was the victim of a violation of these two promises.[3] Although they did not bring perpetual peace to

[1] 18 October 1925, Chamberlain to Tyrrell, AC 52/769; Charles Petrie, *The Life and Letters of the Rt. Hon. Sir Austen Chamberlain*, London, 1939-40, II, 287-90; Emery Kelen, *Peace in Their Time; Men Who Led Us in and Out of War, 1914-1945*, New York, 1963, p. 161; Edgar Stern-Rubarth, *Three Men Tried . . . Austen Chamberlain, Stresemann, Briand and their Fight for a New Europe; a Personal Memoir*, London, 1939, pp. 98-99; Geneviève Tabouis, *They Called Me Cassandra*, New York, 1942, p. 64.

[2] Harold Nicolson, *King George the Fifth; His Life and Reign*, London, 1952, p. 209.

[3] A recent printing of the text of the treaties signed at Locarno: William J. Newman, *The Balance of Power in the Interwar Years, 1919-1939*, New York, 1968, pp. 205-27.

Europe, these agreements—particularly the Treaty of Mutual Guarantee, sometimes called the Rhineland Pact—are of major historical significance. "Locarno," one historian has written, "was the turning point of the years between the wars. Its signature ended the first world war; its repudiation eleven years later marked the prelude to the second."[4]

Locarno was not merely one of many interwar conferences, and the following series of negotiated settlements dealing with German League membership, disarmament, reparation, and military occupation was not a simple honeymoon interlude. The Locarno era—the year preceding the signature of the Rhineland Pact and the four years that followed—was the hinge on which the relations between Germany and the West turned between the wars. It ended the period of confrontation following one war, and during the early thirties it gave way to an age in which each of the settlements of the Locarno era collapsed or was repudiated, placing Europe on the threshold of another war. Moreover, it was an era in which the extent and the limits of great power consensus were tested by a variety of conflicts. From the very beginning, consensus was tried by the conflicting considerations which brought the makers of German, British, and French foreign policy to Locarno, and thereafter it was strained by the divergent views these men held of what they accomplished at Locarno and what their achievement meant for the future.

The deliberations and negotiations which led to Locarno began nine months earlier, in January 1925. At that time Gustav Stresemann, the German Foreign Minister, in consultation with a few senior Foreign Ministry officials, decided to propose a series of nonaggression, arbitration, and military agreements between "those powers interested in the Rhine," a proposal which was delivered in London on January 20 and in Paris on February 9.[5] Stresemann's proposition amounted to an acceptance of the 1919 peace settlement in the West, a renunciation of recourse to war with France (the defender of Versailles), and an agreement to submit to arbitration disputes with Poland, the possessor of Ger-

[4] A.J.P. Taylor, *The Origins of the Second World War*, New York, 1961, p. 57.
[5] The text of the memoranda sent to London and Paris: Edgar (Lord) D'Abernon, *An Ambassador of Peace; Pages from the Diary of Viscount D'Abernon*, London, 1929-30, III, 276-79.

man lands and peoples in the East. Stresemann made his proposal both in pursuit of the objectives which had controlled his foreign policy since 1923 and to meet the new situation which faced him in January 1925.

Since coming to office in August 1923, Stresemann had devoted himself to defending the unity of the Bismarckian Reich from possible disintegration under the impact of the Ruhr invasion and Rhenish separatism. In 1924 he had accepted the Dawes plan in order to prompt the withdrawal of the French from the Ruhr and to promote American investment in Germany. Then, after he proposed the Rhineland Pact, he justified his action as a continuation of both policies. During the economic recession which began in mid-1925, deepened the following autumn, and lasted until the next spring, he spoke of Germany's need for additional American loans, which would be granted, he stated, only if the security pact were concluded.[6] On other occasions Stresemann played on the political trauma suffered by the German people two years earlier when a disarmed, demilitarized, and half-sovereign Reich had been unable to prevent the French from invading the Ruhr and supporting Rhenish separatists and autonomists. He defended the Rhineland Pact as a measure by which the French renounced a policy of invasion and military sanctions, admitted that the lands of the Rhine were a German possession, and recognized the territorial integrity and unity of the Reich—all guaranteed by Great Britain, of course.[7] In so doing, Stresemann perhaps exaggerated both French intentions as of 1925 and the scope of the opportunity open to Paris to continue an aggressive Rhine-Ruhr policy. But his statements carried a propaganda advantage: within Germany, approval of the Rhineland Pact would appear to be a dire

[6] Stresemann's objectives in 1923-24: Jacques Bariéty, "Der Versuch einer europäischen Befriedung; von Locarno bis Thoiry," in Helmut Rössler and Erwin Hölzle (eds.), *Locarno und die Weltpolitik, 1924-1932*, Göttingen, 1969, pp. 34-40. Stresemann on loans and security: 15 July 1925, Cabinet Protocol, 1835/3543/765348-49; Gustav Stresemann, *Vermächtnis; der Nachlass in Drei Bänden*, Berlin, 1932-33, II, 149-50, 151, 154, 218. President Coolidge told the British ambassador that new American loans would depend on the conclusion of the pact, and Chamberlain disseminated the information in Europe: 27 June 1925, Chamberlain to Crewe, AC 52/221; 7 July 1925, Chamberlain to Crewe, AC 52/224.

[7] Stresemann, *Vermächtnis*, II, 68-69, 111-12, 159, 172; ADAP, B, I-1, p. 748; Henry A. Turner, Jr. (ed.), "Eine Rede Stresemanns über seine Locarnopolitik," *Vierteljahreshefte für Zeitgeschichte*, 19 (1967), pp. 417-18, 425-26, 428.

military necessity, and abroad Stresemann's policy would seem a measure of defense against invasion and dismemberment.

Within Foreign Ministry circles the Rhineland Pact was viewed not simply as a defense measure, but as a means of achieving the chief objectives of German foreign policy in 1925. As we shall see, Stresemann aimed at the prompt evacuation of Allied troops from Cologne and the Rhur, and ultimately, at freedom from all foreign occupation and the preservation of Germany from the designs of the French. He wanted a compromise settlement of the problem of German disarmament and, ultimately, the negotiated rather than the enforced application of the Treaty of Versailles. He desired to protect Germany from international institutions of supervision and inspection. The Inter-Allied Military Control Commission (IMCC) was to be withdrawn, and the permanent international commissions, which were being promoted by Paris to govern the disarmament of Germany and the demilitarization of the Rhineland, were not to be established.[8] The Rhineland Pact was proposed, as a top Foreign Ministry official privately stated three months later, with the expectation that the British would lead the French to accept these three objectives.[9] The actual proposal of the pact was prompted, according to available evidence, by two situations which became acute in December 1924: the nonevacuation of Cologne and rumors of an impending Anglo-French military alliance.[10]

[8] Michael Salewski, *Entwaffnung und Militärkontrolle in Deutschland, 1919-1927*, Munich, 1966, pp. 268-70; F. G. Stambrook, "'Das Kind'—Lord D'Abernon and the Origins of the Locarno Pact," *Central European History*, 1 (1968), pp. 251-52. For a discussion of the international commissions, see below, pp. 91-97.

[9] Jürgen Spenz, *Die diplomatische Vorgeschichte des Beitritts Deutschlands zum Völkerbund, 1924-1926; ein Beitrag zur Aussenpolitik der Weimarer Republic*, Göttingen, 1966, pp. 72-74.

[10] Although the records of the German Foreign Ministry have been available for a decade, they have as yet been used to investigate only scattered topics relating to German relations with the Western powers during 1924-25. See, Robert Gottwald, *Die Deutsch-Amerikanischen Beziehungen in der Ära Stresemann*, Berlin, 1965, pp. 12-63; Salewski, *Entwaffnung und Militärkontrolle*, pp. 240-325; Spenz, *Beitritts Deutschlands zum Völkerbund*, pp. 13-121; Stambrook, "'Das Kind,'" pp. 249-52. Other useful accounts of German Locarno policy based on the published or unpublished Stresemann papers are Henry L. Bretton, *Stresemann and the Revision of Versailles*, Stanford, 1963, p. 90; Gordon A. Craig, *From Bismarck to Adenauer; Aspects of German*

In the years following the First World War, Germany was repeatedly penalized for not complying with the Treaty of Versailles, frequently by the application of military sanctions. In 1920 French troops had invaded Frankfort a. M. and the surrounding area; in 1921 they had occupied three cities in the Ruhr—Düsseldorf, Duisburg, and Ruhrort; in 1923 French and Belgian troops had taken over the rest of the Ruhr district.[11] In December 1924 penalty was levied once again, this time by continuing the military occupation of German territory beyond the scheduled date for evacuation. Under the terms of the Treaty of Versailles, the German Rhineland was occupied by Allied troops as a way of assuring compliance with the provisions of the treaty. The area of occupation had been divided into three zones, centered on Cologne, Coblenz, and Mainz; one zone was to be evacuated every five years (1925, 1930, and 1935) provided the German government faithfully carried out its treaty obligations. On September 8, 1924, four months prior to the scheduled evacuation of the first zone (Cologne and the surrounding area), the IMCC began a general inspection of German factories and military installations in order to determine whether Germany had complied with the disarmament provisions of Versailles. By mid-December the IMCC had largely completed its efforts and submitted an interim report stating that the treaty provisions had not been fulfilled. On December 27 the Conference of Ambassadors, the Allied institution responsible for overseeing the application of the treaty, decided that the evacuation of Allied troops from Cologne would not begin on January 10 as scheduled.[12] In this manner the French, supported by the English, the Belgians, and the Italians,

---

Statecraft, New York, 1958, 1965, pp. 51-61; Erich Eyck, *A History of the Weimar Republic*, Cambridge, Mass., 1962-63, II, Chap. 1; Hans W. Gatzke, *Stresemann and the Rearmament of Germany*, Baltimore, 1950, Chaps. 2, 6; George A. Grün, "Locarno; Idea and Reality," *International Affairs*, 31 (1955), pp. 482-84; Newman, *Balance of Power*, pp. 78-88; Harold Schinkel, *Entstehung und Zerfall der Regierung Luther*, Berlin, 1959, pp. 143-45; Annelise Thimme, *Gustav Stresemann; eine politische Biographie zur Geschichte der Weimarer Republic*, Hannover, 1957, pp. 74-89, and Thimme, "Gustav Stresemann; Legende und Wirklichkeit," *Historische Zeitschrift*, 181 (1956), pp. 314-23.

[11] French military sanctions and Stresemann's reaction to them: Bretton, *Stresemann and the Revision of Versailles*, pp. 54-71; Royal J. Schmidt, *Versailles and the Ruhr; Seedbed of World War II*, The Hague, 1968, Chaps. 2, 3, 7.

[12] Salewski, *Entwaffnung und Militärkontrolle*, pp. 271-81, 285.

made clear their intention to enforce the Versailles Treaty by continued occupation.

The decision of the Conference of Ambassadors, officially communicated to the German government on January 5, 1925, had been forecast by earlier events. In August 1924 Edouard Herriot and Ramsay MacDonald, the French and British Prime Ministers, had agreed that the evacuation of Cologne would depend on the outcome of the general inspection conducted by the IMCC, and Stresemann was informed of this soon thereafter. Stresemann and Wilhelm Marx, the German Chancellor, asked the Reichswehr to cooperate with the IMCC for the sake of Cologne. They met with no success, and by early December the German embassies in Paris and London were warning the Wilhelmstrasse that Cologne would not be evacuated on schedule. In the middle of the month, Berlin tested Allied willingness to withdraw in spite of the reported lapses in disarmament. The reports which came back (December 20-24) indicated that the French would make no such high-policy compromise, that they would demand consideration of the details of German disarmament, and that the British and Italians would join them in a declaration of German default and in a refusal to evacuate.[13] Stresemann, who regarded "the sovereignty of Germany on German soil" as the first objective of German policy,[14] found progress toward his goal blocked by Herriot's unwillingness to compromise French military security.

In 1925 French security against a German attack rested on two bases, the disarmament of Germany and the occupation of the Rhineland, both of which prevented the Reichswehr from threatening France. In Paris these two deterrents were viewed as being all the more important in the absence of a third—a defensive military alliance signed by Great Britain. The question facing the Herriot government in late 1924 was whether they should begin to dismantle the barrier of occupation at a time when German disarmament was not complete and without a guarantee of military assistance from Britain. A decision to do so would have caused the government severe political difficulties, and on January 28 Herriot announced to the Chamber of Deputies what had long been suspected throughout Europe—that French insistence

[13] *Ibid.*, pp. 260-68, 281-85, 289.
[14] Stresemann, *Vermächtnis*, II, 445.

on the continued occupation of Cologne was motivated not only by a policy of strict treaty enforcement, but also by the essential security needs of France.[15]

Although Stresemann regarded French concern over military security as irrational, he was willing to give Paris written assurances against "the nightmare of a future German attack," as he called it.[16] He did so to prompt the evacuation of Cologne and the negotiation of a compromise disarmament settlement. Caught between the Reichswehr, which would not cooperate with the IMCC in the disarmament of Germany, and the Allies, who would not evacuate until it did so, Stresemann saw one avenue of escape—a compromise settlement providing for Allied evacuation in exchange for a German promise to correct the most important disarmament violations. To promote this compromise, and to break the link between occupation and treaty enforcement, Stresemann proposed an alternative form of military security—a pact of nonaggression and a treaty of guarantee.[17] Hopefully, Herriot's *Cartel de Gauches* government would be led to evacuate Cologne and so begin the withdrawal of foreign troops from Germany. Then future French governments would be less tempted than those of the immediate past to extend or continue military occupation either as a means of treaty enforcement or as a barrier against German attack. The first step toward Stresemann's objective—the sovereignty of Germany on German soil—would be taken.

The second factor in the January 1925 situation prompting

[15] Edouard Bonnefous, *Histoire politique de la troisième république*, Paris, 1956-62, IV, 70-71; Michel Soulié, *La vie politique d'Edouard Herriot*, Paris, 1962, pp. 207-208.

[16] Stresemann, *Vermächtnis*, II, 67-68.

[17] Viscount D'Abernon, the British ambassador to Berlin, had suggested such a compromise in early December. The Allied governments would select only the essential disarmament violations and the Germans would agree to remove them. Then both Cologne and the Ruhr, which was scheduled for evacuation in August 1925, would be evacuated in May. Thus, Cologne would be freed four months later than scheduled and the Ruhr three months earlier: Salewski, *Entwaffnung und Militärkontrolle*, p. 282. Also Stresemann, *Vermächtnis*, II, 35-36; 28 June 1928, Seeds to Chamberlain, FO. 371/12916/87; Stambrook, " 'Das Kind,' " n. 41; Schmidt, *Versailles and the Ruhr*, pp. 228-29. The purpose of the Rhineland Pact, the German ambassador later admitted to Chamberlain, was to facilitate the evacuation of Cologne and the solution of the disarmament question: 19 March 1925, Chamberlain to D'Abernon, AC 50/54. Also Eyck, *Weimar Republic*, II, 4.

Stresemann to action was the prospect that French security needs would be met in a manner unfavorable to Germany—by an Anglo-French military alliance. Such a bilateral alliance would give London and Paris both the incentive and the opportunity to cooperate on a wide variety of world problems and to collaborate behind Germany's back in the application of Versailles and in other matters of interest to the Reich. Germany would be confronted with a hostile coalition in the West, and Stresemann would be forced to choose between diplomatic isolation or greater dependence on the Soviet Union.[18] Rumors that Austen Chamberlain intended to conclude an alliance with France began to reach the Wilhelmstrasse as early as December 10, 1924, and on December 29, Lord D'Abernon, the British ambassador, warned Carl von Schubert, State Secretary of the German Foreign Ministry, that the French were pressing an alliance on Chamberlain, and he suggested that the Germans intervene with a Franco-German nonaggression pact.[19] D'Abernon's suggestion came at a crucial time: on the same day the German cabinet was meeting to discuss Berlin's response to the Allied decision not to evacuate Cologne, and rumors of an entente, based on British support for French Rhineland policy in exchange for French support of British colonial policy, were being reported to the Wilhelmstrasse.[20] Within two weeks the Germans were ready to propose the Rhineland Pact, and thereafter Stresemann repeatedly stated that the prevention of an Anglo-French alliance was one of his chief objectives in proposing a security pact of his own.[21] He could well regard a Rhineland Pact as the least objectionable way of giving France security. Certainly it was preferable to a military alliance between France and England, the prolonged occupation of Cologne, and the strict enforcement of the disarmament provisions of the Treaty of Versailles—a set of eventualities which confronted his foreign policy with the possibility of a serious setback.

As seen from Berlin, the events of December 1924—the non-evacuation of Cologne and the rumors of an impending Anglo-

[18] Craig, *Bismarck to Adenauer*, p. 55.

[19] Stambrook, " 'Das Kind,' " pp. 237, 247, 250.

[20] Salewski, *Entwaffnung und Militärkontrolle*, p. 286. Stresemann took the rumors seriously: Stresemann, *Vermächtnis*, II, 13; Thimme, *Gustav Stresemann*, pp. 80-81.

[21] Stresemann, *Vermächtnis*, II, 66, 112, 261; Stambrook, " 'Das Kind,' " pp. 250-51.

French alliance—appeared to indicate an abrupt change in the course of German relations with the West and to forecast a reverse for Germany. On September 26, 1923, six weeks after Stresemann came to office and took over the direction of German policy, he had ended passive resistance to the French seizure of the Ruhr. Next, at the London conference in August 1924, he had agreed to fulfill a reparation payment plan drawn up by Allied and American financial experts, and in return Herriot promised to evacuate the Ruhr by August 15, 1925. Then came the December setbacks. After negotiating a reparation settlement with the Germans, the Allies were apparently reverting to a policy of enforcement, sanctions, and imposed settlements. From the non-evacuation of Cologne it appeared that they were about to settle the disarmament problem without considering German interests; the proposed Anglo-French alliance indicated that the security question was to be resolved without consulting Berlin either. "The policy of the London conference," Stresemann told the cabinet on January 6, "carried with it not only the idea of an economic and financial settlement, but a settlement of the whole world-political situation. The nonevacuation of Cologne puts the continuation of this policy in the greatest danger."[22]

All this boded ill for German foreign policy. December's reversals would make it difficult for Stresemann to represent his policy to the German Reichstag as one which brought direct benefits and led to political recovery. In December the German ambassadors to London and Paris were instructed to argue that an Allied refusal to negotiate a Cologne settlement would have an extremely adverse impact on the German public: the majority of the German people would assume that the French had not given up their designs on the Rhineland, that the British were unwilling to oppose them, and that the Allies were determined to keep Germany in chains in spite of German desire for understanding. They would conclude that Stresemann's efforts in behalf of the London policy had been wasted, and that the policy itself was a failure.[23] Stresemann's policy and position as leader of German foreign policy were at a crisis point. If his policy was to have credence, and if the heavy investment he had made in it since 1923 was to be protected, the Allies must begin to withdraw from

[22] 6 January 1925, Cabinet Protocol, 1832/3543/762966.
[23] Salewski, *Entwaffnung und Militärkontrolle*, p. 283.

11

Germany, and Germany must be included in the discussions of security and disarmament. To this end he first threatened the Allies: "If the question of evacuation was not made a matter for negotiations and compromise," he told the press on December 30 "it would mean the complete bankrupty of the policy on which the execution of the Dawes plan was based."[24] Then, in January, he sent a copy of his Rhineland Pact to London.

2. *England Between Victor and Vanquished*

Stresemann communicated his proposal to London through Lord D'Abernon, the British ambassador to Berlin, who, as he later said, had a "considerable share in the inception of the proposals."[25] Since 1923 D'Abernon had urged various schemes for what amounted to Franco-German nonaggression pacts upon the Wilhelmstrasse and commended such agreements to London. By December 1924 he had settled on a multilateral nonaggression pact between Germany, France, Britain, and Italy of the type first proposed by German Chancellor Wilhelm Cuno in 1922. D'Abernon was leery of British involvement in European alliances, and none of his schemes featured any special British commitment to the defense of France, Germany, or the demilitarized zone. Most of all he was "violently opposed," as he put it, to the Anglo-French military alliance favored by Chamberlain. To prevent the conclusion of such an agreement and to promote the evacuation of Cologne, he visited Schubert on December 29, and without authorization from London, he suggested that the Wilhelmstrasse propose a multilateral nonaggression pact.[26] D'Abernon's advice was based on two mistaken assumptions—that the rest of the British government would follow Chamberlain into a French alliance and that Paris would accept a pact which offered no formal British guarantee. But his advice came at the time of the nonevacuation of Cologne and in the midst of rumors of an Anglo-French alliance, and Stresemann mistakenly believed that D'Abernon was speaking with the authorization of his government. Therefore, his

[24] London *Times*, 31 December 1924; Salewski, *Entwaffnung und Militär-kontrolle*, p. 287.

[25] 22 October 1925, D'Abernon to Chamberlain, AC 52/301.

[26] Stambrook, " 'Das Kind,' " pp. 240-48. Chamberlain subsequently suspected that Stresemann's proposal had originated with D'Abernon, but he was not certain of this at the time the pact was being negotiated: 4 November 1925, Chamberlain to D'Abernon, D'Abernon papers 48929.

proposal was welcomed and led to the more elaborate German proposal of three weeks later.

By January 14 Stresemann and Schubert had decided to subordinate D'Abernon's suggestion for a multilateral nonaggression pact to a scheme prepared by Friedrich Gaus, the legal expert at the Wilhelmstrasse—an international guarantee of Rhineland demilitarization and the *status quo* in Western Europe. At the same time, it was decided to inform London of the scheme before notifying Paris and to have D'Abernon communicate it to Chamberlain unofficially rather than having the German ambassador in London make an official démarche. This was suitable to D'Abernon, who was most interested in deflecting his own Foreign Secretary's policy of alliance with France, and to the Germans who feared that leaks to the Paris press would result in quick rejection of the proposal. On January 19 Hans Luther, the new German Chancellor, gave assent to the proposal—the rest of the German cabinet was not informed until later. The next day Schubert gave D'Abernon the text of the German proposal for a Rhineland Pact, and D'Abernon dispatched it to London.[27]

Stresemann's proposal aroused Chamberlain's suspicion. He suspected that Stresemann intended to make the conclusion of a Rhineland Pact dependent upon the complete evacuation of the entire Rhineland. And he concluded that behind Stresemann's request to keep the proposal from the French lay an attempt to initiate secret Anglo-German negotiations, to divide the British from the French, and to prevent an Anglo-French alliance. The proposal, he wrote a month later, was "an endeavor to entrap me into conversations unknown to our Allies."[28] So cool was the For-

[27] Stambrook, " 'Das Kind,' " pp. 252-59.

[28] 3 February 1925, Chamberlain to D'Abernon, AC 52/256 (original in D'Abernon papers 48928); 3 March 1925, Chamberlain to R. Graham, AC 50/51. The Chamberlain papers contain copies of his correspondence with D'Abernon, with other British diplomats, and with other members of the British policy-making elite in and out of the government. The D'Abernon papers contain copies of his correspondence with Chamberlain and with other British ambassadors, particularly G. Grahame in Brussels. Petrie, *Chamberlain*, II, 245-94, reproduces excerpts from a few of the many items found in the Chamberlain papers. In his *An Ambassador of Peace*, D'Abernon has published the text of many of his letters to Chamberlain and has paraphrased many of Chamberlain's letters to him. These items are, however, reproduced in such a way as not to reveal what has been printed verbatim, what has been paraphrased, and who authored and received each. These two works are the best printed sources on British reaction to Stresemann's

eign Office toward the German initiative that Eyre Crowe, the Permanent Under-secretary, first tried to postpone the official delivery of the proposal in London, and when Chamberlain did see the German ambassador, Friedrich Sthamer, on January 30, he all but rejected it. Concerned about British relations with France, Chamberlain indicated to Sthamer that Anglo-German negotiations "behind the back of France" as he put it, would endanger French confidence in England, and he refused to "consent to be put by Germany under any obligations of secrecy toward our Allies." The French would not be receptive to a German proposal "until the attitude of Great Britain towards French security is more clearly defined." Thereby, Chamberlain indicated that no German interference would be welcomed while Britain and France were arranging for the security of Western Europe. Although he did express mild appreciation for Stresemann's regard for French security, he told Sthamer that the German overtures were premature and inopportune, and he even declined to let Sthamer report to Berlin that he favored the German proposal in principle.[29] Chamberlain was initially very cautious about Stresemann's proposal, and it was only after prolonged debate in London that he and the rest of the government came to accept it.

The debate on security within the Baldwin government began on December 4, 1924, when the Committee of Imperial Defense (CID) met to consider, and to discard, the Geneva Protocol. The proposed protocol was rejected unanimously from the onset; the only real issue in the debate, which continued in the CID until February 19, was the form in which British rejection was to be

initiative and on the policy which led to Locarno. Chamberlain's own account: Austen Chamberlain, *Down the Years*, London, 1935. Secondary accounts of Chamberlain's Locarno policy can be found in Martin Gilbert, *The Roots of Appeasement*, London, 1966, pp. 111-16; Douglas Johnson, "Austen Chamberlain and the Locarno Agreements," *University of Birmingham Historical Journal*, 8 (1961), pp. 62-81; Newman, *Balance of Power*, pp. 92-97; F. S. Northedge, *The Troubled Giant; Britain among the Great Powers, 1916-39*, New York, 1967, pp. 248-72; Stambrook, " 'Das Kind,' " pp. 259-63; Arnold Wolfers, *Britain and France between Two Wars; Conflicting Strategies of Peace since Versailles*, New York, 1940, Chaps. 14-16.

[29] 30 January 1925, Chamberlain to D'Abernon, AC 50/31; 3 February 1925, Chamberlain to D'Abernon, AC 52/256 (original in D'Abernon papers 48928); 29 September 1930, Selby to Chamberlain, AC 39/2/31; 1 October 1930, Chamberlain to D'Abernon, AC 39/2/38; Petrie, *Chamberlain*, p. 256; Stresemann, *Vermächtnis*, II, 112-13.

made public at the impending meeting of the League Council in March 1925. All agreed that a simple statement of rejection would expose the government to the charge that Britain was an obstacle to the resolution of the security problem and to the pacification of Europe, but they disagreed among themselves as to what alternative constructive suggestion should be proposed. On December 16 the task of devising a substitute acceptable to Britain was assigned to a subcommittee, chaired by Maurice Hankey, Secretary to the cabinet and the CID.[30]

The task was complex, and it was February 13 before the Hankey subcommittee reported—suggesting that the Covenant of the League of Nations be amended and that the amendments be put in the form of a new protocol. At the same meeting Arthur Balfour submitted a paper putting forth Britain's reasons for rejecting the protocol and stating that Britain would consider "special agreements to meet special needs." When this paper was subsequently read by Chamberlain at Geneva on March 12, 1925, the mention of "special agreements" seemed to indicate British support for Stresemann's proposal, but this is not what Balfour had in mind in February. He strongly opposed any British commitment to France: "I am so cross with the French," he said. "I think their obsession [with security] is so intolerably foolish. . . . They are so dreadfully afraid of being swallowed up by the tiger, but they spend all their time poking it."[31] The most Balfour was willing to offer Paris was an assurance that the British government would consult with France about a security arrangement if and when Germany actually did pose a military threat. In his lack of sympathy for French security demands and his rejection of binding commitments, he was supported by most of the rest of the CID, led by Lords Curzon and Birkenhead.

Neither the Geneva Protocol, the substitute protocol suggested by the Hankey subcommittee, nor Balfour's vague allusion to future consultations were formulas acceptable to Austen Chamberlain, the Foreign Secretary. He favored something much more definite, binding, and specific—a Tripartite military alliance in

[30] The Geneva Protocol: Northedge, *Troubled Giant*, pp. 239-47; F. P. Walters, *A History of the League of Nations*, New York, 1952, pp. 268-76, 283-85. Lord Curzon, the chairman of the CID, summarized the basic reasons for rejection: Cab 2/4/190 (4 December 1924); Cab 2/4/192 (16 December 1924).

[31] Cab 2/4/195 (13 February 1925).

which Britain would guarantee the security of France and Belgium against German aggression. Chamberlain was, in his own words, "the most pro-French member of the government."[32] Since before World War I, he had zealously supported various Anglo-French alliance proposals; more recently, in July 1924, he had told the House of Commons that "the cardinal object" of British foreign policy should be the "maintenance of the entente with France."[33] In December, one month after taking office, Chamberlain began to implement this policy. To end long-standing colonial rivalries, Herriot and Chamberlain each instructed their ambassadors to adopt what Chamberlain termed "a new spirit of cooperation."[34] And when the French in turn pressed Chamberlain for a military alliance, he listened with sympathy.

Herriot's *Chef de Cabinet* told Walford Selby, Chamberlain's private secretary, in early December that the French would still press for a supplementary Anglo-French alliance even if the Geneva Protocol were concluded, an assertion which Herriot himself shrewdly refused to confirm or deny in a personal conversation with Chamberlain on December 5.[35] Chamberlain was anxious, as he wrote in January, to "find some means of giving a sense of security to France," and he was convinced that "a particular and specific guarantee" was the only way of "relieving French fear."[36] On December 16 he told the CID that the Geneva Protocol would not satisfy the French demand for security, and he urged consideration of an Anglo-French alliance, terming the Balfour-Curzon policy of offering no substitute for the protocol "an absolute disaster." The no-substitute policy would not, he stated, educate the British public regarding their country's obligations and responsibilities; it would not deter the Germans who, he predicted, would be ready to renew the attack by 1960 or 1970; it would not soothe the French and lead them to make the German situation tolerable; in short, it would lead to 1914 once

[32] 20 February 1925, Chamberlain to Crewe, AC 52/191.

[33] Quoted in Johnson, "Chamberlain and Locarno," p. 65.

[34] 15 January 1925, Chamberlain to Crewe, AC 52/180; Walford Selby, *Diplomatic Twilight, 1930-1940*, London, 1953, p. 151.

[35] Cab 2/4/192 (16 December 1925). Also 24 February 1925, Chamberlain to Crewe, AC 50/47; Petrie, *Chamberlain*, II, 256; Chamberlain, *Down the Years*, p. 179. Chamberlain visited Herriot in Paris on December 5 on his way to the League Council meeting in Rome, December 8-11.

[36] Quoted in Johnson, "Chamberlain and Locarno," p. 71; 16 February 1925, Chamberlain to Crewe, AC 52/189.

again. In the CID, Chamberlain's plea for a Tripartite alliance found little support and much opposition which included Winston Churchill, Leo Amery, and Samuel Hoare, as well as Curzon, Balfour, and Birkenhead.[37]

Bent on meeting French requirements, Chamberlain was initially unwilling to include Germany in the Anglo-French alliance system. Germany might enter into a similar pact at a later date, he told the CID on December 16; but the French, he said, would "never agree" to include Germany in the original document. Thus, when Stresemann's proposal came in January, Chamberlain told Sthamer it would have to await the conclusion of bilateral Anglo-French arrangements. Even after Stresemann had submitted his proposal to Paris on February 9, and Herriot told Crewe that he had no objections to including Germany in the security arrangements, Chamberlain remained reserved, hesitant, and cautious. On February 13, when he mentioned the German proposal to the CID as an indication of Stresemann's regard for French security and his willingness to renounce aggression, Curzon asked him to prepare drafts of an agreement for a four-power security pact which would include Germany along with Britain, France, and Belgium. But when asked for these drafts at the meeting of February 19, Chamberlain declined to produce them. The Foreign Office, he stated, saw no reason for Britain to offer reciprocal guarantees protecting Germany as well as France against aggression. He promised instead to circulate to the government a document written by Eyre Crowe and Harold Nicolson under his own supervision and direction—a proposal for an Anglo-French alliance.[38] Although by mid-February he was "more favorably disposed to the German suggestion" (in the words of his biographer) than he had been initially, Chamberlain held out for the Anglo-French alliance and did little to promote Stresemann's proposal in London, Paris, or Berlin. The most he had done was to write to D'Abernon and Crewe, his ambassador at Paris, a letter designed to keep the Rhineland Pact alive in the face of continued opposition in London to a Tripartite alliance: "I would consider it would be a great mistake for the

[37] Cab 2/4/92 (16 December 1925); Cab 2/4/195 (13 February 1925); Cab 2/4/196 (19 February 1925).

[38] Cab 2/4/192 (16 December 1925); Cab 2/4/195 (13 February 1925); Cab 2/4/196 (19 February 1925).

Germans to withdraw it or for the French not to consider it with all the serious and even appreciative attention it demands."[39]

Among members of the British government, the only favor shown a four-power regional pact like Stresemann's proposal was expressed by Winston Churchill, the Chancellor of the Exchequer. He strongly opposed Chamberlain's Anglo-French alliance which would, he predicted, encourage the French to continue antagonizing Germany and ultimately lead Britain into a war which would destroy both nations. On December 4, six weeks prior to the German proposal, Churchill recommended to the CID "regional agreements under the League of Nations to protect special points of danger . . . making definite tracts of country demilitarized zones which would be kept free of all troops and military works. In the first instance, such a zone might be drawn up between France and Germany and various powers might be induced to guarantee the sanctity of such a zone. Whichever of the two powers, France or Germany, was the first to violate this zone, that power would then become 'the aggressor,' and would be dealt with by the powers who were signatory to the regional agreement." Churchill did not, however, favor the immediate conclusion of such an agreement; in fact, he strongly opposed it. He wanted to wait two or three years until the French, observing the revival of German power and growing increasingly anxious for a British guarantee, were "in a much better state of mind" and the British government was "in a position . . . to procure from the French concessions to Germany of a far more sweeping character than they contemplate at the present time." At that time, he thought, German territory should be completely evacuated and Germany's eastern frontiers should be revised; then there could be a Franco-German-Belgian security agreement which Britain could join as a "guarantor" or "partner." In his espousal of a postponed regional pact, Churchill was supported by Curzon, Birkenhead, and Amery, the Colonial Secretary, who thought it would be mid-1925 before the dominions could be fully consulted; all flatly opposed a prompt British commitment.[40]

[39] 16 February 1925, Chamberlain to Crewe, AC 52/189; DDB, II, 28; Petrie, *Chamberlain*, II, 257-60.

[40] Cab 2/4/190 (4 December 1924); Cab 2/4/195 (13 February 1925); Cab 2/4/196 (19 February 1925); 23 February 1925, Churchill to Chamberlain, AC 52/155, 156; Johnson, "Chamberlain and Locarno," p. 73; Keith Middlemas and John Barnes, *Baldwin; a Biography*, London, 1969, p. 349.

Thus, the Baldwin government was clearly divided as to what, if any, alternative to propose to France and to the League at the time the Geneva Protocol was rejected. Chamberlain wanted to offer a specific and definite British guarantee to France, and to this end he circulated the Crowe-Nicolson memorandum to his colleagues. He was opposed by the rest of the government, led by conservative imperialists like Churchill, Birkenhead, Amery, Curzon, and Balfour, men who opposed any commitments on the Continent which might restrict Britain's freedom to mediate between the powers.[41] Some of them, like Balfour, opposed any commitment but were willing to allude to "special arrangements for special needs"; others, like Curzon, opposed any mention of a substitute measure, either in Paris or Geneva, until Britain had had time to consider fully various regional pacts and had clearly decided in favor of one of them; most refused to consider an Anglo-French alliance. The conflict between Chamberlain and those whom Crewe termed "the rather stiff anti-French group"[42] was resolved during meetings of the cabinet held on March 2 and 4.

At those meetings the cabinet rejected both the Geneva Protocol and Chamberlain's proposed alternative, an Anglo-French alliance. Confronted with the possibility of going to Paris and Geneva with no European security policy, Chamberlain accepted the suggestion made during the course of the meeting of March 2 (a suggestion made by Churchill, Chamberlain later recalled) to tell Herriot that a quadrilateral pact including Germany "might be of great assurance to the peace of Europe." The cabinet authorized Chamberlain to inform Herriot that he "attached the highest importance to Germany's overture." Because Britain could not participate in a security pact unless Germany were included, Stresemann's proposal "offered the best chance for giving security to France and peace to the world"; "he hoped, therefore, that the proposals would be most carefully considered." Chamberlain's authorization rigidly precluded him from committing the British government to any specific formula for participation in the Rhineland Pact. He could only promise that the govern-

[41] The conservative imperialist school of British foreign policy: D. C. Watt, *Britain Looks to Germany; British Opinion and Policy Toward Germany Since 1945*, London, 1965, p. 20.

[42] 22 February 1925, Crewe to Chamberlain, AC 52/195.

ment would "do its best to make possible such a mutual agreement" and do "its utmost to contribute to the successful
development of this hopeful episode."[43] This wording was most
consistent with the Churchill position—that the French could expect British participation in a regional pact at some future date
and under conditions not yet determined. Denied an Anglo-
French alliance, and with no power to commit the government to
any specific proposal, Chamberlain left for Paris and Geneva,
where he was to announce his government's rejection of the
Geneva Protocol.

When Chamberlain informed Herriot of the cabinet's decision
in conversations held in Paris on March 6-7, the French Premier,
who had already displayed his interest in the Rhineland Pact to
both the British and German ambassadors, was dismayed.[44] Fear-
ing that the Anglo-French entente would suffer irreparable
damage unless Herriot was encouraged and assured, Chamberlain asked Baldwin in London for authority to state that the
British government would definitely agree to a pact based on
Stresemann's proposal. Baldwin, who had not been present at the
meeting of March 4, was unwilling to do this on his own, and he
called an informal meeting of a number of cabinet members on
March 11. There Churchill, Birkenhead, and Amery, three men
who strongly opposed any British guarantee until large concessions had been won from France and until the Treaty of Versailles was revised, refused to allow Chamberlain to commit the
government. Although in sympathy with Chamberlain, Baldwin
did not override the Foreign Secretary's opponents. Hearing this,
Chamberlain telegraphed London on March 12 and threatened
to resign. Baldwin then assured Chamberlain, on March 15, of his
full confidence and personal support and promised to work to
bring Churchill, Amery, and Birkenhead around. Consequently,
on March 20, the cabinet formally accepted the idea of British
participation in the Rhineland Pact, a decision which Chamberlain then announced to Parliament on March 24.[45]

[43] Cab 23/49/12 (2 March 1925); Cab 23/49/13 (4 March 1925); Middlemas and Barnes, *Baldwin*, pp. 350-51.
[44] Cab 2/4/195 (13 February 1925); Petrie, *Chamberlain*, II, 263; Piotr
Wandycz, *France and her Eastern Allies, 1919-1925; French-Czechoslovak-
Polish Relations from the Paris Peace Conference to Locarno*, Minneapolis,
1962, p. 329.
[45] Johnson, "Chamberlain and Locarno," pp. 74-76; Middlemas and Barnes,

In this manner Chamberlain won the Baldwin government to a specific and definite pledge of French security, although not in the form he initially preferred. In the process, he triumphed over Balfour, Curzon, and Churchill, and asserted his control of British foreign policy, a control he retained without serious challenge until the government resigned in 1929. His triumph was of historic significance. It meant that Britain was to guarantee the security of France before the Treaty of Versailles was revised, before its enforcement was relaxed, and while the Rhineland was still occupied. If a British pledge to France was worth anything in terms of French support for a British-oriented German policy, Austen Chamberlain asked for no payment before delivery.

Chamberlain accepted the Rhineland Pact not because he preferred it but because it was the only form in which the cabinet would accept a British guarantee of French security. He told the cabinet, he later wrote, that the mutual pact "was not my policy, but it was a policy which I believed could be worked, and I was prepared to attempt to work it."[46] His acceptance was due in part to the efforts of D'Abernon, whose influence on the course of the negotiations between Germany and England was enormous, and who repeatedly urged the acceptance of Stresemann's proposal on the hesitant and suspicious Chamberlain. D'Abernon pointed out the dangers of an anti-German alliance with France which would, he maintained, revive the European alliance system, give assistance to the strong against the weak, lend support to France's Napoleonic aspirations to dominate Europe, and drive Germany into closer ties with the Soviet Union.[47] The latter argument appealed to Chamberlain, who was as anxious to divide Germany from Russia as Stresemann was to divide Britain from France. The time would come, Chamberlain wrote, when Russia would reemerge as a European great power, but before that happened it would be necessary to "take whatever steps we [the British] could in our power to link Germany up with our Western system

Baldwin, pp. 352-57; Petrie, *Chamberlain*, II, 264; Cab 23/49/17 (20 March 1925); Commons, debates, v. 182, c. 317-22. Also D'Abernon, *An Ambassador*, III, 156.

[46] 11 September 1930, Chamberlain to D'Abernon, AC 39/2/35.

[47] 1 and 2 March 1925, D'Abernon to Chamberlain, D'Abernon papers 48928; D'Abernon, *An Ambassador*, III, 184. Also Stambrook, " 'Das Kind,' " pp. 238-39, 245.

and prevent her from forming an anti-Western block with Russia."[48]

In addition, D'Abernon assured Chamberlain regarding Stresemann's intentions and offset Chamberlain's multiple suspicions— that Stresemann's proposal was a "dodge," a "trick" to evade full disarmament, conditioned upon the prompt evacuation of the entire Rhineland, and an attempt to split the entente, a suspicion he never abandoned.[49] Without becoming convinced of the sincerity and goodwill of the Germans, Chamberlain did accept D'Abernon's notion that the Luther-Stresemann government was both willing and able to negotiate settlements of the disarmament and security problems.[50]

Thus, by mid-February Chamberlain had come to the point of wanting to keep Stresemann's proposal alive; by the time the cabinet met in early March, he regarded the Anglo-French alliance as an arrangement in which Germany would eventually—but only eventually—be included;[51] and by mid-March he was ready to resign unless his colleagues accepted the Rhineland Pact. Chamberlain thus came to the pact slowly, hesitantly, almost inadvertently. In the following months, the months leading to the acceptance of the Locarno Treaties by Commons in November, he had ample opportunity to consider the pact and to justify his decision to accept it.[52]

Above all, Chamberlain found the Rhineland Pact acceptable because it would fill many of the functions of an Anglo-French alliance. The promise of British military assistance to France would silence French demands for security, with their constant reminder of the honor lost when the Treaty of Guarantee of 1919 was not ratified, and reduce the danger of general war by ending

[48] 24 February 1925, Chamberlain to Crewe, AC 50/47; 26 February 1925, Chamberlain to G. Grahame, AC 50/50; Johnson, "Chamberlain and Locarno," p. 79.

[49] 3 February 1925, Chamberlain to D'Abernon, AC 52/256; 7 February 1925, D'Abernon to Chamberlain, AC 52/257; Cab 2/4/195 (13 February 1925); 21 February 1925, D'Abernon to Chamberlain, AC 52/262; D'Abernon, An Ambassador, III, 137; 1 October 1930, Chamberlain to D'Abernon, AC 39/2/38.

[50] 11 February 1925, Chamberlain to Crewe, AC 52/187; 20 February 1925, Chamberlain to Crewe, AC 52/191.

[51] 11 September 1930, Chamberlain to D'Abernon, AC 39/2/35.

[52] Chamberlain presented his Locarno policy in three speeches to Commons on March 24, June 24, and November 18: Commons, debates, v. 182, c. 307-22; v. 185, c. 1555-70, 1652-53; v. 188, c. 419-31, 519-29.

any uncertainty in Berlin as to whether an attack on France would involve Germany in a war with England also. In addition, the pact would provide security for England: by pledging England to keep the German Army behind the Rhine, by going to war if necessary, it gave legal expression to the doctrine that the Rhine was Britain's strategic frontier, the place at which the Channel was to be defended.[53] All this was accomplished in a most felicitous manner; it was done without involving the British in a general treaty of security that would oblige them to submit their own disputes to arbitration and to defend every frontier in Europe. By guaranteeing the security of Western but not Eastern Europe, the Rhineland Pact, like a Tripartite alliance, specified the circumstances in which Britain would act and limited her liability to the defense of the area in which she had a vital interest. Thus, Locarno ratified what had come to be the limits of British commitments.

The Treaty of Mutual Guarantee would at the same time avoid the major disadvantageous consequence of an Anglo-French alliance—the division of Europe into two alliance systems, perpetuating the situation which existed before, during, and following the war, i.e., a continent separated into two hostile camps. The Rhineland Pact would not merely deter Germany and soothe France; it would allow the British to do both without taking sides, without alienating Berlin—leaving open the way to Anglo-German reconciliation.[54] Where an Anglo-French alliance would impose a system of security on Western Europe without German agreement, acceptance of Stresemann's proposal would place German relations with the West on a basis of consent. If Germany voluntarily accepted the *status quo* on the Rhine, as she had voluntarily accepted the Dawes plan, then the military security of the West, like the payment of reparations, would presumably endure without constant Allied enforcement. Chamberlain had no intention of participating in a continued effort "to hold Germany down in a position of abject inferiority and subjection." He saw himself as a "moderator and a reconciler," an "honest broker," turning Stresemann's proposal into something more grand, an agreement

[53] Wolfers, *Britain and France*, pp. 229-30.

[54] British attitudes toward Germany during the 1920's, especially the desire to appease and reconcile: Gilbert, *Roots of Appeasement*, Chaps. 1-12; Watt, *Britain Looks to Germany*, pp. 17-20; Schmidt, *Versailles and the Ruhr*, pp. 67-107, 236-37.

that would "close the war chapter and start Europe afresh as a society in which Germany would take her place as an equal with the great nations." Existing distinctions between victor and vanquished would be removed, and within a society of equals, Chamberlain hoped, a new generation of Germans would come to maturity disinclined to risk another war.[55]

Germany's new status of equality is seen most clearly in Britain's assumption of mutual obligations of military assistance toward both the Reich and France. But, would the British Army in fact fight with Germany against France? Chamberlain told the CID in July that in the event of another Ruhr invasion, Britain was obligated to give military assistance to Germany, and he reportedly told Stresemann that "the last [British] volunteer would be mobilized . . . if it becomes necessary to protect the German frontier on the Rhine guaranteed at Locarno."[56] Chamberlain was, above all, a man of honor who kept his word, and it is difficult to envisage him assuming obligations he did not intend to meet. Yet, it is equally difficult to see him recommending war against France in the event of a Franco-German crisis.[57] Such speculation regarding British action in the event of a French attack on Germany holds great fascination, but it is of little historical interest, for this was not the manner in which the impartiality of British Locarno policy was tested. Instead, it was tried by the way in which Chamberlain handled the more immediate tasks of British policy.

Having promised assistance to both France and Germany, the task of British policy was to maintain good relations between the two countries and prevent war between them; this would spare the British government from having to choose between mobilizing against France and reneging on their obligations to Germany.[58] There were two contradictory methods of doing this. One was to

[55] 20 January 1925, Chamberlain to Crewe, AC 50/28; 19 March 1925, Chamberlain to D'Abernon, AC 50/54; 19 May 1925, Chamberlain to Müller, AC 50/75. The advantages to Britain of being able to balance between France and Germany: Newman, *Balance of Power*, p. 193.

[56] Cab 2/4/201 (1 July 1925); Stern-Rubarth, *Three Men Tried*, p. 179; Stresemann, *Vermächtnis*, II, 218.

[57] When the legal complexities of the pending treaty were examined by the Foreign Office, Germany was still mentioned by name as the potential aggressor and violator of Rhineland demilitarization: 11 July 1925, Memorandum by Cecil Hurst, Cecil papers 51090. "France," Professor Wolfers has written, "still represented the 'friendly power,'" and Germany was still "the potential 'hostile force' which might someday cross the Rhine again": Wolfers, *Britain and France*, pp. 230-31, 260.

[58] *Ibid.*, p. 261.

treat France and Germany impartially, supporting French policy on the Continent according to the merits of each case. D'Abernon, for example, argued that only if France were uncertain of British support, only if Britain were "free to cooperate or not according to the circumstances of the moment would France find it necessary to be amenable to British influence and improve its relations with Germany."[59] Chamberlain, on the other hand, argued that fear of Germany and uncertainty regarding British support had in the past resulted not in a conciliatory France but in the aggressive, independent France of the Ruhr invasion. The way to deal with Paris, he thought, was to "remove the acute fears which distort French policy" and to restore French confidence in England.[60] He tried to do this first by means of an Anglo-French alliance, and although he was dissuaded from this course by the cabinet, he did not regard the substitution of the Locarno Treaties as changing his objectives but as altering his procedure. Chamberlain conceived of his objectives being accomplished in two stages: first, France would be given the security of knowing that Britain was a reliable and faithful ally; then, after the Allies had "secured their own safety," Germany would become again a member of the Concert of Europe.[61] He was convinced that only a secure France would be calm and manageable, and find the restoration of Germany acceptable. And to this end, Chamberlain cooperated closely with Herriot and Briand during the subsequent negotiations leading to Locarno, certain, as he told the cabinet, that once the Rhineland Pact was concluded, Briand would settle other disputes outstanding between France and Germany in a conciliatory manner.[62] "If the French believe you to be their friend," he later wrote, "you can do a great deal with them. If they think you are not their friend you can do nothing." It was "only by the maintenance of this mutual confidence and by close cooperation between our two nations that the rehabilitation of Germany and the restoration of Europe can be achieved."[63]

[59] 28 February 1925, Memorandum by D'Abernon, D'Abernon papers 48928; D'Abernon, *An Ambassador*, II, 238-39; III, 158-59.

[60] 18 March 1925, Chamberlain to D'Abernon, AC 52/264.

[61] 15 May 1925, Chamberlain to D'Abernon, AC 50/71; Johnson, "Chamberlain and Locarno," p. 74.

[62] 10 June 1925, Tyrrell to Chamberlain, AC 52/764; Johnson, "Chamberlain and Locarno," pp. 77-78.

[63] 11 September 1930, Chamberlain to D'Abernon, AC 39/2/35; Chamberlain, *Down the Years*, p. 179.

Chamberlain and his colleagues found Stresemann's proposal acceptable and recommended it to the French because the conclusion of the Rhineland Pact would reduce the danger of general war, provide security for England, and fulfill the unkept British promise to France; and it would do all this while avoiding the dangers of the Geneva Protocol and an Anglo-French alliance. The wartime division of Europe would end; Germany would be reconciled to the Western powers and kept from the clutches of the Soviet Union. The peace settlement in Western Europe would endure because it was based on consent. Most importantly, Britain would assume the role of balancer between France and Germany, and from that position her leaders would be able to keep the peace and thereby avoid giving the military assistance promised in the Rhineland Pact. There are, however, many ways to balance power, and many ways to promote peace. Chamberlain's procedure called first for the restoration of full confidence in Anglo-French relations, and then the recovery of German power. The Anglo-French entente was preserved within the Treaty of Locarno.

3. *The Security of France and Her Allies*

Insofar as the Anglo-French entente was based on full prior consultation between London and Paris, it survived Stresemann's initiative of January-February intact. Chamberlain first denied Stresemann's request for secrecy and informed Herriot of the proposal. And then when Stresemann dispatched his Rhineland Pact proposal to Paris on February 9, with a similar request that London not be informed, Herriot notified Chamberlain of the German action—causing Chamberlain to comment "What earthly object did they [the Germans] think that all this tortuous duplicity would serve?" Herriot did not, however, tell Stresemann that he had in turn divulged their secret to London, a twist which D'Abernon thought "particularly appropriate to the carnival season."[64]

In 1924 Herriot began to liquidate a policy which France had pursued intermittently since the Franco-Russian agreement of 1917, a policy aimed at providing security for France and enforc-

[64] 16 February 1925, Chamberlain to Crewe, AC 52/189; 21 February 1925, D'Abernon to Chamberlain, AC 52/262.

ing the provisions of the Treaty of Versailles through the domination of Western Germany. To this end, some political and military leaders had dreamed of dismembering the Reich, had imposed military sanctions through trans-Rhine invasions, seized mines and factories in the Ruhr, threatened to extend the occupation of the Rhineland beyond 1935, and attempted to alienate the area from Germany by supporting and protecting Rhenish separatists and autonomists.[65] Much of this policy had been rejected by the French public in the elections of May 1924, and for good measure the authors of the Dawes plan had ruled out the imposition of military sanctions unless Germany was in "flagrant" default on her reparation payments and unless all the creditors agreed to them.[66] By accepting the Dawes plan in August, and promising to withdraw French troops from the Ruhr within a year, Herriot implicitly turned from an aggressive and independent Rhine-Ruhr policy toward a policy of military security and the enforcement of the Versailles Treaty in collaboration with other states, especially Britain.[67] This policy then found expression in a number of joint Anglo-French actions during the following months—the proposal of the Geneva Protocol by Herriot and MacDonald, the consideration of a military alliance, and the decision not to evacuate Cologne. It was at this point that Stresemann intervened.

Herriot later wrote that he had never believed in Stresemann's sincerity, but he did not give that impression at the time. Two days after receiving the German initiative, he told Crewe that he believed Stresemann to be "well intentioned and honorable," as Crewe put it.[68] He made no attempt to hide his strong interest in the proposal and informed Chamberlain that he had no objection to mutual guarantees and the inclusion of Germany in the security pact.[69] During the following months, French interest in the Rhine-

[65] Jere C. King, *Foch versus Clemenceau; France and German Dismemberment, 1918-1919*, Cambridge, Mass., 1960; Pierre Renouvin, "Les buts de guerre du gouvernement français (1914-1918)," *Revue historique*, 235 (1966), pp. 9-20; Schmidt, *Versailles and the Ruhr*, pp. 20-66, 232-35.

[66] Carl Bergmann, *A History of Reparations*, Berlin, 1926, pp. 262, 269-70; W. N. Jordan, *Great Britain, France, and the German Problem, 1919-1939*, London, 1943, p. 78.

[67] Herriot specified the objectives of his policy in a letter to Ramsay MacDonald on August 11: Stambrook, "'Das Kind,'" p. 235.

[68] Edouard Herriot, *Jadis*, Paris, 1952, II, 166; Soulié, *La vie politique d'Edouard Herriot*, p. 209; Cab 2/4/195 (13 February 1925).

[69] DDB, II, 22, 27, 30; Wandycz, *France and her Eastern Allies*, pp. 328, 330; Cab 2/4/195 (13 February 1925). Without access to the records of the

land Pact was sustained in spite of the pact's limitations and disadvantages, which were several. Acceptance of the Rhineland Pact would end any prospect of gaining such nearly universal guarantees of the security of France and its Eastern allies as were provided by the Geneva Protocol. It would also end the prospect of an exclusive military alliance with Britain which would have functioned solely to France's advantage. Finally, it would guarantee German territorial integrity and national unity and preclude further unilateral attempts to enforce the provisions of the Treaty of Versailles with military sanctions or augment security through French domination of Western Germany. As Jules Laroche, Political Director of the Quai d'Orsay, said in November 1925, Locarno meant the abandonment of what he called a "policy of magnificence" whereby French governments attempted to assure the nation's security by "territorial aggrandizement in Western Europe"; it meant the acceptance of what he termed "a policy of consolidation," aimed at security through relying on treaties, a détente with Germany, and an entente with England.[70]

For France the Rhineland Pact meant the ratification of decisions taken earlier or elsewhere. The Geneva Protocol was defeated by a decision made in London and announced by Chamberlain in Geneva on March 12. The rejection of a Tripartite alliance, too, was decided in London and communicated to Herriot on March 6-7, with a recommendation that Paris accept Stresemann's proposal. Therefore, in spite of much talk about the Locarno Treaties meeting French security needs, the terms of the Rhineland Pact originated in Germany and were supported by England—the two governments to whom mutual guarantees restricted to Western Europe had special appeal. And, of course,

---

French Foreign Ministry and Council of Ministers it is little easier today than it was forty years ago to penetrate into the formative stages of French policy. If it is now possible to come to some conclusions, it is largely due to insights gained through records of private statements made by French policymakers and kept by the British, German, and Belgian foreign ministries. The best secondary accounts of French policy during the late 1920's are to be found in biographies of three important politicians: Pierre Miquel, *Poincaré*, Paris, 1961; Soulié, *Herriot*; Georges Suarez, *Briand; sa vie—son œuvre avec son journal et de nombreux documents inédits*, Paris, 1938-52, VI. The best accounts of French Locarno policy are: Grün, "Locarno," pp. 483-85; Newman, *Balance of Power*, pp. 88-92; Wandycz, *France and her Eastern Allies*, pp. 328-68; Wolfers, *Britain and France*, Chaps. 2, 4-5.

[70] DBFP, IA, I, 66.

the decision to end the policy of territorial aggrandizement in Western Europe had been implicit in Herriot's August 1924 decision to accept the Dawes plan and liquidate the Ruhr invasion. None of these issues proved to be a barrier to French acceptance. Herriot and his colleagues decided not to reject the German proposal, and on February 20 and April 6, they sent two encouraging but noncommittal replies to Stresemann. Meanwhile, he and Aristide Briand, who succeeded him as Foreign Minister on April 17, sought to assure that the evacuation of Cologne did not take place before Germany was disarmed and a security pact concluded, and that the security of Poland and Czechoslovakia was not neglected.[71]

Briand accepted a series of defeats in attempting to provide for the security of Eastern Europe. Stresemann's Rhineland Pact provided nothing for the East. And the arbitration treaties he offered to Poland and Czechoslovakia did not recognize Germany's Eastern frontiers, nor were they nonaggression pacts excluding the possibility of war in the event an arbitral judgment were not complied with; and when Chamberlain told the House of Commons that Germany was prepared to renounce the use of force in the East, the Wilhelmstrasse quickly corrected him.[72] In addition, the arbitration treaties would have little importance unless the major powers guaranteed them, and in May Chamberlain rejected Briand's attempt to have Britain do so, convinced that the Eastern European settlement did not have the same "durability" as the Western settlement and unwilling to "risk the bones of a British grenadier" for the Polish Corridor.[73] At the Locarno conference Stresemann, assisted by threats from Chamberlain, withstood Briand's attempt to have France guarantee the Polish and Czech arbitration treaties. Briand had to be content to reaffirm unilaterally France's existing alliances with Germany's two Eastern neighbors. Consequently, the negotiations of 1925 added nothing to the security of Eastern Europe. In fact, they diminished it.

[71] Wandycz, *France and her Eastern Allies*, pp. 329-31, 339. The evacuation-security-disarmament nexus is discussed below, pp. 47-59.

[72] Gaines Post, Jr., "German Foreign Policy and Military Planning; the Polish Question, 1924-1929," unpublished doctoral dissertation, Stanford, 1969, pp. 25-28, 85-86.

[73] 14 May 1925, Chamberlain to Crewe, AC 52/70; 16 February 1925, Chamberlain to Crewe, AC 52/189; Petrie, *Chamberlain*, II, 259.

After Locarno the French remained free to come to the military assistance of her two Eastern allies in the event of a German attack on them. Such action would not constitute aggression against Germany under the Rhineland Pact, nor would it provoke armed resistance from Britain or the loss of British assistance. However, in other cases, French freedom of action in Eastern Europe was more limited after 1925 than previously. Before Locarno, France could have given immediate assistance to Poland in any situation; after Locarno, France could immediately invade Germany from the west only if France were first attacked by Germany. Under any other circumstances, the French could aid Poland only after the Council of the League either pronounced Germany an aggressor under Article 16 of the Covenant and called for sanctions by all League members, or failed to come to an agreement, in which case France and those who might support her were free to act alone. But, in this case Britain might decide that France was the aggressor and intervene on the side of Germany. The arrangements made at Locarno, therefore, had the effect of rewriting the Franco-Polish Alliance of 1921 and the French-Czechoslovak Alliance of 1924 in such a way as to limit French freedom in Eastern Europe by making the operation of the French guarantee conditional and delaying it in certain circumstances.[74] Chamberlain recognized these new limits and concluded: "It is all in the German interest and in ours."[75]

The failure to conclude an international guarantee of the security of Eastern Europe was not of immediate importance in 1925. As long as Germany was disarmed and the Rhineland was demilitarized and occupied, the Reich was without adequate military defense; and the French Army, acting alone, could launch an attack on Germany from well within German borders and then conduct successful military operations in the West in support of Poland. If, however, the French Army were to evacuate the Rhineland, it would be less able to conduct a successful offensive without British assistance. No matter what France's legal rights under Locarno might be, her guarantee to Poland would become less credible if her troops left the Rhine. Stresemann understood this and told one German audience that only

---

[74] Briand's attempts to provide for the security of Eastern Europe and the implications of his failure are carefully explored in Wandycz, *France and her Eastern Allies*, pp. 348-68.

[75] 11 August 1925, Chamberlain to D'Abernon, AC 52/291.

the French threat on the Rhine stood in the way of a recovery of German territory and an Anschluss with Austria.[76]

As viewed from Paris and London, the primary issue at stake in 1925 was not the security of Poland but the safety of France. This became evident in late June as Briand and Chamberlain worked out the conditions of British military assistance to France.

At that time, Chamberlain initially tried to interpret British military obligations as they were interpreted by Anthony Eden and Stanley Baldwin a decade later. During the Rhineland crisis of 1936, the British government decided that the garrisoning of troops in the Rhineland without the immediate threat of a German attack was not an occasion for prompt military assistance, but a matter to be submitted to the League Council—with the expectation, incidentally, that the Council would condemn the German action but impose no sanctions. By implication, Locarno was taken to mean that Britain was to come to the immediate military assistance of the French only in the event of an actual German attack on France, or if German troops entered the Rhineland with the obvious purpose of immediately marching across the border and invading French territory.[77]

Similarly, when London and Paris first came to discuss the conditions of British intervention in June-July 1925, Chamberlain and the Foreign Office attempted to limit recourse to war, and immediate British assistance to France and Belgium, to those cases where military action was necessary to defend against actual attack or to "repel invasion." As Cecil Hurst, Legal Advisor to the Foreign Office, saw it, any and all violations of the demilitarized zone, including the construction of fortifications and the assembly of troops, would be referred to the Council of the League of Nations, which would then recommend action only if "it were convinced that Germany intended war." And it was this view of British obligations that the Foreign Secretary presented to the cabinet beginning on June 22 and, in general terms, to Commons on June 24.[78]

There must be no "loophole for war," Chamberlain warned the

---

[76] ADAP, B, I-1, p. 744.

[77] Anthony Eden, *Facing the Dictators; the Memoirs of Anthony Eden, Earl of Avon*, Boston, 1962, pp. 382-405; Wolfers, *Britain and France*, pp. 47-48.

[78] 11 July 1925, Memorandum by Hurst, Cecil papers 51090; Cab 23/50/30 (22 June 1925); Cab 23/50/33 (3 July 1925); Commons, debates, v. 185, c. 1565.

French a few days later, "except in the one case of self-defense against aggression."[79] When the French and Belgians replied that Chamberlain's procedure would allow the Reichswehr time to mobilize in the demilitarized zone unhindered by the armies of the West while the League Council deliberated, Chamberlain and Tyrrell, the Permanent Under-secretary, argued—from the example of July 1914—that acts of mobilization were preceded by a period of acute political tension. During that period, they added, the League Council could be convened and would deliberate, so that when hostilities broke out an immediate decision could be given. Both men opined that, in the event of an actual German attack on French or Belgian territory, Britain would render immediate military assistance. No British government, Chamberlain told the Belgian ambassador, would wait to enter the war until the Germans were at the Channel threatening London. He emphasized the value of this guarantee and warned that it would be jeopardized by French attempts to overcommit Britain. The Rhineland Pact would be ratified by Parliament, he stated, only if the arbitration powers of the League were fully employed and if the British government were free to decide what conditions were serious enough to merit British military intervention.[80]

Briand was not sastified by Chamberlain's assurances, nor was he deterred by his warnings. He agreed that Britain and France should resort to war only in the event of self-defense against aggression, but he shrewdly informed Chamberlain that the word "aggression" would have to be carefully defined. Particularly concerned with preserving the demilitarized zone from German penetration, Briand argued that military action must take place immediately—undelayed by League deliberations—in the event the Reichswehr entered the area. Delay could allow the Germans to stage an attack on France from the Rhineland and gain a significant military advantage over the defenders. Not to lose an important element of the security provided France in 1919, Briand and Henri Fromageot, the legal expert at the Quai d'Orsay, insisted that the Rhineland Pact must clearly specify the various eventualities in which the British guarantee was to have immediate effect.[81] And in late July they took a position at the opposite ex-

[79] 27 June 1925, Chamberlain to Crewe, AC 52/221.
[80] DDB, II, 79, 80, 85.
[81] 5 July 1925, Crewe to Chamberlain, AC 52/222; DDB, II, 79, 80, 85.

treme from Chamberlain and Hurst, asking that the British declare themselves willing to regard any and all violations of the
demilitarized zone as hostile actions.[82]

The Franco-British differences were resolved during personal
conversations between Briand and Chamberlain held in London
on August 11-12. There Chamberlain at first insisted, as he had
promised the cabinet on August 5, that the British Army could
not be engaged over what he called "some trifling infringement."
If the Germans began to construct a fortress or railway line with
possible military uses, no action could be taken until the matter
had been examined by the League Council; British military assistance was to be immediate "only in the event of some serious
threat of an aggressive character which would confer some distinct advantage on the aggressor."[83] As a compromise, the distinction between flagrant and nonflagrant violations of the
demilitarized zone was adopted. The two men agreed that British
military assistance was to be immediate, and take place without
League deliberation, only if Germany resorted to force and committed an unprovoked act of aggression, or if immediate action
were necessary because armed forces had been assembled in the
demilitarized zone.[84]

After the London meetings, Chamberlain spoke of the Rhineland Pact as having modified Articles 42-44 of the Treaty of Versailles. Those articles entitled the British to treat as a "hostile act"
any violation of the demilitarized zone but did not obligate them
to go to war, and Chamberlain was convinced that prior to
Locarno no British government would have acted on that right.[85]
However, under Locarno, he later told Sthamer, hostile acts were
"restricted to a narrowly limited class of flagrant cases, but within
that class we were bound to go to the assistance of France. . . .
Great Britain would be bound to resist the infringement by force
of arms" even though Germany had committed no act of war.[86]

[82] Cab 23/50/43 (5 August 1925).
[83] Cab 23/50/43 (5 August 1925); DDB, II, 85.
[84] Cab 23/50/45 (13 August 1925); 11 August 1925, Chamberlain to D'Abernon, AC 52/291 (original in D'Abernon papers 48929); Petrie, *Chamberlain*,
II, 283; 22 October 1926, Minute by Chamberlain on a memorandum by
William Tyrrell dated 21 October, Balfour papers 49736; Northedge, *Troubled Giant*, pp. 265-66.
[85] DBFP, IA, I, 281.
[86] 4 July 1928, Chamberlain to Nicolson, AC 50/453.

Thus, it is not correct to say that all the British promised to do at Locarno was to assist France in the event an attacking force crossed the Rhine rather than waiting until it crossed the frontier. Britain was not, Chamberlain told the House of Commons in November 1925, prepared "to sit still while the demilitarization of the Rhineland zone is rendered ineffective."[87] In his mind, Britain was obligated to take immediate action in the event troops were assembled in the Rhineland; he assumed that troop assembly would constitute an immediate danger to the other powers, and he used it as an example of such a peril.[88]

British military assistance to France was, thus, limited to grave situations, and even then it was restricted by strategic factors. Immediate military assistance would be possible only by means of prearranged military plans, and how were France and England to coordinate their military efforts against a German army? This question was not urgent in the late 1920s: the Rhineland was occupied; any German force would quickly be engaged by opposing forces; and no military plans were necessary. Thus, the Locarno Treaty itself was not a military necessity at the time it was negotiated; Britain guaranteed the security of France by her military presence in the Rhineland. If the Rhineland were evacuated, however, military plans would become necessary; but their formulation was prevented not only by sentiment in Britain against military conventions and staff talks of the pre-World War I type, but also by the reciprocal nature of the Locarno Treaty. Locarno mentioned no specific opponent, and the conceivable number of victims of aggression was three. If there were to be staff talks, the Germans as well as the French, Belgians, and Italians would have to be included. The general staffs of the five Locarno powers would have to work out jointly three sets of plans and, as Professor Wolfers has pointed out, "military secrecy, quite apart from all political and psychological considerations, made such a procedure inconceivable."[89] Because the British could not plan with the Germans for a war against France while planning with the French for a war with Germany, they decided against

[87] Commons, debates, v. 188, c. 428. Cf. Jordan, *Great Britain, France, and the German Problem*, pp. 194-95; Wolfers, *Britain and France*, pp. 25, 47-48.
[88] 11 August 1925, Chamberlain to D'Abernon, AC 52/291 (original in D'Abernon papers 48929).
[89] Wolfers, *Britain and France*, p. 174. Also Grün, "Locarno," p. 485; Jordan, *Great Britain, France, and the German Problem*, pp. 216-17.

any staff talks at all, and when the Belgians subsequently suggested military staff talks, Chamberlain rejected the idea.[90] The practical effect of the Rhineland Pact on the military security of Western Europe was to render Anglo-French military conversations unfeasible and to eliminate the possibility of immediate British assistance once the Rhineland was evacuated.[91]

From Locarno, then, Briand returned with a pledge of non-aggression from the Germans and a pledge of military assistance from the British; the demilitarization of the Rhineland was guaranteed, and France's borders were apparently secured against even the approach of German troops. This double success was a significant achievement, and it was accepted as an adequate substitute for the unilateral guarantee embodied in an Anglo-French alliance. In spite of Britain's guarantee to Germany, it was unlikely or, as Briand told the Chamber of Deputies, "impossible," that Britain would ever fight side by side with the Germans against France. He expected Britain's guarantee to operate like a unilateral guarantee; he viewed the Rhineland Pact as a replacement for the abortive Treaty of Guarantee and as the culmination of the negotiations he had conducted with Lloyd George in Cannes in January 1922. Briand was victorious where Clemenceau and others had failed. For a success of this dimension, the restriction of the British guarantee to Western Europe and the loss of the right unilaterally to march east of the Rhine—in an effort to enforce the Versailles Treaty with military sanctions, or to augment French security in the West, or to aid the Allies in the East—were calculated to be not too high a price to pay.[92]

4. *Three Images of Locarno*

Three rather different sets of considerations led Stresemann to propose the Rhineland Pact and led Chamberlain and Herriot to

[90] DBFP, IA, I, 143; 24 May 1927, Chamberlain to G. Grahame, FO. 371/12139/143.

[91] Northedge, *Troubled Giant*, p. 268. The only military convention among the Locarno powers was the one which had been concluded between France and Belgium years before: Jonathan Helmreich, "The Negotiation of the Franco-Belgian Military Accord of 1920," *French Historical Studies*, 3 (1964), pp. 360-78.

[92] George Bonnet, *Le Quai d'Orsay sous trois républiques, 1870-1961*, Paris, 1961, pp. 88, 90-91; Walter E. Edge, *A Jerseyman's Journal; Fifty Years of American Business and Politics*, Princeton, 1948, pp. 152-53; Wandycz, *France and her Eastern Allies*, p. 367; Wolfers, *Britain and France*, pp. 43-45, 171-79.

accept it. Different expectations sustained interest in the pact in each capital and brought Briand, Stresemann, and Chamberlain to Locarno in October 1925. Not unexpectedly, each man had a different view of what Locarno meant. Although they did not disagree about the legal provisions of the treaties, each prized the agreements for different reasons, and each had a different notion of what post-Locarno Europe would look like. In their political rhetoric they all spoke of Locarno as being the beginning of a new era, and of that era as being a period of peace. After a great war and a postwar period torn by strife, such assurances from Europe's leading statesmen—publicized by the Geneva correspondents of the American, British, and Western European press —were highly popular with the public. A glance at the rhetoric of Locarno has led some observers to conclude that the three men worked in close harmony for similar ends. This was not so. Each man had a different idea of where the new beginning was to lead and of what was meant by peace.[93]

Austen Chamberlain prized the mutuality of the Rhineland Pact—permitting Britain to guarantee French security without alienating Germany and enabling him to maintain close relations with Paris, which he regarded as the prerequisite to German recovery. He also valued the limited scope of the pact. Locarno was acceptable to him and his government because British responsibilities were limited to coincide closely with the nation's vital interests. Responsibility was limited to Western Europe, and there the new element in the obligations undertaken in 1925 was not the decision to defend France or the Channel ports—something which British governments had done in the past without a prior written promise and would undoubtedly do in the future. The innovation was, aside from the pledge to Germany, the decision to defend France and the Channel at a point 50 kilometers east of the Rhine River, the obligation to come to the aid of France, or Belgium, or Germany in the event the demilitarized status of the Rhineland was violated.[94]

[93] The contradictions between the policies of the three men have been repeatedly observed. See René Albrecht-Carrié, *France, Europe and the Two World Wars*, Geneva, 1960, p. 167; Grün, "Locarno," pp. 481-84; Thimme, *Gustav Stresemann*, pp. 105-106; Walters, *League of Nations*, pp. 345-46; Wolfers, *Britain and France*, p. 65.

[94] A statement by Lord Carvan, Chief of the Imperial General Staff, minimizing Britain's new obligations under the Rhineland Pact: Cab 2/4/201

Technically, Locarno was not a pact of peace but an agreement to go to war in certain eventualities. This is, however, not how it was viewed by most of the Baldwin government who saw in Locarno an agreement to keep Britain out of war rather than to involve her in one. They did not expect it would be necessary to give military assistance to either Germany or France. There was little likelihood of a German attack in the West as long as France remained armed and Germany was disarmed. In the event of a German attack in the East, the British considered themselves in no way obligated to support the French in aiding Poland.[95] Locarno was meant as a deterrent, a way of removing the uncertainty, which may have existed in 1914, as to whether Britain would intervene if France were attacked. "The whole idea of a guarantee," a Foreign Office memorandum of November 1925 stated, "is to prevent a conflict from arising by making the potential aggressor realize that the party whom he attacks will not stand alone."[96] Although the promise of military assistance on the Continent "seemed dangerous in theory," wrote Winston Churchill, "there was little likelihood of such a disaster ever coming to pass."[97] Leopold Amery put it even more bluntly; the situations calling for British action were "so remote and contingent," he wrote to Chamberlain in June, "that we are not likely in fact ever to be called upon to intervene."[98] Locarno was attractive in London not only because of its mutuality, but because it both minimized British obligations and made it unlikely that those obligations would have to be honored. Chamberlain perceived this: he saw in the limitation of British obligations an opportunity to give to France a guarantee that would not be rejected by future governments in which his sentimental affection for France was not represented. He wanted to "give France a national guarantee which every government and every party will be ready to honor"; Locarno was to be "a national document."[99] The foreign policy of the Baldwin cabinet, like its domestic policy, was to promote

---

(1 July 1925). A description of the exact circumstances under which Britain was bound to go to war: DBFP, IA, I, 99. Also Grün, "Locarno," pp. 484-85; Newman, *Balance of Power*, pp. 106-107; Northedge, *Troubled Giant*, p. 269.

[95] Chamberlain to CID, Cab 2/4/201 (1 July 1925); DBFP, IA, I, 99.

[96] DBFP, IA, I, 99.

[97] Winston S. Churchill, *The Gathering Storm*, New York, 1948, 1961, p. 27.

[98] Quoted in Johnson, "Chamberlain and Locarno," p. 77.

[99] 27 June 1925, Chamberlain to Crewe, AC 52/221.

peace and harmony by being unadventuresome. It was the safety of the Locarno Treaty that Chamberlain advertised to the House of Commons during the debate over ratification in November: "I do not think," he said, "that the obligations of this country could be more narrowly circumscribed to the vital national interest than they are in the Treaty of Locarno."[100]

To the French, the Rhineland Pact offered a German pledge of nonaggression and a British promise of military assistance, although it did so at the cost of French freedom to initiate military operations against Germany. Locarno did not, however, protect France from invasion; in fact, it precluded the military staff talks which would have facilitated such protection. Disarmament, demilitarization, and the occupation of the Rhineland protected France from attack and rendered the Locarno Treaty superfluous at the time it was signed. Rather than being a "guarantee against invasion," Locarno was a "guarantee of victory." Although in theory Locarno guaranteed British aid in the event of the assembly of troops in the Rhineland, in practice, once the Rhineland was evacuated, Locarno guaranteed that British troops would return to the Continent to liberate France from the German Army.[101]

Locarno also offered to France the prospect of collaboration with Britain in the application of Versailles and in the pacification of Germany.[102] Cooperation with London, of course, meant that Paris could no longer seek security or treaty enforcement through the exercise of military force beyond the Rhineland, but Poincaré had proved this policy futile, and Briand, who had in 1917 concluded a treaty with the Russians giving the French the Rhineland and who had invaded the three Ruhr towns in 1921,[103] was prepared to adjust to post-1924 conditions. What then was to be done about the expected revival of German power? The answer, found in Locarno, was duplex—entente with Britain and détente with Germany. The alliance with England, disguised as a treaty

---

[100] Commons, debates, v. 188, c. 429.

[101] Jordan, *Great Britain, France, and the German Problem*, pp. 216-17; Wolfers, *Britain and France*, p. 25.

[102] On Briand's German policy see Pierre Renouvin, *War and Aftermath, 1914-1929*, New York, 1968, pp. 222-23; Albrecht-Carrié, *France, Europe and the Two World Wars*, pp. 159-88; Wolfers, *Britain and France*, pp. 62-65.

[103] Renouvin, "Les buts de guerre," pp. 9-20; Schmidt, *Versailles and the Ruhr*, pp. 29-30.

of mutual assistance, would place a preponderance of power behind the established order in Europe and deter Germany from
attempts to revise that order. An attack on France would be
perilous; it might also be rendered unnecessary. Through negotiated settlements for which Stresemann seemed eager, various
points of contention, which otherwise might aggravate Franco-
German relations, could be smoothed out, demonstrating to the
Germans the benefits of collaboration and dissuading them from
a war of revenge. Presumably, if concessions were made to Germany regarding the ephemeral, penal provisions of the Treaty
of Versailles, then Germany might accept the *status quo* established in 1919. The Rhineland Pact offered the prospect of culti-
vating German goodwill and the promise of British aid in case
that goodwill was not forthcoming. To Briand, also, the Treaty of
Locarno opened up the possibility that British military assistance
might not be necessary.

Like Chamberlain, Briand saw Locarno as a guarantee of peace
rather than a provision for war. In his oratory Briand frequently represented Locarno as a measure assuring peace. He
recalled for his audiences the battle of Verdun and the "frightful
things" he saw there: "That abominable butchery filled me with
such horror that I swore to myself that should I after victory, ever
be recalled to power, my heart, my brain, my very being would
be devoted to the cause of peace, that such horrors should never
occur again."[104] However, to view Briand as a simple pacifist,
anxious to avoid another war through indiscriminate concession
to Germany, is to misunderstand what he meant by peace. Philip
Kerr once wrote that when Anglo-Saxons talk of peace they mean
a moral situation. "When the French talk about peace they mean
a juridical situation. Peace to them means the Treaty of Versailles
as the political structure of Europe with irresistible force behind
it."[105] Briand said much the same thing when he told the League
of Nations Assembly in September 1928 that "no special circumstances, no individual aspirations, however justifiable, can be
allowed to transcend the interests of peace. Peace must come before all. If any act of justice were proposed which would disturb
world peace and renew the terrible disasters of yesterday, I
should be the first to call upon those promoting it to stop, to aban-

---

[104] Suarez, *Briand*, VI, 162.
[105] 24 May 1928, Kerr to Houghton, Kerr papers v. 241, pp. 304-305.

don it in the supreme interest of peace."[106] Peace to Briand meant a Europe in which French treaty rights and French leadership of Europe were recognized and accepted—even by the Germans. With his compassionate and conciliatory talk and his willingness to negotiate, Briand worked for the same goals as did Poincaré with his tough talk and intransigence. But he differed from Poincaré; his temperament and experience enabled him to conceive different ways of maintaining French preeminence. Because his methods were pacific, he was able to accept, and later exploit, Stresemann's proposal in a way Poincaré might not have done. To Briand "peace" as a method of French policy meant patient negotiation and the avoidance of the intransigent resistance that would alienate both the former ally that was needed to guarantee French security and the former enemy that might threaten it. "Peace" as an objective of French policy meant first of all a British guarantee, and then German acceptance of the *status quo* in Western Europe, renunciation of force in Eastern Europe, and acceptance of French leadership. "En effet," he reportedly once said, "la France c'est la paix."[107]

Locarno spared Stresemann's policy from a serious reversal, helped to prevent the formation of a hostile Anglo-French alliance, and prompted the beginning of the Allied military withdrawal from both banks of the Rhine. It also averted the cessation of American loans, protected Western Germany from military sanctions, and assured the unity and territorial integrity of the Reich. To this extent the Rhineland Pact was a countermove and a defensive measure.

At the same time, however, Locarno "opened up" what Stresemann called "new prospects."[108] One such prospect was the cultivation of Anglo-French sympathy for the negotiated recovery of territory lost to Poland. Beyond that, Locarno could in effect weaken the Franco-Polish Alliance by increasing French feelings of security on the Rhine and by delaying French military intervention while the League Council deliberated and Paris con-

[106] Records of the Ninth Ordinary session of the Assembly, Plenary Meetings, Text of the Debates, League of Nations, *Official Journal*, Special Supplement, No. 64, Geneva, 1928, p. 83.

[107] Arthur Salter, *Personality in Politics; Studies of Contemporary Statesmen*, London, 1942, p. 200.

[108] Stresemann, *Vermächtnis*, II, 281-82.

sulted with London. Thus, Germany's western flank would receive a measure of protection in the event of a Polish attack on Germany or in case Germany in the distant future were to use force to revise its eastern frontiers—a contingency which neither the Reichwehr nor the Wilhelmstrasse ruled out if attempts at peaceful revision failed. Locarno, thus, offered a potential improvement in Germany's strategic position by reducing the possibility of a two-front war, a war Germany could not win.[109]

In the West Locarno offered the prospect of splitting the entente, of drawing Britain away from France and into the role of arbitrator between Paris and Berlin. Then realization of the immediate objectives of German policy would become feasible: a compromise settlement of the lapses in disarmament reported by the IMCC, the prevention of the establishment of permanent systems of on-site inspection designed by the French to assure the disarmament of Germany and the demilitarization of the Rhineland, and the complete evacuation of all occupation forces from Germany. With France secure from attack, and with "the British draught animals harnessed to the German cart," as one German diplomat put it,[110] the interests of a second-rate military power would be taken into consideration in the resolution of a wide variety of issues.

The complete evacuation of the Rhineland was an issue raised persistently by Stresemann in connection with the negotiations which led to the conclusion of the Rhineland Pact at Locarno, and as early as June he was candidly telling foreigners about this particular new prospect in the West. To Alanson Houghton, the American ambassador, he portrayed the Rhineland Pact as a beginning, a first step which must have as its logical consequence the evacuation of the entire Rhineland—Coblenz and Mainz as well as Cologne—before 1935, the date specified in the Treaty of Versailles.[111] In Stresemann's view, the Rhineland Pact offered to the French peace and security, and for that reason they were free

---

[109] A fascinating analysis of Locarno, German politico-military strategy, and the role of force in Weimar foreign policy is Post's "German Foreign Policy and Military Planning."

[110] 23 June 1925, Memorandum by Dirksen, quoted in Eleanor Bruening, "Germany between East and West, 1921-1926," unpublished D. Phil. thesis, Oxford, 1966, pp. vii/120.

[111] Stresemann, *Vermächtnis*, II, 261-62.

to surrender military control over the Rhine, the means by which they had heretofore sought security. To Houghton, of course, Stresemann emphasized the defensive side of his policy. The withdrawal of all foreign troops from German soil was, he stated, the only sure way to defend against "Herr Foch's policy of conquering the left bank of the Rhine for France" and to put an end to "any fantasies about neutralizing the Rhineland, or trying to turn the feelings of the [Rhineland] populations against Germany." He did not speak of the end of occupation coming as a result of German fulfillment of the Versailles Treaty, but as something to be conceded by France in order to "gain the friendship of a powerful neighbor" and preclude the possibility of "another war in Europe later on." This is significant, for occupation was the means by which German compliance with all the other provisions of Versailles was enforced. Both in his *Kronprinzen-Brief* and in his speech to the Arbeitsgemeinschaft deutscher Landsmann-schaften—two of the most candid statements of his Locarno policy—Stresemann referred to occupation as the "rope of the strangler who has us by the neck."[112] Should the French prove willing to evacuate not only Cologne but the entire Rhineland, and do so in exchange for German friendship rather than for strict German compliance with the peace terms of 1919, then Locarno could be a step toward overcoming Versailles.

To Stresemann, then, Locarno offered the prospect of a wide variety of negotiated settlements—in the East and in the West. And it offered the hope that occupation, the chief means of treaty enforcement on which the British and French could agree, would be terminated. It was to these ends that Stresemann was willing to accept voluntarily the demilitarization of the Rhineland and the relinquishment of Alsace-Lorraine—at least for the foreseeable future. Through such concessions, and through the regular payment of reparations, French fears and suspicions would be allayed, British sympathies would be aroused, and American capital would flow into Germany. And through this rapprochement with the West, the Treaty of Versailles would be revised, and Germany would become strong and great once more. To Stresemann, the revision of Versailles meant not that the Treaty

[112] 7 September 1925, Stresemann to Crown Prince, 3168/7318/159874-75; ADAP, B, I-1, p. 748. The editions of these two documents appearing in Stresemann's *Vermächtnis* are abbreviated.

would be abolished but that it would be "hollowed out"; the chains of Versailles would not disappear but become lighter.[113] To this end he evaded the treaty only so far as evasion did not hamper revision; he met its requirements only so far as fulfillment facilitated revision. He did not refer to his Locarno policy as one of "fulfillment"; he avoided the word, and spoke of his policy as one of "understanding." The reason is evident: "fulfillment" denoted harmony between Germany and the West on Allied terms; "understanding" meant agreement by mutual consent. Stresemann's experience did not indicate that one always made progress with the Allies by always fulfilling the Treaty of Versailles. In his opinion, it was Germany's failure to comply with the reparation clauses of the treaty which had led ultimately to the Dawes plan; and in January 1925, he expressed his confidence that further noncompliance would continue to lead to more negotiated settlements.[114]

The revision of Versailles was to be peaceful, however. Like Briand and Chamberlain, Stresemann saw Locarno as a way of peace. Only in the cause of the recovery of territory from Poland was the use of military force envisaged, and even there it was viewed as probably unnecessary.[115] What was necessary, Stresemann thought, was the "cooperation and understanding" of the powers whose assent was required for the attainment of German aims, and the "actual restriction of these aims and the abandonment of a policy that attempts to advance in all directions at once."[116] These two things—a rapprochement with the West and the concentration of German energies on that which was important and obtainable—led Stresemann to Locarno and were the bases of the policy he conducted thereafter.

It is questionable how much Locarno added to the security of Europe at the time it was negotiated. The application of the

---

[113] Turner, "Eine Rede Stresemanns," pp. 417, 425. On several occasions in October-November 1925, Stresemann stated that Germany had not "morally" renounced the recovery of Alsace-Lorraine but only the use of force in the West. He even added that treaties were valid only so long as the conditions under which they had been concluded remained unchanged. Stresemann, *Vermächtnis*, II, 211-12, 232 and *Essays and Speeches on Various Subjects*, London, 1930, pp. 323-34; Turner, "Eine Rede Stresemanns," p. 425.

[114] Stresemann, *Vermächtnis*, II, 13-14; Thimme, *Gustav Stresemann*, p. 93.

[115] Post, "German Foreign Policy and Military Planning," pp. 300-304.

[116] Stresemann, *Vermächtnis*, II, 172.

treaty was limited to eventualities which were unlikely in 1925—a direct German attack on France or the remilitarization of the Rhineland, both remote as long as Germany was disarmed and the Rhineland occupied; a unilateral French invasion of Germany to enforce the Treaty of Versailles; a French invasion in support of her Eastern Allies without first consulting the League of Nations. To the men who negotiated the Locarno Treaty, it offered prospects other than those of a security agreement providing for the eventuality of war. To Chamberlain it offered an opportunity to meet French demands for protection while at the same time eliminating certain areas and occasions from British concern. To Briand it offered the maintenance and execution of the Versailles Treaty, German renunciation of violent overthrow of the *status quo*, and a British guarantee against the same. To Stresemann it offered the prospect of treaty revision. All saw in Locarno a way of peace, but all thought of peace in different terms. To Briand peace meant a permanently secure and preponderant France; to Stresemann it meant a restored Germany; and to Chamberlain it meant an Anglo-French entente strong enough to keep France from a policy of provocations and unilateral enforcement, and to ameliorate Germany's condition safely. In spite of their long terms in office, Stresemann, Briand, and Chamberlain did not themselves test the adequacy of Locarno as a security pact, nor did they see the achievement of their ultimate goals. Their statesmanship was tested in a more immediate and less spectacular manner, in the way they advanced the interests of their countries by means of the relations, political and personal, they established in 1925.

PART TWO

APPEASEMENT BEFORE AND AFTER LOCARNO

1925-1926

1. *Security, Disarmament, and the Rhineland before Locarno, January-October 1925*

STRESEMANN'S proposal of January-February 1925 raised several crucial issues which were then debated by the powers during the months that followed. The limitation of the British guarantee to Western Europe and its immediate implementation only in cases of attack or flagrant violation of the demilitarized zone was decided on in conversations between London and Paris. Three other points were subject to negotiation between Germany and the West. Two of these pertained to Eastern Europe: would the German arbitration treaties with Poland and Czechoslovakia be guaranteed by France? And would Germany be obligated under Article 16 of the League Covenant to participate in sanctions against Russia and render assistance to Poland? The third related to the Rhineland: would the conclusion of the Rhineland Pact be accompanied by the evacuation of Cologne and followed by the complete withdrawal of Allied troops from Germany? The question of Eastern European security was resolved in Germany's favor prior to the conclusion of the treaties at Locarno in October, but the fate of the Rhineland was not determined until later. The Allies did not formally agree to evacuate Cologne until December 1925, and it was not until 1930 that the occupation of the remainder of the Rhineland was terminated. Because of its duration—and because of its centrality to security and treaty enforcement—the Rhineland issue provides one of the better lenses with which to focus on the relations between Germany and the Western powers throughout the years known as the Locarno era.

The decision not to evacuate the Cologne zone in January 1925 reflected not only Allied willingness to apply sanctions in the enforcement of the Treaty of Versailles but also French reluctance to let the problem of the nation's security continue unresolved. This concern was not without basis. If Cologne, the railway center for North-Central Germany, and Aachen (which was in the same zone) were evacuated, the Holland to Switzerland barrier of military occupation would be broken; the Berlin-Hamburg-Cologne-Liège line of advance would be opened to the Reichswehr, and Belgium and northern France would be accessible to a German attack.[1] Moreover, most of the British Army of the Rhine was stationed in the Cologne zone; if the area were evacuated, Britain's share in the deterrent against Germany would be reduced and her commitment to France thereby diminished.[2]

In discussing Cologne with London, Herriot did not insist that the district remain occupied indefinitely, nor did he assert any legal claim to occupy Cologne until an alternate form of military security was provided France. He did, however, tell Crewe in early February that there was a "moral link" between evacuation and security, that the two issues could not be disassociated, and that the security of France must be considered when Cologne was discussed. This meant, he admitted, that there must be an agreement on security prior to the evacuation of Cologne, an agreement which he hoped to reach by mid-April.[3]

Crewe termed the French attempts to make evacuation dependent on security "a breach of the [Versailles] Treaty," and the reaction of Chamberlain, who suspected that Herriot was trying to "extort" a guarantee of security from England, was no less strong. Although willing to continue occupation in order to enforce German compliance with the disarmament provisions of the treaty, Chamberlain found Herriot's attempt to prolong occupation in order to wrest a guarantee of security from London unacceptable. And in replying to Paris on February 6, he threatened to end his attempts to gain security for France and warned of an Anglo-French break similar to the rupture following the Ruhr invasion.[4] At the same time Chamberlain allowed D'Abernon privately to reassure the Germans that evacuation would take place with the disarmament settlement, and he stated publicly that the Allies intended to fulfill their own obligation under the

[1] Reply by J. H. Morgan to an address by E. L. Spears entitled "The Problem of the Rhineland," *International Affairs*, 4 (1925), p. 130.

[2] In February 1925 Foch pressed the British War Office for a promise to send British reinforcements to France in the event of a German attack after Cologne was evacuated: Cab 2/4/195 (13 February 1925).

[3] 5 February 1925, Crewe to Chamberlain, AC 52/184. The distinction made by Herriot was between *rapport juridique* and *rapport de causalité*: Cab 2/4/195 (13 February 1925).

[4] 14 March 1925, Crewe to Chamberlain, AC 52/195; 6 February 1925, Chamberlain to Crewe, AC 50/39 and AC 52/186; Cab 23/49/5 (3 February 1925); Cab 2/4/195 (13 February 1925). Lord Crewe was British Ambassador at Paris.

Treaty of Versailles.[5] Having warned Paris and reassured Berlin, Chamberlain then continued his efforts to divorce evacuation from security by urging Herriot to negotiate a prompt settlement of the disarmament question and to evacuate Cologne.

Chamberlain wanted to act quickly. Unlike the French, he was not particularly alarmed at the discoveries of the IMCC, and he saw in the Luther-Stresemann government, with its willingness and ability to negotiate on disarmament, a unique but fragile and ephemeral opportunity to arrive at a settlement and end the military control.[6] Beginning in January, he pressed Herriot to proceed with haste toward an evacuation-disarmament settlement: when the IMCC issued a full report on the general inspection of 1924, the discussion of disarmament would be taken out of the hands of the general staffs and the Conference of Ambassadors. Chamberlain and Herriot would promptly meet together, and the two of them would, in Chamberlain's words, show "some consideration for German feeling" and "honestly try to meet their point of view." They would "concentrate on the big questions," and "not insist on trifling matters of no military consequence." "An attitude of unreasonable insistence on small points or a constant succession of irritating incidents" would, Chamberlain threatened, only make it difficult for him to gain a guarantee of French security from his government. The selected "big questions" would then be resolved at a personal meeting between the Allied and German foreign ministers. At that meeting the Germans would be allowed to make reasonable representations and set a date by which they would complete disarmament; in return the Allies would promise to evacuate Cologne by that time. To assure a negotiated disarmament settlement, rather than one which was imposed, Chamberlain wanted the Allies to "communicate personally with the Germans and not by formal note"; he wanted to secure the cooperation of the Germans and "give them the opportunity to offer

[5] Chamberlain declined, however, to follow D'Abernon's suggestion and give Berlin an explicit written promise that evacuation would follow automatically upon disarmament: Edgar (Lord) D'Abernon, *An Ambassador of Peace; Pages from the Diary of Viscount D'Abernon*, London, 1929-30, III, 135; 31 January 1925, D'Abernon to Chamberlain, AC 52/255.

[6] The long-standing division between Paris and London over German disarmament and military control: John P. Fox, "Britain and the Inter-Allied Military Commission of Control, 1925-26," *Journal of Contemporary History*, 4 (1969), pp. 143-49.

any observations which they wish and perhaps to suggest some modifications."[7]

Herriot was thus faced with a dilemma. If he entered into negotiations on disarmament, he would find himself under pressure to conclude those negotiations quickly, especially since Chamberlain was, as Crewe put it, "prepared to stretch a point here and there in favor of Germany, provided she shows a reasonable spirit."[8] The result would be, Herriot feared, the resolution of the disarmament question and the evacuation of Cologne without discussion of substitute security for France. On the other hand, if he insisted on security arrangements prior to evacuation, he ran the risk of alienating Chamberlain and prompting him to cease his efforts to gain a British guarantee of French security. To escape from this dilemma, Herriot withstood Chamberlain's demand for a quick disarmament settlement and prompt evacuation, and in mid-February he insisted on a protracted procedure. The full report of the IMCC was first to be carefully studied in detail by the military experts of the Allied governments; then the Conference of Ambassadors would debate the issue; finally, the Allied foreign ministers would meet in mid-April, decide on the conditions under which Cologne would be evacuated, and communicate their decision to Berlin.[9]

Chamberlain objected. He warned that if Herriot deliberately chose to communicate by note, he would view it as an indication that the French intended to prolong occupation by maintaining their grievances rather than to obtain redress through a satisfactory disarmament settlement. But Herriot was successful. Although Chamberlain did not accept the French thesis that evacuation was dependent on new security, he did agree to postpone the foreign ministers' conference indefinitely while the Rhineland Pact was considered. Thus, the disarmament negotiations were

[7] 9 January 1925, Chamberlain to D'Abernon, D'Abernon papers 48928; 12 January 1925, Chamberlain to D'Abernon, AC 52/253; 16 January 1925, D'Abernon to Chamberlain, AC 52/254; 20 January 1925, Chamberlain to Crewe, AC 50/28; 6 February 1925, Chamberlain to Crewe, AC 50/39; Cab 2/4/195 (13 February 1925); DDB, II, 17; D'Abernon, *An Ambassador*, III, 121, 138-39.

[8] 13 May 1925, Crewe to Chamberlain, AC 52/212.

[9] 5 February 1925, Crewe to Chamberlain, AC 52/184; 13 February 1925, Chamberlain to Crewe, AC 50/41; 17 February 1925, Crewe to Chamberlain, AC 52/190; 22 February 1925, Crewe to Chamberlain, AC 52/212; DDB, II, 21; Michel Soulié, *La vie politique d'Edouard Herriot*, Paris, 1962, p. 209.

spun out, and the evacuation of Cologne was delayed until progress was made toward security. While not insisting on a legal
relationship between evacuation and security, Herriot had implemented a *de facto* link between the two issues. And throughout
1925 the French gave London the impression they were in no
hurry to resolve the disarmament issue and promote evacuation
until French security was guaranteed. Paris was to prove willing
to overlook infractions of the disarmament clauses only as discussion of security advanced.[10]

Although the IMCC submitted its formal report to the Conference of Ambassadors on February 15, it was June 4 before the
Germans received any detailed statement from the Ambassadors'
Conference on the lapses in disarmament which had prompted
the decision not to evacuate Cologne, and it was June 20 before
the French replied to Stresemann's Rhineland Pact proposal.[11]
The long delay was a disappointment to Chamberlain, and he was
dissatisfied with the sequence in which the notes were finally sent
—the note on disarmament being dispatched before the one on
security. The Germans, he expected, would suspect that the reply
to their note on security was being delayed while their disarmament was being arranged. He was also disappointed at the form
of the Allied communication on disarmament—a note rather than
a personal meeting—and saw in it the perpetuation of the old
postwar situation in which the victors imposed the execution of
the peace terms on the vanquished. He felt, however, that there
was little he could do; he was content to urge patience on the
Germans, to urge haste and conciliation on the French, and to assure the British cabinet that once the security pact was concluded, the French would be much more conciliatory.[12]

The French note of June 16, expressing willingness to conclude
a mutual security pact based on Stresemann's proposal, displayed
a careful concern for Allied interests. Belgium was to be a party

[10] 20 February 1925, Chamberlain to Crewe, AC 52/191; DDB, II, 33, 39;
14 March 1925, Crewe to Chamberlain, AC 52/195; 28 May 1925, Crewe to
Chamberlain, AC 52/215; Fox, "Britain and the Inter-Allied Military Commission of Control," pp. 149-50.

[11] Michael Salewski, *Entwaffnung und Militärkontrolle in Deutschland,
1919-1927*, Munich, 1966, pp. 294-99, 302-305.

[12] 7 May 1925, Chamberlain to D'Abernon, AC 52/269; 12 May 1925,
Chamberlain to Crewe, AC 52/211; 21 May 1925, Chamberlain to Crewe,
AC 52/214; 10 June 1925, Tyrrell to Chamberlain, AC 52/764; Cab 23/50/27
(28 May 1925); Salewski, *Entwaffnung und Militärkontrolle*, p. 305.

to the Rhineland Pact; the German treaties of arbitration with Poland and Czechoslovakia were referred to in an ambiguous phrase which left a loophole for a French guarantee of them; Germany was to join the League of Nations and accept the obligations of Article 16 of the Covenant to participate in sanctions against aggressors.[13] Finally, because both London and Paris had suspected from the very beginning that Stresemann intended to make complete Allied withdrawal from the Rhineland a condition of the pact,[14] they insisted that the proposed pact involve no modification of the Treaty of Versailles.

Stresemann found this note unacceptable. He objected to what he saw as a French attempt to guarantee the Eastern arbitration treaties. He had no intention of rendering assistance to Poland under Article 16, either by participating in military or economic sanctions against the Soviet Union, or by permitting the transportation of Allied troops across German territory.[15] And he objected to the notion that the conditions of military occupation would be unaffected by the Rhineland Pact.

Stresemann had proposed the Rhineland Pact to assure the evacuation of Cologne, and the prospect of the early evacuation of the entire Rhineland had sustained his interest in it during his four-month wait for the French reply. The question of evacuation became critical after June 16, when the French indicated serious interest in the pact negotiations and opposition within Germany to further negotiations intensified. This opposition came from various sources: Ulrich von Brockdorff-Rantzau, German ambassador to Moscow, thought Stresemann incapable of maintaining German ties with the Soviet Union while concluding a security pact with the West.[16] General Hans von Seeckt, Chief of the Army, who talked of reconquering the frontiers of 1914 in the

---

[13] *Papers Respecting the Proposals for a Pact of Security Made by the German Government on February 9, 1925*, Cmd. 2435, London, 1925, pp. 48-51; Jürgen Spenz, *Die diplomatische Vorgeschichte des Beitritts Deutschlands zum Völkerbund, 1924-1926*, Göttingen, 1966, pp. 65-66, 78-81; Piotr Wandycz, *France and her Eastern Allies, 1919-1925; French-Czechoslovak-Polish Relations from the Paris Peace Conference to Locarno*, Minneapolis, 1962, pp. 348-49.

[14] 3 February 1925, Chamberlain to D'Abernon, AC 52/256; DDB, II, 27.

[15] Spenz, *Beitritts Deutschlands zum Völkerbund*, pp. 65-66; Wandycz, *France and her Eastern Allies*, pp. 352-54.

[16] Erich Eyck, *A History of the Weimar Republic*, Cambridge, Mass., 1962-63, II, 10-19.

East and in the West, objected to the renunciation of the threat of force in Germany's relations with France and Poland.[17] And most importantly, the leadership of the Nationalist Party (DNVP), under pressure from the extreme right wing within their organization, objected to a variety of things, including what they depicted as a renunciation of German land and people in the East and West, and they attempted to force Stresemann's resignation from the government.[18] To withstand these efforts, to neutralize criticism of his policy, and to win Nationalist support for an affirmative reply to the French note, Stresemann sought both to minimize the importance of German concessions and to demonstrate what he called the "positive advantages" of the Rhineland Pact. He informed the leaders of the DNVP and the cabinet that he would not sign the pact until the Ruhr district, including Düsseldorf, Duisberg, and Ruhrort (the three "sanction towns" occupied in 1921), was evacuated and the withdrawal of troops from Cologne was assured. In addition, he stated that the early evacuation of the entire Rhineland could, and would, follow the conclusion of the treaty.[19]

For Stresemann, the promised evacuation of the Ruhr and the sanction towns symbolized the end of what he called "the futile policy of attempted measures of force against Germany."[20] On June 20 he asked Pierre de Margerie, the French ambassador, for assurance from Paris that the Ruhr would in fact be evacuated as scheduled on August 15. His reasons for doing so, as he presented them to both the French and the Reichstag Foreign Affairs Committee, were that the nonevacuation of Cologne had cast doubt on French intentions to fulfill their treaty engagements; if he was to continue security negotiations, he must know whether "the German nation is to be hoodwinked" with regard to the Ruhr

[17] 24 June 1925, Cabinet Protocol, 1834/3543/765055-57; Hans Meier-Welcker, *Seeckt*, Frankfurt, 1967, pp. 470-77.

[18] Robert Garthwol, "DNVP and European Reconciliation, 1924-1928; a Study of the Conflict between Party Politics and Government Foreign Policy in Weimar Germany," unpublished doctoral dissertation, Chicago, 1968, pp. 112-53.

[19] 2 July 1925, Cabinet Protocol, 1834/3543/765169; Gustav Stresemann, *Vermächtnis; der Nachlass in Drei Bänden*, Berlin, 1932-33, II, 88; Henry A. Turner, Jr., *Stresemann and the Politics of the Weimar Republic*, Princeton, 1963, pp. 189-90; Garthwol, "DNVP and European Reconciliation," pp. 101, 104.

[20] Stresemann, *Vermächtnis*, II, 161.

also. The French reply came in 36 hours: the Ruhr would be evacuated on August 15, earlier if possible.[21] Stresemann then asked, on July 11, that the sanction towns also be evacuated before August 15, but was less successful.[22] In the end, the Ruhr was evacuated two weeks early on July 31, but Briand delayed the evacuation of the three sanction towns until August 25 in an attempt to get a commitment from the Germans to carry out Allied demands for disarmament.[23]

The chances for the evacuation of the Cologne zone would be maximized, Stresemann calculated, if this issue was discussed during a foreign ministers' conference on security. To this end, the German government showed no eagerness to comply with the disarmament demands of the Conference of Ambassadors, and Berlin's reply to their note of June 5 was by design delayed until shortly after the Locarno conference.[24] In addition, Stresemann attempted to persuade the Allies to evacuate Cologne in return for Germany's adherence to the Rhineland Pact. Although he approached the matter somewhat obliquely in his formal note of July 20 (his reply to the French note of June 16), he informed Briand at the same time that the question of evacuation must be settled before the pact was concluded.[25]

Cologne and the Ruhr were not Stresemann's only objectives. He also kept open the question of the prompt evacuation of the entire Rhineland. Much of importance was to be gained through the complete withdrawal of Allied forces from Germany. Stresemann would secure a practical benefit with which he could popularize his policy. The Allies would be unable to enforce German compliance with the Treaty of Versailles by delaying the evacuation of Coblenz in 1930 and of Mainz in 1935; this advantage would not be available to them in their future negotiations with

[21] *Ibid.*, pp. 107-108, 122.

[22] D'Abernon, *An Ambassador*, III, 175; 7 July 1925, Chamberlain to Crewe, AC 50/103.

[23] 14 July 1925, Chamberlain to Crewe, AC 52/255; 15 July 1925, Crewe to Chamberlain, AC 52/266.

[24] Stresemann, *Vermächtnis*, II, 150; Salewski, *Entwaffnung und Militärkontrolle*, p. 315.

[25] *Reply of the German Government to the Note Handed to Herr Stresemann by the French Ambassador at Berlin on June 16, 1925, Respecting the Proposals for a Pact of Security*, Cmd. 2468, London, 1925, p. 7; 18 July 1925, Stresemann to Hoesch, 1514/3123/646166-67; Spenz, *Beitritts Deutschlands zum Völkerbund*, pp. 81-84; Wandycz, *France and her Eastern Allies*, pp. 353-54.

Berlin. And early evacuation was a test of Allied intentions, a way of seeing how much could be expected from the Allies in the future. If Germany accepted the *status quo* in the West, including the demilitarization of the Rhineland, and promised to arbitrate disputes with Poland and Czechoslovakia, then would the Allies in exchange negotiate the application of Versailles rather than imposing penalties on Germany? The French attitude toward Rhineland evacuation would indicate, Stresemann said to Houghton, whether or not they wanted to go on playing the role of "Napoleonic dictator on the continent of Europe."[26]

Consequently, in his note of July 20, Stresemann cautiously objected to the preservation of occupation in any form. The Rhineland Pact, he stated, was so important that "it could not but react on the conditions in the occupied territories and the question of occupation in general."[27] He foresaw complete evacuation not as a result of German compliance with Versailles, but as a product of the new security provided by the Rhineland Pact. "Absolute security," he had said in March, "no longer needs to be strengthened by a ten-year occupation of the Rhineland." It was unlikely, he thought, that Coblenz and Mainz would be evacuated immediately along with Cologne, but if a security pact were concluded, the period of occupation should be shortened.[28] What he hoped for, he had told D'Abernon on June 10, was that the evacuation of the whole of the Rhineland would be one of the items of "corresponding compensation" which the Allies would offer in exchange for Germany's joining the League of Nations. In so doing, Stresemann played the "Rapallo bluff," suggesting that Russia too was bidding for German allegiance and that the West could compete only by offering Germany "something positive."[29] Then, in his July 20 note, he handled the topic of complete evacuation delicately. Because he expected to raise the matter at the confer-

---

[26] Stresemann, *Vermächtnis*, II, 262.

[27] Cmd. 2468, p. 7.

[28] Stresemann, *Vermächtnis*, II, 69, 88. As early as August 18, 1924, Stresemann had informed the minister-presidents of the German *Lande* that complete evacuation was a primary objective of German foreign policy: 1580/3241/705596.

[29] Stresemann noted that D'Abernon told him that "an agreement could be reached regarding a curtailment of the periods of occupation": Stresemann, *Vermächtnis*, II, 102. D'Abernon, on the other hand, reported that he warned Stresemann against raising the subject: D'Abernon, *An Ambassador*, III, 169.

ence, and because he expected strong Allied resistance to any discussion in July,[30] he merely mentioned his expectations and did
not make further negotiations dependent on the complete evacuation of Cologne or the entire Rhineland. Nevertheless, his note
was badly received in London and Paris.

Chamberlain was anxious to see the Cologne zone evacuated,
but he adamantly opposed any discussion of Coblenz and Mainz.
He had almost refused Stresemann's proposal in January because
he suspected that it might be conditioned on a complete withdrawal of all Allied troops from German territory. In March,
when he met Herriot in Paris and urged him to accept Stresemann's offer, he promised him that there would be no reduction
in the fifteen-year period of occupation.[31] He then made a point of
disclosing, in his first full public discussion of the German proposal, D'Abernon's assurances that Stresemann did not intend to
make the early evacuation of zones two and three a condition of
the Rhineland Pact. In mid-June, when Stresemann again tested
Allied sentiment in a conversation with D'Abernon, Chamberlain
warned the German Foreign Minister against raising the evacuation issue,[32] and finally he instructed Berlin in how to reply to the
French note of June 16. The Germans should, he thought, "take
account of what we have done for them . . . and attach importance
to any advice we may tender." He wanted Berlin to send a cordial, simple, and prompt reply, a reply avoiding "petty discussion
of detail" and accepting the principles of the French note "without cavil," as D'Abernon put it.[33]

When Stresemann ignored Chamberlain's advice and raised the
issue of occupation in his note of July 20, the British Foreign Secretary saw the German action as a near breach of promise:
"Either they meant what they said when they presented their
note, and in that case they have no business to raise these extraneous questions, or they did not mean what they said, and in that
case I was wrong to trust their good faith, and the French will be

[30] Stresemann, *Vermächtnis*, II, 149.

[31] 19 March 1925, Chamberlain to Crewe, AC 50/55. Herriot's insistence
on this point: DDB, II, 33.

[32] Commons, debates, v. 182, c. 321 (24 March 1925); 26 June 1926, Chamberlain to D'Abernon, AC 52/280.

[33] 2 April 1925, Chamberlain to D'Abernon, AC 52/256; Charles Petrie,
The Life and Letters of the Rt. Hon. Sir Austen Chamberlain, London,
1939-40, II, 271-74; D'Abernon, *An Ambassador*, III, 169-70.

justified in every suspicion that they entertain." The effect of the German note would be, he added, "to visit the occupation and all the conditions of disarmament and demilitarization more firmly than ever upon Germany. . . . The Germans have gone out of their way to ask for a reaffirmation of the Treaty provisions. They will get it. What fools they are."[34] By this time Chamberlain was publicly referring to the Rhineland Pact as an instrument "on which the peace of the whole world depended," and he did not want negotiations hampered by what he called the Germans' "attitude of mind, their tendency to search for and even to create difficulties."[35] Although D'Abernon objected to Chamberlain's estimate of Stresemann's character, he was forced to tell the German Foreign Minister on August 3 that shortening the period of occupation would be "extraordinarily difficult."[36]

Confident of Chamberlain's support, Briand rejected Stresemann's attempt to associate evacuation of Cologne with the Rhineland Pact. In a note dated August 24, Briand insisted on German acceptance of all the obligations of the League Covenant, and he maintained that the provisions of the Treaty of Versailles, including those dealing with occupation, could not be modified.[37] However, Stresemann was not dissuaded. On September 24 he reassured the cabinet that the evacuation of Cologne and the early evacuation of the entire Rhineland would be considered at the impending conference,[38] and two days later, when he formally accepted an Allied invitation to attend a conference of foreign ministers at Locarno, he rejected the notion of German war guilt, specifically insisted on the evacuation of the Cologne zone prior to the conclusion of the security pact, and then published the text of this declaration in the press.[39] In reply, Chamberlain and

[34] 29 July 1925, Chamberlain to D'Abernon, D'Abernon papers 48929.

[35] Petrie, *Chamberlain*, II, 279; 10 July 1925, Chamberlain to D'Abernon, AC 52/282.

[36] Stresemann, *Vermächtnis*, II, 164-65. D'Abernon on Stresemann's character: 7 February 1925, D'Abernon to Chamberlain, AC 52/257; D'Abernon, *An Ambassador*, III, 174-75. Also F. G. Stambrook, " 'Das Kind'—Lord D'Abernon and the Origins of the Locarno Pact," *Central European History*, 1 (1968), p. 238.

[37] London *Times*, 27 August 1925; Wandycz, *France and her Eastern Allies*, p. 355.

[38] 24 September 1925, Cabinet Protocol, 1835/3242/713884-97; Stresemann, *Vermächtnis*, II, 180-81.

[39] *Proceedings of the Locarno Conference, October 1925*, Nos. 35-37, 43, 45, 51, 54-55 (AC 38/1/4); London *Times*, 30 September 1925; Spenz, *Beitritts*

Briand expressed their agitation at Stresemann's rejection of the war-guilt allegation and insisted that the Cologne zone would be evacuated only when Germany had complied with the disarmament provisions of the Versailles Treaty.[40]

In the eight months prior to the conference at Locarno, the conflicts between Paris and London had been resolved. Briand and Chamberlain had agreed that Britain would in no way guarantee the *status quo* in Eastern Europe but that France would be free to come to the aid of her Eastern Allies without risk of British interference. They also compromised their differences over the conditions under which the British were obligated to come to the immediate military assistance of France. Thus, by the time the Locarno conference was convened, there was little of importance to divide the two delegations.

German negotiations with the Western powers had not, however, produced the same level of agreement. In his note of July 20, Stresemann had withstood French attempts to guarantee the arbitration treaties with Poland and Czechoslovakia and had objected to German assumption of the full obligations of Article 16,[41] but he had not won the consent of Paris and London to his position on either issue. Moreover, he had secured no positive advantages from his initiative; he had not won acceptance for the idea that the Rhineland Pact should facilitate the evacuation of Cologne and shorten the fifteen-year period of occupation. His hints at complete evacuation had been rejected, and, even with regard to Cologne, he had been unable to drive a wedge between military occupation and treaty enforcement. The French, in effect declined to withdraw from Cologne until the British had provided them with security, and at the same time they refused to promise evacuation to the Germans in exchange for the conclusion of a security pact. They insisted that disarmament come first, and the delay in arranging a disarmament settlement allowed them to occupy Cologne until after the security treaty could be concluded at Locarno. Thus, on the eve of the Locarno confer-

---

Deutschlands zum Völkerbund, pp. 87-89. For Stresemann's attitude toward war guilt see Henry L. Bretton, *Stresemann and the Revision of Versailles*, Stanford, 1953, pp. 46-53.

[40] *Proceedings of the Locarno Conference*, Nos. 56, 62, 65; London *Times*, 30 September 1925; *Le Temps*, 1 October 1925. Also DDB, II, 107.

[41] Cmd. 2468, pp. 7-9; Spenz, *Beitritts Deutschlands zum Völkerbund*, pp. 81-84; Wandycz, *France and her Eastern Allies*, pp. 353-64.

ence, Stresemann had made little formal progress toward opening up any new prospects in the West. The only sign of Allied concession—Chamberlain's desire for a negotiated settlement of the disarmament question—actually predated the German initiative on security. Finally, Stresemann's proposed Rhineland Pact cannot be given credit for having prevented the formation of an Anglo-French military alliance; the conservative imperialists within the Baldwin government had done this, and they would have done so even without Stresemann's initiative of January 20.

Significantly, Stresemann had not split the entente. Instead, eight months of negotiation had confirmed in Chamberlain's mind the emotional basis of an Anglo-French alignment against Germany. In negotiations with Briand, Chamberlain found the French Foreign Minister "amazingly reasonable." Briand "has almost taken my breath away by his liberality, his conciliatoriness, his strong and manifest desire for peace." On the other hand, he found the attitude of the Germans "just the contrary—niggling, provocative, crooked." "Your Germans," he wrote D'Abernon, "are very nearly intolerable. From the first to the last, very nearly every obstacle to the Pact negotiations has come from them." Provoked by Stresemann's demand to revise the war-guilt clause, he wrote: "At every stage the Germans sow distrust in my mind. At every stage Briand disproves the common assertion that the difficulty is now with France. I have chosen my path with the limits set to me by forces beyond my control. God forgive me if I have allowed myself to be duped by the Germans, but either Stresemann is crooked and a coward, or the value of any pact which may be made is, for the present, singularly discounted by the opposition which he meets." At the same time, he wrote, "I remain confident, as I have been from the first, that I can count on Briand's good sense, suppleness, liberality, and courage." "It will not be his fault if such difficulties as there are, are not overcome."[42] Chamberlain's suspicion of the Germans had reached its height on the eve of the Locarno conference. Whether Stresemann would be able to overcome this distrust, on the one hand, and chronic French hostility toward Germany, on the other, and then reap practical benefits from his initiative of 1925, would be determined at the conference itself.

---

[42] 15 September 1925, Chamberlain to D'Abernon, AC 52/295; 30 September 1925, Chamberlain to D'Abernon, AC 52/297. D'Abernon did not share Chamberlain's distrust: D'Abernon, *An Ambassador*, III, 189, 192.

2. *The Locarno Bargain, October 5-December 1, 1925*

The conference held at Locarno from October 5 to 16 took place without a major crisis. Most of the issues were defined in Stresemann's original proposal, and others were resolved in the nine months of negotiations that followed. The German representatives at the conference were able to convey an impression of honesty and straightforwardness. Chancellor Hans Luther, who spoke French, held a private conversation with Briand on October 7, and the next day the term "spirit of Locarno" appeared in the press.[43] In the full meetings of the conference, Stresemann was able to win the concessions that had been denied him in negotiations through normal diplomatic channels. He prevented the French from guaranteeing the German arbitration treaties with Poland and Czechoslovakia, and he won exemption from full particpation in the sanctions specified in Article 16 of the Covenant.[44] Because these concessions to Germany were made largely at the expense of smaller Eastern European powers, they were accompanied by little acrimony on the part of the great powers and did not threaten to disrupt the negotiations. Smoothed by feelings of personal confidence between the representatives of the large powers, and facilitated by the sacrifices of the small powers, the conference proceeded amicably.

During the conference the only effective opposition to German demands came during the private informal conversations between Stresemann, Luther, Briand, and Chamberlain on October 12 and 15 when the Germans attempted to secure compensation for their signature of the Locarno Treaties.[45] Stresemann and Luther asked amnesty for those Germans imprisoned by the French during the Ruhr occupation, a lifting of the restrictions

[43] London *Times*, 8 October 1925. Also D'Abernon, *An Ambassador*, III, 195.

[44] Lionel Kochan, *The Struggle for Germany, 1914-1945*, Edinburgh, 1963, pp. 43-44; Spenz, *Beitritts Deutschlands zum Völkerbund*, pp. 96-106. Wandycz, *France and her Eastern Allies*, pp. 359-68. Minutes of the meetings and notes on the conversations held at Locarno can be found in *Proceedings of the Locarno Conference*; Sitzungsniederschriften der Konferenz von Locarno, 5 bis 16 Oktober 1925 (Nachlasse von Stockhausen); Ministerium für Auswärtige Angelegenheiten (DDR), *Locarno-Konferenz 1925; eine Dokumentensammlung*, Berlin, 1962.

[45] The following account is based on the records found in *Proceedings of the Locarno Conference*, Nos. 146, 176. Also Stresemann, *Vermächtnis*, II, 193-203, 215-16; Petrie, *Chamberlain*, II, 287.

on German civilian aviation, and for a lenient interpretation of some of the disarmament demands of the Conference of Ambassadors.[46] Most of their petition, however, pertained to the Rhineland: they asked that the Cologne zone be evacuated, that the regime of occupation in the remaining two zones be eased, that the number of occupying troops in those zones be reduced, that all Black troops be removed from Germany, that the entire Rhineland be evacuated prior to the dates named in the Treaty of Versailles, and that no systems of permanent on-site inspection be established to maintain the disarmament of Germany and the demilitarization of the Rhineland. Stresemann presented this list of demands, which had been unanimously approved by the cabinet prior to the conference, as the *Rückwirkungen* (subsequent effects, or corollaries) of the Locarno Treaty. He asked that the Allies give formal, written assent to them in the Final Protocol of the conference.[47]

He met stiff resistance. Briand stated that Stresemann's demands were startling, amounting to a revision of Versailles, and both he and Chamberlain stated that Stresemann had raised issues too numerous and too difficult to be resolved during the conference. When Stresemann persisted, the atmosphere filled with hostility, and at one point during the conversation of October 15, the negotiations lapsed into "a long and somewhat tense silence."[48] "This attempt at blackmail by the German delegation," Chamberlain wrote to London, "introduced a discordant note into our discussions here, which have hitherto proceeded on a high level of good faith with noteworthy absence of any sort of bargaining."[49] Repeatedly, he and Briand refused to participate in what they characterized as a behind-the-scenes bargain for German assent to the treaty; neither would consider signing any such agreement as a condition of the conclusion of the pact.

[46] In Stresemann's account he mentions asking for the return of the Saar to Germany prior to 1935. There is no indication of this in *Proceedings of the Locarno Conference.*

[47] German opposition to on-site inspection and their demand for alleviations in the regime of occupation were outlined in two *aide-mémoires* presented to the occupying powers on October 14-15: *Proceedings of the Locarno Conference,* No. 162.

[48] *Ibid.,* No. 176. Also Werner Freiherr von Rheinbaben, *Viermal Deutschland; aus dem Erleben eines Seemannes, Diplomaten, Politikers, 1895-1954,* Berlin, 1954, pp. 216-17.

[49] 16 October 1925, Chamberlain to Tyrrell, *Proceedings of the Locarno Conference,* No. 187.

Stresemann and Luther, on the other hand, adamantly refused to propose ratification of the security pact to the Reichstag unless Cologne were evacuated. The Allies in response refused to bypass the Conference of Ambassadors and conclude a Cologne-disarmament settlement at Locarno, but they did promise to negotiate a compromise after the conference was over. It was agreed at Locarno that after their return to Berlin, the Germans would address a note to the Conference of Ambassadors indicating that they had made a serious beginning on disarmament and promising to carry out the most important remaining points. The Allies would then respond, promising to evacuate Cologne by a specified date without waiting for the completion of German disarmament. Chamberlain had favored such a compromise since January, and he urged it on Briand and Stresemann at Locarno; both men accepted it there, Briand with the statement that he would resign if his government did not follow him.[50] With the proposed evacuation of Cologne prior to the full compliance with the disarmament demands of the Conference of Ambassador, Stresemann secured some reward for his acceptance of the Locarno Treaty and achieved one of his objectives of the previous January.

Stresemann was less successful, however, with regard to Coblenz and Mainz. Chamberlain and Briand refused to bind themselves to ease the regime of occupation or to reduce the number of troops. They would not even make arrangements for a settlement to be concluded at a later date; instead they declared themselves generally in favor of such measures and suggested that they be handled through normal diplomatic channels. Briand promised to urge the alleviations and reductions on Paul Painlevé, the Premier and Minister of War, and on the rest of the French government; Chamberlain promised to visit Painlevé in Paris and remonstrate with him to the same end. Both men promised to make public statements regarding the consequences of Locarno for the Rhineland. On the topic of complete evacuation, however, Briand and Chamberlain talked much less readily. Chamberlain was noncommittal, and Briand indicated vaguely that the security pact would have important political consequences and would be followed by a détente which would make all things possible.[51]

[50] *Ibid.*, Nos. 145-46, 164, 196; Salewski, *Entwaffnung und Militärkontrolle*, pp. 315-17.
[51] *Proceedings of the Locarno Conference*, Nos. 146, 158, 164, 176, 195.

After the conclusion of the Locarno conference, the Cologne-disarmanent arrangement agreed upon there was carried out. On October 23 Berlin reported to the Conference of Ambassadors on the status of German disarmanent: some of the measures required by the Ambassadors' Conference in their note of June 4 were fulfilled; others would be fulfilled by mid-November; still others would not be completed until an unspecified later date; and finally, with regard to five specific matters, Berlin declined to give any assurance of compliance.[52]

Chamberlain was content with this formulation because he did not think the remaining lapses contributed to Germany's capacity to wage an aggressive war. However, he was unwilling to initiate concessions to Berlin or to go further than the French to meet the German position. Instead, he was inclined to agree to any conditions acceptable to Paris: knowing the "largeness of Briand's views," he wrote, "I willingly resign leadership in this matter to France."[53]

Briand and Berthelot looked after the delivery of the *Rückwirkungen* to Berlin. Under pressure from Paris, Paul Tirard, the French High Commissioner in the Rhineland, previously hostile to any reform of the regime of occupation, contented himself with initial difficulties. Stronger resistance came from the French High Command, and at a meeting of the Conference of Ambassadors in late October, Marshal Foch argued for a careful and lengthy discussion of the German note of October 23. However, Jules Laroche and René Massigli (acting for Briand) and Crewe (acting for Chamberlain) insisted on a speedy reply in the spirit of Locarno. Between November 6 and 11, Berlin and Paris agreed on the details of how all but one of the five unresolved matters were to be resolved. Foch then offered little resistance at a second meeting held on November 14. Crewe reported that the French Generals "behaved extremely well"; with a joke and a

---

[52] *Correspondence between the Ambassadors' Conference and the German Ambassador at Paris respecting German Disarmament, Evacuation of Cologne Zone and Modifications in the Rhineland Régime, Paris, October-November 1925*, Cmd. 2527, London, 1925; pp. 2-5; Salewski, *Entwaffnung und Militärkontrolle*, p. 318. The five issues were the German police, the High Command, the prohibition of training with certain weapons, the fortifications around Königsberg, and the relations between the Reichswehr and the Verbände (paramilitary organizations).

[53] 4 November 1925, Chamberlain to Müller, AC 50/135; DBFP, IA, I, 1, 15, 21, 35, 50, 89; Fox, "Britain and the Inter-Allied Military Commission of Control," p. 153.

shrug Foch resigned himself to evacuation prior to complete disarmament.[54] On November 16 Briand, acting as chairman of the Conference of Ambassadors, notified Hoesch that the evacuation of Cologne would begin on December 1 "without waiting for the execution [of the German promise of October 23] to be entirely completed." He added that in "making the beginning of the evacuation coincide with the signature of the Locarno agreements, the Conference expresses the confidence of the governments represented upon it that the signature will inaugurate a new era in their relations with Germany."[55] In this way the promise made at Locarno was kept, and in January 1926 the Cologne zone was evacuated—in effect, in exchange for German signature of the Rhineland Pact. The dependence of evacuation on prior compliance with the disarmament provisions of Versailles, put forth by the Conference of Ambassadors in January 1925, was disregarded.

Two days earlier, on November 14, a similar note had announced other *Rückwirkungen*. Although no date was set for withdrawal from the entire Rhineland, the Allies did promise to reduce the number of troops in zones two and three, to meet most of Stresemann's demands for alleviations in the regime of occupation, and to reduce the size of the IMCC.[56] All this was done, in Briand's words, in order that the "peaceful intentions" and the "spirit of goodwill," "confidence," and "appeasement" which inspired the Locarno agreements might be extended to the Rhineland issue.[57]

Thus, a complex bargain was made between Germany and the Western powers in October-November 1925.[58] Germany promised to maintain the *status quo* in the West, to arbitrate disputes in the East, and to join the League of Nations. In return, the British and French exempted Germany from participation in League sanctions against Russia, stopped short of an international

[54] 15 November 1925, Crewe to Chamberlain, AC 52/232; DBFP, IA, I, 2, 12, 33, 41, 56, 89, 102; Salewski, *Entwaffnung und Militärkontrolle*, pp. 320-23.

[55] Cmd. 2527, pp. 12-14; Salewski, *Entwaffnung und Militärkontrolle*, p. 324. Philippe Berthelot was Secretary General at the French Foreign Ministry. Leopold von Hoesch was German Ambassador at Paris.

[56] The withdrawal of the IMCC was to await the complete fulfillment of the German promise of October 23.

[57] Cmd. 2527, pp. 10-11; Hugh Spender, "The Fruits of Locarno," *Fortnightly Review* (January 1926), pp. 50-51.

[58] The term "Locarno bargain": William J. Newman, *The Balance of Power in the Interwar Years, 1919-1939*, New York, 1968, p. 98.

guarantee of Germany's Eastern frontiers, and promised to evacuate Cologne. This part of the Locarno bargain was soon brought to a conclusion, but other parts of the bargain, although arranged in the autumn of 1925, were not immediately implemented, and their fulfillment was the subject of negotiation for two years after Locarno. Agreed upon but not completed was the compromise disarmament settlement by which Germany would fulfill some but not all the Allies' disarmament requirements and the Allies would in return abolish the IMCC and reduce the strength of their armies in the remaining zones of occupation. The entire Locarno bargain was, of course, not formulated in terms of a crude *do ut des* agreement; Chamberlain and Briand were sensitive about any notion of payment being made for Germany's signature; consequently, Allied concessions were spoken of as measures to promote an atmosphere of goodwill, peace, and harmony. Finally, one element—the complete withdrawal of Allied troops from the Rhineland—was completely excluded from the Locarno bargain.

Stresemann regarded complete evacuation as the ultimate goal, "the end point," of his Locarno policy, and in early November he asked both Briand and Chamberlain to make public declarations concerning Germany's right to the early evacuation of the entire Rhineland. The ratification of the Locarno Treaty by the Reichstag would be greatly facilitated, he stated, by statements that the improved international atmosphere, along with German compliance with the Treaty of Versailles, would result in the shortening of occupation.[59] Briand declined to do so, as did Chamberlain, who commented: "There is a limit beyond which we cannot go; they are in grave danger of falling into their usual error of opening their mouths too wide."[60] Consequently, Stresemann had to tell the cabinet on November 16 that the Allies would make no binding promises regarding early evacuation. Convinced that the Allies would not depart the Rhineland for a year, and noting that "politics is the art of the possible," Stresemann did not make the evacuation of Coblenz and Mainz a condition of German ratification, nor did he mention the topic when he met Chamberlain and

[59] Henry A. Turner, Jr. (ed.), "Eine Rede Stresemanns über seine Locarnopolitik," *Vierteljahreshefte für Zeitgeschichte*, 19 (1967), p. 428; DBFP, IA, I, 43, 68; Stresemann, *Vermächtnis*, II, 225.

[60] DBFP, IA, I, 53, 56.

Briand in London on December 1 for the signature of the treaty. Instead, he pressed for a reduction in the number of occupying troops, which he described to the cabinet as "the beginning of a subsequent final evacuation."[61]

The Locarno bargain was not well received in Berlin. In the Reichstag debate on the treaty (November 23-27), those parties which voted for ratification accepted the *Rückwirkungen* with no particular enthusiasm, and the DNVP, which had withdrawn from the cabinet on October 26 and voted against ratification, was more critical of the continued occupation of Coblenz and Mainz than of the terms of the treaty itself.[62] Disappointment in the bargain was largely due to the dangerous political tactic, pursued by the Luther government, of emphasizing the importance of the *Rückwirkungen*. This was tactically useful, both in the campaign to secure ratification of the treaty and in persuading the Allies to reward Germany before the treaty was actually signed on December 1. But, it had the unintended consequence of raising the expectations of the German public. Prior to November 14, while the negotiations were actually in progress, Stresemann publicly mentioned the evacuation of the Cologne zone but discussed the other *Rückwirkungen* in vague terms. This lack of specific information gave rise to much speculation that the entire Rhineland would be evacuated. When this did not happen, popular disappointment resulted, which was then intensified by the tactics employed by the government in its negotiations with the Allies. To maintain pressure on the Allies for further concessions, Berlin assumed an attitude of official disappointment, and the press was told that the *Rückwirkungen* were short of German requirements. Stresemann, meanwhile, noted in his diary that the concessions of November 14 satisfied him completely while he played down the importance of securing *Rückwirkungen* in a speech to his party colleagues on November 22.[63]

Berlin's official disappointment in turn alienated the Allies.

[61] 16 November 1925, Cabinet Protocol, 2273/4509/130375-76; Stresemann, *Vermächtnis*, II, 238; 17 December 1925, Stresemann to Hoesch, 1491/3087/619872; ADAP, B, I-1, 1, 16.

[62] Eyck, *Weimar Republic*, II, 39-41; Garthwol, "DNVP and European Reconciliation," pp. 213-15, 223, 243.

[63] Stresemann, *Vermächtnis*, II, 215-16, 223-26, 246-48; Turner, "Eine Rede Stresemanns," pp. 417, 427.

D'Abernon had recommended the *Rückwirkungen* to London, hoping they would produce a good effect on German public opinion.[64] Chamberlain was more pessimistic. Before the *Rückwirkungen* were announced, he predicted that Luther and Stresemann might well make the "grave mistake of treating concessions, which would have appeared impossible to them a month ago, as valueless from the moment they were offered, or of allowing themselves and their public to think that nothing was of any value except that which was refused."[65] When they were announced and received no enthusiastic response, D'Abernon remarked bitterly, "The art of expressing gratitude . . . is one which the Germans do not practice. Directly they are granted anything, they not only ask for more, but they criticize what has been given them as inadequate satisfaction of their unquestionable rights."[66] The final blow came with the debate over ratification. The negative vote of the DNVP and the lukewarm reaction of the other parties disappointed Chamberlain: "It is borne in upon me once again that to a German no concession is of any value from the moment it has been made." Suspecting that Stresemann might intend to ask for complete evacuation when the Treaty of Locarno was signed in London on December 1, he instructed D'Abernon to warn Stresemann that "this is not the moment for them to press for further concessions from us."[67]

Stresemann himself felt somewhat trapped by the reaction to the Locarno bargain within Germany. He needed tangible benefits to popularize his policy, and he was willing to use the popular demand for compensation in an attempt to gain reward from the Allies, but he could not demand more than the Allies would grant, and this exposed him to criticism at home as an ineffective representative of German foreign policy. In the face of disappointment, created by demands which he had promoted and publicized, Stresemann could only preach patience. Confronted with Allied resistance, he could not even raise the question of complete evacuation when he met with Chamberlain and Briand in London.

[64] Stresemann, *Vermächtnis*, II, 226.

[65] 5 November 1925, Chamberlain to D'Abernon, AC 50/140.

[66] DBFP, IA, I, 69; D'Abernon, *An Ambassador*, III, 207-208. Colonel Ryan, acting British High Commissioner in the Rhineland, and Joseph Addison, Counselor at the British embassy in Berlin attributed this ingratitude to the "German mentality": DBFP, IA, I, 44, 141.

[67] DBFP, IA, I, 120.

3. *The League Council Crisis and the Beginning of Locarno Diplomacy, March 1926*

One element of the Locarno bargain was that Germany join the League of Nations and receive a permanent seat on the Council under conditions that would do minimal damage to relations between Berlin and Moscow. When the German government formally applied for membership on February 8, 1926, Poland, Spain, and Brazil quickly put forth claims to permanent Council seats also. The Polish claim found some support in London and Paris, but strong opposition in Berlin. The result was the first post-Locarno crisis, a crisis which was eventually resolved by offering the three other powers semi-permanent Council seats. Poland accepted this, while Spain threatened to withdraw from the League and Brazil actually did so. Meanwhile, the admission of Germany was delayed from the League Council meeting of March 1926 to the Assembly meeting the following September.[68] The means by which the Locarno powers tried to deal with this crisis are of particular interest and significance, for they established a diplomatic procedure which persisted throughout the Locarno era.

Austen Chamberlain was concerned that both Paris and Berlin be given a fair and equal hearing. He was anxious that Germany's case be heard and that no solution be imposed by a League Council of which Germany was not yet a member. Even more he feared that Germany might gain admission under conditions which would be regarded as a German triumph over France and Poland. Either eventuality would, he thought, "split the Locarno powers into two camps on the old lines" and bring an end to the work of conciliation begun in October, something which he thought would be "a disaster of unequalled magnitude."[69] His objective, as he had stated it in March 1925, was "the restoration

[68] David Carlton, "Great Britain and the League Council Crisis of 1926," *Historical Journal*, 11 (1968), pp. 354-64; Spenz, *Beitritts Deutschlands zum Völkerbund*, pp. 125-71; F. P. Walters, *A History of the League of Nations*, New York, 1952, 1960, pp. 316-27.

[69] 26 February 1926, Chamberlain to D'Abernon, D'Abernon papers 48929; 18 March 1926, Chamberlain to Baldwin, AC 53/51; 29 March 1926, Chamberlain to D'Abernon, AC 53/218; W. N. Jordan, *Great Britain, France, and the German Problem, 1919-1939*, London, 1943, p. 99.

of the Concert of Great Powers in Europe,"[70] and the way to achieve concert, he thought, was through personal across-the-table conversations between Germany and the Allies. During the security pact negotiations he had urged Briand to abandon the exchange of formal notes in favor of personal conversations with the Germans,[71] and at Locarno major problems had been discussed in informal private conversations between the heads of the French, British, and German delegations. The results of this method now led Chamberlain, Briand, and Stresemann to assume that personal discussion was the most effective way to reach an equitable and lasting resolution of the League Council crisis. Chamberlain took the initiative and proposed that "the Locarnites," as he called them, meet at Geneva in March for "a round table discussion of the real Locarno kind." Briand, Stresemann, Mussolini, and Emile Vandervelde of Belgium readily agreed.[72] And on four occasions during the League Council meeting (March 7-17), the Locarnites met in Chamberlain's hotel room at his summons to discuss, without complete success, the competing claims of the four powers to Council seats.[73]

The example was set, and for the next three and one-half years there persisted a pattern of negotiation by means of meetings of the representatives of the Locarno powers, usually meetings of the Locarno Big Three—Stresemann, Briand, and Chamberlain. As often as four times a year these three men met in Geneva, or wherever the League Council was convened, and there in one another's hotel rooms, they privately discussed the disarmament of Germany, the evacuation of the Rhineland, the settlement of the reparation question, and other matters affecting the relations between their nations. They also arbitrated the affairs of the rest of Europe and coordinated their policies on matters considered by the League Council. As a result, these "Geneva tea parties," as

[70] 19 March 1925, Chamberlain to D'Abernon, AC 50/54. Also Austen Chamberlain, "Great Britain as a European Power," *International Affairs*, 9 (1930), p. 188.
[71] 7 July 1925, Chamberlain to Crewe, AC 52/224; 11 August 1925, Chamberlain to D'Abernon, AC 52/291.
[72] DBFP, IA, I, 282, 287, 289-90, 321; 25 February 1925, Chamberlain to G. Grahame, AC 50/173; Petrie, *Chamberlain*, II, 298.
[73] DBFP, IA, I, 327, 330, 332, 334, 336; ADAP, B, I-I, 145, 148, 153, 166; Spenz, *Beitritts Deutschlands zum Völkerbund*, pp. 139-51.

they were derisively called, became far more important than the meetings of the League which occasioned them. And they came to surpass negotiations through normal diplomatic channels, which were utilized largely to handle low-level or routine matters, or, at best, to prepare for future foreign ministers' meetings and to follow up those previously held.

The unique qualities of the Locarno diplomatic method were the exclusiveness, secrecy, and informality of the meetings and their frequency and regularity; they were convened periodically and held even if there were no prospect of conclusive results. The Locarnite meetings were criticized at the time, largely by supporters of the League and advocates of open diplomacy, as a return to secret diplomacy dominated by a few great powers. And since then, historians have criticized Locarno diplomacy and the conference system of the 1920's in general, as an example of unsystematic procedures and inadequate preparation for meetings. Nevertheless, the Locarnites found the tea parties appealing. They saw in personal conversations the best way to promote further détente among their states, and their meetings permitted them to use the extemporaneous verbal facility and other persuasive powers developed during years of experience as party-parliamentary politicians. From their frequent personal contact, there developed among the men of Locarno a brotherhood of foreign ministers, a set of personal-political relationships to which they could appeal when there were issues to be resolved and favors to be asked.[74]

To be sure, the relationship between Stresemann and his two colleagues grew slowly. Chamberlain, for example, was slow to recognize that Stresemann was the man who made German policy and the man with whom he would have to deal. Prior to the Locarno conference, Chamberlain had attributed the German proposal on security to Luther and referred to the Rhineland Pact as "Luther's policy."[75] Stresemann impressed Chamberlain as being "rather cold and austere" while Luther, who could speak French with Briand and Chamberlain, impressed them all with

[74] For a fuller discussion of the Locarno diplomatic method, its critics, and its appeal to the Locarnites, see my "The Conduct of Locarno Diplomacy," *Review of Politics*, 34 (1972).

[75] 27 April 1925, Chamberlain to Crewe, AC 52/207.

what D'Abernon called his "honesty and straightforwardness."[76] It took some time, as D'Abernon knew, to develop an appreciation for Stresemann, and at the March 1926 meeting of the League, Chamberlain still found Luther "conciliatory" and Stresemann "unyielding."[77] Stresemann could be aloof and harsh, and this impression was heightened by his hoarse baritone voice and his coarse features. Harold Nicolson, who observed Stresemann while First Secretary of the British embassy at Berlin, described the impression which Stresemann's appearance conveyed: "The thick neck reminded observers that he was the son of a Berlin publican; the bald, bullet head suggested Prussian obstinacy and rage; the paled face and delicate white hands denoted sensitiveness and refinement; the small, watchful, restless, pink-lidded eyes flashed suspicion; the way his tongue would at moments dart between red lips indicated almost reptilian quickness and resource."[78]

What success Stresemann achieved with Briand and Chamberlain was due to the force of his character, the strength of his convictions, and the persistence, earnestness, and passion with which he conveyed those convictions to the others. With his quick, clear, shrewd mind, time and time again he took the initiative in the Locarnite meetings, presented his aspirations in idealistic, and even sentimental and emotional terms, and won sympathy for himself and acceptance for his policies. His success was not due to brilliant innovation, long-range planning, or tactical duplicity; it was due to the flair with which he took the rather simple political notions of treaty revision common to most Germans and

[76] 20 December 1927, Chamberlain to M. Lampson, AC 54/326; D'Abernon, *An Ambassador*, III, 195. Also Antonia Vallentin-Luchaire, *Stresemann*, New York, 1931, p. 199; Eyck, *Weimar Republic*, II, 32; Edgar Stern-Rubarth, *Three Men Tried . . . Austen Chamberlain, Stresemann, Briand and their Fight for a New Europe; a Personal Memoir*, London, 1939, p. 112.

[77] D'Abernon, *An Ambassador*, III, 195; 9 March 1926, Chamberlain to Tyrrell, AC 53/511. Also 13 April 1926, Chamberlain to Howard, AC 53/368; DBFP IA, I, 330, 337, 340.

[78] Stern-Rubarth, *Three Men Tried*, pp. 221-22; Emery Kelen, *Peace in Their Time; Men Who Led Us In and Out of War, 1914-1945*, New York, 1963, pp. 154, 160; Harold Nicolson, *King George the Fifth; His Life and Reign*, London, 1952, p. 408. The official biographical sketch filed by the British embassy in Berlin mentions Stresemann's "frog-like face and harsh metallic voice": FO. 371/12886/339. For a more complimentary description of Stresemann's features see Vallentin-Luchaire, *Stresemann*, pp. 16, 100.

molded them into something convincing and persuasive.[79] Too, his forcefulness, his congeniality, and his gently sarcastic sense of humor were valuable assets in personal conversations, as was his long, political experience as a member of the Reichstag since 1907 and chairman of the German People's Party (DVP) since its formation in 1918.

Briand's experience as a parliamentary politician—on March 9, 1926, he had formed the ninth cabinet of his long career—made him effective in hotel-room conversations also, and he liked them for that reason. An extraordinarily persuasive speaker, Briand was one of the greatest orators of the interwar years. Most people, including Chamberlain, who heard him speak in large public meetings regarded him as the best speaker they had ever heard.[80] He was equally persuasive in the small meetings of the Locarno powers where he sat, stout and slouching, hair, moustache, and clothes in disorder, chain-smoking his forty to fifty cigarettes a day while recounting anecdotes and explaining his policies. He disarmed his listeners with his engaging and expressive voice, with the mocking smile in the corners of his eyes, the elegant gestures of his slender hands, and his biting wit and ironic humor.[81] All this gave his discourse what one frequent attendant of the Locarno tea parties called a "strange power of seduction and persuasion."[82] In both public speeches and informal conversations, Briand employed his unmatched facility to extemporize. He did not rely on mastery of details, careful analysis, or involved logic. He read and wrote very little. Reports prepared by his subordinates were usually read to him or paraphrased for him, either

[79] Herbert von Dirksen, *Moscow, Tokyo, London; Twenty Years of German Foreign Policy*, London, 1951, pp. 46, 61; Stern-Rubarth, *Three Men Tried*, p. 157; Vallentin-Luchaire, *Stresemann*, pp. 13, 29.

[80] Austen Chamberlain, *Down the Years*, London, 1935, p. 185; Duff Cooper, *Old Men Forget; the autobiography of Duff Cooper (Viscount Norwich)*, New York, 1954, p. 163; Arthur Salter, *Personality in Politics; Studies of Contemporary Statesmen*, London, 1942, pp. 199-200.

[81] Robert (Lord) Cecil, *All the Way*, London, 1949, p. 201; Kelen, *Peace in Their Time*, pp. 154, 174; Vallentin-Luchaire, *Stresemann*, pp. 199-200.

[82] Paul Hymans, *Mémoires*, Brussels, 1958, II, 599. Anthony Eden came away from one meeting "completely convinced" by Briand, and even Stresemann reportedly once jokingly said that in private conversations Briand possessed "something supernatural which completely prevented him from controlling himself." Anthony Eden, *Facing the Dictators; the Memoirs of Anthony Eden, Earl of Avon*, Boston, 1962, p. 10; August Bréal, *Philippe Berthelot*, Paris, 1937, p. 211.

in long conversations with Philippe Berthelot, the Secretary General, or in quick briefings just prior to a meeting or speech. He then used those reports in a highly selective manner. Abhoring the use of notes, he would remember a few phrases from a document, use them to express the essentials of his position, and give an appearance of having mastered the issue under discussion. Gaps in his knowledge were covered by avoiding precise explanations.[83]

Had Briand thoroughly prepared himself, he might have deprived himself of his major asset as a negotiator—his ability to phrase what he had to say in the manner most convincing to his audience. Briand had, one League official wrote, "flair without profound knowledge, magnetism without industry, eloquence without exactitude."[84] The expansiveness of his ideas, their vagueness, and their incompleteness was an important part of his political method, for it allowed him to present his policy in such a way as to achieve a consensus. It permitted him to emphasize the reasons for agreement on any issue rather than the causes for division; it allowed him to achieve compromise and promote conciliation, to practice a policy which he called "appeasement." He could reconcile divergent opinions and conflicting demands in a way that would have been difficult by means of definitive statements. In a search for consensus, Briand avoided the direct confrontation of issues; "he preferred to circumnavigate an obstacle rather than attempt to steer through it."[85] Contemporary observers attributed Briand's methods to age, fatigue, and laziness,[86] but in avoiding unnecessary struggles, especially those from which he might not emerge victorious, Briand was serving the interests of France. He could at the same time call for peace and reconciliation, postpone Stresemann's demands for action with

[83] Richard D. Challener, "The French Foreign Office; the Era of Philippe Berthelot," in Gordon A. Craig and Felix Gilbert (eds.), *The Diplomats, 1919-1939*, Princeton, 1953, p. 79; Jules Laroche, *Au Quai d'Orsay avec Briand et Poincaré, 1913-1926*, Paris, 1957, pp. 41-42; Emmanuel de Peretti de la Rocca, "Briand et Poincaré (Souvenirs)," *Revue de Paris*, 4 (1936), pp. 767, 788; A. C. Temperley, *The Whispering Gallery of Europe*, London, 1938, p. 98.

[84] Salter, *Personality in Politics*, p. 198. Also Chamberlain, *Down the Years*, pp. 185-86; Carlo Sforza, *Makers of Modern Europe; Portraits and Personal Impressions and Recollections*, Indianapolis, 1930, p. 234.

[85] Emile Ludwig, *Nine Sketched from Life*, New York, 1934, pp. 101-102.

[86] Sforza, *Makers*, pp. 228-29; Stern-Rubarth, *Three Men Tried*, p. 170; Temperley, *Whispering Gallery*, p. 38.

statements of goodwill, and protect France's rights under the Treaty of Versailles. When spoken, his statements had a hypnotic, intoxicating quality, but when carefully analyzed, it became apparent that with all his verbiage Briand had actually said very little and left most everything unresolved. However, Briand's sensitivity to his audience—large or small—does not mean that he drew the inspiration for his policy from his audience, or that he formulated policy during the course of a speech or discussion as he read the expressions on his listeners' faces, as has been alleged.[87] Briand improvised, but he improvised within defined limits. The danger of Briand's mode of operation was not that he would depart widely from a political course consistent with French interests; he was far too experienced a politician for that. The danger was that he might leave large areas of ambiguity.

At first glance, it would appear that Austen Chamberlain did not fit into the informality of the Locarno tea parties. His formality in dress—morning coat, well-pressed trousers, boutonniere, top hat, and monocle attached to a black shoe lace—his very correct bearing, and his "stiff and forbidding manner of speaking," as Eden described it, gave Chamberlain an appearance of aloofness and an air of conceit which set him off from other people—even his colleagues in Parliament.[88] He *was* conceited and pompous, but this was only a part of him; other qualities made him effective at the meetings. His correctness covered a boyish enthusiasm, sincerity, and optimism, qualities which eased the negotiations of 1925 and did as much to promote the spirit of Locarno as did Briand's oratory.[89] Chamberlain was a good public speaker; although he had none of the hypnotic intoxication of Briand, or even the power and drama to which Stresemann sometimes rose, he was capable of a clarity, logic, and precision that escaped Baldwin and MacDonald. He was an experienced and adroit politician and a talented diplomat. Throughout the Locarno era he played on two chess boards, as Crewe put it; he played a German

[87] Ludwig, *Nine Sketched from Life*, pp. 99-131.
[88] Eden, *Facing the Dictators*, p. 8; Kelen, *Peace in Their Time*, p. 154; Harold McMillian, *Winds of Change, 1914-1939*, New York, 1966, pp. 174-75; Harold Nicolson, *Diaries and Letters*, London, 1966-68, I, 49; Josiah Wedgwood, *Memoirs of a Fighting Life*, London, 1940, p. 203.
[89] John Connell, *The "Office"; a Study of British Foreign Policy and its Makers, 1919-1951*, London, 1958, pp. 70-71; Nicolson, *King George the Fifth*, p. 408.

game and a French game.[90] Being industrious, meticulous, and exact, he played both with great skill; never once did he get his moves confused. Chamberlain's effectiveness with Briand and Stresemann was due also to what he called "loyalty," and it has been said of him that he held "the old-fashioned belief that it was necessary to conduct one's self in politics like a man of honor."[91] "Warm hearted, considerate, and generous, . . . incapable of a mean action,"[92] he treated his associates, Stresemann and Briand included, in a fair and just manner. His major limitation was his susceptibility to the personal charm and magnetism of others. He fell under the spell of Lloyd George; he was nearly uncritical in his admiration of Mussolini; and to Briand he offered unqualified affection and loyalty.[93] Between the two men there developed what Chamberlain called a "close and affectionate intimacy" based on Chamberlain's long-standing sentimental attachment for France, the sway of Briand's oratory, and Briand's deference to English policy during the negotiation of the Locarno Treaties.[94] This same regard was extended less readily to Stresemann.

The relationship between Stresemann, Briand, and Chamberlain was a relationship of three party-parliamentary politicians accustomed by parliamentary debate to expressing their views orally, accustomed by interparty negotiation to making compromises, and accustomed by democratic politics to tolerating opposition. It was not an association based on three similar personalities; even less was it based on three identical views of the future of Europe. It was not a relationship in which the three men consistently duped, tricked, or deluded each other; but neither was it one of continuous harmony. The course of the diplomatic relations between the Locarno powers after 1925 is largely a story of the conflict between three men and the policies they con-

[90] 17 February 1925, Crewe to Chamberlain, AC 52/190. Also 16 February 1925, Chamberlain to Crewe, AC 52/189.

[91] Edward Francis-Williams, *A Pattern of Rulers*, London, 1965, pp. 18, 20-21. As Birkenhead cruelly said of Chamberlain, "Austen always played the game, and he always lost it": Lord Beaverbrook, *Men and Power, 1917-1918*, London, 1956, p. xiii.

[92] Eden, *Facing the Dictators*, p. 8.

[93] Alan Cassels, *Mussolini's Early Diplomacy*, Princeton, 1970, pp. 310-14; D. H. Elletson, *The Chamberlains*, London, 1966, pp. 266, 245; Arthur Salter, *Memoirs of a Public Servant*, London, 1961, p. 203, and Salter, *Recovery; the Second Effort*, London, 1932, p. 254.

[94] Chamberlain, *Down the Years*, pp. 180, 184.

ducted. The dispute in 1926 over the implementation of the Locarno bargain, exaggerated by the Russo-German Treaty of Berlin, is a case in point.

4. The Military Occupation of Germany and the Treaty of Berlin, January-August 1926

During the nine months following the signature of the Treaty of Locarno, the most persistent source of conflict between the Locarno powers was the Rhineland. While Stresemann, Briand, and Chamberlain were successfully arranging for the seating of Germany on the League Council, and while the three men were establishing the forms of personal diplomacy by which they were to conduct their relations during the next three years, they were disagreeing sharply over the size of the forces which were to occupy the Rhineland. In their note of November 14, 1925, the Allies had promised, as part of the Locarno bargain, to reduce the number of troops occupying Coblenz and Mainz "to a figure approaching the normal." Stresemann contended that the term "normal figure" meant 46,000 men, the number which normally comprised the German garrison in the area prior to 1914, and this was the figure he and Luther had proposed at Locarno and at the signature ceremonies at London. The French, on the other hand, contended that the term "normal figure" meant at least 72,000 men—the number of Allied troops stationed in zones two and three on December 1, 1925, the day the Locarno Treaty had been signed; and in London, Briand had indicated that the post-Locarno forces of occupation would number 75,000 men.[95] To the British the term meant 55-60,000 men: they contended that the number of troops on December 1, 1925, was 64,000 rather than 72,000, and they insisted that the November 14, 1925 promise called for a sensible reduction below that level.[96] This disagreement over the prospective size of the armies of occupation exer-

[95] *Proceedings of the Locarno Conference*, Nos. 146, 150, 203; DBFP, IA, I, 122, 191; Stresemann, *Vermächtnis*, II, 250-51. On occasion the French even claimed that 80,000 men was a normal figure; this, they maintained, was the size of the forces normally stationed in zones two and three before French forces in the Rhineland had been "depleted" during the summer of 1925 by the dispatch of troops to North Africa to quell the Rif rebellion: DBFP, IA, I, 505.

[96] 4 March 1927, Memorandum by Central Department, FO. 371/12148/116-17.

cised the Locarno powers until August 1926, when the French at last promised to reduce the size of their army by 6,000 men, and while it did so, this apparently trivial issue exposed the fundamental suspicions and hostilities which existed among the members of the Locarno Triplice.

The conflict over the size of the occupying army first took on major proportions in mid-January 1926 when a subcommittee of the Conference of Ambassadors recommended that an occupying force of 75,000 men be maintained in zones two and three after the occupation of Cologne was terminated on January 31. The French maintained their garrison at 60,000, while the Belgians and the British moved additional troops into the Coblenz and Mainz zones as they evacuated Cologne. Consequently, the total number of troops in zones two and three was increased from 64,000 or 72,000 (depending on whether one accepts the British or French figures) to 75,000, and there were more troops in Coblenz and Mainz after the signature of Locarno than before. When Stresemann discovered this, on January 13, he immediately protested to D'Abernon, demanding that the forces of occupation be reduced to the size of the prewar German garrison (46,000); he then formalized this protest in written notes handed to the occupying powers on January 18 and 24.

The argument developed by Stresemann in January was one which he was to repeat frequently, with minor variations, as the dispute over troop reduction extended into the spring and summer of 1926: the maintenance of an oversized army of occupation was incompatible with the Treaty of Locarno, an agreement which renounced the use of force on the Rhine; failure to reduce the number of occupying troops was a violation of the Allied promise of November 14, 1925; if that promise were not kept, he could not continue his Locarno policy, and he could not recommend to the Reichstag that Germany apply for admission to the League of Nations; only a sizeable and *en masse* reduction would popularize the Locarno policy within Germany and enable him to continue in office; otherwise he would have to resign.[97]

Stresemann's threats to resign and to delay German application for League membership had some effect on the Allies. Although they did reject his prewar German garrison formula (46,000), they

[97] DBFP, IA, I, 189, 192, 202, 207; Stresemann, *Vermächtnis*, II, 432-34, 436-38, 444-45.

reaffirmed the promise of November 14, 1925, denied that the armies of occupation would be maintained at a level of 75,000 men, and vowed to reduce their forces to the "lowest practical level."[98] Stresemann accepted this formula, and although he continued to demand that the pledge be performed and that the armies actually be reduced in size, little more was heard from Berlin about the 46,000 figure.[99] On January 28 Stresemann informed the Reichstag of the Allied promise and survived a DNVP sponsored vote of no confidence. And as President Hindenburg and many members of the Reichstag Foreign Affairs Committee had wanted to make troop reduction a condition of Germany's joining the League, the assurance cleared the way for application to Geneva on February 8.[100]

On January 28, while Stresemann was addressing the Reichstag, Chamberlain and Briand were meeting privately in Paris to coordinate their League Council policies and discuss troop reduction. Following the conversation, Briand told the press that the size of the French Army of the Rhine would be reduced only if the Germans fulfilled their promise to disarm, and then only to the extent consistent with French interests, and without impairing French military security.[101] These stipulations reflected Briand's readiness to defer to the French military, and in particular to the generals of the occupying army, men who had expressed their hostility to the Locarno Treaty and their opposition to any subsequent concessions in the Rhineland.[102] General Guillaumat, the Commander of the Army of the Rhine, opposed troop reduction, as did General Debeney, the Chief of Staff, who considered a large occupying force essential to French military security; and these two generals had the passive support of Marshal Foch, who refused to override Debeney without direct instructions from the government.[103] Briand, in turn, hesitated to ignore the generals and simply order large reductions, as the

[98] Cuno Horkenbach, *Das Deutsche Reich von 1918 bis heute*, Berlin, 1930, p. 219.

[99] Stresemann, *Vermächtnis*, II, 251, 437-38, 463, 479.

[100] DBFP, IA, I, 206; Stresemann, *Vermächtnis*, II, 435-36; Eyck, *Weimar Republic*, II, 54; Andreas Dorpalen, *Hindenburg and the Weimar Republic*, Princeton, 1964, p. 98; Horkenbach, *Deutsche Reich*, p. 219.

[101] Ibid., p. 220.

[102] DBFP, IA, I, 12, 432.

[103] 29 June 1927, Phipps to Tyrrell, FO. 371/12148/179; 6 July 1927, Phipps to Tyrrell, FO. 371/12148/186.

army could easily find support for its position in the Chamber of Deputies. Briand's eighth, ninth, and tenth governments (November 28, 1925-July 17, 1926) were unstable and vulnerable due to their inability to stop the fall of the franc; and Briand, who was almost continually threatened with defeat, was unwilling to add to his difficulties the political repercussions of a conflict with the army.[104] In the matter of troop reduction, Briand found "military opposition and parliamentary difficulties formidable," as Crewe wrote in April,[105] and as a consequence the French Premier did little to meet the demands of the Germans in the months after the signature of the Locarno Treaty.

Military and political opposition was not the only reason Briand delayed troop reduction, however. He was himself not convinced that troop reduction was desirable or that it would reconcile to the Locarno policy the German Nationalists on whom the evacuation of Cologne had apparently made no impression. As early as December, Crewe had become impressed by "the firmness of his [Briand's] manner and by his reluctance to make any concessions to Germany which could possibly be avoided. There is in fact an increasingly strong undercurrent of distrust of Germany in official circles here, or an undercurrent which has gathered strength since, and in spite of, the Locarno conference."[106] Berthelot was convinced that Briand himself, not the military or the parliamentary situation, was preventing troop reduction. He found Briand "inclined to shilly-shally," as Crewe put it, and he thought that with pressure from Chamberlain, Briand could be brought to order a sizeable and immediate reduction.[107]

At their meeting of January 28, Chamberlain did persuade Briand to approve, privately and informally, the idea of a 15,000-man reduction,[108] and for the next six months he did urge Briand to carry out that reduction. He viewed the November 14, 1925 note as an Allied promise to reduce the number of troops below 75,000, and he was concerned that the increase in troop strength in the Coblenz and Mainz zones would allow Berlin to charge Paris and London with bad faith.[109]

[104] ADAP, B, I-1, 46, 48; DBFP, IA, I, 28; Stresemann, *Vermächtnis*, II, 434-35.
[105] DBFP, IA, I, 295.   [106] DBFP, IA, I, 161.
[107] Stresemann, *Vermächtnis*, II, 434-35, 437-38; DBFP, IA, I, 223.
[108] DBFP, IA, I, 236.
[109] Cab 23/53/35 (2 June 1926); DBFP, IA, I, 191, 196, 203, 505.

Chamberlain's entreaty to Briand was limited, however; he declined to "embarrass" Briand by pressing him "unduly." He feared troop reduction would only add to Briand's political difficulties, expose him to attack, and bring about his fall from office. Chamberlain therefore publicly stated his "warm sympathy and affection for France" after his January 28 meeting with Briand, and thereafter he pursued what he characterized as a policy of "close and continuous cooperation with France."[110]

"The spirit of Locarno is a spirit of reciprocity," Chamberlain declared after his meeting with Briand,[111] and he was convinced that the Germans were not reciprocating for what the Allies had done for them since Locarno. Chamberlain was influenced by Lord Kilmarnock, British High Commissioner in the Rhineland, who reported that Mayor Konrad Adenauer had responded to the evacuation of Cologne with a speech referring to the sufferings of the German people under British occupation, and that German officials in the Rhineland and Berlin continued to encourage popular resistance against the regime of occupation and special propaganda against it even after it had been relaxed. Believing that "the German understands only two methods of conduct—to browbeat or be browbeaten," Kilmarnock recommended that no more unilateral concessions be made to the Germans in the Rhineland.[112] Chamberlain agreed: Allied concessions, "our every endeavor to act in the Locarno spirit," are acknowledged, he complained, not by some reciprocal step toward disarmament, but by uncooperative behavior from German authorities in the Rhineland, by "vituperative abuse" from the German press and some German politicians, and by "ever growing demands, put forward almost as ultimatums." With the Germans "clamouring for a further reduction of troops," Chamberlain shared Kilmarnock's resistance to further unilateral concessions.[113] Until the Germans were more grateful for past concessions and did more toward disarmament, Briand could not reasonably be expected to urge troop reduction on the French military, Chamberlain believed. Until then, there was little he could do for them; the Germans, he had

---

[110] DBFP, IA, I, 231, 236, 386; Horkenbach, *Deutsche Reich*, p. 220.
[111] *Ibid.*, p. 220.
[112] Kilmarnock's reports, dated February 3, March 23, April 15, April 20: DBFP, IA, I, 241, 371, 432.
[113] DBFP, IA, I, 231, 236, 268.

said earlier, were "the most difficult people in the world to help."[114]

In April, Chamberlain at last instructed D'Abernon to complain to Stresemann of his dissatisfaction with Berlin's post-Locarno policy. At the same time, he spoke of his hopes for improved relations between Germany and the West in the past tense: "I *had* looked forward to steady progress in the path of concession and conciliation."[115] What led Chamberlain to make his complaints heard in Berlin and to refer to the uneven progress toward better relations was the information he had received from Berlin on April 1: the Germans were preparing to sign a treaty of limited neutrality with Soviet Russia.[116]

In London and Paris news of the Russo-German limited neutrality agreement, the Treaty of Berlin, provoked both dismay and suspicion. On April 6 the British and French ambassadors arrived at the Wilhelmstrasse seeking—and receiving—assurance that Germany would continue the policy which had led to Locarno and would honor its obligations under the League Covenant.[117] Numerous retaliatory measures were considered on the Quai d'Orsay—exclude Germany from the League, attempt to delay the signature of the Berlin Treaty, deliver a formal protest to Berlin. But with their careers tied to the détente between Germany and the West, Chamberlain and Briand did not even dare criticize the treaty in public. Chamberlain in particular took upon himself the difficult task of defending German policy.[118] To do otherwise, he argued, would only "drive Germany further into the arms of Moscow."[119]

The Berlin Treaty was formally signed on April 24. The next day Chamberlain wrote to D'Abernon: "The cost will be borne

[114] 29 March 1926, Chamberlain to D'Abernon, AC 53/218; 21 October 1925, Ryan to Lampson, D'Abernon papers 48929.

[115] 23 April 1926, Chamberlain to D'Abernon, AC 53/222; DBFP, IA, I, 434, 455.

[116] Schubert informed D'Abernon of the pending treaty on March 31, and the Quai d'Orsay was notified on April 3: DBFP, IA, I, 391, 392; ADAP, B, II-1, 99-101, 104.

[117] ADAP, B, II-1, 108; DBFP, IA, I, 398.

[118] Cab 23/52/15 (14 April 1926); DBFP, IA, I, 412, 421, 475, 477, 486, 491, 492, 497, 506, 511, 516.

[119] DBFP, IA, I, 418.

by Germany, and I think she is a fool to pay the price, but that is her business."[120] The bill for the Treaty of Berlin—to be paid in terms of occupation—was presented to Berlin in late April. Berthelot told Hoesch that, because of the Treaty of Berlin, Briand could do nothing about troop reduction. Then in a series of conversations between April 26 and 30, D'Abernon delivered Chamberlain's stinging rebuke of German ingratitude and informed Stresemann and Schubert that "it was not possible to press for a reduction of the French garrison just after a new Russo-German agreement had been signed."[121] Indeed, in the face of the French reaction against the Berlin Treaty, Chamberlain wrote to D'Abernon: "My earnest desire was to make progress with the changes which Locarno had rendered possible. At the present moment, however, it would be useless to talk of further concessions. . . . In the excitement and perturbation caused by the Russo-German negotiations, we could make no progress."[122]

Chamberlain was, then, in a difficult position. On the one hand the Germans were not behaving with the loyalty he expected from his Locarno partners. And on the other hand, he felt that the French had "behaved badly" by raising troop levels after Locarno, that all the occupying powers were "guilty of a very ugly breach of faith," and that London was honor bound to perform the promise of November 14, 1925, and promote troop reduction. This complicated his German policy and his position in Parliament, where he had to defend a policy of delayed troop reduction "which I and all British opinion hold to be radically indefensible." Consequently, as the furor over the Berlin Treaty died down, Chamberlain continued to instruct Crewe to speak to Briand about troop reduction. But his entreaty with Briand still took a rather relaxed form: Crewe was to discuss troop reduction with Briand informally, and at a moment of his own choosing.[123]

Events did not reach a critical point until late July, when the German ambassadors in London and Paris made a formal démarche asking for action on troop reduction.[124] By this time Chamberlain was anxious lest the issue go unresolved until Sep-

[120] DBFP, IA, I, 464.

[121] ADAP, B, I-1, 197; DBFP, IA, I, 484; 28 April 1926, D'Abernon to Chamberlain, D'Abernon papers 48929; D'Abernon, *An Ambassador*, III, 251.

[122] DBFP, IA, I, 435, 486.

[123] DBFP, IA, I, 487; 11 May 1926, Chamberlain to Crewe, AC 53/170.

[124] 28 July 1926, Chamberlain to D'Abernon, AC 50/227.

tember, when resentment in Berlin against Allied occupation policy might interfere with Germany's entrance into the League. He feared also that Stresemann might actually raise the issue before the League Council, and that he would be forced by British public opinion to side with the Germans against the French.[125] The German démarche, therefore, led Chamberlain to address a personal letter to Briand on July 29, urging troop reduction in order that the two of them not find themselves in public opposition when they met the Germans at Geneva. When finally threatened with a split in the entente, Briand responded, and in August he promised to reduce the size of the French Army of the Rhine by 6,000 men, a reduction which was then carried out during September.[126] This reduction was far short of the 15,000 men discussed by Briand and Chamberlain on January 28, and consequently, London as well as Berlin refused to regard it as a satisfactory final resolution of the issue. More importantly, it was not accompanied by an agreement among the Locarnites over their fundamental political differences.

The dispute over troop reduction was more than an argument over the number of troops which constituted a normal figure; it was a conflict over the meaning of the Locarno bargain. To the Germans, troop reduction was part of their reward for signing the Rhineland Pact, and as such an Allied promise had not been fulfilled. To the French, it was part of another bargain by which the Germans must first disarm, and in 1927 they were to continue to use German requests for reductions in the size of the occupying forces as occasions to press for complete disarmament. To Chamberlain, troop reduction was to be withheld pending a change in German attitude. These basic differences were not resolved in 1926, although one spectacular attempt was made to do so when, in their conversation at Thoiry on September 17, Briand and Stresemann deliberately suspended discussion of troop reduction, a partial solution to the Rhineland problem, and projected instead a comprehensive settlement of all the outstanding differences between France and Germany.

[125] 26 July 1926, Chamberlain to Crewe, AC 53/181. D'Abernon reported rumors from Berlin that Hindenburg favored keeping Germany out of the League until the reduction had been made: 19 July 1926, D'Abernon to Chamberlain, AC 53/231; D'Abernon, *An Ambassador*, III, 256-57.

[126] 29 July 1926, Chamberlain to Briand, AC 53/81; 3 January 1927, Kilmarnock to Chamberlain, FO. 371/12128/197-99; 4 March 1927, Memorandum by Central Department, FO. 371/12148/116-17.

5. Allied Withdrawal from the Rhine? The Thoiry Conversation, September-October 1926

The scheme discussed by Briand and Stresemann during their famous private conversation at Thoiry on September 17, 1926, called for the return of the Saar to Germany without the plebiscite of the Saar population provided for in the Treaty of Versailles and for Germany to repurchase the Saar mines from France for approximately 300 million marks. The IMCC would be withdrawn, and the German government and the Conference of Ambassadors would settle their differences over disarmament. France would, in addition, raise no objection if Germany purchased the return of Eupen-Malmedy from Belgium. Most importantly, the Rhineland would be completely evacuated within a year and in exchange France would receive reparation payment in advance of the annuities scheduled under the Dawes plan. This payment would be made possible by the public sale (capitalization) of a portion of the bonds posted by Germany as security for its reparation obligations. Under the provisions of the Dawes plan, bonds with a face value of 16 billion marks had been deposited with the Reparation Commission; of these, 11 billion represented a lien on the German National Railways, and 5 billion represented a mortgage on German industry. The Thoiry scheme provided for the sale of 1.5 billion marks worth of railway bonds. The proceeds of this sale would go to Germany's creditors and be deducted from Germany's total reparation debt. Approximately one-half of the proceeds, 780 million marks, would go to assist France in balancing the budget and stabilizing the franc.[127]

[127] There are two firsthand accounts of the Thoiry meeting. The fullest, Stresemann's, appears in his *Vermächtnis*, III, 17-23. The notes of Professor Hesnard, Briand's translator, are less complete: Georges Suarez, *Briand; sa vie—son oeuvre avec son journal et de nombreux documents inédits*, Paris, 1938-52, IV, 203-28. Briand himself made no record of the Thoiry conversation, and Hesnard's other papers reportedly contain no reference to Thoiry: Jacques de Launay, *Major Controversies of Contemporary History*, Oxford, 1965, p. 119. Briand did, however, make a rather full oral report of what had been discussed at Thoiry to Austen Chamberlain, and Chamberlain's record of this account bears somewhat more resemblance, at significant points, to Stresemann's version than it does to that of Hesnard: 6 October 1926, Memorandum by Chamberlain, AC 50/236. A description of the Dawes bonds can be found in Carl Bergmann, *A History of Reparations*, New York, 1927, pp. 276-78; and Harold G. Moulton, *The Reparation Plan*, New York, 1924, pp. 24-28.

The meeting at Thoiry has some times been wrongly described as an act of impetuosity. The week before it took place Briand had welcomed Germany to the League of Nations with a speech at Geneva which surpassed his usual eloquence; exhilarated by this event, the two men held a personal meeting. Taking elaborate measures to elude the press, they arrived at a hotel in a small village in the French Jura across the border from Geneva. A meal of fine food and wine added to their feeling of well-being, and they formulated a scheme which came to nothing because of its grandeur and impracticality.[128]

Actually, a personal meeting between the two men had been planned before they arrived in Geneva, and the items they discussed at Thoiry, including the exchange of early evacuation for prior reparation payment—the heart of the Thoiry bargain—had been under consideration for some time.[129] In 1925—before, during, and following the Locarno conference—Stresemann had informally and cautiously raised the issue of early evacuation with the French and British. Although Briand and Chamberlain had refused to enter into formal negotiations or to make the public assurances Stresemann requested, Berthelot, who strongly favored a comprehensive settlement of Franco-German differences, began to speak during the month of November of early evacuation, and he persistently advanced a scheme calling for financial compensation in exchange.[130] Pressed by Berthelot, aware that

[128] Maurice Beaumont, *La faillite de la paix*, Paris, 1960, p. 325; Theodor Eschenburg, *Die improvisierte Demokratie*, Munich, 1963, pp. 208-11; Vallentin-Luchaire, *Stresemann*, pp. 239-43.

[129] The discussions of Eupen-Malmedy, the Saar, disarmament, and military control—before, during, and after Thoiry—have been carefully examined elsewhere, and the following account makes no effort to repeat those efforts. See Klaus Pabst, *Eupen-Malmedy in der belgischen Regierungs-und Parteienpolitik, 1914-1940*, Aachen, 1964, pp. 453-81; Salewski, *Entwaffnung und Militärkontrolle*, pp. 332-43; Maria Zenner, *Parteien und Politik im Saargebiet unter dem Völkerbundsregime, 1920-1935*, Saarbrücken, 1966, pp. 231-33. All these accounts are based on the records of the German Foreign Ministry and surpass earlier accounts based on the Stresemann papers. Robert Gottwald has used the records of the German Foreign Ministry and the Department of State to discuss the bond mobilization scheme in *Die deutschamerikanischen Beziehungen in der Ära Stresemann*, Berlin, 1965, pp. 73-88.

[130] 12 November 1925, Hoesch to AA, 2254/4502/116778; ADAP, B, I-1, 2, 8, 41, 61, 67. Berthelot was so open in his advocacy of the project that it was soon referred to at the Wilhelmstrasse as "Berthelot's plan": unsigned, undated memoranda, 2273/4509/130708. According to Crewe, Berthelot made "no secret of favoring" the scheme: 7 February 1926, Crewe to Chamberlain, AC 53/145. Also DBFP, IA, I, 188.

occupation did not provide long-term military security, and intrigued by the idea of a post-Locarno Franco-German entente, Briand himself privately indicated an interest in the scheme in early December.[131] Throughout the first half of 1926, Chamberlain encouraged Paris to discuss complete evacuation with Berlin, although he did so quietly and without perseverance, angered as he was by German ingratitude.[132] Then in July, as the value of the franc fell to its interwar low point and the need for foreign financial assistance became urgent, Raymond Poincaré, who became Premier and Finance Minister on the 23rd, showed a strong interest in advance reparation payment in exchange for early evacuation, and he and his new National Union government authorized Briand to conduct an exploratory conversation with Stresemann.[133]

By this time, although the Locarnites had found themselves unable to agree on troop reduction, they had concurred on the efficacy of negotiations conducted by means of informal foreign ministers' meetings. The notion of settling outstanding Franco-German differences by personal conversation, rather than through normal diplomatic channels, attracted both Stresemann and Briand. From the time of the Locarno conference onward, both men talked repeatedly of a conversation *à deux*, to be held away from the press and across the border from Geneva following Germany's admission to the League.[134] Final preparations for this meeting were worked out between August 3 and September 11.[135]

---

[131] ADAP, B, I-1, 15, 67. Also DBFP, IA, I, 236, 505.

[132] 19 May 1926, Chamberlain to D'Abernon, AC 50/204; DBFP, IA, I, 236, 415, 487, 511.

[133] On the decline of the franc see Edouard Bonnefous, *Histoire politique de la troisième république*, Paris, 1956-62, IV, 155-59, 164-72; Eli Schwartz, "Monetary Experience of France, 1919 to 1939," *World Affairs Quarterly*, 27 (1956), p. 59. On Poincaré's interest and approval see DDB, II, 131; 8 October 1926, Crewe to Chamberlain, AC 53/184; 23 June 1928, Memorandum by Schubert, 2544/5138/297396. Even Berthelot commented on Poincaré's lack of opposition to Briand's policy: 13 October 1926, Crewe to Chamberlain, AC 53/186.

[134] ADAP, B, I-1, 1, 15, 225; Stresemann, *Vermächtnis*, II, 437-38, 453, 446, 471; III, 16.

[135] 3 August 1925, Hoesch to AA, 1333/2406/504333; Stresemann, *Vermächtnis*, II, 463-66; 22 August 1926, Memorandum by Stresemann, 3146/7331/162330-41 (the text in Stresemann's *Vermächtnis*, II, 466-73 is abbreviated); 26 August 1926, Hoesch to AA, 2246/4501/115692-93; 2 September

At the time the Thoiry meeting was held, both men regarded it as an exploration of the most significant difficulties affecting Franco-German relations. Stresemann had told the cabinet on September 2 that he would conclude no agreements at Thoiry, and they authorized him to conduct a comprehensive discussion.[136] Briand consulted his colleagues also, and he too went to the luncheon not to conclude agreements but to seek German agreement to a project which he could then present to Poincaré.[137] Although Stresemann questioned the ease with which the Dawes bonds could be sold, and Briand was not certain how soon German demands could be met, both agreed at Thoiry that they preferred a prompt and all-inclusive settlement of Franco-German differences to a piecemeal handling of problems and incidents as each became critical. They also decided to ask their governments to consent to further negotiations and to have the technical details of bond sale and advance reparation payment studied by their respective financial experts who would make specific proposals which could then be presented for governmental approval. Both men, then, regarded Thoiry as a first step which would lead to steady progress; neither expected the abrupt termination of discussions which soon took place.

The success of the Thoiry scheme depended on the willingness of private investors to purchase bonds secured by the German railways. If they were to be persuaded, they would need to be assured that German reparation payment—the interest on their investment—could be transferred to their accounts in currencies they could use. Private investors would be unwilling to suspend transfer of payment in order to protect the mark during periods of financial difficulty as was the case with German payments under the Dawes plan. At Thoiry, Stresemann agreed to waive transfer protection over the interest on a small portion of the bonds. But this permission to change the form of the indebtedness

---

1926, Hoesch to Stresemann, 2246/4501/115727-30; 11 September 1926, unsigned memoranda, 2254/4502/116899, 903.

[136] 2 September 1926, Cabinet Protocol, 1840/3543/769979-80.

[137] Stresemann's conversations with Briand and Hesnard on 11 September: unsigned memoranda, 2254/4502/116899, 903. According to Hesnard, Briand believed he would eventually succeed in concluding a comprehensive settlement although he expected further difficulties from the Council of Ministers: 3 September 1926, unsigned memorandum, 2273/4509/131113-14.

was the extent of the projected German contribution to the reparation-evacuation scheme. German banks could not purchase the bonds. The only suitable market was in the United States, and access to it was restricted. Flotation of new foreign issues on Wall Street was supervised by the American Treasury, which had established a policy of not approving private loans to countries which had not settled their war debts. The Franco-American (Mellon-Berenger) Debt Funding Agreement, negotiated in April 1926, had not yet been ratified by the National Assembly, and as the Thoiry scheme amounted to an American loan for the benefit of France with the German railways as security, Washington withheld approval pending ratification of the Mellon-Berenger agreement.[138]

Further opposition came from London, where the British Treasury faced no financial crisis, had no need for immediate cash, and did not want to sacrifice future income by selling bonds at a discount.[139] On October 14 Chamberlain, who thought the bond sale impractical and had never approved it, informed de Fleuriau of British opposition.[140] In Paris, Poincaré did not find it necessary to overcome Anglo-American opposition to the bond sale project, nor did he find it worth the effort. Since coming to office he had gradually raised the value of the franc, finally stabilizing it in early December. He did this through a conservative fiscal policy, without risking a vote of no confidence in the Chamber over the ratification of the unpopular Mellon-Berenger agreement, without American financial assistance, and without having to purchase with political concessions German cooperation in a scheme which would have yielded a mere 780 million marks in advance repara-

[138] Joseph Brandes, *Herbert Hoover and Economic Diplomacy; Department of Commerce Policy, 1921-1928*, Pittsburgh, 1962, pp. 153, 171-76; Lester V. Chandler, *Benjamin Strong, Central Banker*, Washington, D.C. 1958, pp. 366-70; Benjamin H. Williams, *Economic Foreign Policy of the United States*, New York, 1929, pp. 87-92. On the Mellon-Berenger agreement see Etienne Weill-Raynal, *Les réparations allemandes et la France*, Paris, 1947-49, III, 376-80.

[139] 27 September 1926, Treasury Memorandum entitled "Note on the Commercialization of German Reparation Bonds. . . ," FO. 371/12877/92-95; 20 September 1928, Memorandum by Lieth-Ross, FO. 371/12878/75-79. Capitalization, Chamberlain later pointed out to Stresemann, "might be very costly to the creditors": 6 December 1926, Chamberlain to Tyrrell, AC 53/568.

[140] 14 October 1926, Chamberlain to Crewe, AC 53/189. Also 10 October 1926, Tyrrell to Chamberlain, AC 53/564; 6 October 1926, Memorandum by Chamberlain, AC 50/236. Aime de Fleuraiu was the French Ambassador to London.

tion payment.[141] Finally, the Germans were not eager to see the bond project succeed because it would jeopardize the prospects for downward revision of the Dawes plan. The Wilhelmstrasse expected a favorable resettlement of the entire reparation question within two or three years, and they recognized that if Germany were to waive a measure of transfer protection in 1926, the creditor powers would raise their opinion of German transfer capabilities and would demand accordingly larger payments when the reparation debt was eventually revised.[142]

Faced with these obstacles and difficulties, Stresemann and Briand agreed on October 28 to abandon their plan for expert discussions of bond sale, and to hold instead periodic conversations between Briand and Hoesch to discuss Franco-German relations and the realization of the type of comprehensive settlement proposed at Thoiry. Initially, both Stresemann and Briand expected these conversations to show some progress by December. Stresemann, hoping that the French National Assembly would ratify the Mellon-Berenger agreement in early 1927, expected definite results in a year.[143] He did not believe that the exact date of evacuation was of great significance; the important thing, he told an American, was that France had accepted the principle of early evacuation.[144] As Chancellor Marx told the Center Party leaders on October 31, "The great advantage of Thoiry is that in the future France will be unable to uphold a recalcitrant attitude with respect to the occupation of the Rhine-

---

[141] Bonnefous, *Histoire politique de la troisième république*, IV, 167-71, 180-82; Benjamin D. Rhodes, "Reassessing 'Uncle Shylock'; the United States and the French War Debt, 1917-1929," *Journal of American History*, 55 (1969), pp. 800-802; Weill-Raynal, *Réparations allemandes*, III, 394-95. Berthelot called the proposed payment "une compensation dérisoire": DDB, II, 137. As William Tyrrell, Permanent Under-secretary of the British Foreign Office put it, advance payment would require "a mountain of work to give birth to a mouse": DDB, II, 143.

[142] 17 September 1926, unsigned memoranda, 2254/4502/116935-39; ADAP, B, I-1, 116, 271; DDB, II, 132; 11 October 1926, Poole to State, 751.62/59.

[143] 28 October 1926, Hoesch to Stresemann, 2257/4502/119538-42. Stresemann became highly agitated when Seydoux suggested that it would be many years before evacuation took place: Stresemann, *Vermächtnis*, III, 45-51, 53-57. He told Rudolf Breitscheid of his hope for progress: Stresemann, *Vermächtnis*, III, 44. And he reportedly told the Foreign Affairs Committee of the Reichstag of the one-year delay in results: *Berliner Tageblatt*, 4 November 1926.

[144] 29 October 1926, Poole to State, 751.62/71.

land. Germany can demand that their territory be liberated from foreign occupation as soon as the right financial solution is found."[145] The right solution proved to be more remote than Berlin expected, however. On November 11 Briand brought to an end all hope that the bonds could be sold at any time in the foreseeable future, and he suspended further discussions: Briand declared that "the prompt fulfillment of the Thoiry idea had been crushed by technical obstacles; for that reason we face an unavoidable standstill."[146]

The abortion of the Thoiry scheme was a historic turning point. In 1926 the Germans had dreamed of purchasing their freedom from Versailles. Not only would the Rhineland be evacuated and the Saar returned to them in exchange for capital payments, but territory lost to Poland would be regained in return for financial assistance to Warsaw.[147] Such schemes—in which Hjalmar Schacht played a prominent role—were entertained largely because Germany held a significant financial advantage at the time. Because the mark was stable, Germany began to receive sizeable American loans in early 1926. On the other hand, the French franc, the Belgian franc, and the Polish zloty were unstable, thereby making these three countries unattractive sites for foreign investment. This situation did not last for long, however. The Polish and Belgian currencies recovered, and, most importantly, Poincaré stabilized the franc in December 1926. Thereafter, Paris did not need foreign financial assistance, and the Germans, along with the Americans and British, lost the leverage they had once tried to exert by attaching conditions to loans to France. Then during the following months, Emile Moreau, the Governor of the Bank of France, was able to acquire large holdings of foreign currency in New York, London, and Berlin, Consequently, when reparation and evacuation issues were to come up again for settlement in 1929, it would be the French, with their holdings of dollars, marks, and pounds, who would be able to take the lead in the game of financial diplomacy and exert political pressure on Berlin and London.

[145] Quoted in 1 November 1926, Poole to State, 751.62/82.

[146] 11 November 1926, Hoesch to Stresemann, 2257/4502/119560.

[147] Pabst, *Eupen-Malmedy*, pp. 464-81; Josef Korbel, *Poland between East and West: Soviet and German Diplomacy toward Poland, 1919-1933*, Princeton, 1963, pp. 197-200.

6. *Permanent Surveillance of Germany and the End of Military Control, November-December 1926*

Before meeting Briand at Thoiry, Stresemann promised the German cabinet that he would continue his efforts to wrest piecemeal concessions from Paris in the event no comprehensive settlement was reached with the French.[148] This he did. In November-December 1926, with Rhineland evacuation delayed by the impracticality of the bond sale, he successfully pressed Paris and London to isolate the question of German disarmament from the other issues discussed at Thoiry and then to withdraw the IMCC. A year earlier, in their note of November 16, 1925, the Conference of Ambassadors had promised to end military control; but they had not done so because the Germans had not carried out their side of this part of the Locarno bargain by satisfying the disarmament requirements of the Allies. Berlin and the Ambassadors' Conference had continued to discuss these unsatisfied requirements during 1926, and at Thoiry Briand and Stresemann had agreed to make the disarmament question a matter of high policy. Encouraged by this, Stresemann pressed his advantage: in a conversation with de Margerie on November 1, he insisted that a date must be set for the withdrawal of the IMCC during the December meeting of the League Council. Otherwise, he stated, the policy of understanding would be jeopardized and he would have to resign from office.[149]

When the comprehensive settlement was delayed, Briand, too, focused on specific questions. He pressed for some arrangement to assure French military security in the event Allied troops were indeed withdrawn from the Rhineland. After all, French security rested in part on the maintenance of a demilitarized buffer zone in Western Germany. Under Articles 42 and 43 of the Treaty of Versailles, Germany was forbidden to construct any fortifications or assemble troops west of a line 50 kilometers east of the Rhine River; Article 44 stated that a violation of Article 42 or 43 would be considered a hostile act by the Allied powers; the Treaty of Locarno assured France of British military support in case Ger-

---

[148] 2 September 1926, Cabinet Protocol, 1840/3543/769979-80.
[149] Salewski, *Entwaffnung und Militärkontrolle*, pp. 326-50; Hans Gatzke, *Stresemann and the Rearmament of Germany*, Baltimore, 1954, pp. 61-68; Stresemann, *Vermächtnis*, III, 45-51.

many committed such a hostile act. All these arrangements were automatically enforced as long as the Rhineland was occupied by French and British troops; minor German violations could be observed by the occupying forces, and major ones would engage the Reichswehr in an act of war with both the British and French Armies of the Rhine.

However, when the Rhineland was evacuated, British military assistance would be immediate only if the British government was convinced that the German Army had committed a flagrant violation; in the event of a nonflagrant violation, the French could not legally act against Germany, and the other Locarno powers could not join her in sanctions, until called upon to do so by the League Council. This was cumbersome and time-consuming: If not then in session, the League Council would have to be convoked. It would have to decide on an investigation and appoint a committee of inspection. The committee would have to conduct the inspection and report to the Council. The Council would then have to call upon its members to fulfill their obligations under the League Covenant. This protracted procedure raised two dangers. The Council might not be able to verify a serious act of remilitarization with sufficient promptitude to protect French security. And, in the event of a minor violation, the French government might be unwilling to seek League sanctions; the other members of the Council might be unwilling to impose them; a series of ignored minor infractions might thereby result in the gradual remilitarization of the Rhineland. Thus, while the Treaty of Locarno guaranteed perpetual demilitarization, it provided no efficient means to preserve it. To fill this void, which he termed "a gap in the Locarno Treaty," Joseph Paul-Boncour, a prominent Socialist Deputy and a French delegate to the League, advocated a permanent, resident, civilian, commission of inspection, appointed and empowered in advance, which could quickly and automatically bring into effect the guarantees held by France against remilitarization.[150]

French efforts to establish a Rhineland inspection commission under League Council auspices had begun even before Strese-

---

[150] Salewski, *Entwaffnung und Militärkontrolle*, pp. 355-56. This proposal was so closely identified with Paul-Boncour that it became known in the German Foreign Ministry as "Boncour's idea." For one indication of Paul-Boncour's attitude toward evacuation and permanent inspection see DBFP, IA, I, 213. Also Stresemann, *Vermächtnis*, III, 42-44.

mann proposed the Rhineland Pact. Initially, in 1924, Paris had sought to impose its project without German consent, maintaining that Article 213 of the Treaty of Versailles, which bound Germany to accept incidental inspection when the majority of the League Council deemed it necessary, provided the basis for both the permanent inspection of German disarmament and a resident commission in the Rhineland. However, during 1925 both Chamberlain and Stresemann had resisted French efforts, and Briand was compelled to agree that no inspection schemes would be adopted until Germany had joined the League.[151] If there was to be permanent on-site inspection, then, Briand would have to persuade Stresemann to accept it voluntarily. After Germany joined the League Council, he attempted to do so (at Thoiry) and continued his efforts during the League Council meeting of December 1926.

At the Geneva meetings (December 5-12), Briand suggested that he and Stresemann "freely negotiate" an agreement providing for a commission of civilians, which would remain in the Rhineland after the troops had departed, observe conditions there, and report violations to the League Council.[152] Briand was somewhat apologetic in this request; he expressed an unwillingness to take responsibility for the proposal, stating that his hands were tied by Paul-Boncour, the author of the plan, and by "people in France." The desire for such precautions he admitted to be "ridiculous"; however, he maintained that both he and Stresemann should try to understand French public opinion. Briand expressed confidence in the effect a Rhineland inspection commission would have: if a commission remained, "French public opinion, which had been alarmed by the recent reports out of Germany regarding Russian munition deliveries and lapses on the part of the Reichswehr, would be able to accept the evacuation of the Rhineland."[153]

[151] Salewski, *Entwaffnung und Militärkontrolle*, pp. 268-70; Spenz, *Beitritts Deutschlands zum Völkerbund*, pp. 14, 30-31, 53-54, 106-108; Stambrook, " 'Das Kind,' " pp. 251-52; DBFP, IA, I, 185; *Proceedings of the Locarno Conference*, Nos. 157, 162, 176.

[152] The conversations at Geneva: 5 December 1928, Memorandum by Stresemann, 1344/2466/156550-54; 8 December 1928, Stresemann to Marx and Hindenburg, 1344/2466/156555-57; Cab 23/53/65 (15 December 1926); DBFP, IA, II, 326, 333, 345, 352, 353, 355; Salewski, *Entwaffnung und Militärkontrolle*, pp. 358-64; Fox, "Britain and the Inter-Allied Military Commission of Control," pp. 161-63.

[153] On these reports, see Gatzke, *Stresemann and Rearmament*, pp. 72-76.

Chamberlain, too, decided to make evacuation dependent on permanent resident inspection. He wanted "no more Thoiry but a little sober English sense,"[154] and he regarded Rhineland inspection as a more practical form of compensation than selling reparation bonds. At Geneva he spoke explicitly to Stresemann of the immediate evacuation of zone two and of setting a definite date for the early evacuation of zone three. It would be "a very good bargain from the German point of view," he said, if in return for evacuation, Stresemann permitted "a few gentlemen to kick up their heels in the Rhineland."[155] Chamberlain did not, however, enter into any formal agreement regarding early evacuation, and Briand, who still considered advance reparation payment a prerequisite to advance evacuation, apparently made no suggestions as explicit as those of Chamberlain.

Even had he been promised the complete evacuation of the Rhineland, Stresemann would not have agreed to permanent inspection. Franco-German relations, he had told the Reichstag on November 23, must be conducted "on the sole basis of mutual confidence"; there could be "no question of replacing occupation by an arrangement of a political character."[156] It would degrade the work of Locarno, he then told Briand and Chamberlain at Geneva, to establish a commission in order to ascertain if one country was going to attack another in spite of having signed the Rhineland Pact. If the Reichswehr attacked, he added, it would be evident without being announced by civilians "standing in the Rhineland with a magnifying glass." Behind this combination of moral indignation and ridicule were considerations which Stresemann did not reveal to Chamberlain and Briand. Time, he wrote to President Hindenburg and Chancellor Marx, was on his side; the evacuation date provided for in the Treaty of Versailles was growing nearer, and as it did, the value of evacuation as an instrument of barter diminished; as the French came to recognize this, they would become increasingly disposed to further compromise. Provided the Germans did not inflate the value of evacuation by insisting on it anxiously, the problem would become increasingly easy to solve. Stresemann, therefore, was

154 21 December 1926, Minute by Chamberlain, FO. 371/12125/144.
155 6 December 1926, Chamberlain to Tyrrell, AC 53/568.
156 Stresemann, *Vermächtnis*, III, 64.

willing to postpone further consideration of permanent resident inspection and of evacuation until the next League meeting in March 1927. He was intent, however, on setting a date for the withdrawal of the IMCC, and because he agreed to meet the disarmament requirements of the Conference of Ambassadors and to undertake further discussion of permanent inspection in March, Chamberlain and Briand agreed on December 11 to withdraw the control commission by January 31.

By December 9, negotiations in Paris between the Germans and the Conference of Ambassadors had resolved all but two of the outstanding points of disarmament, one of which was the existence of 88 fortifications the Germans had constructed at Königsberg, Kusten, and Glogau.[157] Briand insisted that these be destroyed; he could not permit them to exist, he told Stresemann, without risking reproach for deserting his Polish allies. However, the other lapses in disarmament, which had disrupted German relations with the West since the general inspection of 1924, were regarded as settled. Briand told Stresemann that both he and Chamberlain saw the end of military control from the standpoint of the "great understanding" with Germany. Military control was an obstacle, he said, which must be removed "so that we can walk more freely on the road to Thoiry."

For his part, Chamberlain was "most anxious to get rid of [military control] at the earliest possible moment," as he wrote to one of his ambassadors in mid-November. He was convinced that Germany was in effect disarmed; the matters presently at issue were, he thought, "of little or no intrinsic importance" and posed no threat to Allied security. Unless there were general disarmament, Chamberlain thought, "law or no law, treaty or no treaty, no power on earth can keep Germany disarmed indefi-

---

[157] Salewski, *Entwaffnung und Militärkontrolle*, pp. 357-58. The fortifications at Kusten and Glogau were apparently the beginnings of an extensive system of fortifications on the right bank of the Oder River designed to protect German troops while they crossed the river and took up positions on the other side in preparation for an attack on the Polish Corridor. The fortifications at Königsberg were apparently designed to permit the dispatch of German troops to East Prussia by sea, permitting a small force to cover the debarkation and concentration of troops at the port in preparation for an advance into open country: 24 December 1927, G-2 report by W. W. Harts, 862.20/506-507. Also Salewski, *Entwaffnung und Militärkontrolle*, pp. 369-72.

nitely."[158] In the meantime, he relied on Stresemann who, he was convinced, wanted to observe the military clauses of the Treaty of Versailles and would have an easier time doing so now that Seeckt no longer commanded the Reichswehr.[159] In the settlement of disarmament, Chamberlain employed two distinct strategies, one in Berlin and one in Paris. He urged the Germans to meet the requirements of the Conference of Ambassadors, and to the French he recommended that concessions be made to the Germans on minor points in order to win Berlin's agreement on essentials. Above all, he urged Paris to encourage Berlin to comply with those essential points by promising to withdraw military control.[160]

Under the terms of the contract negotiated by the Locarnites at Geneva on December 11—and then honored by them—the German government and the Conference of Ambassadors would agree, prior to January 31, 1927, on which of the Königsberg fortifications would be destroyed, and the IMCC would be withdrawn by that date.[161] Each Allied power was empowered to appoint a special military expert to its Berlin embassy to deal with German authorities on disarmament matters after January 31, but these experts were not authorized to conduct on-site investigations.[162] Thus, special Allied rights to inspection came to an end.

Moreover, the Locarnites established no procedure to maintain the demilitarized status of the Rhineland. Having earlier accepted the Anglo-German position that the Treaty of Versailles did not provide for a permanent, resident commission of inspection in the Rhineland, or anywhere else in Germany, without the

[158] 19 November 1926, Chamberlain to G. Grahame, AC 50/253; DBFP, IA, I, 264; Fox, "Britain and the Inter-Allied Military Commission of Control," pp. 156-61.

[159] 6 December 1926, Chamberlain to Tyrrell, AC 53/567. Seeckt resigned his command on October 8, 1926: Gatzke, *Stresemann and Rearmament*, p. 59. On Seeckt's image abroad see Salewski, *Entwaffnung und Militärkontrolle*, pp. 345-46.

[160] DBFP, IA, I, 250, 277, and II, 275; 3 December 1926, Chamberlain to Tyrrell, AC 53/565.

[161] 1 February 1927, Crewe to FO., FO. 371/12117/183-84; Salewski, *Entwaffnung und Militärkontrolle*, pp. 365-71. The IMCC published its final report on February 28, 1927.

[162] This was the opinion of Cecil Hurst, Legal Advisor to the British Foreign Office: 30 June 1928, Memorandum by Huxley, FO. 371/12296/239-40.

consent of the German government, Briand was unable to persuade Stresemann to accept such inspection provisions at Geneva. Instead, the Superior Council of National Defense in Paris was authorized to draft a scheme for Rhineland inspection which would be presented for the consideration of the German government when negotiations on evacuation began.[163] Consequently, the only means the Allies would have at their disposal to verify German disarmament after January 31 was their right under Article 213 of the Treaty of Versailles, which authorized them, in specific instances of suspected violation, to go before the League Council and present a case for a special *ad hoc* commission of inspection. Likewise, unless a special inspection commission was subsequently agreed upon, the only means the Allies would have of verifying the demilitarization of the Rhineland, once the occupying troops were withdrawn, was the same right to incidental inspection under Article 213. Such rights, of course, meant very little. Incidental inspection, one English diplomat wrote a year earlier, "is never going to be really effective. Short of force (which we are certainly not prepared to employ) you cannot keep a nation of over 60,000,000 inhabitants permanently subject to foreign tutelage in this matter of her armament." In supporting the French in the maintenance of this right, the British, thought this same diplomat, were speaking "to some degree with our tongues in our cheeks."[164]

So, by January 1927 Stresemann had won the compromise disarmament settlement which had prompted him to propose the Rhineland Pact two years before, and at the same time he had secured the abolition of one system of on-site inspection and prevented the establishment of two others. The Allies had first evacuated Cologne and then withdrawn the IMCC before the Germans had actually performed their disarmament promises. However, the magnitude of Stresemann's accomplishment was not as great as it might seem, for in the end Berlin did not escape compliance with the terms of the negotiated settlement. The Allies kept military occupation at their disposal as a means of enforcing compliance with the agreement of December 1926; during the months

[163] League of Nations, *Official Journal*, February 1927, p. 162; *Survey of International Affairs, 1927*, p. 99; Gatzke, *Stresemann and Rearmament*, pp. 70-71; Eyck, *Weimar Republic*, II, 46-48.
[164] DBFP, IA, I, 201.

large part due to events which took place in Paris early in 1927. reductions; and in 1927 Paris and London proved willing to reduce the level of occupying forces only after Berlin had fully performed its disarmament contract. This Allied intransigence, which contrasts sharply with the concessions of 1925-26, was in large part due to events which took place in Paris early in 1927.

PART THREE

THE DECLINE OF THE SPIRIT OF LOCARNO
1927

1. *Briand's Retreat from Thoiry, December 1926-February 1927*

ON DECEMBER 14, 1926, almost immediately after the close of the League Council meeting, Stresemann announced to the press his intention to demand the complete withdrawal of Allied troops when he returned to Geneva in March. Privately, he still hoped to attain his goal as soon as the Mellon-Berenger agreement was ratified, and his December meetings with Chamberlain and Briand had given him some reason to hope for productive conversations in the near future. The two men had remained willing to discuss anticipatory evacuation even though the bond sale scheme had proved to be unworkable, and their goodwill, shown in their willingness to abolish the IMCC, seemed to indicate that the prospects for further concessions were bright.[1]

Stresemann's plans were not to be realized. The Allies refused to open formal negotiations on early evacuation in March 1927, and it was not until the September 1928 session of the League Assembly, eighteen months later, that they did so. Soon after the full potential of Allied appeasement had been explored at Thoiry, it came to an abrupt halt, and German revisionism was stalemated. The reason? Between December 1926 and March 1927 there developed in Paris strong opposition not merely to the terms of the Thoiry proposal but to the principle of early evacuation itself.

Within one week after his return from Geneva in December, Briand began to encounter opposition within the Council of Ministers. Until then the financial emergency had enabled Poincaré to keep the diverse elements of his National Union government unified in support of his program of currency stabilization, with German help if necessary. By December 8, however, the franc was being exchanged at 25 to the dollar, the best price since 1925 and the rate at which it was eventually legally stabilized. With the end of the financial crisis, the National Union could afford division, and at the cabinet meeting of December 21 the first serious opposition was raised against Briand's policy. It was led by Louis Marin, Minister of Pensions, a right-wing Deputy, an

[1] Gustav Stresemann, *Vermächtnis; der Nachlass in Drei Bänden*, Berlin, 1932-33, III, 74; Wilhelm Marx, *Der Nachlass des Reichskanzlers Wilhelm Marx*, Cologne, 1968, I, 462.

101

ardent French patriot, and a Germanophobe. He was apparently supported by Louis Barthou, Vice President of the Council of Ministers, and by André Tardieu, Minister of Public Works. Their attack on Briand was occasioned by his decision to withdraw the IMCC.

What is known of this meeting and those which followed comes from Philippe Berthelot, who informed Hoesch of them, asking that his comments be kept "strictly secret." According to Berthelot, Briand was severely criticized within the cabinet for promising to withdraw the IMCC prior to the complete settlement of the disarmament question. As a result, the strength of his political position was badly damaged; he now had to be very careful about compromising himself; he could not speak in favor of early evacuation before the Chamber of Deputies and still stay in office. "Under these conditions," Berthelot reported, "one must sadly say that we have regressed in the policy of understanding, especially with regard to the evacuation problem." He thus clearly indicated that the prospects for an end to occupation were dim, although he did not tell Hoesch, as he told Eric Phipps of the British embassy, that evacuation could not take place for two years. Berthelot did, however, threaten Berlin with something far more damaging to the future of German revisionism: an end to the Locarnite meetings. He said that opposition to Briand within the cabinet made it "impractical that Briand go to Geneva four times a year and there, in the peaceful international atmosphere, conduct negotiations from the standpoint of high political ideals and enter into binding agreements which afterwards had to slowly be made workable. . . . In the future, Briand would go to Geneva only in the autumn."[2]

With his policy of early evacuation opposed in the cabinet and criticized in the National Assembly and in the press, Briand was repudiated by Poincaré, who told Henri Simond, the owner of the *Echo de Paris*, that Briand had exceeded the cabinet instructions

[2] 22 December 1926, Hoesch to Stresemann, 1344/2466/516558-59; 13 January 1927, Hoesch to Stresemann, 1344/2466/516577-80; 20 January 1927, Crewe to FO., FO. 371/12116/169-70. Berthelot, an old school diplomat who had no liking for the Geneva tea parties, frequently took upon himself the task of dampening the hopes which Briand engendered in Stresemann during their personal conversations: Ernst Geigenmüller, "Botschafter von Hoesch und die Räumungsfrage," *Historische Zeitschrift*, 200 (1965), p. 611.

at the Thoiry conversation.[3] So Briand retreated. On January 19 he went before the Foreign Affairs Committee of the Chamber of Deputies, abandoned what the American ambassador called his "somewhat platitudinous optimism,"[4] and renounced support for early evacuation. He had entered into no obligations to evacuate the Rhineland, Briand insisted; from the standpoint of formal diplomatic procedure the question had not even been raised. He, himself, would not open formal negotiations; Berlin alone would have to take the initiative. And he would respond favorably to that initiative only if French rights to security and reparation under the Treaty of Versailles were guaranteed. Thereby Briand ended any prospect that the occupied area would be evacuated in return for any minor compensation such as permission to sell German bonds. Finally, he promised that the cabinet and the Chamber of Deputies would be consulted before any future negotiations took place. This statement, unanimously approved by the cabinet the day before, brought Franco-German relations to a post-Locarno low point, but it saved Briand from loss of his office. "Had he tried to go further with the Locarno policy," Hoesch reported, "he would have suffered defeat."[5]

Briand's statements of January 19 seemed to imply that it was Stresemann's fault that the evacuation question was not being pursued, and to this the German Foreign Minister reacted by threatening to make a formal demand for an immediate end to occupation.[6] Under the terms of Article 431 of the Treaty of Versailles, Germany had a legal right to early evacuation provided Berlin "complies with all the undertakings resulting from the present Treaty"; and on February 9 Hoesch suggested to Briand that Stresemann might press this claim at the March session of the League Council. This statement forced Briand to reveal his own attitude. He refused to promise Stresemann any help

---

[3] *Echo de Paris*, 4 January 1927; 4 January 1927, Crewe to Chamberlain, AC 54/110; 13 January 1927, Hoesch to Stresemann, 1344/2466/516558-59. Also Michel Soulié, *La vie politique d'Edouard Herriot*, Paris, 1962, p. 298.

[4] 3 January 1927, Herrick to State, 751.00/15.

[5] *Le Matin*, 20 January 1927; Stresemann, *Vermächtnis*, III, 78-79; London *Times*, 20 January 1927; 20 January 1927, Hoesch to AA, 1344/2466/516592-94.

[6] On the dispute between Stresemann and Briand regarding responsibility for the failure of the Thoiry scheme see my "The Conduct of Locarno Diplomacy," *Review of Politics*, 34 (1972).

with his efforts and even threatened open opposition. Alluding to nationalist opposition within France, Briand stated that formal demands would have no practical results other than to provoke a public controversy which would anger both sides and work injury. He cautioned Hoesch that the European public must not be led to believe that every session of the League Council or Assembly must be accompanied by some significant event. Stresemann must not be disappointed, Briand stated, if he did not return from Geneva in March with a success similar to the December decision to withdraw the IMCC. Consequently, a compromise was struck: Briand promised to come to Geneva in March, and Hoesch informed Briand that Stresemann would not formally raise the evacuation issue there.[7]

2. French Rhine Policy in 1927: Occupation and Security

The opposition to evacuation which Briand encountered in Paris was based on the notion that the occupation of the Rhineland, among its multiple advantages, afforded France an essential measure of military security against a German attack.[8] France, it was stated, was vulnerable because her frontiers were not yet protected by permanent fortifications and because her army was being reduced in size; and without French troops on the Rhine, there was no way to protect the nation against the Reichswehr which, it was alleged in Paris, was capable of striking at France and inflicting severe damage. This argument, advanced by Marshal Foch and other French military planners, received wide circulation during 1927, and it was largely responsible for the resistance to the Quai d'Orsay project for early evacuation. The execution of the Thoiry scheme was hindered by the impracticality of bond sale, but the extensive and persistent opposition to evacuation which followed in 1927 was based on the notion that occupation was so important to the security of France that it could not be abandoned no matter what the terms of exchange might be.

[7] 9 February 1927, Hoesch to AA, 1344/2466/516623-27; 5 March 1927, Hoesch to Stresemann, 1344/2466/216630-34.

[8] For general discussions of the advantages offered France by military occupation see André Tardieu, The Truth About the Treaty, Indianapolis, 1921, pp. 145-201; Paul Tirard, La France sur le Rhin; douze années d'occupation rhénane, Paris, 1930, pp. 450-53.

In August 1926, the month before Thoiry, the French government had proposed to the National Assembly legislation designed to reorganize the army, to reduce the term of service from eighteen to twelve months, and to mobilize the resources of the entire nation in time of war. The bill to mobilize the nation was presented to the Army Commission of the Chamber of Deputies in January 1927, and it was debated and passed during the month of March. (Due to opposition in the Senate, the legislation never became law.) The bill to reorganize the army was discussed by the Chamber in May-June 1927 and became law on July 13. The one-year term of service was also debated in 1927, although the bill was not passed by the Chamber until January 1928 and did not become law until March of that year.[9]

These three bills were not the only pieces of defense legislation placed on the agenda of the National Assembly in 1927. In meetings held on December 17, 1926 and January 18, 1927, the Superior Council of War approved a project to build a fortified barrier along the northern and northeastern frontiers of France. This was the decisive event in the long history of the origins of the Maginot Line, for it committed the War Ministry, the Chief of Staff, and the Superior Council of War, i.e., Painlevé, Debeney, and Marshal Henri Pétain, to construction of the fortifications system.[10] The decision to build the Maginot Line reflected the "lessons" derived by the French military from the experience of World War I—the superiority of defense, the supremacy of fire power, and the invincibility of permanent concrete fortifications like those at Verdun. The decision was actually taken, however, in February 1927, after years of study and delay; and it was taken for reasons which were pressing at that time.

The French government and military committed themselves to the Maginot Line at a time when the one-year service law was pending and it seemed that fortifications must be constructed to compensate for the reduced size of the standing army.[11] The

[9] Edouard Bonnefous, *Histoire politique de la troisième république*, Paris, 1960, IV, 208-12, 240-41, 244-45; Shelby Davis, *The French War Machine*, London, 1927, pp. 70, 73.

[10] Paul-Emile Tournoux, *Haut commandement, gouvernement et défense des frontières du nord et de l'est, 1919-1939*, Paris, 1960, pp. 125-26, and Tournoux, "Les origines de la ligne Maginot," *Revue d'histoire de la deuxième guerre mondiale*, 9 (1959), p. 3.

[11] The following discussion of the origins of the Maginot Line, its *couverture* function, and the role played by the one-year service law and the im-

effect of the one-year service law would be to create an army composed of very short-term conscripts and of 106,000 professionals who were for the most part engaged in training the conscripts. The law was passed over the opposition of the Superior Council of War, which looked with concern to the "lean years" of 1935-42 when the declining population of eligible males would further reduce the number of troops immediately available for combat at any moment.[12] This manpower dilemma was to be met with fortifications and fire power; with the Maginot Line, France could be better defended with fewer men.

The second consideration which prompted the decision to construct the Maginot Line was the pending termination of military occupation. The evacuation of Cologne indicated that the rest of the Rhineland would be evacuated more or less on schedule, and the conversation at Thoiry suggested that all French troops might be withdrawn early. In French strategic planning, military occupation and the Maginot Line were both intended to serve the same function—to provide *couverture*. The notion of *couverture* applied to any of several means of defending French territory during the initial stages of a German attack. During the late 1920's the task of *couverture* was assigned to a combat-ready force of 32 active divisions stationed in the Rhineland and in the frontier regions of France. Their function was to prevent German forces from penetrating into the French interior and there interfering with the mobilization and deployment of the mass reserve army. When the reserves had mobilized, they could then protect the industrial and mineral resources of eastern France while the French economy was being converted to military production and while France's allies were arriving to join the con-

---

pending evacuation of the Rhine in the decision to build it is based on Richard D. Challener, *French Theory of the Nation in Arms, 1866-1939*, New York, 1955, pp. 220-24; Irving I. Gibson (pseud.), "Maginot and Liddell Hart; the Doctrine of Defense," in E. M. Earle (ed.), *The Makers of Modern Strategy; Military Thought from Machiavelli to Hitler*, Princeton, 1943, pp. 171-72, and Gibson, "The Maginot Line," *Journal of Modern History*, 17 (1945), pp. 133-39, 146; Enno Kraehe, "Motives behind the Maginot Line," *Military Affairs*, 8 (1944), pp. 110-17; Stephen Ryan, *Pétain the Soldier*, South Brunswick, N.J., 1969, pp. 245-60; Tournoux, *Haut commandement*, pp. 126-27 and Tournoux, "Les origines de la ligne Maginot," pp. 3-4.

[12] Philip Bankwitz, *Maxime Weygand and Civil Military Relations in Modern France*, Cambridge, Mass., 1967, pp. 41-42; Challener, *French Theory*, pp. 170, 178-81; Ryan, *Pétain*, pp. 220-22.

flict.[13] At a time when the one-year service law complicated the *couverture* problem by reducing the number of effectives under arms at any one time, fortifications were seen as a way of permitting this smaller number of troops to perform the task. The Maginot Line was conceived of not as a substitute for covering troops but as a supplement to them, as a way of organizing their efforts more efficiently; it was not to be a wall against invasion, but a way of allowing a small covering force to hold out while a large force was mobilizing in safety.[14]

The occupation of the Rhineland provided *couverture par excellence*, or, as General Debeney put it, "couverture de prémier ordre." According to official French military doctrine, the Army of the Rhine, which was deployed on the right bank of the river and controlled the bridgeheads, was to defend against a German attack until the remainder of the active army arrived on the Rhine. Then the total force would cross the river and penetrate deep into German territory. Such a campaign, conducted entirely on German soil, would not only leave French territory inviolate during mobilization, it would also allow France to come to the military assistance of Poland or Czechoslovakia if necessary. During the late 1920's, however, the French High Command became disposed to use the Army of the Rhine not as an offensive spear but as a defensive shield. It could, Debeney maintained, prevent a German attack from breaking into French territory even though the Reichswehr might be initially successful during the period of mobilization. To be sure, the evacuation of Cologne diminished the value of occupation as a defensive barrier: Belgium and northern France were opened to an offensive mobilized in northern Germany and advancing along the Hamburg-Cologne-Aachen-Liège line, and French troops centered on Coblenz would find their left flank exposed and their backs against the middle Rhine with its comparatively disadvantageous terrain and communications.[15] For this reason, the most important advantage

---

[13] Bankwitz, *Weygand*, pp. 42-43. The need for *couverture* was a widely accepted precept of French military thought in the 1920's: Challener, *French Theory*, pp. 178-81. General Debeney wrote extensively on the problem; for example: "Armée nationale ou armée de métier?," *Revue des deux mondes*, 53 (15 September 1929), pp. 260-63.

[14] Kraehe, "Motives behind the Maginot Line," p. 117; Gibson, "Maginot and Liddell Hart," pp. 349-70, and Gibson, "The Maginot Line," p. 141.

[15] Debeney, "Armée nationale," p. 260; Gibson, "The Maginot Line,"

which occupation offered to the French after 1925 was the prospect of blowing up the Rhine bridges immediately, delaying the German advance, and withdrawing to the Lorraine frontier to await the main French armies.

What the French hoped to achieve through occupation can be seen in the way in which the Rhineland was divided at Versailles for purposes of evacuation. The third zone with the Mainz bridgehead was selected by General Henri Mordacq, who drew up the plan for occupation at Paris, as the last area for evacuation because of its significance to both an offensive and defensive strategy. He decided that the occupying armies should be evacuated from Germany in three successive stages from north to south, rather than in three successive withdrawals westward away from the Rhine. By controlling Mainz to the very end, the French Army would be able to launch an offensive campaign up the Main Valley and into the heart of Germany for as long as occupation lasted.[16] The boundaries of the Mainz zone were then drawn to maximize its defensive benefits. It was by far the largest zone, defending the entire Franco-German border from Landau in the south, north along the Rhine to midway between Mainz and Coblenz, and extending north-westward to a point near Aachen. Thus, it covered most of the Rhine, the Moselle, the Saar, the industry of the Briey-Longwy basin, and such militarily significant points as Metz, Verdun, and Sedan. Occupation thus provided the French with *couverture* for mobilization—for either an offensive or a defensive military campaign; and at the same time it deprived the Reichswehr of a staging area next to the French border. Were the Rhineland evacuated, France would lose the barrier that protected the interior during the period of mobilization; and with the Rhine undefended, the Reichswehr would encounter no resistance until it arrived in France. French troops, unaided by prepared defenses and unable to fall back from the Rhine, would have to retreat to the Somme, the Seine, or even the Loire to await reinforcement from their allies; northeastern France, rather than the German Rhineland, would be overrun. The *couverture* afforded by occupation was especially important

---

p. 136; Ryan, *Pétain*, p. 248. Reply by J. H. Morgan to an address by E. L. Spears entitled "The Problem of the Rhineland," *International Affairs*, 4 (1925), p. 130.

[16] J.-J. Henri Mordacq, *Le ministère Clemenceau; journal d'un Témoin*, Paris, 1930-31, III, 214-15; W. N. Jordan, *Great Britain, France, and the German Problem, 1919-1939*, London, 1943, pp. 186-87.

in early 1927, when the one-year service law threatened to reduce the size of the active army and when the construction of the Maginot Line had not been approved by the National Assembly. Such was the argument of those French generals, led by Marshal Foch, who opposed evacuation in early 1927 and afterward.

Foch was by no means certain that the Germans had reconciled themselves to the settlement of 1918. Within Germany, he thought, there were "good and bad instincts contending," and it was impossible to tell which would win out. If the instinct for revenge won out over the instinct for reconciliation, Germany would not lack means to devastate France and Belgium once again. German industry, he argued, could be rapidly changed over to war production, and reserve soldiers could be combined with the efficient small professional force to form "a very powerful instrument of war." Occupation, Foch maintained, was the one way of bringing Germany to reason in the event Berlin refused to pay reparations or threatened the peace of Europe. It was, indeed, France's only measure of security. Due to the impending one-year service law and the declining population, France would soon have no army. Until the fortifications were completed, France would have no frontiers, To evacuate the Rhineland at a time when France was without an army and without frontiers, and when Germany was resisting disarmament would be, he concluded, a "crime against the country." On October 11, 1926, Foch dispatched to Poincaré and President Doumergue a memorandum insisting on the maintenance of occupation until 1935, and on November 1 his views were published in an anonymous article in the *Revue de France*. He was supported by Marshals Joffre and Pétain and by General Debeney, and together they convinced the French policy-making elite that the Rhine could not be evacuated until the frontier fortifications were completed.[17] According to Berthelot, Briand "stood all alone"

[17] The text of Foch's note to Poincaré: Maxime Weygand, *Mémoires*, Paris, 1950-57, II, 504-507. His published statement: Anon., "Un crime de lèse-patrie; l'évacuation anticipée," *Revue de France*, 6 (1 November 1926), pp. 5-11. Regarding the authorship of the article: 12 January 1929, Dawson to State, 862t.01/1269; Bankwitz, *Weygand*, pp. 28-29. Other indications of Foch's views on early evacuation in 1927 are found in Charles Bugnet, *Foch Speaks*, New York, 1929, p. 287; Raymond Recouly, *Foch; My Conversations with the Marshal*, New York, 1929, pp. 289-90; Weygand, *Mémoires*, II, 328-29. On Joffre: 11 February 1927, Hoesch to AA, 5684/L1659/492528. On Debeney: 4 April 1927, Dawson to State, 800.00/101. On Pétain, who apparently considered resigning over the issue: Pierre Bourget, *Un certain Philippe Pétain*, Paris, 1966, pp. 127-28.

in his willingness to evacuate the Rhine in the near future.[18]

In fact, the Locarno era Reichswehr did not pose a substantive threat to France sufficient to require the continuation of occupation and the construction of an elaborate and costly system of fortification. Even the multifold evasions of the Treaty of Versailles did not provide Germany with the number of men, heavy artillery, planes, and tanks necessary to threaten her neighbors.[19] By 1926-27 the German Ministry of Defense and the Army Command had accepted the limits of German power, rejected Seeckt's fantasies of a war of liberation against France, recognized that the Reichswehr was incapable of fighting a defensive war in the West—much less an offensive one—and adamantly opposed any war with France. Although they expected secret rearmament to put Germany in a stronger position by 1933, the most they expected of the Reichswehr during the late 1920's was a short-lived defensive holding action, well within German territory, in the unlikely event Poland alone attacked Germany.[20] It was not until late in the 1930's that the threat of a German military offensive ceased to be potential and became actual and immediate.[21] What France had to fear was not present German military capability but her potential power and future intentions.

Nevertheless, past experience with German invasions and German demographic and industrial superiority led to chronic apprehension in France during the interwar years, and even during the

[18] 13 January 1927, Hoesch to Stresemann, 1344/2466/516579.

[19] This was the opinion of the British and American military attachés in Berlin and of the Chief of the Imperial General Staff: 11 January 1926, Schurman to State, 751.62/43; 15 January 1928, "Germany, Combat Estimate," 862.20 MID/1: 3 January 1929, Rumbold to Lindsay, AC 55/434; 6 December 1928, Secretary of State for War to CID, "The Military Situation in Germany," FO. 371/12889/110-14. Wolfgang Sauer argues that illegal rearmament was futile and counter-productive; it jeopardized German relations with the Western powers while not significantly augmenting German military security: Karl Dietrich Bracher, et al., Die nationalsozialistische Machtergreifung; Studien zur Errichtung des totalitären Herrschaftssystems in Deutschland, 1933/34, Cologne, 1960, pp. 766-84. A description of German evasions: F. L. Carsten, The Reichswehr and Politics, 1918-1933, Oxford, 1966, pp. 220-38, 272-74, 305-306, 351-59.

[20] Gaines Post, Jr., "German Foreign Policy and Military Planning; the Polish Question, 1924-1929," unpublished doctoral dissertation, Stanford, 1969, pp. 127, 188, 198, 207, 298-300, 304-305.

[21] William J. Newman, The Balance of Power in the Interwar Years, 1919-1939, New York, 1968, pp. 112-27, 132-35.

Locarno era there developed what has been termed "an emotional, almost fanatical fear of Germany."[22] Fear is seldom expressed rationally; and from the justifiable belief that the German Army was potentially both able and willing to attack France, it was imagined that the Reichswehr could attack in the near future and could, under some circumstances, inflict severe damage. In the France of the late 1920's it was widely presumed that the Reichswehr was capable of launching a surprise attack with a highly mobile, well-armed, and even numerically superior army. This attack, referred to as the *attaque brusque* because of the elements of surprise and mobility in the suspected German strategy, was the starting point for most French strategic thought after 1919, and it was expounded with great consistency not only in the writings of the French military, but also in the press and in parliamentary debates.[23]

French apprehension fed on the notion that the Reichswehr, in spite of the restrictions placed upon it by the Treaty of Versailles, held certain advantages over the French Army. In January 1927, B. H. Liddell Hart publicly praised the mobility and offensive capability of the highly trained, professional German Army and pointed out the vulnerability of the cumbersome French Army of mass reserves to the deep offensive thrusts of a rapidly maneuvering Reichswehr.[24] General Hans von Seeckt elaborated on this topic in his *Moderne Heere* published two years later.[25] Within France, Colonel Jean Fabry, *rapporteur* of the Chamber Army Commission, and others, put forth exaggerated estimates of the number of combat-ready effectives in Germany—400,000 men. And, assuming that Germany would rearm secretly and then

[22] Kraehe, "Motives behind the Maginot Line," p. 111.

[23] Challener, *French Theory*, pp. 139, 190, 223, 245; Gibson, "Maginot and Liddell Hart," pp. 369-70, and Gibson, "The Maginot Line," p. 137; Kraehe, "Motives behind the Maginot Line," pp. 111-13.

[24] Liddell Hart's articles, in which he suggested that France remodel its army after the German example, appeared in the *Daily Telegraph* on January 11, 14, 15, and 18, and were reprinted in his book, *The Remaking of Modern Armies*, London, 1927. Also B. H. Liddell Hart, *The Memoirs of Captain Liddell Hart*, London, 1965, I, 103-104; Robin Higham, *The Military Intellectuals in Britain, 1918-1939*, New Brunswick, N.J., 1966, p. 85. Liddell Hart's estimate of the effectiveness of the German Army was shared by the American military attaché in Berlin, who held that "the present German army, within its limit of 100,000, is better than the German army of 1914 and the best the world has ever known": 2 October 1926, Poole to State, 751/62/64.

[25] Hans von Seeckt, *Gedanken eines Soldaten*, Berlin, 1929, pp. 51-61.

catch France by surprise with only 240,000 active troops and a minimum of stockpiled weapons, they predicted that large areas of France would be lost to the enemy before the reserves were mobilized and that the country's heavy industry, located close to the German border, would be captured in the early stages of a German attack as had happened in 1914. These notions were accepted somewhat uncritically, and during the Locarno era they became the orthodox French view of German military capacity. Together with the statements of Liddell Hart and Seeckt, they reinforced what many French Generals and politicians were prepared to contend—that the Reichswehr possessed an offensive capability which posed an immediate as well as a potential threat to France.[26]

Alarm over the presumed offensive effectiveness of the Reichswehr had multiple effects. The reform of the French Army and the construction of the Maginot Line at great expense were both based in part on the fear of the *attaque brusque* and justified by the argument that they would provide the most efficient method of defending France against that attack. In turn, the debates over army reform and the Maginot Line, which took place from 1927 to 1929, tended to focus public attention on the German military threat, and thereby offered the French occasions for more intense expressions of insecurity. Most importantly, fear of the *attaque brusque* played into the hands of those in France who saw security primarily in military terms: because Germany posed a serious military threat, France required a military barrier of its own design. In the absence of frontier fortifications, the *couverture* provided by Rhineland occupation was indispensable to the solution of the problem of defending France.

Briand also believed that occupation played an essential role

[26] To the 100,000-man Reichswehr, Fabry added 300,000 men from the German police, paramilitary, and veterans of past service: Chambre débats, 1928, pp. 2972-75, 4770; Gibson, "Maginot and Liddell Hart," p. 269. Because the Republican Guard and the colonial troops would not be available for combat during the initial stages of the war, Fabry predicted that France would have to rely on 110,000 professionals and 130,000 conscripts. Although the annual contingent numbered 260,000, only half of it would be sufficiently trained at any given time to engage in combat: Chambre débats, 1928, pp. 2972-75. The surprise attack, it was feared in Paris, would allow the Germans time to convert their industry to wartime production while that of France was still on a peacetime basis: Challener, *French Theory*, pp. 161, 189-90. On the importance of the industrial regions of eastern France to French war effort see Challener, *French Theory*, pp. 95-97; Gibson, "The Maginot Line," p. 137.

in the French security system, but the role he envisioned differed from the one assigned to it by the army. His willingness to substitute a commission of inspection for occupation suggests that he saw occupation in terms of a trip wire rather than of a barrier. If German troops were to attack across the Rhine or remilitarize the Rhineland, they would quickly be engaged by Allied occupation forces, and a state of war would exist between Germany and France and England. The inspection commission would serve a similar function; Paris would have incontrovertible evidence of remilitarization which could be used to invoke the guarantees of the Locarno ally across the Channel. In either case, Britain's entry into the war would be virtually automatic, taking place regardless of the mood of English politicians and public. Implicit in Briand's Locarno policy was the notion that French security depended on the support of her allies rather than on occupation which was temporary, or on fortresses which, he believed, would soon be rendered obsolete by rapidly changing military technology.[27] Consequently, a few years of occupation could be exchanged for an institution that would perpetually guarantee British support for the preservation of the Rhineland as a demilitarized buffer.

There was, then, a difference of viewpoints in Paris over the function which military occupation was to play in the French security system. And during 1927, the opposition of the General Staff and others who believed that France must depend on her own resources for security led Briand publicly to renounce support for early evacuation on January 19, to warn Stresemann on February 9 against any formal démarche at the pending League Council session, and to adopt the military's view of the role of occupation. The evacuation of the Rhineland—particularly the third zone—was a matter of great military significance, Briand told Chamberlain later in the year.[28]

3. *The Crisis of Franco-German Relations and the Personal Estrangement between Stresemann and Briand, March-May 1927*

The March 1927 meeting of the League Council has been viewed as one of the most successful episodes of Franco-German

[27] 9 February 1927, Hoesch to AA, 1344/2466/516624.
[28] 13 October 1927, Memorandum by Chamberlain, AC 50/372.

cooperation between the wars.[29] The issues discussed before the Council—the number of troops guarding the Saar railroads and the use of the German language in the schools of Upper Silesia—were settled amicably, and it seemed that progress was being made in the adjustment of German relations with the rest of Europe. Stresemann acted as chairman of the Council for the first time, and it appeared that harmony was being facilitated by the admission of Germany to the status of full partner in the Concert of Europe. However, on the more important issues, discussed in secret among the Locarnites, there was no progress and little goodwill. Actually, the League meeting in March was the high point of the post-Thoiry estrangement between Stresemann and Briand.

Although Stresemann did not demand early evacuation publicly and formally at Geneva, he did raise the matter in the private meetings of the Locarnites.[30] He found Briand unyielding. Although the Frenchman talked optimistically of evacuation at some future date, he maintained that he could do nothing for the present. Stresemann then tried to split the entente, asking Chamberlain, who had no serious domestic opposition with which to contend, to evacuate British troops from Coblenz without waiting for the French to do so. However, Chamberlain was concerned over Briand's vulnerable position vis-à-vis his critics in France and refused to jeopardize it further by separating himself from Briand. Instead, he suggested that if Stresemann wished to facilitate evacuation, he should agree to civilian inspection of the Rhineland. Faced with a solid Anglo-French front, Stresemann retreated. He accepted what amounted to an indefinite postponement of formal action on the Rhineland question; neither he nor Briand suggested a definite date when evacuation discussions might take place. And he accepted the formula for discussions put forth by Briand in Paris on January 19. The two men agreed that when early evacuation was discussed, Germany would base its

---

[29] F. P. Walters, *A History of the League of Nations*, London, 1960, pp. 337-38.

[30] 6 March 1927, Memoranda by Stresemann, 1335/2406H/504969-73 and 1344/2466/516635-42; 7 March 1927, Stresemann to Hindenburg and Marx, 1344/2466/516643-47; 10 March 1927, Memorandum by Stresemann, 1344/2466/516648-51; 12 March 1927, Stresemann to Hindenburg and Marx, 1344/2466/516652-53; Stresemann, *Vermächtnis*, III, 108-19, 15 March 1927, Chamberlain to Lindsay, AC 54/335.

legal claim on Article 431 of the Treaty of Versailles which provided for early evacuation in the event Germany fulfilled the treaty conditions. Although Stresemann reserved the right to argue that Locarno provided a "moral basis" for early evacuation, this was little more than a face-saving measure. In effect, what emerged from the March meetings was a three-power agreement that evacuation would be postponed until it could be discussed in terms of France's Versailles Treaty rights to security and reparation. This marked a full retreat from the conciliation and the appeasement of Locarno and Thoiry which had prompted both the evacuation of Cologne and the withdrawal of the IMCC.

Stresemann, in an attempt to gain compensation for his acceptance of delayed evacuation, asked for a reduction in the size of the armies of occupation. This too was denied. Chamberlain, who strongly favored troop reduction, admitted to Stresemann that he had a "very bad conscience" about the excessive strength of the occupying force and promised to use his good offices with Briand. However, neither Chamberlain nor Stresemann made any progress. Briand replied that he was still working to win over the opponents of troop reduction at home. Caught between Stresemann and Chamberlain on the one hand and the French General Staff on the other, Briand denied Stresemann's request. The spirit of Locarno was in sharp decline; at Geneva and during the weeks that followed there was little of the good personal feeling which had accompanied previous Locarnite meetings.

In opposing the German claims put forth at Geneva, Briand went beyond what Stresemann was willing to attribute to the necessities imposed by the political situation in France. Briand had been unaccommodating in the secret conversations, and Stresemann had expected this. What Stresemann was unwilling to pardon was what he termed Briand's "unnecessarily unfriendly and malicious tone" and his repeated disavowal of any involvement in the plans for the evacuation of the Rhineland. Seeking an explanation for this, Stresemann concluded that Briand was personally responsible for the lack of progress at Geneva and that Briand himself had become a barrier to Franco-German understanding. He admitted that Briand's hostility may have been partially due to ill health, but he was more inclined to attribute Briand's attitude to what he called a lack of "the decisive will and the firm trust which is necessary to carry the Franco-German

understanding to a successful conclusion." In view of this, Stresemann's first impulse was to retaliate. He suggested to Hoesch that
"we observe a certain reserve toward Briand personally. It can't
hurt anything if he feels that lack of accommodation by the
French will, in the end, cause a reaction in Germany, and that the
continuing regard which I have shown for Briand's situation since
Thoiry cannot go without reciprocation."[31]

Hoesch admitted that Briand had, of late, been "extraordinarily
unfriendly" toward him also, but he did not agree with Stresemann's analysis of the causes of Briand's behavior. "If at present
[Briand] appears to lack resolution and confidence," Hoesch replied to Stresemann, "it is not because of a lack of will." Rather,
Briand was observing the limits of the possible while using some
rather unscrupulous methods to overcome his opponents in Paris.
At present, Hoesch opined, Briand's methods included a public
display of hostility toward Stresemann and a public disavowal of
his role in the evacuation discussions. This, Hoesch recommended, should be overlooked in Berlin, for it was only by such
tactics that Briand could remain in office, and the ultimate success
of German policy depended on just that. Briand wanted peace;
he realized that peace was not possible without an understanding
between France and Germany; he knew that understanding was
impossible unless German claims were satisfied. From no other
French statesman could as much be expected, Hoesch calculated;
therefore Briand deserved Berlin's assistance.[32]

To an extent, Stresemann took Hoesch's advice and aided
Briand by temporarily lowering the intensity of his demands. In
late March he backed away from any initiative on early evacuation. He would continue not to make formal demands for it, and
in addition, he decided not even to press for it in informal conversations with Briand. All further action on complete evacuation

[31] 18 March 1927, Stresemann to Hoesch, 1344/2466/516668-69. Briand had
been showing signs of fatigue and emotional instability since early January,
and Stresemann, Schubert, and Chamberlain had noticed that Briand was
tired, listless, humorless, and apparently ill during the March Council session: 3 January 1927, Crewe to Chamberlain, AC 54/109; 15 March 1927,
Chamberlain to Lindsay, AC 54/335; 23 March 1927, Lindsay to Chamberlain, FO. 371/12127/111-12; Stresemann, *Vermächtnis*, III, 111. Stresemann had
been bothered by Briand's "lack of will" since the previous November; see
his "A Will and a Way" speech to the Reichstag on 23 November 1926:
Stresemann, *Vermächtnis*, III, 58-64.
[32] 28 March 1927, Hoesch to Stresemann, 1344/2466/516670-74.

would be postponed until the number of Allied forces of occupation had been decreased as promised on November 14, 1925. At first Stresemann only reminded Briand informally of France's obligations. But, when Paris responded with noncommittal replies and no action, he became convinced that his relations with Briand had reached the point of crisis. And on April 23 he instructed the German embassy in Paris to make a formal démarche at the Quai d'Orsay demanding troop reduction as compensation for the postponement of complete evacuation and threatening to resign and thereby discontinue the policy of Franco-German understanding unless his demands were met.[33]

The German ambassador was instructed to complain to Briand that the understanding with France, which Stresemann had made the central point of his whole foreign policy, was not progressing due to the deferment of the Rhineland question. His Locarno policy would, Stresemann wrote, "be seriously endangered," "appear ridiculous," and "become a laughing stock," if something did not happen soon "which can be taken as evidence that the French government intends to continue it." Public support for his policy was being undermined by open criticism which he had to admit was justified.[34] His critics in the Reichstag accused him, he complained, of having become the "dupe" of his own policy and of having been deceived by the Allies who had not fulfilled their promises of November 1925. He threatened to resign rather than face the Reichstag once more with no progress on troop reduction. Stresemann chose troop reduction as the touchstone of French willingness to put an end to what he called the "uncertainty" and "risk of stagnation" pervading Franco-German relations. If Briand could not reduce the number of occupying troops, Hoesch was to say, Stresemann would have to conclude "that the conditions for a rapprochement between Germany and France are completely absent on the French side." "If my policy of

[33] 1 April 1927, Stresemann to Hoesch, 1344/2466/516676; 8 April 1927, Hoesch to Stresemann, 1344/2466/516681-87; 23 April 1927, Stresemann to Hoesch, 1344/2466/516703; Stresemann, *Vermächtnis*, III, 128-30, 132-33; Geigenmüller, "Hoesch und die Räumungsfrage," p. 611.

[34] In the Reichstag debate of March 22 and 23, during which Stresemann pessimistically recounted the setbacks which had taken place since December, he was sharply criticized, even by Werner von Rheinbaben, a member of his own party, for his lack of success at Geneva earlier that month: Stresemann, *Vermächtnis*, III, 120-21.

understanding with France is condemned to failure, I would rather draw the consequences of it now than have to reproach myself for continuing to put off the German people with all manner of false hopes."[35]

Stresemann's plea for troop reduction, along with his dramatic portrayal of the crisis in Franco-German relations and his threatened resignation, was delivered to Briand by Kurt Rieth, chargé d'affaires, in a series of conversations, held at the Quai d'Orsay, between May 4 and May 11.[36] Briand dealt with the German démarche in the manner which was becoming customary for him: he insisted that he could do nothing to promote evacuation at the present time, but he assured Stresemann that he wished to continue the policy of understanding, and he offered the hope that progress would be made in the future. He claimed to have won a large part of the French public and a majority of the Council of Ministers over to his views during the period since his troubles of December,[37] and he promised to persist in his efforts to convince the remaining cabinet members and the General Staff to undertake a reduction in troop strength. But he would do so, he told Rieth, only if Stresemann permitted the military experts, who had been attached to the Allied embassies in Berlin after the withdrawal of the IMCC, to conduct an on-site inspection of the fortifications around Königsberg to verify that they had been destroyed as agreed, and to certify that Germany had at last complied fully with Allied disarmament demands.

The demand to inspect the Königsberg fortifications indicated a new and tougher line in Briand's German policy. He was now unwilling to grant Stresemann's demands simply to demonstrate his goodwill and to confirm the policy of understanding, and he was not willing to make material concessions in return for promises and assurances from Berlin. Instead he insisted, as he told Crewe, that there could be no troop reduction until Berlin had fulfilled its disarmament contract with the Conference of Ambassadors "to the full."[38] Faced with the choice of rebuffing Stresemann and

[35] 23 April 1927, Stresemann to Hoesch, 1344/2466/516703-07; Stresemann, *Vermächtnis*, III, 138-40.

[36] Records of these conversations: 1344/2266/516716ff. Also Geigenmüller, "Hoesch und die Räumungsfrage," pp. 611-12.

[37] Poincaré evidently could not be included among Briand's supporters, for in a speech given on May 2 at Bar-le-duc he favored a retention of the guarantees of security afforded France under the Treaty of Versailles: *Le Matin*, 3 May 1927.

[38] 12 April 1927, Crewe to Chamberlain, AC 54/126.

Chamberlain, who continued to press troop reduction on Briand,[39] and risking further reaction against his policy at home, he chose to deny Stresemann's plea. Moreover, in making troop reduction dependent on disarmament, Briand was demanding more than was legally due to France. The Allied note of November 14, 1925, in which troop reduction was promised, mentioned nothing of German disarmament.[40] And, as Briand knew full well, the military experts in Berlin had no legal right to make visits or conduct on-site investigations; their sole function was to give expert advice to the Allied ambassadors on the status of German disarmament. If Briand wanted a special inspection, it would have to be authorized by the League Council.[41] Briand was, thus, attempting to strike a political bargain: if Stresemann were to make a concession going beyond Germany's legal obligations, then he would urge troop reduction on the French Army and cabinet. From a legal standpoint, the Allies were "clearly in the wrong" in delaying troop reduction, and the Germans had an "unanswerable case" in demanding it, as Chamberlain told Briand.[42] How, then, would Chamberlain and Stresemann respond to Briand's new policy? Would they insist on strict French compliance with her legal obligations, or would they negotiate with Briand a compromise settlement of the type which Briand had concluded with Berlin in 1925 and 1926? Chamberlain, for one, proved willing to yield to Briand.

4. Chamberlain and the Entente: The Rhineland, Russia, and "the Anglo-French Thoiry" of May 18, 1927

On May 16, the President of France, Gaston Doumergue, arrived in England for a state visit with George V. He was accompanied by Aristide Briand, who had a two and one-half hour conversation with Austen Chamberlain at the Foreign Office on

[39] 6 April 1927, Chamberlain to Crewe, AC 54/124.

[40] The evacuation of Cologne, not troop reduction, was promised to the Germans in exchange for past and future disarmament: *Correspondence between the Ambassadors' Conference and the German Ambassador at Paris respecting German Disarmament, Evacuation of Cologne Zone and Modifications in the Rhineland Régime, Paris, October-November 1925*, Cmd. 2527, London, 1925, pp. 10-14.

[41] 8 June 1927, Memorandum by Central Department, FO. 371/12120/173-78.

[42] 15 March 1927, Chamberlain to Lindsay, AC 54/335.

May 18. The King found Doumergue "a nice man and easy to get along with,"[43] and the public statements of the two heads of state contained references to a renewal of the Entente Cordiale and to the "close collaboration" of their two countries. The short communiqué issued following the Chamberlain-Briand conversation likewise referred to the "solidarity of the Entente Cordiale."[44]

On the Wilhelmstrasse the use of such expressions evoked memories of the agreement which had been concluded 23 years earlier in 1904. Why, it was asked in Berlin, was the term "Entente Cordiale" used, a term which implied exclusive Anglo-French cooperation? Why was the term "spirit of Locarno," which implied cooperation between the ex-Allies and Germany, omitted? Could it be that the Entente Cordiale of 1927 involved specific agreements on a wide variety of issues which might be directed against Germany or operate to the detriment of German interests? Prior to the state visit it had been rumored in the press that Britain and France were about to conclude a number of specific agreements,[45] and after the meeting of May 18, the rumors reappeared. Some newspapers reported that Chamberlain had agreed to support French policy on Rhineland evacuation, and Briand had agreed in turn to support the British position on a number of issues, including the Russian question. This agreement, it was added, rendered Locarno little more than a memory.[46] These rumors pre-

[43] Harold Nicolson, *King George the Fifth; His Life and Reign*, London, 1952, p. 427.

[44] London *Times*, 17 and 19 May 1927; *New York Times*, 19 May 1927; 17 May 1927, Sthamer to AA, 5138/K1821/458718.

[45] On April 22 the Ullstein chain of newspapers in Germany published a sensational report from their London correspondent to this effect. He based his report on information from what he called "an absolutely reliable diplomatic source." Schubert instructed both the London and Paris embassies to find out if this report was based on fact. Investigation established that the London correspondent of the Ullstein press had been informed by the London correspondent of the *Chicago Tribune*, who had misunderstood a statement by A. B. Houghton, the American ambassador in London. Houghton denied the rumor; the London press put no stock in it; Sthamer reported to Berlin that it was conjecture without serious foundation: 22 April 1927, Schubert to London, 5386/K1982/513934; 25 April 1927, Schubert to Paris, 5386/K1982/513936; 25 April 1927, Sthamer to AA, 5386/K1982/513937; 28 April 1927, Sthamer to AA, 5386/K1982/513953-55. Also 26 April 1927, Schurman to State, 741.51/46.

[46] Again, the source of these rumors turned out to be the London correspondent of the *Chicago Tribune*: 20 May 1927, Rieth to AA, 5183/K1821/458731-33; 22 May 1927, Rieth to AA, 5183/K1821/458758-59.

pared Stresemann for the worst: "Was Germany being offered as a sacrifice to please the French on the occasion of M. Doumergue's visit?" he asked Sir Ronald Lindsay, the new British ambassador.[47] And when Sthamer reported that the Rhineland and Russia had probably been the chief topics of conversations between Chamberlain and Briand, the Wilhelmstrasse responded with an anxious telephone call to the London embassy asking for more information and stating that any Anglo-French discussion of Russia and the Rhineland was of the "greatest importance for us."[48]

Little information was forthcoming, however. The Foreign Office and the Quai d'Orsay were careful not to reveal the content of the Briand-Chamberlain conversation of May 18; both merely denied the rumors of a Rhineland-Russia deal and insisted that the only purpose of the Doumergue-Briand visit, and its only result, was to increase public support in Britain and France for amicable relations between the two countries. When questioned by Sthamer, Tyrrell denied that the conversation had produced any specific agreement, or even that specific questions had been discussed, although he did admit that Briand had been in a very "serene, reasonable, and agreeable" mood and that the conversation had produced a harmony of outlook.[49] Chamberlain authorized Lindsay to tell Stresemann that "no new engagement was undertaken or sought by either side on any subject," and he personally told Sthamer that the Russian question had scarcely been mentioned and assured him that he and Briand would continue to follow the Locarno policy. When Sthamer asked why the term "Entente Cordiale" had been used in the communiqué instead of the hallowed term "spirit of Locarno," Chamberlain weakly replied that the latter words had been overworked by too frequent usage.[50] In Paris, Berthelot allowed that the Doumergue visit had rekindled enthusiasm for the entente, but he denied that the

[47] 15 May 1927, Lindsay to Chamberlain, FO. 371/12120/84-87.

[48] 19 May 1927, Sthamer to AA, 5183/K1821/458726; 20 May 1927, Sthamer to AA, 5183/K1821/458726; 20 May 1927, record of telephone call, 5386/K1982/513956.

[49] 20 May 1927, Sthamer to AA, 5386/K1982/513957-60; 27 May 1927, Chamberlain to Lindsay, FO. 371/12120/109.

[50] 24 May 1927, Chamberlain to Lindsay, FO. 371/12120/89; 25 May 1927, Sthamer to AA, 5183/K1821/458762-63. A month later Chamberlain gave Stresemann a partial report on the conversation: Stresemann, *Vermächtnis*, III, 148-49.

Briand-Chamberlain conversation had altered the European diplomatic situation.[51] Consequently, uninformed as to the content of the conversation, the Germans formed their own opinions of its implications for British-German relations. Sthamer, who three weeks earlier had discounted the practical political significance of the prospective state visit,[52] came away from his interview with Tyrrell with a distinctly pessimistic reaction:

> My impression of the conversation was very unfavorable. It is my conviction that England has declared to France a kind of disinterest in German-French relations, probably for concessions in other areas. At least I don't believe that any kind of help from England with regard to Paris can be counted on. I also feel that the Locarno policy has suffered a severe blow. I was not able to ascertain [from Tyrrell] on this occasion if this attitude of England's was partially directed at exerting pressure on Germany in order to make [Germany] more pliant to England's anti-Russian policy. However, it appears [to me] that this is so.[53]

Chamberlain's notes on his conversation with Briand indicate that the talk was neither as innocent as he maintained nor as sinister as the Germans feared.[54] The two men discussed, as Chamberlain put it, "all the major problems of the moment"—the Franco-Spanish conflict over Tangier, the resistance of France's ally Yugoslavia to Mussolini's pressure on Albania, the threat of the Kuomintang to European interests in China, and Briand's veiled suggestion that the French might limit their naval armaments in exchange for a British guarantee of France's position in the Mediterranean. Neither man pursued the idea of a Mediterranean Pact, but the conversation did reveal what Chamberlain called "a very general agreement as to the objects to which our efforts should be directed and even as to the means by which those objects may be pursued."

The Rhineland and Russia received much more thorough discussion than Chamberlain indicated to the Germans. The raid on

[51] 20 May 1927, Keller to AA, 5183/K1821/548743-44; 22 May 1927, Rieth to AA, 5183/K1821/458758-59.

[52] 28 April 1927, Sthamer to AA, 5386/K1982/513953-55.

[53] 20 May 1927, Sthamer to AA, 5386/K1982/513957-60.

[54] 21 May 1927, Memorandum by Chamberlain, AC 50/336.

the offices of Arcos Limited and the Soviet Trade Delegation in London, which had begun on May 12, had been completed just three days before, and British relations with Russia and China were Chamberlain's primary concern at the time. He described to Briand the Soviet and Kuomintang threat to the British Empire. He also continued to support Briand's Rhineland policy. A week earlier, when approached regarding troop reduction, he had stated that inspection of the Königsberg fortifications must come first,[55] and he reaffirmed this position in his conversation with Briand. However, there is no evidence of the kind of crude bargain rumored in the press: Chamberlain did not ask Briand for any active collaboration in Britain's Russian policy in exchange for the assistance he gave to Briand's German policy.

Chamberlain's entente policy had its inherent dangers. Might not the Germans, faced with Anglo-French cooperation in the West, desert to the Russian camp? Speaking of himself and Briand, Chamberlain said to the French Foreign Minister on May 18: "We are battling with Soviet Russia for the soul of Germany. We had won a success at Locarno. We had confirmed it when Germany entered the League; but the more difficult our relations with Russia became, the more important was it that we should attach Germany solidly to the Western Powers." Of necessity, then, Berlin was handled delicately. Chamberlain strove to hold Berlin in the Western orbit, not by coercing the Germans, but by pressing Briand to take action on troop reduction. "It was absolutely necessary," he said, "that we should give the Germans the satisfaction to which they were entitled in this matter and that we should prevent them from succumbing to the temptation offered by the redoubled efforts to win them which the Soviet Government [are] certain to make."[56] However, because of his commitment to the entente, Chamberlain's pressure was restrained. By May 1927 Briand could be certain that Chamberlain would not insist on evacuation or depart from him on troop reduction; he could delay concessions on the Rhine without jeopardizing his good personal relations with London or risking the loss of British support for his German policy. He reportedly believed that Chamberlain's resentment over German financial and military aid to Russia would prevent the British Foreign Sec-

[55] 11 May 1927, Chamberlain to Crewe, AC 50/531.
[56] 21 May 1927, Memorandum by Chamberlain, AC 50/336.

retary from doing any favors for Stresemann,[57] but the reason for Chamberlain's support of Briand's Rhineland policy lay deeper than this. It rested on a fundamental agreement between the two men as to how to deal with the German problem.

Lord Crewe later wrote that the year 1927 was "a very satisfactory one for Franco-British relations, certainly the most satisfactory since the war. Indeed, it is difficult to remember a period when the cooperation between the two governments has been so close."[58] For three years Chamberlain had nurtured the entente initiated by Herriot and MacDonald. From the beginning he had settled Anglo-French differences first so a united front could be presented to the Germans. Although he imagined himself to be an honest broker, Chamberlain tried to moderate French policy by persuasion rather than by coercion, by a "steady gentle pressure on the French," as he described it.[59] He hoped that growing French confidence in England would make Paris receptive to concessions suggested by London and that Locarno would be the beginning of the appeasement of Germany. But, by 1927 those in Paris who looked for security in occupation and fortifications were in a position to shape the policy of France, and consequently Chamberlain's Locarno guarantee and subsequent support did not greatly increase London's influence over French policy and induce complete evacuation, or even troop reduction. In January 1925 Churchill had predicted that Britain would squander her bargaining power by guaranteeing French security, because France in return would do little more than evacuate Cologne.[60] By 1927 it seemed that his forecast was coming true. Certainly, Chamberlain was no longer the leader of the Anglo-French entente; he became the follower, the one who tried to smooth out French differences with Germany as they arose. The close cooperation praised by Crewe was largely on French terms.

[57] In February Briand reportedly told Vandervelde that German aid to Russia, from which the Nationalists in China indirectly benefitted, had made the British Foreign Office sufficiently opposed to evacuation that he, Briand, need do nothing about it: 8 February 1927, Keller to Stresemann, 1344/2466/516621-22.

[58] 12 January 1928, Crewe to Chamberlain, FO. 371/13344/252.

[59] 21 December 1926, Minute by Chamberlain, FO. 371/12125/144.

[60] 24 January 1925, Churchill to Chamberlain, AC 52/452.

Chamberlain's support of Briand's policy has met with two forms of criticism. At the time, he was charged with being deliberately partisan, and he was accused of ignoring the need for a fair and equitable accommodation of Germany which would have promoted lasting peace in Europe. Historians since then have suggested that Austen Chamberlain, like his half brother Neville, abandoned Britain's traditional policy of balance of power: in dealing with France and Germany, each man, in order to avoid armed conflict, supported the stronger power, or the power most able or willing to risk the use of force in attaining its objectives.[61] Actually, Austen Chamberlain was something of an exception to that long line of British statesmen from Lloyd George to Neville Chamberlain who, disregarding French interests, approached the Germans directly to arrange an accommodation with them. Austen Chamberlain worked through Paris. He did so because of the role which he envisioned for himself in the Locarno arrangements, and also because of his high regard for Briand, his personal affection for France, and his distaste for the Germans.

Chamberlain did, as he said, "love France like a woman,"[62] and by contrast he had a rather low opinion of the German character. Within three months after assuming office, he had come to the opinion that the Germans were blundering, thick-headed, and politically inept at best, and in early 1927 he still found them "a very disagreeable people."[63] At their worst the Germans were the people who had conducted the "evil policy" which led to the outbreak of the First World War;[64] at their best they were a very difficult people to help, and this was an opinion Chamberlain held throughout the Locarno era. "They cringe or they bully; they speak like master or servant and seem incapable of behaving as equals, simply and naturally, or of believing that they are not

[61] Joseph Rothschild, *Pilsudski's coup d'état*, New York, 1966, p. 302; Arnold Wolfers, *Britain and France between Two Wars; Conflicting Strategies of Peace since Versailles*, New York, 1940, pp. 270-72.

[62] Charles Petrie, *The Life and Letters of the Rt. Hon. Sir Austen Chamberlain*, London, 1939-40, II, 304.

[63] 11 February 1925, Chamberlain to D'Abernon, AC 52/258; 25 January 1927, Minute by Chamberlain, FO. 371/12131/125. Also 28 September 1925, Chamberlain to Cecil, Cecil papers 50178; 19 February 1926, Chamberlain to D'Abernon, AC 53/213.

[64] 19 May 1925, Chamberlain to Muller, AC 50/75.

again top dog if anyone treats them as such."[65] The Germans were ungracious, intransigent, and ungrateful for what their British friends did for them. They were, he told one German diplomat in December 1926, "a nation of Poincarés."[66]

Chamberlain eventually came to regard Stresemann as a German of exceptional loyalty and courage, a "merry companion" of the Geneva parties, and a statesman who honestly pursued a peaceful policy; and after the German Foreign Minister died, he expressed his personal affection for him and admitted admiration for the skill with which he won concessions from the Allies.[67] But during the opening months of 1927, Chamberlain remained deeply disappointed with the course of German policy and with what he regarded as Stresemann's violation of the principles of fair play. His complaints were much what they had been a year earlier. By conducting a deliberate policy of propaganda against occupation and doing nothing to prevent demonstrations in the Rhineland against the occupying troops, the Germans were reverting to "the policy of ill will and aggravation which preceded Locarno." Stresemann himself displayed none of the spirit of give and take that Chamberlain thought necessary to the improvement of relations between Germany and the West. Having been granted the withdrawal of military control, Stresemann constantly demanded more concessions such as troop reduction and complete evacuation while not reciprocating by completing German disarmament. This convinced Chamberlain that one simply could not treat Germans as one treated Englishmen,[68] and this conviction strongly influenced his German policy in 1927. Early in the year he instructed Lindsay to deliver to Stresemann a protest regarding German ingratitude and intransigence, a protest completely different in tone from the mild reproaches Chamberlain sometimes sent to Briand, and one so condemnatory that it

[65] 25 April 1926, Chamberlain to Mary Carnegie, AC 4/1/1269; 19 December 1930, Chamberlain to Cecil, Cecil papers 51079.
[66] 9 December 1926, Chamberlain to Tyrrell, AC 53/569.
[67] 20 December 1927, Chamberlain to M. Lampson, AC 54/326; 10 October 1930, Chamberlain to D'Abernon, AC 39/2/38; Austen Chamberlain, *Down the Years*, London, 1935, pp. 172, 178; Daniel Elletson, *The Chamberlains*, London, 1966, pp. 245-46.
[68] Because of the German mentality, Chamberlain wrote, "you cannot count on the same reactions to any particular policy as you could if that policy were applied to Englishmen"; 19 January 1927, Chamberlain to Hugh Spender, AC 54/453.

prompted Stresemann to reply with a written protest to London.[69] At the same time Chamberlain decided not even to approach Paris on occupation "until the Germans show a clearer appreciation of the part which they must play in the work of pacification."[70] Then in May he sided with Briand in favor of on-site inspection at Königsberg prior to troop reduction. Thus, by implication Chamberlain asserted that Berlin, not Paris, was responsible for the decline of the spirit of Locarno, and he rejected Stresemann's contention that Briand was responsible for the cessation of appeasement after Thoiry.

It was not difficult for Chamberlain to defer to Briand on the German question. Whether the Königsberg fortifications were inspected or not was not vital to British interests. Even the larger questions—German disarmament, troop reduction, evacuation—were of minor concern to Chamberlain, the Foreign Office, and the British Parliament in 1927. Non-Continental affairs—the attacks on Britian's position in China, the break in relations with Russia, the Geneva Naval Conference with the United States—were more pressing and more important, and they occupied Chamberlain's time and energy to the exclusion of almost everything else.[71] During the years between 1924 and 1926—the years of the Dawes plan, the Locarno negotiations, and the admission of Germany to the League of Nations—German affairs received close attention in London, but in 1927 Russia, China, and the United States pushed Germany into the background of British foreign policy.[72] "We have," Sthamer reported in October, "recently become relatively uninteresting here."[73]

Preoccupied with the responsibilities of a world empire,

[69] DBFP, IA, II, 392, 400, 417; 17 January 1927, Stresemann to Sthamer, 5540/K2090/567681-715; 20 January 1927, Sthamer to Stresemann, 1344/2466/516589-91.

[70] DBFP, IA, II, 395.

[71] China alone, Chamberlain complained, left him "little freedom of time or mind for other problems": 22 January 1927, Chamberlain to Balfour, Balfour papers 49736. Also 11 April 1927, Chamberlain to Cecil, Cecil papers 51079.

[72] In the 21 months between December 1926 and September 1928 the cabinet had on its agenda matters pertaining to German affairs only once. On British relations with Russia, China, and the United States see F. S. Northedge, *The Troubled Giant; Britain among the Great Powers, 1916-39*, New York, 1967, pp. 292-302, 310-18, 332-37.

[73] 22 October 1927, Sthamer to AA, 5138/K1825/459096.

Chamberlain left the German question to Briand, and in so doing, risked little opposition at home other than a few interpolations in the House of Commons, and he encountered no resistance from those who aided and advised him. Baldwin had complete confidence in Chamberlain and his pro-French policy, relied heavily on his Foreign Secretary, and intervened rarely in foreign policy-making. Walford Selby, Chamberlain's private secretary, was a strong advocate of the entente, and so was Tyrrell, formerly Lord Grey's private secretary and now Permanent Under-secretary at the Foreign Office.[74] D'Abernon, who had long been the major spokesman for German interests in the British foreign service, retired in October 1926; he was replaced by Sir Ronald Lindsay, who did not plead the German cause with the diligence of his predecessor. The German ambassador in London, Friedrich Sthamer, was a man in whom Chamberlain had very little confidence and with whom he was frequently on bad terms.[75] Other than through the Locarno tea parties, German interests were not effectively represented in London.

There was, thus, no need for the specific Rhineland-Russia agreement rumored by the press, suspected by Sthamer, and feared by Stresemann. For a variety of reasons Chamberlain deferred to Briand without demanding *quid pro quo*.

5. *Germany Between East and West* *June 1927*

In spite of Chamberlain's concern with keeping Germany aligned with the West as Britain broke off relations with Russia,

---

[74] Keith Middlemas and John Barnes, *Baldwin; a Biography*, London, 1969, pp. 342-43, 345; Walford Selby, *Diplomatic Twilight, 1930-1940*, London, 1953, pp. 131, 149-50.

[75] In 1925 Chamberlain wrote to D'Abernon that Sthamer was "not a clever man, and I do not think that I should ever be able to negotiate effectively through him": 26 March 1925, Chamberlain to D'Abernon, D'Abernon papers 48928. His opinion remained much the same through 1927, when he told Lindsay that because of Sthamer all important communications with the Germans would have to be handled through the British embassy in Berlin: 19 January 1927, Chamberlain to Lindsay, AC 54/333. Also Douglas Johnson, "Austen Chamberlain and the Locarno Agreements," *University of Birmingham Historical Journal*, 8 (1961), p. 72. For more beneficent evaluations of Sthamer see G. P. Gooch, *Under Six Reigns*, London, 1958, p. 214; Hajo Holborn, "Diplomats and Diplomacy in the Early Weimar Republic," in Gordon A. Craig and Felix Gilbert (eds.), *The Diplomats, 1919-1939*, Princeton, 1953, p. 152; Annelise Thimme, "Gustav Stresemann; Ledgende und Wirklichkeit," *Historische Zeitschrift*, 181 (1956), p. 324.

there was, in 1927, little basis for closer Russo-German ties.[76] Primarily because Stresemann had succeeded in coming to an accommodation with the West in 1924-25, Germany no longer shared with Russia a "community of fate," a common weakness, isolation, and exclusion from the Concert of Europe. Nevertheless, Stresemann maintained ties with Moscow because of their potential and immediate value. One day Germany might benefit from a Russo-Polish war, and in the meantime the Treaty of Berlin served as a counterbalance to Dawes and Locarno. By means of a careful balance between Russia and the West, Stresemann hoped to avoid becoming diplomatically or militarily dependent on one side or the other, a dependence which could lead to the expenditure of Germany's meager resources in the defense of Russia against the West or the West against Russia.[77] He had initiated his Locarno policy to protect and secure the Rhineland; evacuation remained his first priority, and he would not, as he wrote in 1925, "expose the Rhineland to perpetual vexations in order to please Russia."[78] On the other hand, he would not purchase freedom for the Rhineland by adopting an exclusively Western orientation and joining England in an anti-Bolshevik campaign or joining France in a military alliance against Russia, as Arnold Rechberg repeatedly suggested.[79] His objective was to

[76] The historical literature on Stresemann's Eastern policy published prior to 1958 is summarized in Christian Höltje, *Die Weimarer Republik und das Ostlocarno-Problem, 1919-1934; Revision oder Garantie der deutschen Ostgrenze von 1919*, Würtzburg, 1958, pp. 106-13. Subsequent and more detailed accounts based on the archives of the German Foreign Ministry are found in E. H. Carr, *A History of Soviet Russia*, London, 1950, VII, 46-69, 248-82, 425-39; Harvey L. Dyck, *Weimar Germany and Soviet Russia, 1926-1933; a Study in Diplomatic Instability*, London, 1966; Kurt Rosenbaum, *Community of Fate; German-Soviet Diplomatic Relations, 1922-1928*, Syracuse, 1965; Jürgen Spenz, *Die diplomatische Vorgeschichte des Beitritts Deutschlands zum Völkerbund, 1924-1926*, Göttingen, 1966, pp. 40-50, 67-72, 89-95, 111-14.

[77] Stresemann, *Vermächtnis*, II, 554. The literature on the problem of the Eastern versus Western orientation of Stresemann's policy is vast. Shrewd comments on the problem have recently been made by Christoph Kimmich, *The Free City; Danzig and German Foreign Policy, 1919-1934*, New Haven, 1968, pp. 70-73, and Spenz, *Beitritts Deutschlands zum Völkerbund*, pp. 118-21. On the strategic potential of the Russian tie see Post, "German Foreign Policy and Military Planning," pp. 281, 289-304.

[78] Quoted in Carr, *Soviet Russia*, VII, 255. Also Marx, *Nachlass*, I, 462.

[79] Rechberg and his elaborate schemes for Franco-German industrial cartels, a military alliance between the two countries along with a common General Staff, cancellation of war debts, reduction of reparations, the return of the Rhineland, Saar, Danzig, and the Corridor to Germany, a treaty of guarantee

obtain what he could from each side while remaining independent of both and not becoming the tool of either.

In 1925 it had been believed on the Wilhelmstrasse that a balance between Russia and the West, i.e., a détente in the West without a military alliance or a renunciation of German ties with Russia, offered the best means of achieving the objectives of German policy both in Eastern Europe and on the Rhine. Stresemann recognized that "the fact that the Western powers are still preoccupied by the dangers of a Russo-German understanding is a political asset of considerable value for Germany."[80] However, by 1927 there was little he could do to exploit this asset. Russia, still weak, isolated, and antagonistic toward Britain, was of little immediate and direct help to Germany among the European powers. As Herbert Dirksen was later to lament, "we never learned to make political hay out of the Moscow sunshine."[81]

The one alternative to balance, debated on the Wilhelmstrasse in 1927, was a strategy for renouncing the tie with Russia as worthless and dangerous and falling in behind Britain's anti-Soviet policy. If London would support Germany against France and would make major concessions in exchange for German support against Russia, then Germany would separate completely from the Soviet Union.[82] Had it been tried, this policy would not have worked. Chamberlain was not interested in winning Germany over to an anti-Soviet coalition.[83] He had neither the power

---

for Poland, and an Anschluss with Austria: Eberhard Vietsch, *Arnold Rechberg und das Problem der politischen West-orientierung Deutschlands nach dem 1. Weltkrieg*, Coblenz, 1958. The Wilhelmstrasse explained privately whenever necessary that Rechberg had no official standing and was not to be taken seriously: 28 March 1928, Schurman to State, 651.6211/5. There seems little need to have done so. J. G. Schurman, the American ambassador, described Rechberg's ideas as "extravagant and unreal"; Briand called him a "muddle head"; and Poole dismissed him as a "crank": 21 March 1928, Schurman to State, 800.51 W89 France/518; 5 March 1929, Memorandum by Stresemann, 2258/4502/120351; 1 October 1928, Poole to State, 862.00/2434.

[80] Quoted in Carr, *Soviet Russia*, VII, 258.

[81] Harvey L. Dyck, "German-Soviet Relations and the Anglo-Soviet Break, 1927," *Slavic Review*, 25 (1966), pp. 71-74; Herbert Dirksen, *Moscow, Tokyo, London; Twenty Years of German Foreign Policy*, Norman, Okla., 1952, p. 67.

[82] Dyck, "German-Soviet Relations," pp. 81-82.

[83] "It has *always* been clear to me," Chamberlain wrote the next year, "that any attempt to remedy the Russian evil by a combination of the so-called Western Powers against Russia could only defeat its own object by playing directly into the hands of the Bolsheviks": 8 May 1928, Chamberlain to Stamfordham, AC 55/183.

nor the desire to return Polish territory to Germany, part of Stresemann's price for an alignment with England.[84] And he left very little room between himself and Briand for Stresemann to maneuver. As Dirksen put it, "The principle that the English will approach us only so far as this is possible without encroaching on Anglo-French relations has run like a red thread through our foreign policy during the past few years." Brockdorff-Rantzau said much the same thing when he wrote that weakening the ties with Russia would mean "losing the East without gaining the West."[85]

When the British government severed diplomatic relations with Russia on May 27, 1927, Stresemann was not forced to choose between East and West. He was able to declare Germany neutral in the dispute and to assure George Chicherin, Commissar for Foreign Affairs, that he would not allow the transport of Allied troops across Germany in the event the British encouraged Poland to attack Russia—actions which Moscow feared, or pretended to fear.[86] Conceivably, Chamberlain might have threatened to oppose troop reduction or evacuation in order to stop German arms shipments to Russia, to terminate German economic assistance which, he had complained to Stresemann in March, provided Moscow with funds to conduct Communist propaganda against the British Empire,[87] or to press Berlin into following London in breaking diplomatic relations with the Soviet Union. But Chamberlain showed no interest in forcing Berlin into a pro-British alignment or using the Locarno Triplice as an anti-Russian front.[88] Therefore, he had no reason to bribe Stresemann with complete evacuation, to threaten him with a tougher Rhine policy, or to delay concessions out of resentment of German neutrality. Bribes would have alienated the French; bargaining with occupation would have been inconsistent with Chamberlain's conception of fair play among the Locarno powers and dis-

[84] Dyck, "German-Soviet Relations," p. 83.

[85] Quoted in *ibid.*, pp. 82-83.

[86] *Ibid.*, pp. 75-76; Adam Ulam, *Expansion and Coexistence; the History of Soviet Foreign Policy, 1917-67*, New York, 1968, pp. 154, 165-66.

[87] Polish Army Intelligence informed the British Foreign Office that German ships were carrying arms to Russia for trans-shipment to China: 8 February 1927, Warsaw to Central Department, FO. 371/12139/36-40. Chamberlain's complaint: 6 March 1927, Memorandum by Stresemann, 1344/2466/516638-39.

[88] Stresemann, *Vermächtnis*, III, 150.

rupted the Locarnite relationships he valued so highly; threats would have alienated the Germans. As Sthamer observed, the British Foreign Office feared that Germany would only move closer to Russia if the promises of Locarno were not kept.[89]

On only one occasion did Chamberlain ask Stresemann to choose sides. On June 8 the Russian legate at Warsaw was murdered, and there was some fear that Moscow might send an ultimatum to Poland.[90] Chamberlain took advantage of this; on June 14 during the League Council meeting at Geneva, he asked Stresemann to caution Chicherin on behalf of the Locarno powers against aggravating the conflict with Poland. Stresemann was unable to find a way to reject Chamberlain's request without disrupting the harmony of the Locarno Triplice, and he consented, possibly without considering the impact of his action on Russo-German relations.[91]

For hazarding German neutrality in what has been called "the Anglo-Soviet cold war" of 1927,[92] compensation on the Rhine was neither offered nor asked. Stresemann had come to Geneva with no intention of asking for complete evacuation. His goal was troop reduction, and he had known for weeks at what price this could be purchased—on-site inspection of the Königsberg fortifications by the military experts attached to the Allied embassies in Berlin. Briand had demanded this in early May, and Chamberlain had assured him of British support during their May 18 conversation in London. Stresemann had every legal right to reject further inspection of German disarmament, and he had done so for months. Then at Geneva on June 15, a compromise was struck: a visit to Königsberg would be made not by the entire body of Allied experts, but by only two or three individuals. In spite of this, Stresemann was not able to win from Briand a binding promise to reduce the occupying army by a specific date. Briand told him the same day that he could not be rushed; he complained of further trouble with the General Staff which con-

[89] 4 May 1927, Sthamer to Stresemann, 1344/2466/516721.

[90] There was, in fact, little likelihood of aggressive Soviet action toward Poland: Ulam, *Expansion and Coexistence*, pp. 154, 165-66.

[91] Stresemann, *Vermächtnis*, III, 150-53; Marx, *Nachlass*, II, 64-65; Dyck, "German-Soviet Relations," pp. 77-79.

[92] Robert D. Warth, "The Arcos Raid and the Anglo-Soviet 'Cold War' of the 1920's," *World Affairs Quarterly*, 29 (1958), p. 115.

tended that there were additional matters regarding German disarmament to be settled.[93]

Austen Chamberlain was more considerate. His sense of loyalty was aroused by Stresemann's contention that the Allies had broken their promise of November 14, 1925, and he admitted to him that the Allies did not have "clean hands" in the matter. Separating himself from the ambiguous statements of Briand, he assured Stresemann that "if England makes a declaration, she will stick by it." When Briand was forced to leave Geneva because of illness, Chamberlain and Stresemann met alone on June 18, and the British Foreign Secretary agreed to make to the House of Commons a statement reaffirming his commitment to troop reduction, a statement to which Stresemann could then refer in the Reichstag.[94] Chamberlain did so not only because of his bruised conscience, but also out of gratification at the harmony the Locarno powers displayed during the Geneva conversations. Stresemann's contribution to that harmony—his acceptance of one-time, limited inspection and his agreement to deliver a Locarnite warning to Chicherin—raised Chamberlain's estimation of the German. Stresemann was, he wrote, "most reasonable and conciliatory, and he showed in my opinion an increasing appreciation of other people's difficulties and an increasing tact in handling them."[95] Chamberlain, it seems, was willing to spare Stresemann the fate of returning to Berlin with completely empty hands out of gratitude for having been saved from complete isolation on the Russian question. In exchange for a statement from Berlin disapproving of Russian policy, London made a statement implicitly disapproving of French policy. This was destined to remain the limit of exclusive Anglo-German cooperation during the Chamberlain-Stresemann period.

Although Stresemann refused to commit Berlin to either an exclusively Western or Eastern orientation, German foreign policy had become more dependent on the West than the Soviet Union. Stresemann's reaction to Chamberlain's plea of June 14, his adoption of what has been described as a position of "cautious

[93] Stresemann, *Vermächtnis*, III, 154-56; 16 June 1927, Stresemann to Chamberlain, FO. 371/12121/4; Marx, *Nachlass*, II, 61-62, 65-67.

[94] Stresemann, *Vermächtnis*, III, 160-61; Marx, *Nachlass*, II, 67-68.

[95] 17 June 1927, Chamberlain to Tyrrell, AC 54/477. Also 20 June 1927, Chamberlain to Mary Carnegie, AC 4/1/1272.

neutrality with an edge in favor of London,"[96] reflected the dependency of German revisionism on Allied goodwill. Stresemann was, as he wrote to Hoesch in March 1927, preparing the way for evacuation of the Rhineland, the return of the Saar, and the revision of the Dawes plan;[97] and negotiations with the West, especially the understanding with France discussed at Thoiry, offered the prospect of progress toward these goals. In addition, the League of Nations provided machinery through which German minorities in Eastern Europe could be protected, and it was preparing for a disarmament conference in which German claims to equality of arms could be put forth. Finally, if the German-Polish border was to be revised, as Stresemann hoped, then the approval of Briand and Chamberlain was requisite; and Stresemann sought and won some assurance of this in December 1927.[98] From 1925 to 1927, Paris and London drew ever more promising pictures of what Germany could expect from collaboration with the West. The attractiveness of the bait dangled by the Allies contrasted sharply with Berlin's less rewarding relations with Moscow. So Stresemann looked more to the West than to the Soviet Union as a way of achieving Germany's objectives. He did so although few of his objectives had been realized by mid-1927; in fact, Stresemann's program was stalemated at the stage of troop reduction.

On July 3 the Conference of Ambassadors agreed to the compromise worked out at Geneva on June 15. The military experts attached to the French and Belgian embassies in Berlin would visit Königsberg, and guided by a German general, they would verify that the fortifications and gun emplacements there had been destroyed. This inspection was completed on July 8, and the last major question regarding German disarmament was resolved. On July 22 the Conference of Ambassadors formally announced that the IMCC had been dissolved on January 31, 1927. Allied rights to direct enforcement of the disarmament provisions of the Treaty of Versailles were at an end.[99]

A reduction in the number of occupying troops did not follow immediately; it continued to be delayed by a dispute between

[96] Dyck, "German-Soviet Relations," p. 68.
[97] 16 March 1927, Stresemann to Hoesch, 1344/2466/516662.
[98] See below, p. 156.
[99] *Survey of International Affairs, 1927,* pp. 100-101.

London and Paris over the size of the reduction each country would make. In July 1927, there were approximately 70,000 foreign troops on the Rhine—not many fewer than the 72,000 men the French claimed were in zones two and three at the time the Locarno Treaty was signed. Of these 56,000 were French, 7,500 were British, and 6,500 were Belgian. Chamberlain wished to reduce the total size of the occupying armies to 56,000 men. And to this 14,000-man reduction he wanted the French to contribute 11,000 which would bring their contingent to 45,000.[100] However, General Guillaumat, Commander of the French Army of the Rhine, insisted that French forces could not be reduced below 50,000 men without impairing the security of France. This was the absolute minimum *couverture* needed to hold the Rhine bridgeheads while France's reserves mobilized. Briand therefore urged on Chamberlain a smaller reduction of 10,000, maintaining the total force at 60,000 men. The French, he stated, would reduce by 5,000 men and the British and Belgians would make up the difference, a measure which would have reduced the small 7,500-man British contingent—already outnumbered by the French by 8 to 1—to a few thousand men. Chamberlain continued to press Briand for larger total reductions; but he was unsuccessful. On August 6 Briand went before the Council of Ministers and, supported by Poincaré, promised that the size of the occupying armies would be reduced by no more than 10,000 men.[101] Chamberlain then had to content himself with securing reductions in proportion to the sizes of the existing armies, and here he was more successful. At the end of August, the French agreed to reduce their army by 8,000 men to a level of 48,000, a minor victory for Briand over Guillaumat and Foch. The British and Belgians each contributed reductions of about 1,000 men. On September 5 Briand sent a note to Stresemann stating that the forces of occupation would be reduced by 10,000 men, and that in the future, the Allies would station no more than 60,000 troops on the Rhine.[102]

[100] 15 July 1927, Memorandum by Sargent, FO. 371/12148/205. German figures on troop strength: *Bericht des Reichskommissars für die besetzen rheinischen Gebiete* (1927), Bundesarchiv, R43/1/198/348-59.

[101] 30 July 1927, Chamberlain to Crewe, FO. 371/12148/229; 7 August 1927, Phipps to Tyrrell, FO. 371/12148/264-67.

[102] 25 August 1927, Chamberlain to Crewe, AC 50/354; Cab 23/55/49 (25 August 1927); 22 October 1927, Chamberlain to G. Grahame, FO. 371/12129/29.

It had taken two years to resolve all the issues raised during the year of Locarno. The German government had spent 25 months satisfying the Allies on the points pertaining to German disarmament raised in June 1925. Slightly less than two years were spent by the Allies performing the *Rückwirkungen* of Locarno promised in November 1925. If Stresemann's Locarno policy was in part an attempt to remove certain penal and regulatory provisions of the Treaty of Versailles without acceding to the disarmament demands of the Allies, then one significant phase of the Locarno era came to an end in September 1927, and it came to an end short of complete success for Stresemann. He had not succeeded in evading the Allied demands of 1925. To be sure, Russo-German military collaboration was not allowed to interfere with the progress of the disarmament negotiations, and a number of matters on which the British and French military would have liked to have insisted were written off, but those restrictions which were generally agreed to be of importance were imposed on the German Army. Germany was in effect disarmed to the level specified in the Treaty of Versailles. It is hard to argue with the conclusion arrived at independently by both British and German military planners: although the Versailles Reichswehr with its illegal augmentations provided a basis for subsequent improvement and expansion, it had little present value.[103]

More significantly, two years of negotiations had not produced the consensus among the Locarnites for which so much hope had been publicly expressed in 1925. Along with the rest of the government, Stresemann was by no means satisfied with the 10,000-man reduction; he did not consider the maintenance of a Rhineland garrison of 60,000 men to be a fulfillment of the Allied promises of November 1925. He told Briand so at Geneva in September 1927,[104] and his dissatisfaction was reflected throughout the entire spectrum of opinion represented in the German press.

Meanwhile, the means, if not the ends of Briand's policy of understanding with Germany had been altered. Throughout 1927, Briand had referred to his problems with the French cabinet and General Staff, denied that his own attitudes had changed since Thoiry, and asserted that he would resign before he would

---

[103] See above, p. 110, n. 19.
[104] Stresemann, *Vermächtnis*, III, 218-19.

abandon his attempts to reach an understanding. He had, however, become more cautious. The private discussions in Geneva in March and June 1927 indicated that Briand was no longer willing to make concessions out of regard for the spirit of Locarno and Thoiry. Before he was willing to fulfill further the promises made in November 1925, the Germans had to actually carry out their own promise to disarm. By the autumn of 1927 Briand was no longer satisfied with Stresemann's verbal assurances of future compliance as a reason for dismantling the machinery by which the Allies controlled and enforced the application of the Treaty of Versailles. And he was no longer willing to discuss with Stresemann concessions which might not be supported by the opinion of the French public, the Council of Ministers, or the General Staff.

As the French position on Rhineland evacuation was hardening, the German position was being reoriented, and the result was a widening gulf between Paris and Berlin on the issue of Rhineland occupation. When, on July 22, the Conference of Ambassadors declared itself satisfied that the German government had met the disarmament demands of the Allies, it began to be unofficially asserted in Berlin that Germany had fulfilled the Treaty of Versailles. By disarming and by making regular reparation payments the Germans had met their Treaty obligations. It was now time for the Allies to fulfill their reciprocal obligation to evacuate the Rhineland. Germany was no longer the debtor of the Allies; rather, the Allied debt to Germany had fallen due. The Allies had obligations to meet, and failure to fulfill them placed *them* in violation of the Treaty of Versailles.[105] No longer could Germany be represented as being the violator of the peace treaty, and the notion that Germany was the innocent victim of Versailles gained a new measure of credibility. The way was prepared for a new offensive of German revisionism.

The launching of the offensive was delayed, however. It was not until September 1928, one year later, that Berlin took formal diplomatic action demanding the withdrawal of all Allied troops. In September 1927, at the Geneva meetings of the Locarnites,

[105] Examples of this argument: *Berliner Tageblatt*, 10 July 1927; Richard Wolff (ed.), *Unser Recht auf Räumung; Stimmen führender Politiker und Kundgebungen der deutschen Öffenlichkeit zur Rheinlandräumung*, Berlin, 1927.

Briand refused to talk of evacuation, stating that the Council of Ministers had expressly forbidden him to discuss it. Although Poincaré was coming to accept the idea, Louis Marin was still opposed; consequently, a Thoiry-type Rhineland-reparation settlement could succeed only after the Right was weakened and the Left strengthened in the French elections of 1928, he stated. Had Stresemann persisted, he would have found neither Briand nor Chamberlain receptive to his initiative. Privately, the two men concurred that discussion of evacuation was, in Chamberlain's words, an "obvious impossibility" at that time. And neither of them anticipated total evacuation in the near future.[106] Chamberlain accepted the idea that France's eastern frontiers would have to be fortified prior to evacuation; his major concern, as he expressed it privately to Briand a month later, was that delays in construction might necessitate the extension of evacuation beyond 1930 and 1935; and he urged Briand to "get on with the defense of the new frontier" so that the Allies could anticipate the treaty dates for evacuation "if possible." Briand admitted that the Superior Council of War had delayed fortification, hoping that occupation could be prolonged beyond 1935; however, he hoped that the fortifications would be complete in a few years and that the 1930 and 1935 dates for evacuation could be anticipated by at least a year.[107]

Assured that negotiations would be possible after the French elections, Stresemann remained willing to postpone formal action on complete evacuation. He had not insisted that it be made one of the *Rückwirkungen* of Locarno in 1925, and in 1926 he had delayed suit until the negotiations on troop reduction were concluded. He did not then respond, however, to the September 1927 announcement of troop reduction with a demand for new concessions. Instead, he followed the advice which Hoesch had given him for months: postpone claims to evacuation until after the French elections; any earlier action would yield no results and would only strengthen the hand of Briand's political opponents by enabling them to call attention to the size of the German

[106] 14 September 1927, Chamberlain to Tyrrell, FO. 371/12153/261; Marx, *Nachlass*, II, 69-70.
[107] 13 October 1927, Memorandum by Chamberlain on a conversation with Briand held on 7 October, AC 50/372.

appetite for concessions and the futility of any attempt to satisfy it.[108]

There were risks in gearing the pace of German foreign policy to French electoral politics, and Stresemann understood them. His opponents in Germany could criticize his lack of continued success; the French might come to assume that Berlin was willing to wait indefinitely for evacuation. Suspending the campaign for concessions, he wrote, "might well prove a serious handicap to our home and foreign policy in the near future."[109] It was to hedge against these risks that Stresemann launched a propaganda campaign directed at the immediate evacuation of the Rhineland during the winter of 1928.

[108] Nachlass Koch-Weser 37/55 (4 February 1928); 10 August 1927, Cabinet Protocol, 1845/3543/773605; 20 December 1927, Cabinet Protocol, 1846/3543/775116-17; 9 February 1927, Hoesch to AA, 1344/2466/516625; Stresemann, *Vermächtnis*, III, 167-70, 195-98; Geigenmüller, "Hoesch und die Räumungsfrage," pp. 614-16.

[109] Stresemann, *Vermächtnis*, III, 195-98.

PART FOUR

FREEDOM FOR THE RHINELAND
JANUARY-JULY 1928

1. *The German Offensive on Evacuation: The Winter Debate, January-February 1928*

DURING the winter of 1927-28, the three issues which most decisively affected relations between the Locarno powers—evacuation, security, reparations—were reopened to public discussion. In December 1927, Parker Gilbert, the Agent General for Reparation Payments, called for a new and final reparation settlement. A month later Joseph Paul-Boncour again proposed the establishment of an international institution to protect France against the remilitarization of the Rhineland. And on January 30 and February 1, 1928, in two speeches to the Reichstag, Stresemann declared an end to German patience and demanded a prompt end to military occupation. There followed a public exchange of views on the Rhineland question, a discourse thereafter referred to on the Wilhelmstrasse as the "winter debate": Briand replied to Stresemann from the rostrum of the French Senate on February 2, and the British and Belgian governments publicly stated their official positions on evacuation later in the month. These events were a milestone in Germany's relations with the West. They ended the long post-Thoiry period of quietude, during which discussion of a comprehensive settlement had lain dormant. They were to lead, in September 1928, to a three-part German-Allied agreement to discuss a final reparation settlement, to negotiate the complete evacuation of the Rhineland, and to consider an institution of surveillance for the demilitarized zone. In turn, this agreement led to The Hague conference of August 1929 at which the Young plan was adopted and the Allies agreed to end the military occupation of Germany.

It was in his third annual report on the Dawes plan, published on December 10, 1927, that Gilbert proposed that Germany's reparation debt be fixed in the form of a definitive schedule of payments, that transfer protection be canceled, and that foreign supervision over German finances, including the office of the Agent General and its functions, be abolished. For a number of reasons, not all of which were mentioned in his published report, Gilbert believed that the time had come to revise the Dawes plan in this manner.[1]

[1] The following description of Gilbert's reparation policy is based on his published report of December 10, his oral statement to the Reparation Com-

Because of German economic and financial instability in 1924, the Dawes experts had not attempted to design a final and definitive settlement specifying Germany's total reparation obligation and assigning a schedule of payments by which the debt could be paid off. Instead, they had proposed a temporary measure to facilitate Germany's economic and financial recovery, a plan which was to be revised when that recovery had taken place. To allow time for Germany's recovery, they had established a schedule of annuities which increased gradually from 1 billion marks in 1924-25 to a standard Dawes annuity of 2.5 billion marks to be paid beginning in September 1928. And they had provided for transfer protection, the suspension of the transfer of reparation receipts to the accounts of Germany's creditors when necessary in order to protect the value of the Reichsmark. In 1927 Gilbert came to the conclusion that investor confidence in the German economy had been restored, thereby permitting the formulation of a definitive settlement. He also thought that the higher standard Dawes annuity would draw so heavily on Germany's foreign exchange reserves, already strained by interest payments on Germany's large foreign loans, that transfer might well have to be suspended. In that case, Germany's reparation creditors would in effect be forced to pay, by means of diminished receipts, damage done to the exchange position of the mark by what Gilbert considered to be the fiscal irresponsibility of German borrowers. If such a transfer crisis, a "Dawes crisis," was to be avoided, transfer protection must be abolished, which would in turn force Germany to reduce its borrowing. Moreover, the cancellation of protection and the adoption of a definitive schedule of payments would permit the sale of German reparation bonds to private investors, offering the creditors the prospect of advance payment.[2] But, if the German reparation debt was to be so capitalized, then it must be done promptly, Gilbert be-

---

mission on January 14, and his written report to the commission on January 24: Allied Powers, Reparation Commission, Official Documents, *Report of the Agent General for Reparation Payments*, Berlin, 10 December 1927, pp. 169-72; 17 January 1928, Blanesburgh to Treasury, FO. 371/12876/35-38; 24 February 1928, Gilbert to Reparation Commission, FO. 371/12876/168-81; 24 February 1928, Wilson to State, 462.00 R296/2162; Etienne Weill-Raynal, *Les réparations allemandes et la France*, Paris, 1947-49, III, 254-56, 400-403, 867-68.

[2] See above, p. 87 and below, p. 161, n. 42.

lieved, for the sale of other German securities was rapidly exhausting German credit and absorbing the market for reparation bonds. Gilbert was less explicit about what the Germans might receive in exchange for the suspension of transfer protection. He did not propose a new and lower schedule of payments. He only stated that if private bankers were to purchase reparation bonds, they must have the assurance of knowing that German payments —their interest income—were within what Germany could pay and transfer unconditionally, without protection.[3]

One month after Gilbert proposed a revision of the interim solution which the Dawes experts had found for the reparation problem in 1924, Joseph Paul-Boncour suggested what amounted to a reexamination of the arrangements which had been made for the security of Western Europe at Locarno in 1925. Paul-Boncour had long maintained that there was a gap in the Locarno Treaty: although Locarno gave specific international guarantees to the demilitarization of the Rhineland, once Allied troops left the area, there would be no means to prevent violations of its demilitarized status. On January 14, 1928, in an interview published in *Paris Midi*, he called for permanent civilian inspection of the Rhineland. As Paul-Boncour was Rapporteur for the Chamber Foreign Affairs Committee and a French delegate to the League of Nations, it was assumed in Berlin that his statement reflected official French policy. It provoked much discussion in the German Reichstag where Stresemann, who intentionally made no public comment on Gilbert's call for a final reparation settlement, vigorously rejected the idea of permanent surveillance.

Stresemann's comments were made during the course of two long speeches delivered to the Reichstag on January 30 and February 1, speeches which opened what one Belgian diplomat termed "a German offensive" aimed at the complete evacuation of the Rhineland.[4] Although Stresemann had publicly claimed evacuation before, these speeches were of particular significance because he spoke, as the American ambassador said, "more boldly than he has done on any previous occasion."[5] He publicly explained the German position on military occupation with unprecedented directness, and he gave a comprehensive presenta-

[3] See n. 1 above; 27 July 1928, Schubert to Köpke, 2332/4492/101160.
[4] 1 March 1928, Chamberlain to Knatchbull-Hugessen, AC 50/424.
[5] 31 January 1928, Schurman to State, 762.00/32.

tion of what were to be the German arguments for evacuation throughout the months of negotiations which followed. Using Paul-Boncour's statement as a pretext to break what Briand regarded as their gentlemen's agreement of September 1927 not to discuss evacuation in public prior to the French elections,[6] Stresemann abandoned the restraint and patient waiting which had characterized his foreign policy during the previous year and inaugurated a campaign of impatient and outspoken demands for Rhineland evacuation.

The explanation for Stresemann's action is not difficult to find. His Locarno policy had been sharply attacked in the Reichstag on January 30 when Axel von Freytagh Loringhoven, a member of the right wing of the DNVP, charged that Stresemann's policy had climaxed at Thoiry and had since come to a complete standstill. Instead of trying to disguise that standstill as a pause before renewed success, Stresemann should, Freytagh contended, admit that the Locarno policy had come to an unsuccessful conclusion.[7] With Reichstag elections pending, elections which would subject Stresemann's Locarno policy to a vote of the German people for the first time, such criticism could not go unanswered. It was politically necessary for Stresemann to depict his policy as active, certain, and potentially productive. So, he vigorously asserted German claims to a free Rhineland.

Stresemann put forth an ingenious argument:[8] Germany had a legal right to immediate evacuation because the preconditions for early evacuation, as specified in Article 431 of the Treaty of Versailles, had been met. The disarmament clauses of the treaty had been fulfilled as of July 1927, and the reparation clauses were being fulfilled by the regular payment of the Dawes annuities. Germany need not actually pay every mark of reparation to merit evacuation. Had this been the intention of the authors of the Versailles Treaty, then the provision they had made for early evacuation would make no sense, as Germany could never pay off her reparation obligations in less than fifteen years.

Stresemann recognized, however, French interest in additional guarantees of security and reparation payment, and to attract

[6] 17 February 1928, Hoesch to Schubert, 2244/5138/297344; 6 March 1928, Memorandum by Stresemann, 1336/2406/505984-85.

[7] Reichstag, *Verhandlungen*, v. 394, s. 381, pp. 12509-12.

[8] *Ibid.*, v. 394, s. 371, pp. 12490-95; s. 394, pp. 12556-60.

Paris to early evacuation, he suggested that their requirements might be met. He did "not reject on principle" a discussion of Thoiry-like proposals for advance payment of the Dawes annuities. And while rejecting the Paul-Boncour scheme for permanent inspection, he hinted at temporary surveillance lasting until 1935, the normal end date for military occupation specified by the Versailles Treaty. He also indicated that if Paris wished to obtain such advantages in exchange for early evacuation, negotiations must be opened soon. As the term of occupation came closer to expiration, the value of early evacuation decreased, and the time was approaching when Germany would be willing to offer nothing at all in exchange.

Stresemann dealt pointedly with the objection, put forth in Paris after Thoiry, that evacuation would leave France defenseless against German attack. With Germany disarmed, the Versailles Reichswehr posed no threat to France, he stated, and there was no basis for French fears of an *attaque brusque*. Moreover, France possessed the security of the guarantees given at Locarno which, Stresemann said, rendered military occupation a political "anomaly." Referring to Briand's famous speech to the League Assembly in September 1926, he said: "Much has been said about discarding machine guns and cannons, but machine guns and cannons are still staring [Germany] in the face in the Rhineland." Behind French concern for security beyond Locarno "there lurks a certain amount of hypocrisy [*ein stück Heuchlei*] which can no longer be tolerated by the public opinion of the world." Germany, not France, was disarmed, defenseless, and vulnerable.

Stresemann maintained that continued occupation had caused the hopes and the spirit of Locarno to subside. Occupation stood as "the insurmountable obstacle" to the termination of the Franco-German antagonism which had for so long disturbed the peace of Europe. By perpetuating Franco-German hostility, occupation prevented the Locarno Treaty from fulfilling its promise to alter relations between France and Germany, to create understanding and cooperation between the two countries, and to open a new era of lasting peace in Europe. Occupation produced among the German people "a psychological obstacle" to understanding with France. And if France did not take into account what Stresemann called "political psychology" and leave the Rhineland, an "iron curtain" (*eiserner Vorhang*) would continue to hang between the two countries; they would be permanently alienated, and Franco-German conflict would once again threaten the peace of Europe.

With this argument Stresemann depicted occupation as a moral wrong by which the government of France selfishly and hypocritically deprived the people of Germany, France, and Europe of the lasting peace that would result from evacuation. His suggestion that Germany would make anticipatory reparation payments and permit the inspection of the Rhineland until 1935 might entice the French government, but the notion that occupation was a legal injustice, a political anomaly, and an obstacle to peace was clearly designed to make evacuation seem acceptable and even morally necessary to the general public. Much of the justification for military occupation rested on the notion that German malice, exhibited before and during the First World War, might be repeated—either through armed aggression, or through a willful failure to fulfill the Treaty of Versailles. Counteractively, Stresemann conducted a propaganda offensive, asserting that it was not Berlin but Paris which disturbed the peace of Europe. Would not the pressure of European and American public opinion then be brought to bear on the makers of French policy? He candidly told Briand the next time he saw him personally: "The voices which turn against the Allies for maintaining occupation are much stronger than those which Germany has to fear in this matter."[9]

"I was horrified at your speeches," Briand later told Stresemann; "they stood my hair on end."[10] Briand's position in the French government and his influence over the Chamber of Deputies rested on the belief that Locarno had been the first step in the pacification of Germany; therefore, Stresemann's statements—his expression of dissatisfaction with their joint Locarno enterprise, his threat that it could end in failure with the alienation of Germany from France, and his allegation of hypocrisy—cut the ground from beneath Briand's foreign policy and his political position at home. Shocked and irritated, Briand was provoked into a public defense of his policy, and on February 2 he gave Stresemann a direct reply from the rostrum of the French

[9] 6 March 1928, Memorandum by Stresemann, 1336/2406/505988.
[10] 6 March 1928, Memorandum by Stresemann, 1336/2406/505984.

Senate.[11] Carrying on what he characterized as "a sort of dialogue . . . over the frontier," Briand spoke with little of the vague and eloquent optimism usually evident in his oratory.[12]

Briand's Senate speech was an adroit compromise between a hard and a soft line. On the one hand, he accepted the idea of early evacuation and even suggested that it might take place in the not distant future, something he had been unwilling and unable to do a year earlier. Thereby, he openly accepted the primary objective of German policy, and he also made his foreign policy acceptable to the French Left with its desire for international conciliation and justice. On the other hand, he rejected the notion that occupation should be ended to preserve the spirit of Locarno and to create an atmosphere of understanding; he insisted on France's treaty-given rights to security and reparation. Thereby, Briand protected himself from the accusation of the French Right that he was betraying the national interests of France while side-stepping Stresemann's reproach that he was betraying the spirit of Locarno.[13]

The Treaty of Locarno alone, even with its spiritual attributes, was not sufficient to produce evacuation, Briand told the Senate and Stresemann. Promises of goodwill could not prevent the remilitarization of the Rhineland; so, alluding to civilian surveillance, Briand called for "a simple instrument of registry or quick recording, intended to put in play eventually the mechanism of international guarantee." Nor did Germany's past record of payment under the Dawes plan constitute satisfactory assurance of French rights to reparation; therefore, Stresemann must propose some means of anticipatory payment as was discussed at Thoiry.

[11] Briand's speech: Sénat débats, 1928, pp. 64-72. His reaction to Stresemann's speeches: 17 February 1928, Hoesch to Schubert, 2544/5138/297344-45; Gustav Stresemann, *Vermächtnis; der Nachlass in Drei Bänden*, Berlin, 1932-33, III, 340.

[12] Hoesch noticed the difference in Briand's speaking style, as did Myron Herrick, the American ambassador, who reported that Briand was less vague and indefinite than usual and less prone to deal in "brilliant and smooth generalities": 3 February 1928, Hoesch to AA, 2455/5138/297331; 6 February 1928, Herrick to State, 751.00/20.

[13] Hoesch's analysis of Briand's speech: 3 February 1928, Hoesch to AA, 2544/5138/297331-32, 35-37; 15 June 1928, Hoesch to Schubert, 2257/4502/119071. For the attitudes of the French Right and Left toward evacuation see François Goguel-Nyegaard, *La politique des parties sous la IIIe république*, Paris, 1958, p. 298.

Thus asserting France's right to reparation and security, Briand insisted that both must be augmented if the occupation troops were to leave the Rhineland before 1935.

In his speech Briand explicitly rejected the notion that the evacuation of the Rhineland should follow from the mutual confidence which existed between Stresemann and himself, and he showed himself unwilling to abandon the certain benefits of military occupation in the hope of removing psychological barriers between the French and German people. By implication Briand refused to base his German policy on anything as intangible, transitory, circumstantial, and voluntary as personal confidence and "political psychology." The occupation of the Rhineland guaranteed that Germany would pay reparation and not threaten France through rapid rearmament, remilitarization of the Rhineland, or invasion. If evacuation took place, France's financial and military security would be subject to the ravages of time and circumstance, changes in German public opinion, and the designs of future German leaders. The evacuation of Coblenz and Mainz was to be exchanged for assurances of reparation and security which were permanent, independent of German goodwill, and institutional rather than personal. For Briand the spirit of Locarno was as mortal as the men who made it; it was not to be the basis for long-term investments.

To Briand's mind, Locarno had not abolished Versailles and relieved Germany of the treaty obligations to be fulfilled prior to evacuation. Instead, it accomplished "the humanization of the Versailles Treaty"; by allowing France and Germany "to speak directly instead of fighting at a distance, it permitted them to make the execution of the Treaty possible." Locarno for Briand was not the first step toward the revision of Versailles, but the first step on the road to compliance. The difference between himself and Stresemann, Briand admitted, was an honest one: the German Foreign Minister simply emphasized the spirit of Locarno and the concessions which must be made to Germany in order to sustain it. "Stresemann is a man who in this international undertaking for peace does not lose sight of the particular interests of his country," Briand said. "While walking in the olive garden of Locarno [he] has the tendency to put out his hand to take rather than to give."

In the winter debate two very different views of the future of

Franco-German relations were put forth. One came to be known as the "German thesis" and the other as the "French thesis." According to Stresemann, the time had come for France, in the interest of European peace and harmony, to relinquish the gains made in 1919. Briand, on the other hand, held that this could not be done because the assurances nominally made to France in 1919 had not yet been realized and executed. These two theses grew, in turn, from the equivocality of Locarno, the two discrepant views held by Stresemann and Briand of what Locarno meant.

The public debate among the Locarno powers was continued on February 8-9 when the British government defended its foreign policy in the House of Commons. Speaking on February 8, Chamberlain dealt exclusively with Britain's relations with Russia, China, and the United States and said nothing of Germany and the Continent, in spite of the statements by Stresemann and Briand one week earlier.[14] When questioned the next day regarding the government's policy on early evacuation, Godfrey Locker-Lampson, Parliamentary Under-secretary for Foreign Affairs, stated that the government would welcome evacuation but rejected the idea of unilateral British withdrawal.[15] The statements of Chamberlain and his Under-secretary indicated the press of matters other than German affairs on Chamberlain's time,[16] his deference to French Rhineland policy with its demand for *quid pro quo*, and his refusal to inconvenience Briand with public criticism or opposition. In 1928 he continued to pursue what he had earlier termed a policy of "intimate cooperation with France"; he refused, as he said, to "press the French government too hard upon this issue."[17] Although he wished to see occupation terminated early, Chamberlain declined to aid Stresemann's campaign for evacuation either by independent withdrawal, by public disapproval of French policy, or by persistent private pressure on Briand.

This public exchange of views on the enforcement of Versailles and on early evacuation, an exchange to which Paul Hymans, the

[14] Commons, debates, v. 213, c. 115-23.

[15] Commons, debates, v. 213, c. 262.

[16] In February Chamberlain regarded Anglo-American relations as his most urgent problem, and he devoted most of his time to them: 12 February 1928, Chamberlain to M. Lampson, AC 55/303.

[17] 19 November 1926, Chamberlain to G. Grahame, AC 50/253; 15 May 1928, Chamberlain to Howard, AC 55/270.

Belgian Foreign Minister, contributed on February 21,[18] was a watershed in Germany's relations with the West. The winter debate ended the ban on public discussion of early evacuation, and it opened the way to subsequent negotiations by demonstrating that the Rhineland problem was negotiable. In the months after Thoiry, the French cabinet and Chamber had regarded occupation as indispensable and non-negotiable. However, in February 1928, Briand was able to go before the French Senate, state that France had no misgivings about early evacuation provided Germany offered compensation, and receive an almost unanimous vote of confidence. Somewhat surprised by the favorable reaction to his speech, Briand told Stresemann in March that "there is no opposition at all, as a matter of principle, to the evacuation of the Rhineland."[19]

2. *Evacuation and Security*

The end of foreign occupation became a political possibility in February 1928; this in itself was, Hoesch wrote, "a step along the difficult road to our freedom."[20] But it was only the first step, for freedom had become possible only in return for compensation. Typically, Briand did not make explicit in his Senate speech what compensation would be asked; instead, he referred to the actual form of compensation only in the most vague and general terms, a practice to which he conformed during the months following the winter debate. While Briand was well aware that occupation was an asset which must be liquidated while it still had some value,[21] he declined to discuss specific proposals with Stresemann

---

[18] Speaking at length to the Belgian Senate, Hymans expressed views similar to those of Briand. In addition, he insisted that Germany compensate Belgium for the currency issued to the Belgian population by the German Army during the war, currency subsequently redeemed by the Belgian government after the Armistice: Sénat. Compte rendu analytique, 1928, pp. 189-95. Since 1918 the German and Belgian governments had agreed on two occasions on the amount and method of German compensation to Belgium for this expense, but these agreements had not been ratified by the German Reichstag: Klaus Pabst, *Eupen-Malmedy in der belgischen Regierungs-und Parteienpolitik, 1914-1940*, Aachen, 1964, pp. 454-56.

[19] 6 March 1928, Memorandum by Stresemann, 1336/2406/505984; Stresemann, *Vermächtnis*, III, 340.

[20] 3 February 1928, Hoesch to AA, 2544/5138/297336.

[21] DDB, II, 167; Georges Suarez, *Briand; sa vie—son oeuvre avec son journal et de nombreux documents inédits*, Paris, 1938-52, VI, 214.

prior to the French elections in April. Briand's vagueness made it difficult for Berlin to read French policy during the first half of 1928, and these difficulties were compounded by a glaring lack of unity and direction in Paris. For example, all the important spokesmen for French policy—Poincaré, Berthelot, Briand, and Paul-Boncour—expressed such different attitudes toward civilian surveillance of the Rhineland that the Wilhelmstrasse could not discern who spoke for France.

As far as Berlin was concerned, the crucial issue was not civilian surveillance as such but its form and its duration. Stresemann, supported by the Reichstag delegations of most of the German parties, was prepared to hasten the evacuation of the Rhineland by consenting to international inspection under certain specified conditions: the inspection commission must be composed of civilians; Germany must be represented on it; it must not be a standing commission but one convened only when it had business to conduct; and it must cease to exist in 1935. The last point—termination in 1935—was the crux. Stresemann and the spokesmen for all the German parties emphatically rejected Paul-Boncour's proposal of a commission of inspection in perpetuity.[22]

Paris gave the Wilhelmstrasse every reason to believe that it would not support "the Boncour idea." Poincaré recognized that the Treaty of Versailles made no provision for permanent surveillance of the demilitarized zone, and convinced by this legalism, he deprecated the idea in private conversations with various German politicians.[23] Berthelot discarded Paul-Boncour's project, telling Hoesch that it was "worthless and absurd," a mechanism

[22] German Socialists like Hermann Müller and Rudolf Breitscheid openly urged the acceptance of inspection as a way of gaining early evacuation: Reichstag, *Verhandlungen*, v. 394, s. 363, p. 12258; s. 371, pp. 12502-503; Hermann Müller, "Die Deuteten der Luxemberger Beschlüsse," *Rheinischer Beobachter*, 1 February 1928. The German Nationalists were most outspoken on their rejection of a perpetual commission: Reichstag, *Verhandlungen*, v. 394 s. 363, pp. 12257-58; s. 371, p. 12504.

[23] DDB, II, 184; 12 January 1928, Hoesch to AA, 4506/K936/239962-64 (Erich Koch-Weser, DDP); 26 January 1928, Memorandum by Schubert, 2544/5138/297314-15; 27 January 1928, Hoesch to Schubert, 2544/5138/297322-26 (Joseph Wirth, ZP); 23 February 1928, Rieth to AA, 4506/K936/240035; 27 February 1928, Memorandum by Schubert, 2756/5881/430270-72 (Otto Hoetzsch, DNVP). As part of a campaign to win Poincaré to the idea of a Franco-German understanding, Briand and Stresemann had arranged for the French Premier to meet a series of moderate German party leaders: Wilhelm Marx, *Der Nachlass des Reichskanzlers Wilhelm Marx*, Cologne, 1968, II, 61-62.

which would add nothing of practical value to the security of France.[24] Briand, by contrast, supported the idea unequivocally in a conversation with the Belgian ambassador but did not make his position evident to Berlin. He did not clearly adopt *permanent* inspection in his Senate speech, and in subsequent conversations with Hoesch and Stresemann he was critical of Paul-Boncour for publicizing the project without authorization; he suggested that Paul-Boncour's mind could be changed, and he admitted that a commission with permanent status was pointless, having value only as a concession to French public opinion. From these vague and conciliatory statements Hoesch concluded that Briand did not know his own mind on Rhineland inspection.[25]

In Berlin, Schubert read the reports from the Paris embassy, decided that the French would not make perpetual surveillance a precondition of evacuation, and told the cabinet in late February that the issue had been completely excluded from consideration.[26] Berlin, left in the dark regarding Briand's attitude, was to be surprised the following September when he adamantly insisted on permanent international inspection of the Rhineland.

As had been the case in 1925, measures for security of Eastern Europe received less serious attention than did safety on the Rhine. Auguste Zaleski, the Polish Foreign Minister, did attempt to make early evacuation dependent on new guarantees of Polish security. On May 25, 1928, he announced to the Foreign Affairs Committee of the Polish Senate that Warsaw had interests to defend in the evacuation of the Rhineland, and on June 11, while visiting Paris, he publicly suggested that evacuation should be delayed until there were sufficient guarantees of Poland's security.[27] But his efforts received no official support in London and Paris, and they were resolutely resisted in Berlin.

[24] 1 February 1928, Hoesch to AA, 2544/5138/297328; 4 February 1928, Hoesch to Stresemann, 2544/5138/297341.

[25] DDB, II, 167; 26 January 1928, Memorandum by Schubert, 2544/5138/297317; 1 February 1928, Hoesch to AA, 2544/5138/297327; 3 February 1928, Hoesch to AA, 2544/5138/297333-34; 4 February 1928, Hoesch to Stresemann, 2544/5138/297341; 17 February 1928, Hoesch to Stresemann, 2544/5138/297346; 6 March 1928, Memorandum by Stresemann, 1336/2406/505988.

[26] 28 February 1928, Cabinet Protocol, 1696/3573/776253.

[27] *Le Temps*, 14 June 1928; Christian Höltje, *Die Weimarer Republik und das Ostlocarno-Problem, 1919-1934; Revision oder Garantie der deutschen Ostgrenze von 1919*, Würzburg, 1958, p. 188; Josef Korbel, *Poland between*

Stresemann looked forward to the restoration of Danzig, the Polish Corridor, and Upper Silesia to the Reich, perhaps by peaceful means, but by force if one day circumstances should permit. But his first concerns were to come to a political understanding with France and to free the Rhineland from foreign control. Then, he hoped, the Western powers might give their cooperation and support to revision in Eastern Europe. Until they did so, Stresemann steadfastly refused to recognize the German-Polish border of 1922, and he continually obstructed attempts to arrange an international guarantee of it. Consequently, Zaleski's pronouncements met what the American ambassador to Berlin called "a solid wall of press criticism" and a declaration by the German government that Berlin's attitude toward an Eastern Locarno remained what it always had been—negative.[28]

Chamberlain did not expect the Germans to renounce their claims to the ceded areas, and he looked forward to the day—long after he had ceased to be Foreign Secretary—when the Germans and Poles would agree to modification of their frontiers. Meanwhile, in response to Zaleski's statements, he made it clear to Warsaw, Paris, Berlin, and the House of Commons that England would make no guarantees of European security beyond Locarno and that, as far as he was concerned, Poland had no right to extract new guarantees as the price of early evacuation.[29]

East and West: Soviet and German Diplomacy toward Poland, 1919-1933, Princeton, 1963, p. 245; J. W. Wheeler-Bennett and Hugh Latimer, *Information on the Reparation Settlement*, London, 1930, p. 62.

[28] On the objectives of Stresemann's Polish policy and the détente in the West as a means to revision in the East see Zygmunt J. Gasiorowski, "Stresemann and Poland after Locarno," *Journal of Central European Affairs*, 18 (1958), pp. 292, 294-95, 298-300, 303-304, 312-13; Höltje, *Ostlocarno-Problem*, pp. 114, 124-30, 189-91; Christoph M. Kimmich, *The Free City; Danzig and German Foreign Policy, 1919-1934*, New Haven, 1968, pp. 72-77, 154-64; Korbel, *Poland between East and West*, pp. 197-200, 212, 232-33. On the role of war and peace in Germany's Polish policy see Gaines Post, Jr., "German Foreign Policy and Military Planning; the Polish Question, 1924-1929," unpublished doctoral dissertation, Stanford, 1969, pp. 96-99, 281, 289-304. On the primacy of the Rhineland see 16 December 1927, Stresemann's speech at Königsberg, 3173/7372/166866-73; Stresemann, *Vermächtnis*, II, 445. Reaction to Zaleski's statements can be found in 16 June 1928, Schurman to State, 760c. 6215/474; Reichstag, *Verhandlungen*, v. 423, s. 6, p. 92.

[29] 12 January 1927, Chamberlain to Roberts, AC 50/269; 8 May 1929, Chamberlain to Erskine, AC 50/503; 29 June 1928, Chamberlain to Erskine, AC 50/458; 29 June 1928, Memorandum by Chamberlain, AC 50/459; 5 July 1928, Sthamer to AA, 2257/4502/119173-74; Commons, debates, v. 219, c. 509.

In Paris, Briand made no consistent attempt, either before or after Zaleski's statements, to make the evacuation of the Rhineland dependent on a new guarantee for Poland. Characterizing the arrangements for Eastern Europe made at Locarno as "final and satisfactory," he had told Hoesch in 1926 that to make evacuation dependent on Eastern Locarno was "absurd" and would "only impede or prevent a Franco-German settlement."[30] In 1927 Briand, along with Chamberlain, had privately and informally approved Stresemann's right to seek territorial revision prior to any multilateral guarantee of Eastern European security, and he had joined with Chamberlain to aid Stresemann in thwarting a Polish scheme for what Berlin regarded as an Eastern Locarno in disguise.[31] Although one statement made by Berthelot in February 1928 led Hoesch to report that Paris intended to insist that Poland and Czechoslovakia participate in any discussions of evacuation, in fact the French did not respond to Zaleski's statements with an attempt to link evacuation with an Eastern Locarno. Berthelot himself reacted to Zaleski's declarations with impatience, telling Chamberlain that Zaleski "talked a great deal too much."[32]

In the end Zaleski's efforts produced no results, and the Paul-Boncour scheme for permanent inspection of the demilitarized zone received little support in Paris, except from Briand, who disguised his position. The French were hesitant indeed to propose to Berlin new guarantees of security to substitute for that afforded by military occupation.

3. The Price of Freedom: Gilbert, Poincaré, and the Origins of the Young Plan, January-April 1928

Although Poincaré and Berthelot attached little importance to the schemes of Zaleski and Paul-Boncour, neither hesitated to claim financial compensation for early evacuation. Poincaré

---

[30] 28 October 1928, Hoesch to Stresemann, 2257/4502/110542-43.

[31] 12 December 1927, Memorandum by Chamberlain, AC 50/404; Stresemann, *Vermächtnis*, III, 172-98; Gasiorowski, "Stresemann and Poland," pp. 307, 310-12; Höltje, *Ostlocarno-Problem*, pp. 115, 185; Korbel, *Poland between East and West*, pp. 214-17, 240-43.

[32] 1 February 1928, Hoesch to AA, 2544/5138/297328; 3 February 1928, Hoesch to AA, 2544/5138/297334; 5 February 1928, Hoesch to Stresemann, 1335/2406/505945-46; 29 June 1928, Memorandum by Chamberlain, AC 50/459.

agreed with Parker Gilbert on the desirability of a completely new and final reparation settlement and made it a condition of complete evacuation. Berthelot shared this policy objective and told Berlin so clearly, but unofficially. Meanwhile Briand, the official spokesman for French foreign policy, either declined to clarify his views or referred vaguely to the revival of the Thoiry scheme—anticipatory payment without revision of the Dawes plan. Consequently, viewed from Berlin, French reparation policy, too, lacked definition and direction.

Speaking of financial compensation in his February 2 Senate speech, Briand referred to the Thoiry scheme and optimistically forecast a European financial settlement by the end of the year. Then, in conversations with Hoesch and the Belgian ambassador shortly afterward, he predicted that the new French parliament, to be elected in April, would ratify the Franco-American War Debt Funding agreement of 1926; Wall Street would then be opened to the sale of the Dawes bonds, and advance reparation payment could be arranged at a foreign ministers' conference to be held in Paris. But he firmly declined to formulate any specific proposals, telling Hoesch that reparation and war debts were "very unsure ground for him."[33] Then, on March 5 in a Geneva conversation with Stresemann, he abruptly renounced any support for the Thoiry scheme and merely promised to listen to proposals from Stresemann after the French elections.[34] Further inquiry in Paris evoked no definition of Briand's reparation policy, and Hoesch concluded in June that Briand had no plans; the Senate speech reflected only his "wishes and hopes."[35]

Berthelot did not share Briand's hope for a simple, quick Rhineland-reparation settlement. At times he expressed to German diplomats some disdain for Briand's vague and unsure conception of a Franco-German settlement and claimed for himself a superior grasp of the details and complexities involved. Berthelot's self-confidence led him to engage in personal di-

[33] Chambre débats, 1928, pp. 70-71; 17 February 1928, Hoesch to Stresemann, 2544/5138/297347; DDB, II, 167.

[34] 6 March 1928, Memorandum by Stresemann, 1336/2406/505987-88; Stresemann, *Vermächtnis*, III, 341. Berthelot told Schubert that Briand had not meant to revive the Thoiry scheme in his Senate speech; Briand was only airing an idea without defining his real goals: 6 March 1928, Memorandum by Schubert, 2544/5138/297365.

[35] 15 June 1928, Hoesch to Schubert, 2257/4502/119082-83.

plomacy, and in March he repeatedly presented to Hoesch his own elaborate plan for a Franco-German settlement—a scheme with which, he admitted, Briand did not completely agree.[36]

Carefully, directly, even bluntly, Berthelot instructed Hoesch in the conduct of German foreign policy. To promote German freedom, France was willing to evacuate the Rhineland and return the Saar, but Paris would do so, he added, only as part of a much more comprehensive settlement—a final and permanent reparation agreement including advance payment, a definitive settlement of France's inter-Allied war debts, "some formula" for the security of Eastern Europe, and a resolution of the Anschluss question acceptable to all parties. The Polish and Austrian questions were matters of secondary importance to him, Berthelot admitted, and Paul-Boncour's scheme was of no value. The crucial issue was France's financial security: he insisted on a Gilbert-like final reparation settlement and threatened to prolong the negotiations of a Rhineland settlement until he got the price he wanted from Germany. Any attempt by Stresemann and Briand to arrange evacuation in exchange for simple financial compensation, a Thoiry-like one-time capital payment, would only produce "discord and disappointment," he warned.

Berthelot thus promoted a sweeping new European settlement which would replace the arrangements of 1919 as the basis of

---

[36] Although Berthelot destroyed his personal papers, published no memoirs, and made few public statements, the outline and details of his German policy emerge clearly from his discussions with German diplomats, in particular his frequent, confidential, and candid conversations with Hoesch. This summary of Berthelot's policy in early 1928 is based on the following records of conversations with him found in the German Foreign Ministry Archives: 1 February 1928, Hoesch to AA, 2544/5138/297327-30; 4 February 1928, Hoesch to Stresemann, 2544/5138/297338-43; 5 February 1928, Hoesch to Stresemann, 1335/2406/505945-46; 27 February 1928, Memorandum by Schubert, 2756/5881/430269-73; 6 March 1928, Memorandum by Schubert, 2544/5138/297363-69; 3 April 1928, Hoesch to Schubert, 2544/5138/297370-91. On Berthelot's tendency to extenuate those proposals made by Briand with which he did not agree see Ernst Geigenmüller, "Botschafter von Hoesch und die Räumungsfrage," *Historische Zeitschrift*, 200 (1965), pp. 612-13; Emmanuel de Peretti de la Rocca, "Briand et Poincaré (Souvenirs)," *Revue de Paris*, 4 (1936), p. 773. His personality, his hauteur, sarcasm, and peremptory manner of speaking are described in 26 August 1928, Hoesch to Schubert, 1366/2406/506267; August Bréal, *Philippe Berthelot*, Paris, 1937, pp. 207-209; Richard D. Challener, "The French Foreign Office; the Era of Philippe Berthelot," in Gordon A. Craig and Felix Gilbert (eds.), *The Diplomats, 1919-1939* Princeton, 1953, p. 71; Peretti de la Rocca, "Briand et Poincaré," pp. 773-75.

Germany's relations with the West. In what would amount to a new peace conference, Germany, the Allies, and the United States would collectively negotiate a final settlement, simultaneously putting an end to the Rhineland, reparation, war debt, and other questions. At a "single stroke," Berthelot said, Germany would be free, and the way would be opened to "European peace through the cooperation of all the European great powers and America."[37] When Hoesch and Schubert each skeptically suggested that attempts at a comprehensive settlement might create more difficulties than could be resolved, Berthelot replied reassuringly. The most complex difficulties could be solved by "wearing out the problems"; by repeatedly coping with the problems, thinking about them, and discussing them, they would become ripe for solution—by 1930, he estimated.[38]

Like Berthelot, Poincaré was interested in a definitive reparation-war debt settlement, largely because he wanted to insure the future of French finances. In 1928, almost ten years after the end of the war, neither France's reparation income nor her war debt payments had been finally determined, and this introduced a large measure of uncertainty into both French domestic finances and her political relations with Germany and her former Allies. Although Paris had negotiated war debt funding agreements with both London (Caillaux-Churchill) and Washington (Mellon-Berenger) in 1926, neither had yet been ratified by the National Assembly, largely because the former had no "safeguard clause" limiting French war debt payments to what Paris received in reparation from Berlin. By 1928 ratification had become a matter

---

[37] In addition to above, see 8 September 1928, Hoesch to AA, 1775/3642/ 807843. Berthelot's disdain for the Treaty of Versailles, the revision of which he regarded as inevitable; his commitment to Franco-German understanding; and his predilection for a comprehensive settlement which he promoted again in 1931 are discussed in Edward W. Bennett, *Germany and the Diplomacy of the Financial Crisis, 1931*, Cambridge, Mass., 1962, pp. 61, 111-12; Bréal, *Berthelot*, pp. 70, 209; Ernst Geigenmüller, "Botschafter von Hoesch und der deutsche-österreiche Zollunionsplan von 1931," *Historische Zeitschrift*, 195 (1962), pp. 591-92, and Geigenmüller, "Hoesch und die Räumungsfrage," pp. 609-10.

[38] In addition to above, see 29 January 1929, Hoesch to Schubert, 2258/ 4502/120323. For Berthelot's preference for the slow-paced old diplomacy and the skill, patience, and resourcefulness with which he conducted negotiations see Bréal, *Berthelot*, pp. 67, 207-208; Challener, "The French Foreign Office," pp. 71-72, 73; Harold Nicolson, *Diplomacy*, New York, 1939, 1964, p. 81; Peretti de la Rocca, "Briand et Poincaré," p. 775.

of some urgency; unless it was completed by August 1, 1929, the French Treasury would have to pay to Washington what amounted to a penalty of 400 million dollars.[39] Yet, even a finance minister of Poincaré's ability and prestige could not risk proposing ratification without assurance that France's reparation income would cover her war debt payments, and he had no such assurance to offer. France had only the Dawes plan, a temporary schedule of payments, subject to suspension in the event of transfer difficulties, and liable to breakdown or modification at some future date.

To resolve this problem and to give France what he called "absolute financial security," Poincaré gave his approval to Gilbert's suggestion for a new and final reparation settlement in a conversation with the Agent General on January 18.[40] He expected this settlement to meet three specifications:[41] 1) It must be negotiated in the winter-spring of 1929 in order to meet the deadline imposed by the 400-million-dollar penalty. 2) Both the term and the amount of the reparation settlement must be adequate to cover French war debt payments, and an additional amount must be included to indemnify France for war damages. 3) The Ger-

[39] In 1919 the French government had purchased a quantity of clothing, food stuffs, building materials, motor vehicles, and weapons from the American Army at a cost of 400 million dollars. This obligation, referred to as the "war stocks debt," was to be paid in full on August 1, 1929, ten years after purchase, unless the Mellon-Berenger agreement were ratified first. In that case, it would be credited to the total French war debt account to be paid off during the course of 62 years: Wildon Lloyd, *European War Debts and Their Settlement*, New York, 1934, pp. 37-38; Harold G. Molton and Leo Pasvolsky, *World War Debt Settlements*, New York, 1926, p. 365; Jacques Chastenet, *Histoire de la troisième république*, Paris, 1952-63, v, 178, and Chastenet, *Raymond Poincaré*, Paris, 1948, p. 282.

[40] Weill-Raynal, *Réparations allemandes*, III, 404.

[41] Poincaré's conversations with Phipps, Wirth, Hoetzsch, and Hoesch: 10 January 1928, Phipps to Sargent, FO. 371/12875/145-46; 26 January 1928, Memorandum by Schubert, 2244/5138/297314-15; 23 February 1928, Rieth to AA, 4506/K936/224035; 27 February 1928, Memorandum by Schubert, 2756/5881/430272; 12 July 1928, Hoesch to AA, 2544/5138/297405-408. Also Edouard Bonnefous, *Histoire politique de la troisième république*, Paris, 1956-62, IV, 274-75; Chastenet, *Troisième république*, v, 176-78, and Chastenet, *Poincaré*, p. 282; Jean-Baptiste Duroselle, *Histoire diplomatique de 1919 à nos jours*, Paris, 1962, p. 101; Pierre Miquel, *Poincaré*, Paris, 1961, pp. 599-600; Pierre Renouvin, *War and Aftermath, 1914-1929*, New York, 1968, pp. 245-46.

man debt must be commercialized and capitalized in order to guarantee payment and to provide for advance payment.[42]

It was to attract Berlin to cooperation in this enterprise that Poincaré, the man who in 1923 had threatened Germany with occupation beyond 1935, was now prepared to offer to Berlin the prospect of early evacuation. In conversations with several prominent German politicians during the first six months of 1928, Poincaré demonstrated extreme sensitivity about his reputation for militant anti-Germanism, anxiously disassociated himself from his postwar policies, pointed out the need for a Franco-German understanding, and spoke readily but vaguely of early evacuation in exchange for financial compensation.[43] During the Locarno era even Poincaré decided that the best way to insure the payment

[42] Commercialization involved the alteration of the technical status of the German reparation debt to correspond to the type of external debt which governments normally owed, a debt represented by negotiable bonds held by a government's foreign creditors. Once the debt was commercialized, it could be capitalized, i.e., bonds could actually be sold to the public on the international market, with the proceeds of the sale going to the treasuries of the creditor governments: Denys P. Meyers, *The Reparation Settlement, 1930*, Boston, 1930, pp. 108-109. Commercialization and capitalization were disadvantageous to Germany and beneficial to the creditors. Once the German debt was commercial rather than intergovernmental and Germany was the debtor of private institutions such as American banks, downward revision or suspension of transfer would be almost impossible. Any failure to pay as scheduled would ruin the commercial credit on which the Reich, German states, cities, and private enterprises were dependent. Moreover, the treasuries of France and the other creditor countries could collect reparation revenue in advance by selling German reparation bonds to the public; they would then have in hand funds from which to make war debt payments: Bennett, *Diplomacy of the Financial Crisis*, pp. 6-7; Moulton and Pasvolsky, *World War Debt Settlements*, pp. 134-36; Wheeler-Bennett and Latimer, *Reparation Settlement*, p. 103.

[43] DDB, II, 184; 12 January 1928, Hoesch to AA, 4506/K936/239962-64 (Koch-Weser); 26 January 1928, Memorandum by Schubert, 2544/5138/297314-15; 27 January 1928, Hoesch to Schubert, 2544/5138/297322-36 (Wirth); 27 February 1928, Memorandum by Schubert, 2756/5881/430270-72; 23 February 1928, Rieth to AA, 4506/K936/2400035 (Hoetzsch). Poincaré all but repudiated "Poincarism." To Rudolf Breitscheid he stated that the outbreak of World War I was not Germany's sole responsibility, that he, Poincaré, had opposed the annexation of German territory in 1919; that he had been forced into the Ruhr invasion by his cabinet; that he had always favored Franco-German reconciliation; and that he had originated the Thoiry idea: 23 July 1928, Memorandum by Schubert, 2544/5138/297398. Also Erich Eyck, *A History of the Weimar Republic*, Cambridge, Mass., 1963, II, 177.

of reparation was not by continuing or extending occupation but by ending it.

While Poincaré had in mind some general objectives, he declined to make specific proposals, either to foreign governments or to the French public. During the electoral campaign of March-April, he was content to give notice of his conciliatory attitude toward Germany and his desire for a financial settlement. At Carcassone on April 1, he endorsed the foreign policy of the Republican Left, associated himself with the attitudes of Herriot and Briand, expressed his hope for a speedy settlement of reparation and war debts, and mentioned the possibility of selling German reparation bonds.[44] These statements were brief, general, and noncommittal, but clearly Poincaré was attempting to win support for his National Union in the Radical Socialist areas of southern France and trying to indicate to Berlin, and perhaps to Washington, his interest in a final settlement of war-incurred intergovernmental indebtedness. He was not, however, suggesting that negotiations be opened; in fact he stated that immediate discussions would be premature. Unprepared to propose terms for a settlement to guarantee the financial security he desired for France, Poincaré, too, waited for proposals from Germany.[45]

The evolution of Poincaré's reparation policy was greatly influenced by the efforts of Parker Gilbert and his deputy, Pierre Jay.[46] Gilbert conferred with Poincaré on January 18 and again on March 21, prior to the Carcassone speech. The two men agreed that a new and final reparation settlement was desirable and that it must precede any attempt to commercialize the German debt and sell reparation bonds. On the latter occasion,

[44] *Journal des Débats*, 2 April 1928.

[45] Gilbert told Schubert on July 27 that Poincaré had no definite plan for a reparation settlement in mind: Memorandum by Schubert, 2544/5138/297425.

[46] The following description of Gilbert's activities, his influence in Paris, and his proposals for a final reparation settlement is based on accounts of his conversations in Paris and Berlin: 6 February 1928, Memorandum by Schubert, 2756/5881/430267-68; 28 February 1928, Memorandum by Schubert, 2544/5138/297349-62; 28 March 1928, Memorandum by Schubert, 2332/4492/101160; 27 July 1928, Schubert to Köpke, 2544/5138/297412-25; 18 August 1928, Schubert to Köpke, 2544/5138/297426-33; 13 April 1928, Fletcher to State, 462.00 R296/2229; Emile Moreau, *Souvenirs d'un gouverneur de la Banque de France; histoire de la stabilisation du franc (1926-1928)*, Paris, 1954, pp. 519, 528, 552, 557; Weill-Raynal, *Réparations allemandes*, III, 403-405.

Gilbert presented to Poincaré what Emile Moreau, the Governor of the Bank of France, called "the Gilbert plan," a procedure for the settlement of reparations and war debts. And Poincaré soon thereafter expressed to Moreau his hope for the plan's success.

After suggesting a new and final reparation settlement in December 1927, Gilbert worked energetically toward that goal during the first half of 1928. He traveled between Berlin, Paris, the capitals of the other reparation creditors, and the United States, where he discussed his plan at the Treasury (the indirect recipient of most reparation funds) and with American bankers, the potential purchasers of reparation bonds. In this manner Gilbert learned what each party expected from any new reparation settlement. This knowledge, and his position as Agent General— the foremost expert on all the technical details of the reparation problem—enabled him to define for all concerned the limits of negotiation and to put forth a procedure of his own design.

In Europe Gilbert warned both the Germans and the creditors against engaging in any financial negotiations without the informal consent of the United States government, consent which would not be forthcoming until after the November elections. There would be no American support for a new settlement at all, he added, if the European powers attempted to discuss inter-Allied war debts at the same time reparations were being decided. Washington would suspect that her debtors were trying to involve the United States in the reparation problem and attempting to make American war debt claims appear responsible for the demands of the Allies on Germany. Finally, Gilbert advised against any attempt to revive the Thoiry scheme for a quick sale of the Dawes bonds. Washington would not approve such a sale until the National Assembly ratified the Mellon-Berenger agreement,[47] and New York bankers, knowing that the Dawes plan would soon be revised, would withhold their funds until a permanent payment plan was established. Therefore, Gilbert insisted, the German debt could be commercialized and capitalized only after a definitive settlement was reached.

Having issued these warnings, Gilbert proposed his own grand design for a final settlement of war-incurred international indebtedness. First, Germany would accept the French demand for a reparation settlement prior to evacuation and initiate discus-

---

[47] See above, pp. 87-88.

sions of a new and final payment plan. Germany's total obligation would then be determined, and transfer protection would be abolished. After the American elections, Poincaré would go before the National Assembly and gain ratification of the Mellon-Berenger agreement. A private loan to capitalize the reparation debt could then be authorized by the American government. And some time after the American elections and prior to the inauguration of the new American president, the French and other creditors could go to the American Treasury and ask for a substantial discount of their war debts in return for prepayment. Reparation bonds would then be sold over a five-year period.[48]

Stresemann did not object to giving France financial compensation in order to expedite the early evacuation of the Rhineland.[49] He had been willing to do so at Thoiry. Then, when he opened his campaign for early evacuation during the winter debate, he alluded to the Thoiry scheme; and on March 5 at Geneva he tried to get Briand to commit himself to renew discussion of the Thoiry proposals. Stresemann saw in the Thoiry scheme—a public sale of the Dawes bonds—the quickest, simplest, and least ambitious way to raise the capital sum which he hoped would prompt the French to leave the Rhine. It was, then, the resurrection of the Thoiry scheme alone which Stresemann spoke about when he discussed financial compensation during the early months of 1928.

Privately, Stresemann also looked forward to a new and final reparation settlement. Although he instructed his ambassadors to avoid the use of the phrase, he regarded "the revision of the Dawes plan" as one of the three primary objectives of his policy

[48] The importance of settling the French war debt prior to the inauguration was pointed out by Gilbert to Moreau and to Lindsay. Hoover would drive a hard bargain, and his election would make the settlement much more difficult, Gilbert stated. Benjamin Strong, Governor of the New York Federal Reserve Bank, told Moreau that Hoover would attempt to raise France's payments above those scheduled in the Mellon-Berenger agreement: Moreau, *Souvenirs*, pp. 528, 567; 30 May 1928, Lindsay to Chamberlain, FO. 371/12877/145-51. On Hoover's attitude toward debt payment see Robert H. Ferrell, *American Diplomacy in the Great Depression; Hoover-Stimson Foreign Policy, 1929-1933*, New Haven, 1957, pp. 32-37.

[49] The following discussion of Stresemann's reparation policy is based on 30 January 1928, Stresemann to American and Western European embassies, 2332/4492/101079-90; 6 March 1928, Memorandum by Stresemann, 1336/2405/505987-88; 15 March 1928, Cabinet Protocol, 1696/3575/776476-78.

of understanding. (The other two were the evacuation of the Rhineland and the return of the Saar.)[50] However, Stresemann did not favor the elaborate schemes of Berthelot and Gilbert. He hoped to open Rhineland negotiations with Paris in June, immediately after the French and German elections, and he wanted financial compensation to expedite rather than to retard the pace of those negotiations. A complete and final settlement of both reparations and French war debts would only complicate matters by introducing the ingredient of American participation and approval and thereby delay serious negotiations until mid-1929 while the new American president was elected, inaugurated, and settled in office. Consideration of a final reparation payment plan rather than the simple Thoiry scheme would make anticipatory payment and the freedom of the Rhineland dependent on the slow pace of American politics.

Moreover, the adoption of a definitive reparation settlement would place German negotiators at a tactical disadvantage. With French troops on the Rhine, Paris could delay evacuation in an attempt to press Germany for a larger reparation settlement, and this would, as Schubert told Gilbert, lead to "some very disagreeable cattle trading."[51] The tactical advantage Paris had over Berlin would be further increased if settlement of French war debts was included in the negotiations, as Berthelot wished. France would then be able to use the United States and Germany against each other. If the Americans refused to reduce their demands for debt payment, the French could shift the responsibility for large reparations from themselves to the United States; and if settlement were delayed due to American refusal to renegotiate or alter the Mellon-Berenger agreement, Paris could use this as an explanation for continued occupation. As early as February 1928, Hoesch made it known in Paris that Berlin objected to evacuation being made dependent on the generosity and the goodwill of the United States. Berthelot replied that he could envision no other solution; America "had the money bag at its disposal."[52]

How were such complications, delays, and tactical disadvan-

[50] 30 January 1928, Stresemann to American and Western European embassies, 2332/4492/101089; 16 March 1927, Stresemann to Hoesch, 1344/2466/516662.

[51] 28 February 1928, Memorandum by Schubert, 2544/5138/297353.

[52] 4 February 1928, Hoesch to Stresemann, 2544/5138/297340.

tages to be avoided? Stresemann's answer was to keep the arrangements for evacuation and financial compensation simple by separating them from a final reparation-war debt settlement and making them first. He had explained this in his famous *Kronprinzen-Brief* of September 1925: in order to secure a reparation settlement which was favorable to Germany, it was first necessary to release the strangle hold of military occupation from Germany's neck.[53] He reaffirmed his belief in this tactic in January 1928 when he instructed his ambassadors regarding his position on Gilbert's proposed revision of the Dawes plan. Warning them that his words were not to be mentioned to anyone outside the German foreign service, Stresemann wrote that any German statements calling for a revised reparation settlement would only convince the French to occupy the Rhineland until their reparation receipts were defined and secured. To prevent this, Stresemann was determined to pursue a passive, watch-and-wait tactic, to make no public or official response to Gilbert's proposal, and to "strive to postpone the final reparation solution until after the solution of the Rhineland question."[54] Consequently, Berlin, like Paris, declined to initiate specific proposals for a final solution of the reparation problem.

Thus, Parker Gilbert's call for a new reparation settlement raised expectations and objections but led no one to deal openly with the crux of the problem: how much would Germany pay each year, and for how long? If Germany was voluntarily to accept a new and final schedule of payments, then the term of the debt would have to be short enough to be attractive in Berlin. And if transfer protection was to be abolished, the size of each annuity would of necessity be limited to what Germany could transfer each year without difficulty. The Germans could not be expected to jeopardize the value of the Reichsmark by larger payments, and the American investors who were to purchase the reparation debt would not do so unless they were certain that German payments could be made unconditionally.[55] One British Treasury official privately estimated that payments of 1.5 billion

[53] 7 September 1925, Stresemann to Crown Prince, 3168/7318/159874-75.

[54] 30 January 1928, Stresemann to American and Western European embassies, 2332/4492/101082, 88. Schubert agreed that evacuation was the first task of German diplomacy: 21 February 1928, Schubert to Stresemann, 3432/9101/226268-91.

[55] See above, pp. 87-88.

marks for 36 years might be acceptable to both German politicians and New York bankers.[56] However, this schedule would not meet the requirements of Paris and London. Poincaré needed 62 annuities, not 36, to cover French war debt payments to the United States and England for their full term. And the debt payment needs of the British Treasury required German reparation annuities of 2 billion marks because the English received a much smaller share of each German payment than did the French.[57] Thus, the combined needs of both treasuries seemed to require 2 billion marks for 62 years.

If there was to be a final settlement, whose interests would be sacrificed? Would the United States cancel part of its war debt claims? If not, would one or more of the European creditors accept less in reparation than they paid in war debts? If not, would the Germans make reparation payments which were above what could be paid without transfer difficulties? If so, would American bankers purchase the reparation debt knowing that transfer of the interest on their bonds was not secure? Given all these unanswered questions, it is understandable that no one proposed a schedule of payments. This was a problem for financial experts, and the politicians of the Locarno era willingly surrendered it to them. In September 1928 they were to agree to appoint an international committee of experts, and in 1929 the Young committee was to meet and deliberate a final reparation settlement.

4. The Müller Government and the Evacuation of Coblenz, April-July 1928

By mid-1928, the complex difficulties obstructing further adjustment in Germany's relations with the West had become apparent. Unless the American government reduced its war debt claims on France and Britain, there was little hope that a new reparation settlement would include a significant downward revision of the Dawes plan. The French would insist on a final settlement as the price of evacuation—unless Briand was both willing and able to persuade the government and Chamber to withdraw

[56] 20 September 1928, Memorandum by Lieth-Ross, FO. 371/12878/75-99.
[57] Under certain circumstances Berlin and Paris might have agreed on a 1.5 billion mark 36-year schedule of payments, but this would not have met London's requirements: See below, pp. 203-204 and n. 54.

French troops from the Rhine in exchange for a lesser form of financial compensation similar to the one-time capital payment discussed at Thoiry. In Germany, Stresemann was compelled to press for the evacuation of the Rhineland in order to demonstrate the practical benefits of his policy of understanding. How long could he content his constituency by pointing to past achievements (the belated evacuation of Cologne, the withdrawal of military control, and the reduction of troop strength) and by expressing his impatience at the delay of further concessions? In this situation, Berlin faced an important policy decision: should the freedom of the Rhineland be purchased at the price of making the Dawes plan permanent? Those who made policy in Berlin did not reply to this question directly. Instead, in July the German government was to decide to demand complete evacuation and to refuse to offer recompense. And they were to do so knowing that the French would demand compensation and planning to advertise French demands as a wrong perpetrated against Germany by the Allies. This decision was taken over the opposition of Leopold von Hoesch who recommended an alternative: postpone German demands for complete evacuation in order to avoid French counter demands for an exorbitant reparation settlement and meet the demand within Germany for a foreign-policy success with partial evacuation—the anticipatory evacuation of the Coblenz zone alone.

For months a German diplomatic initiative demanding evacuation had been delayed until after the French elections; ironically the results did not improve the prospects for German success. The elections, held on April 22 and 29, were largely a national vote of confidence in the policies of Poincaré's National Union government, a Right-Center coalition supported by all the parties except those on the extreme Right and the Socialists and Communists on the Left. During the campaign Poincaré spoke from a platform of anti-Communism, fiscal responsibility, and a foreign policy of conciliation with careful regard for the treaty rights of France. He was victorious. The National Union emerged with a clear majority, and Poincaré obtained a mandate for his conservative fiscal policy and his cautious foreign policy. By contrast, support for Briand's influence within the government diminished. The parties of the *Cartel des Gauches* suffered from their electoral opposition to Poincaré and the National Union; both the

Socialists, the one group favoring the immediate and unconditional evacuation of the Rhineland,[58] and the Radical Socialists,
who strongly supported Briand's policy of understanding with
Germany, lost seats in the Chamber of Deputies. Meanwhile, on
the moderate Right, the parties of André Maginot and Louis
Marin, opponents of Briand, gained representation in the Chamber and increased influence in the National Union.[59] The
strengthened Right, Hoesch predicted, would drag like a "dead
weight" on the mechanism of Franco-German understanding,
would make Stresemann's work even more difficult, and would
obstruct progress toward the objectives of German policy.[60] His
estimate was confirmed when the new National Union government came to present its foreign policy to the Chamber on June 7.
The government's declaration insisted that there would be no
changes in French policy, omitted reference to the spirit of Locarno, expressed suspicion regarding the revisionist objectives of
German policy, and voiced concern for French treaty rights. Provided Germany harbored "no mental reservation concerning the
revision of treaties" and did not deny to France her right to security and reparation, France was ready to discuss in a friendly
and conciliatory manner any petition Berlin might submit.[61] After
the French elections of April 1928, the Left was weaker; Briand
was no more influential; Poincaré's careful regard for the rights
of France was endorsed; and the Right, which looked across the
Rhine with suspicion and hostility, was stronger. At a time when
Berlin was looking impatiently for the prompt evacuation of the
Rhineland, there was little hope that French troops would depart
with only minimal counterconcessions.

In contrast, the German elections of May 20 did not confirm in
power those parties which had previously governed the country,
nor did they produce a stable coalition for the future. Since
November 1923, Germany had been governed by two different
combinations: either by the *Bürgerbloc*, a coalition of three non-
Socialist parties (the Democratic, Center, and People's parties)
supported in the Reichstag by the Social Democrats, or by majority right-wing cabinets which included the Nationalists. How-

---

[58] *Populaire*, November 23, 1928.

[59] Bonnefous, *Troisième république*, IV, 247-53; Chastenet, *Troisième
république*, V, 170-71; Goguel-Nyegaard, *La politique des parties*, pp. 245-58.

[60] 30 April 1928, Hoesch to AA, 1336/2406/506147-48.

[61] *European Economic and Political Survey*, 3 (1928), pp. 631-32.

ever, in the elections of May 1928, the *Bürgerbloc* lost 21 of its 152 Reichstag seats; the Nationalists, who had participated in the government since February 1927, lost 33 of their 111 seats; and the Social Democrats, who had not assumed responsibility, gained in representation. Consequently, neither of the combinations which had governed Germany for almost five years was possible any longer. The losses of the Nationalists precluded right-wing majority governments, and minority cabinets of the middle were infeasible because the *Bürgerbloc* was an even smaller minority than previously, and because the growth in Social Democratic representation (to almost twice the size of the next largest party) made it unlikely that the SPD would be content with exclusion from office and toleration of non-Socialist governments. While debarring governments of the Right and Center, the elections did not make possible a government of the Left. In spite of the large Socialist gains, the Weimar Coalition (Social Democratic, Democratic, and Center parties) was seven votes short of a majority. The only possible majority government was a cabinet of the Great Coalition which extended all the way from the Social Democrats on the Left to the People's Party on the Right. Because various differences among these parties prevented the formation of such a government, on June 28, Herman Müller, a Social Democrat, formed a "cabinet of personalities" composed of men from the Great Coalition parties.[62]

The Müller government was not an effective political coalition of parties bound by prior agreement to support the cabinet's decisions in the Reichstag. Instead, it was an assemblage of personalities who might possibly be able to influence their party delegations to follow the government on crucial issues. What held the government together was the personality and policies of Gustav Stresemann. His political ability brought the People's Party to support a Socialist Chancellor, and the objectives of his foreign policy were the single important issue on which all the

---

[62] Karl D. Bracher, *Die Auflösung der Weimarer Republik*, Stuttgart, 1957, pp. 287-88; Werner Conze, "Die Krise des Partienstaates in Deutschland 1929/30," *Historische Zeitschrift*, 178 (1954), pp. 52-54; Eyck, *Weimar Republic*, II, 155-61; Alfred Milatz, *Wähler und Wählen in der Weimarer Republik*, Bonn, 1965, pp. 122-23; Helga Timm, *Die Deutsche sozialpolitik und der Bruch der grossen Koalition im März 1930*, Düsseldorf, 1952, pp. 79-86; Henry A. Turner, Jr., *Stresemann and the Politics of the Weimar Republic*, Princeton, 1963, pp. 238-44.

Great Coalition parties could agree in advance. With the Social Democrats, larger than all the other government parties combined, divided from the others on a variety of domestic issues, the execution of Stresemann's foreign policy became the *raison d'être* of the Müller government.

On July 3 the new German government presented its foreign policy to the Reichstag and committed itself to the three primary goals of Stresemann's policy of understanding. Their declared program included—along with the promotion of general disarmament—the immediate and unconditional evacuation of the Rhineland, the return of the Saar to Germany, and a reparation settlement within Germany's capacity to pay.[63] Although it quickly became apparent in Berlin that this program would be opposed by the other Locarno powers, the cabinet defiantly resolved not to alter the announced goals of German policy.[64] And on July 12 Hoesch visited Raymond Poincaré and brought the government's declaration to his attention.

In Hoesch's opinion, the July 3 program of the Müller government was premature; he saw large obstacles barring the way to a Rhineland settlement and continued to caution against any German diplomatic initiative aimed at securing one. Hoesch had made his views known in a long personal letter to his friend Carl von Schubert dated June 15.[65] There he stated, as he had done before, that German diplomacy had made no practical progress toward freedom for the Rhineland since the defeat of the Thoiry scheme. To be sure, the Quai d'Orsay, the French government, and the National Assembly had accepted the principle of early evacuation; but with the exception of the Socialists, all major political groups in France insisted on compensation. In Paris the Rhineland was still regarded as a "pawn" to be returned to Germany for recompense; "vague promises" and verbal assurances, Hoesch warned, would not be regarded as satisfactory. However, there was no compensation, Hoesch continued, which Germany could offer. The Reich could do nothing to realize French

---

[63] Reichstag, *Verhandlungen*, v. 423, s. 4, pp. 38-39.

[64] Austen Chamberlain voiced serious objections to the entire program: 4 July 1928, Sthamer to AA, 2257/4502/119104-106; 9 July 1928, Cabinet Protocol, 1697/3575/777263.

[65] 15 June 1928, Hoesch to Schubert, 2256/4502/119070-2257/4502/119094; Geigenmüller, "Hoesch und die Räumungsfrage," pp. 616-18.

"fantasies" of additional security in Eastern or Western Europe. And financial compensation was not feasible in the near future. Paris was no longer ready to accept a one-time capital payment (the Thoiry scheme); Gilbert insisted that the Dawes plan be revised before any reparation bonds were sold, and a final settlement was remote and would be very expensive to Germany. For these reasons, Hoesch concluded, "the prospect of early evacuation does not exist at the present time."

In Hoesch's estimation, German insistence on prompt and complete freedom for the Rhineland was to no avail; it only led the French to overestimate the value which Berlin placed on evacuation and encouraged Paris to put forth exaggerated demands for compensation. To correct this impression, he recommended to Schubert that Berlin not represent evacuation as the central objective of German policy and as the epitome of Germany's requirements; it should instead state that Germany was prepared to endure occupation until 1935. The ambassador admitted that this would not bring immediate evacuation, but it would, he contended, lead eventually to a settlement favorable to Germany. Confronted with the possibility of gaining no benefit from evacuation as the 1935 deadline approached, Paris would be led to initiate negotiations, placing Germany in the advantageous position of being able to demand the withdrawal of Allied troops. Hoesch recognized the disadvantages of this tactic: abandonment of the campaign for immediate total evacuation might disappoint the German public, leave the government open to the charge that they had suffered a setback, and expose Stresemann to the criticism that his Locarno policy was without practical benefits. To alleviate these difficulties, Hoesch recommended a way to make partial progress toward freedom from occupation. He knew that both Briand and Poincaré were considering a project to evacuate the Coblenz zone alone, not in exchange for material compensation from Germany but as a reward to the German people for defeating Nationalists and electing Socialists.[66] Convinced of the futility and the dangers of negotiations on complete evacuation,

[66] On June 5-6, both men had discussed this project with Rudolf Breitscheid, the foreign-affairs expert of the recently victorious Social Democratic Party. Briand promised to propose it to the Council of Ministers, and Poincaré said he would discuss it in a "benevolent manner": 23 June 1928, Memorandum by Schubert, 2544/5138/297398. Also 6 June 1928, Hoesch to Stresemann, 1344/2466/517236; Eyck, *Weimar Republic*, II, 177.

Hoesch was intrigued by the prospect of the immediate evacuation of Coblenz. He recommended the idea to Schubert on June 15, and engaging in a bit of personal diplomacy, he suggested it to Poincaré.

In speaking with the French Premier on July 12, Hoesch first presented Poincaré with the Müller government's declaration of July 3, and he then supported the German demand for unconditional evacuation with the German thesis and the arguments set forth by Stresemann in the winter debate.[67] Poincaré, however, refused to discuss the question in those terms. Propounding the French thesis, Poincaré insisted that the Rhineland could be evacuated only after the German reparation debt had been settled and commercialized. Then, as German bonds were gradually sold and Paris received advance payment, French troops would gradually be withdrawn from German soil. To this Hoesch responded by expressing his disappointment that Poincaré was not willing to evacuate the entire Rhineland immediately as a gesture of French goodwill, and he suggested that the Coblenz zone be vacated promptly as a demonstration of French confidence in the new German government.

Poincaré replied that the unconditional evacuation of Coblenz was impossible. Speaking of the French public as if it were a reflection of himself, he said: "Because of their legalistic and logical way of thinking, the French people would not understand if France, suddenly out of high heaven, made direct sacrifices to Germany"; there must be an occasion, and the German elections "were scarcely such an occasion." When Hoesch suggested that the French would obtain reconciliation with Germany in return for evacuation, Poincaré replied that "the French people demanded clearer reasons." The French public opposed, he said, "any acts of spontaneous accommodation because of ill feeling over the German attitude toward the Alsatian autonomy movement." Hostility between the Alsatians and the French government was particularly acute at this time,[68] and Poincaré, who as Briand said, was "extraordinarily sensitive and gruff" on matters

[67] 12 July 1928, Hoesch to AA, 2544/5138/297403-11.
[68] In May 1928 the French Ministry of Justice brought to trial on charges of sedition 22 leaders of the Alsatian Autonomist Party: Anon., "The Problem of Alsace-Lorraine," *European Economic and Political Survey*, 4 (1929), pp. 393-405; C.J.H. Hayes, *France, a Nation of Patriots*, New York, 1930, pp. 281-88.

concerning Alsace-Lorraine, maintained that some Germans still wanted to revise the settlement of 1919 in the West, and that some German officials supported the autonomy movement and worked actively for the return of Alsace to Germany.[69] He then brought out what Hoesch referred to as Poincaré's "hobbyhorse": under the terms of the Treaty of Locarno, Germany had not renounced Alsace-Lorraine, but only its forceful recovery; when the time for evacuation came, Poincaré stated, he would demand a *Locarno supplémentaire*, by which the German government would renounce Alsace forever, declare that it was solely the concern of French domestic policy, and state that the present status of the area was final and unchangeable.[70]

In suggesting the evacuation of the Coblenz zone to Poincaré, Hoesch was pursuing a policy of his own and acting without authorization from Berlin. In fact, Schubert had previously warned him, on June 30, of the dangers of partial evacuation. The evacuation of the Coblenz zone, Schubert thought, was of little importance to Germany. Expecting complete evacuation, the German public would not regard the evacuation of Coblenz as a remarkable diplomatic success; it would be apparent that Berlin was being "put off with a token," and the position of the new government would not be strengthened. The greatest danger Schubert foresaw was that the French would use the evacuation of the second zone as a pretext for the continued occupation of zone three (Mainz). Paris, he suspected, would depict the evacuation of Coblenz eighteen months early as a great concession and expect the Germans to silence their demands for further concessions for some time to come. To preserve Germany's tactical position and to prevent what he called an "intolerable breach" in the campaign for complete evacuation, it was necessary to beware of "gifts

[69] Poincaré made such charges not only to Hoesch but also to Breitscheid in June and to Stresemann in August: 23 June 1928, Memorandum by Schubert, 2544/5138/297399-400; Stresemann, *Vermächtnis*, III, 357-66. Other indications of Poincaré's attitude toward Alsace in mid-1928 are to be found in his speeches at Strasbourg on May 5 and at Metz on May 6: London *Times*, 7 May 1928.

[70] The qualifications which Stresemann had placed on the renunciation of Alsace-Lorraine during the course of several speeches in late 1925 (see above, p. 43, n. 113) subsequently received much public attention in Paris after being mentioned in a magazine article: Anon. (Frederick Eccard), "L'irrédentisme allemand et l'Alsace-Lorraine," *Revue hebdomadaire*, 11 June 1927, p. 122.

borne by the Greeks." Schubert sharply criticized Hoesch for his lapse into personal diplomacy; and, supported by Stresemann and Müller, he decided that Germany must be "extraordinarily cautious" regarding the evacuation of Coblenz. If the French offered to evacuate the area in an effort to "prop up" the German government, Berlin would accept the gift, while making it clear that German demands were in no way satisfied. However, nothing was to be done to promote the idea.

Unlike Hoesch, Schubert did not regard French expressions of willingness to evacuate the Coblenz zone as an opportunity to be seized at a time when the fruit of complete evacuation was not ripe. He saw it as an indication that the French were aware that their position on the Rhine was untenable. Encouraged by this, he resolved that the immediate objective of German policy should be the withdrawal of all foreign troops from Germany, and he, Stresemann, and Müller decided that formal negotiations on the Rhineland were to be opened during the September meeting of the League Assembly.[71] In mid-July Schubert prepared a long memorandum on the objectives and tactics of German Rhineland policy. And a series of events were to follow: the Allied governments were informed of the impending German initiative in early August. The cabinet endorsed the step on August 22. Stresemann personally presented the German case to Poincaré in Paris on August 27, and in mid-September Müller opened formal negotiations with the five Allied powers in Geneva.

5. The End of Locarnite Collaboration? The German Denkschrift of July 20, 1928

The decision to demand the complete withdrawal of Allied forces from Germany, which was taken over Hoesch's objections, was not a sudden one.[72] For a year, Stresemann had planned to open formal negotiations in June 1928, after the French and German elections. He had been unable to do so because both he and

---

[71] 30 June 1928, Schubert to Hoesch, 1336/2406/506209-12; 14 July 1928, Schubert to Stresemann, 3432/9101/226449-50; 21 July 1928, Schubert to Hoesch, 2257/4502/119145-47; 21 July 1928, Memorandum by Schubert, 2257/4502/119148; unsigned, undated memorandum, entitled "Guidelines for the Impending Discussion of the Rhineland Question," 2544/5138/297444-45; Stresemann, *Vermächtnis*, III, 352-53.

[72] Hoesch's objections: Geigenmüller, "Hoesch und die Räumungsfrage," p. 618.

Briand had been ill and could not travel to Geneva, and because the French government had not received its vote of confidence until June 7, and the German government did not take office until early July.[73] Then during July, preparations for the opening of negotiations had been further delayed by the slow recovery of Stresemann's health and his absence from Berlin.[74]

With Stresemann disabled, Schubert found himself responsible for performing the duties of the Foreign Minister as well as those of the State Secretary. He explained foreign policy to the cabinet, led the German delegation to Geneva in June, wrote and signed the instructions dispatched to the German missions abroad, and at the same time devoted himself conscientiously, methodically,

[73] Stresemann had not been in good health since 1924, and there was speculation in 1926-27 that he might leave office. He became ill with bronchial influenza in December 1927 and was unable to work for a month. He was in a noticeably weakened condition during the winter debate and took a leave of absence on the French Riviera which lasted from early February to early March. After some preliminary symptoms, he became seriously ill with a kidney infection on May 9. Although he was out of danger within a few days, the attack was so serious that he was forced to discontinue his election campaign: Max von Stockhausen, *Sechs Jahre Reichskanzlei; von Rapallo bis Locarno; Erinnerungen und Tagebuchnotizen, 1922-1927*, Bonn, 1954, p. 250; Stresemann, *Vermächtnis*, III, 72, 499, 501.

[74] Stresemann was, Lindsay observed, "a rather pathetic spectacle, very weak and entirely unfit for work. He has got much thinner and looks like a partially deflated air balloon, with transparent hands. . . . After a quarter of an hour, I found him mopping his forehead from the mere exhaustion of sitting in a chair and talking quietly to me about nothing in particular": 22 June 1928, Lindsay to Chamberlain, AC 55/311. On June 20 Stresemann left Berlin for the sanitorium at Bühlerhöhe, where his recovery was not rapid. There were rumors that he would not return to the Wilhelmstrasse when the new government was formed, and he did, in fact, consider retirement for the first time in his career in mid-July. He suffered a relapse in August— his first stroke, which left his speech temporarily impaired. Except for a trip to Paris in late August, which was preceded by a brief stay in Berlin, Stresemann moved from spa to spa for the next six months. While convalescing away from Berlin, Stresemann was unable to formulate policy; he could not read routine official documents and dispatches, and it was difficult for the Foreign Ministry to communicate with him except by courier: Stresemann, *Vermächtnis*, III, 298, 505, 514, Part 4, Chap. 2; *New York Times*, 19 May 1928; Lewis Hertzman, "Gustav Stresemann; the Problem of Political Leadership in the Weimar Republic," *International Review of Social History*, 5 (1960), p. 375; Gerhard Stroomann, *Aus meinem roten Notizbuch; ein Leben als Artz auf Bühlerhöhe*, Frankfurt, 1957, 1960, pp. 133-35; 21 July 1928, Memorandum by Schubert, 2257/4502/119149; 31 July 1928, Strohm to Boltze, 2257/4502/119224.

and painstakingly to the routine tasks of the State Secretary.[75] Schubert found his unaccustomed responsibilities burdensome since he was unable to take things easily and tended to allow the details of his work to overwhelm him. He complained repeatedly that his manifold and difficult tasks deprived him of the time necessary to ponder German Rhineland policy and give it the co-ordination and direction necessary to prevent Hoesch's personal diplomacy and to open formal negotiations.[76]

Despite Stresemann's illness and Schubert's predicament, the opening of negotiations could be delayed no longer. During the first weeks of July, the governments of the occupying powers responded to Müller's July 3 claim to immediate evacuation. Briand, Chamberlain, and Hymans rejected Müller's demand and sought to escape criticism for continuing occupation by contending that no German government, including the Müller cabinet, had ever formally demanded an end to occupation.[77] These statements disturbed Schubert, Müller, and Hoesch, for they were, as one British diplomat privately admitted, "slightly disingenuous": Chamberlain and Briand first privately urged Stresemann to make no formal demands for evacuation, and then they avoided

---

[75] Although he was an efficient and knowledgeable assistant to Stresemann, Schubert did not feel at home in the world of high policy. His rather stiff and clumsy manner and a lack of extemporaneous verbal facility, both of which he covered with a sardonic sense of humor, put him at a disadvantage in the world of Locarno diplomacy: Nachlass Koch-Weser 37/211 (23 August 1928); 27 August 1925, D'Abernon to Chamberlain, D'Abernon papers 48929; 13 August 1929, Memorandum by Schubert, 2241/4498/107693; Edgar (Lord) D'Abernon, *Portraits and Appreciations*, London, 1939, pp. 151-52; G. P. Gooch, *Under Six Reigns*, London, 1958, pp. 232-33; Hajo Holborn, "Diplomats and Diplomacy in the Early Weimar Republic," in Gordon A. Craig and Felix Gilbert (eds.), *The Diplomats, 1919-1939*, Princeton, 1953, p. 154; Georg Schreiber, *Zwischen Demokratie und Diktatur; Persönliche Erinnerungen an die Politik und Kultur des Reiches (1919 bis 1944)*, Münster, 1949, p. 100.

[76] Herbert von Dirksen, *Moscow, Tokyo, London; Twenty Years of German Foreign Policy*, Norman, Okla., 1952, p. 43; Geneviève Tabouis, *They Called Me Cassandra*, New York, 1942, pp. 68-69; 13 July 1928, Memorandum by Schubert, 2257/4502/119137; 14 July 1928, Schubert to Stresemann, 3432/9101/226350; 21 July 1928, Schubert to Hoesch, 2257/4502/119144; 24 July 1928, Schubert to Hoesch, 2257/4502/119159.

[77] 5 July 1928, Briand to Council of Ministers: 10 July 1928, Hoesch to AA, 1336/2406/506218-19. 6 July 1928, Hymans to Chamber: *European Economic and Political Survey*, 3 (1928), p. 712. 18 July 1928, Chamberlain to Commons: Commons, debates, v. 220, c. 386-88.

full public justification of their own policies by suggesting that Berlin was not pressing the Rhineland problem. These statements placed responsibility for the continuation of occupation on the Germans rather than on the Allies, thereby reducing Germany's propaganda advantage. And they implied that Stresemann's policy was quiescent, an impression which damaged its appeal to the German public.[78] It was to counter this appearance of inactivity, to deprive the Allies of recourse to evasive tactics, and to compel them to clarify their position on evacuation that Berlin decided to make a formal demand for the opening of evacuation negotiations. In preparation for this démarche, Schubert wrote a lengthy *Denkschrift* on German Rhineland policy which he completed on July 20.[79]

Analyzing the course of events since 1925, Schubert perceived that the Locarno diplomatic method and the spirit of Locarno had conferred some distinct advantages on France and imposed some serious liabilities on Germany. There had been no open confrontation between Germany and the West since Locarno, and since Thoiry the discussion of potentially divisive problems like military occupation had been largely limited to confidential conversations at Geneva. This secrecy and inactivity had fostered an illusion of harmonious Franco-German relations—the spirit of Locarno—which provided Briand with a "covering cloak" beneath which he perpetuated occupation, enforced the Treaty of Versailles, and preserved French war gains (*Kriegspfand*) without suffering the resentment and criticism of those who opposed such policies both in France and abroad. What Schubert called "the prevailing situation of stagnation and vague conversations without results" had in turn introduced ambiguity into German rela-

---

[78] 6 July 1928, Pünder to Schubert, 2257/4502/119110; 14 July 1928, Schubert to Stresemann, 3432/9101/226346-48; 24 July 1928, Hoesch to Schubert, 2257/4502/119165-67; 17 July 1928, Minute by Huxley, FO. 371/12902/142.

[79] Schubert's memoranda had a reputation for thoroughly exploring every aspect of a problem, mastering every detail, and then making clear and definite recommendations: D'Abernon, *Portraits*, pp. 152-53. His memorandum on evacuation was no exception. German Rhineland policy is described in the following documents: 28 July 1928, Schubert to London, Paris, Brussels, and Rome, 2257/4502/119214-22; unsigned, undated note, written by Schubert and entitled "Guidelines for the Impending Discussion of the Rhineland Question," 2544/5138/297436-48; 22 August 1928, Cabinet Protocol, 1698/3575/777781-90 and 1592/3242/714791; a final draft of the guidelines, 1775/3642/807600-608; unsigned, undated commentary on the guidelines, possibly the work of Stresemann, 1775/3642/807609-15.

tions with the West and complicated German domestic politics. And if Stresemann continued to talk and defer action on military occupation, his arguments would soon lose their impact, and German demands would no longer be taken seriously. The way to escape from this situation, Schubert argued, was to destroy the illusion that "when all is said and done," the German government "will accept the presence of foreign troops on German territory without German-French relations being seriously affected." Rather than continuing to respect Briand's difficulties with his opponents, Germany must formally demand complete evacuation without compensation and force the Allies, emphatically and publicly, to consent or refuse.

The arguments which Schubert outlined in his *Denkschrift* to support the German demand were similar to the German thesis put forth by Stresemann in the winter debate: evacuation was not a "mere gesture of accommodation, but a real political necessity." Only by withdrawing from the Rhine could the French reach their ultimate national objectives—the elimination of German hostility as a threat to the peace of Europe and permanent Locarnite cooperation on all important questions of European diplomacy.

Schubert also elaborated the legalistic argument for evacuation. All the requirements of the Treaty of Versailles were fulfilled. Germany had disarmed; France was secure; the Reich had made the Dawes payments regularly and would continue making them. The framers of the Treaty of Versailles had not intended that Germany do the financially impossible and actually pay the entire reparation debt prior to evacuation. Rather, the "Tripartite Agreement on Occupation," signed by Wilson, Clemenceau, and Lloyd George on June 15, 1919, provided for evacuation prior to 1935 provided Germany "has given proofs of her goodwill and satisfactory guarantees to assure the fulfillment of her obligations."[80] Calling attention to this statement, the Germans were

[80] *Declaration of the Governments of the United States of America, Great Britain and France in Regard to the Occupation of the Rhine Provinces,* Cmd. 240, London, 1919. This was an agreement among the Allies alone, and Germany, therefore, had no legal right to demand its fulfillment. Stresemann, nevertheless, alluded to it at Locarno, and thereafter the Wilhelmstrasse saw to it that it received wide attention in the German and foreign press: *Proceedings of the Locarno Conference,* No. 146; Karl Mehrmann, "Rhein-Main-und Ruhrgebiet," in Heinrich Schnee, *et al., Zehn Jahre Versailles,* Berlin, 1929-30, III, 141-44.

prepared to argue that they had shown goodwill and given guarantees by accepting the Dawes plan in 1924 and by fulfilling it since. Therefore, Germany had a legal right to evacuation without entering into additional agreements. Evacuation was not a gift; the Germans had paid for it in advance by disarming, by meeting their reparation obligations, and by guaranteeing France's frontier at Locarno.

Considering the strategy of the German diplomatic initiative, Schubert did not expect the Allies to concede complete evacuation without compensation at once. Berlin was not prepared, however, to be denied the attainment of the immediate objective—"to force the other side to make themselves clear on evacuation and to state their possible conditions." Should the Allies decline to clarify their position at Geneva in September, the Germans would bring the full pressure of public opinion to bear upon them. They would publicly announce the inconclusive results of the meeting and publicize their argument for evacuation without compensation. At the same time, the Allies would be informed that the inconclusive results of the Geneva discussions "cannot be without influence on the position of Germany in pending or emerging questions of international politics."

Was Schubert recommending that Berlin depart from the practice of cooperation with the other Locarno powers? He did not specify what steps might be taken, but he did suggest that Germany would no longer seek the agreement of the Locarnites on every important diplomatic issue. If Germany no longer had to show special consideration to the occupying powers over the Rhineland question, Berlin could "adopt a somewhat harder line on specific questions" and gain "a certain freedom in the direction of foreign political independence." The impending discussions could thus lead to an estrangement between Germany and the Western powers, but Schubert expected that estrangement to benefit Germany. If the conflict between Germany and the Allies over occupation were defined, publicized, and dramatized by the abandonment of Locarnite collaboration, then the governments of France and Britain would be embarrassed in the presence of world opinion. London and Paris would have cause to reexamine their policies and be led to hasten the freedom of the Rhineland.

The crux of the negotiations, Schubert predicted, would be French demands for compensation and German refusal to make any. Although he was not certain what compensation France would demand, he asserted that no concessions could be offered. An Eastern Locarno and permanent on-site inspection of the Rhineland were both "out of the question." If Paris demanded financial compensation, the German response would be negative. For a number of reasons, none of which were Germany's fault, financial compensation was infeasible, possible only in the "distant future," after the inauguration of the American president. Consequently, Paris must consider the termination of military occupation "only from the general political point of view"; the continuation or the cessation of Locarnite cooperation must be the only determining consideration.

What would the Germans do in the event the Allies insisted on financial compensation? Schubert's strategy provided for several eventualities. If Germany's creditors insisted that Berlin make specific proposals providing satisfactory financial compensation, the Germans would refuse to take any initiative in an enterprise so impractical. However, if the creditors were willing to make proposals themselves and were able to demonstrate that their proposals could be accomplished quickly and easily, then Berlin would not break off negotiations. The creditors would be given an opportunity to demonstrate the feasibility of financial compensation, and the way would be left open to possible agreement. Schubert was willing to engage in simultaneous, parallel negotiations on reparation and evacuation, but the two issues must be kept separate; under no circumstances would the Germans recognize a juncture between the two.[81] If the French were not content with this formula and insisted that a final reparation settlement be concluded prior to evacuation, thereby postponing evacuation indefinitely, the Germans would unequivocally assert their opposition. They would not promise to cooperate in the search for a financial settlement, and they would proclaim that the German people had no choice but to sustain occupation until 1935. Upon the Allies would fall "the responsibility for the inevitable cessation of the appeasement process," and unencumbered by concern over evacuation, Berlin would pursue a more independent policy. The whole foreign policy of the Reich must not be allowed to suffer, Schubert wrote, just because the impracticality of compensation made it impossible to satisfy France's "vast desires."

[81] 18 August 1928, Memorandum by Schubert, 2244/5138/297428.

Having prepared the arguments and strategy of German policy, Schubert instructed his ambassadors to notify the Allies that Berlin would open the Rhineland problem at Geneva in September and that Stresemann would conduct preliminary negotiations in late August when he visited Paris to sign the Kellogg-Briand Pact.[82] This was done between July 31 and August 3. In London, Sthamer spoke with Ronald Lindsay, who had recently been appointed Permanent Under-secretary. Privately, Lindsay was convinced that occupation "may be very useful in the reparations question later on, as a means of pressure on the Germans to induce them to agree to a high enough figure."[83] However, in speaking with Sthamer, he did not mention British interest in coercing Berlin into a generous reparation settlement. Instead, he convinced Sthamer that he was not personally opposed to evacuation and indicated that the only real obstacle lay in Paris, where Berthelot opposed the opening of Rhineland negotiations in September. "The tempo of evacuation," Lindsay said, "was dictated by the slowest moving partner."[84]

Britain's partner was moving very slowly indeed. Berthelot told Hoesch that the action the Germans proposed was "ill advised," for opposition within the Council of Ministers would prevent Briand from agreeing to evacuation. Briand himself then admitted as much to Hoesch: "The results of the [German] proposal were uncertain"; German unwillingness to offer compensation, he said, "considerably impeded prospects for solution."[85] Thus, from these soundings in London and Paris Schubert had every reason to believe that the French would reject any formal demand for immediate and unconditional evacuation and that the British would support them.

"The success of the action appears doubtful," Schubert reported to the German cabinet on August 22. Nevertheless he, Stresemann, and Müller decided to proceed as planned and insist that negotiations with the Allies take "definite form" in September. The cabinet approved the decision, recognizing the demand

---

[82] 28 July 1928, Schubert to London, Paris, Brussels, and Rome, 2257/4502/119214-22.

[83] 9 August 1928, Minute by Lindsay, FO. 371/12902/186.

[84] 3 August 1928, Sthamer to AA, 1775/3642/807103-104; 11 August 1928, Cushendun to Rumbold, FO. 371/12902/191.

[85] 1 August 1928, Hoesch to AA, 1775/3642/807109-11; 3 August 1928, Hoesch to AA, 1775/3642/807105-106.

within Germany for an aggressive foreign policy. "The general political situation," as Schubert termed it, made some action "unavoidable."[86]

As it turned out, August-September 1928 was not an auspicious time for Berlin to initiate negotiations, the success of which depended heavily on Allied goodwill. In July, while Schubert was preparing Germany's petition for the end of military occupation, Chamberlain and Briand were secretly concluding an agreement on military and naval armaments which completely disregarded German interests. This agreement, the Anglo-French Disarmament Compromise, indicated that London and Paris would not hesitate to collaborate at Berlin's expense, and thereby it forecast the course which the relations between the Locarno powers were to take during the second half of 1928.

[86] 22 August 1928, Cabinet Protocol, 1698/3575/777781-90 and 1592/3242/714791.

PART FIVE

COMPENSATION FOR THE ALLIES
AUGUST-DECEMBER 1928

1. The Disarmament Compromise and the Opening of the Rhineland Question, August-September 1928

IT WAS a short statement, a few dozen words. The British and French governments, Chamberlain said, had formulated a scheme designed to remove the differences between them which had deadlocked the deliberations of the League of Nations Preparatory Commission on Disarmament since late 1926. He did not divulge the details of the proposed agreement, which must, he said, first be communicated to the other interested powers. He only stated, in reply to a direct question, that the proposals pertained exclusively to the limitation of naval armaments.[1] In this manner Austen Chamberlain announced to Commons on July 30, 1928, what came to be known as the "Anglo-French Compromise on the Limitation of Armaments."

Under the terms of the Compromise, the two powers agreed that in future multilateral agreements on naval disarmament, limitations would be placed on heavy cruisers and large submarines; by omission, no limitation would be placed on the construction of light cruisers and small submarines.[2] The British thereby gained the support of the French, who had previously opposed them at Geneva, against the United States in the Anglo-American conflict over naval disarmament. In this dispute the British asserted their right to maintain a large number of light cruisers with six-inch guns to protect their extensive imperial commerce, and the United States claimed parity in total cruiser tonnage, a tonnage level to which they intended to build in eight-inch gun cruisers which could defeat the more lightly armed British ships. In exchange for French support, the British government agreed to support the French position on the restriction of land forces, a matter which Chamberlain deceptively did not mention to Parliament. The French wanted no limitations placed on their

[1] Commons, debates, v. 220, c. 1837-38.
[2] The terms of the agreement were embodied in three notes exchanged between Britain and France during June and July 1928. The texts of these notes and other documents pertaining to the Compromise were printed, sometimes in an abbreviated form, in *Papers Regarding the Limitation of Naval Armaments*, Cmd. 3211, London, 1928. For the history of the Compromise, see David Carlton, "The Anglo-French Compromise on Arms Limitation, 1928," *Journal of British Studies*, 8 (1969), pp. 141-62, which does not completely supersede the account in *Survey of International Affairs, 1928*, pp. 61-81.

large numbers of trained reserves, and the German government, denied a large reserve army by the Treaty of Versailles, opposed granting France this special consideration. The British, who had heretofore opposed French attempts to exclude this category of military manpower from limitation, now withdrew their opposition. In essence, the Disarmament Compromise was a crude and simple deal: a "concession to our views on naval matters," Chamberlain said when he discussed the scheme with Berthelot on June 29, "would enable us to withdraw our opposition to [the French] view on military reserves."[3] The Compromise was, thus, an Anglo-French arrangement to reserve from limitation the categories of armaments and manpower in which each was particularly interested, and to do so at the expense of Germany and the United States.

The Anglo-French proposal, which arrived in Washington on July 31—without any mention of the accompanying British concessions on trained reserves—was never debated or even considered by the American government. To the Americans, who had opposed a British attempt to limit heavy cruisers at the Geneva Naval Conference of 1927,[4] it appeared that Britain, having failed to achieve its objectives in direct negotiations with the United States a year before, was now attempting to maintain naval supremacy, and to compel American agreement to it, by means of a secretly negotiated *fait accompli*. This American suspicion of European duplicity and collusion brought Anglo-American relations to a twentieth-century low point.[5]

The terms of the Compromise were kept secret. The other naval powers—Italy and Japan as well as the United States— were asked to consider the naval agreement, without being given the Anglo-French correspondence in which it was embodied, and as the British and French did not publish this correspondence

[3] 29 June 1928, Memorandum by Chamberlain, FO. 371/13351/219.
[4] David Carlton, "Great Britain and the Coolidge Naval Disarmament Conference of 1927," *Political Science Quarterly*, 83 (1968), pp. 573-98.
[5] Robert H. Ferrell, *American Diplomacy in the Great Depression; Hoover-Stimson Foreign Policy, 1929-1933*, New Haven, 1957, p. 73; Ferrell, *Frank B. Kellogg, 1925-1929 and Henry L. Stimson, 1929-1933*, New York, 1963, p. 168; and Ferrell, *Peace in their Time; the Origins of the Kellogg-Briand Pact*, New Haven, 1952, pp. 203-205, 209; D. C. Watt, *Personalities and Policies; Studies in the Formation of British Policy in the Twentieth Century*, London, 1965, pp. 39-40, 218, and Watt, "Anglo-American Arms Relationships," *Review of Politics*, 25 (1963), p. 280.

until October 22, there was no official public disclosure of the details of the naval agreement until the State Department did so unilaterally on September 28.[6] Nevertheless, the press quickly and correctly guessed the terms of both the naval and military parts of the Compromise, and during August there occurred what has been described as a "general outburst of anger and suspicion."[7] The press, without official information, and fed by rumors from Paris, attributed an importance to the Compromise that went beyond that of a technical agreement on disarmament. In what has been called "an imaginative orgy," it was erroneously speculated that the Compromise contained secret clauses providing for military consultations of the type which had existed prior to 1914.[8] This combination of official secrecy and extravagant public rumors made it necessary for the British and French governments to offer private assurances and public denials of the existence of any secret clauses or special arrangements directed at other nations.[9]

Such denials did not, however, remove opposition to the Compromise among members of the Labour and Liberal parties in Britain, where it was viewed as an indication of the willingness of the English and French governments to obstruct general disarmament in order to protect particular interests and derive special benefits.[10] It appeared also that the age of secret diplomacy had returned, and that political agreements and military conventions had been made which might once more lead to war.[11] In addition, the notion of a secret deal between two great

---

[6] Cmd. 3211, pp. 27-28, 34-38.

[7] *New York Times*, 1 August 1928; *Manchester Guardian*, 3 October 1928. On September 21, the *New York American* published the text of a note, obtained surreptitiously at the Quai d'Orsay, which described the naval agreement in detail. This was the first of a series of unofficial, semi-official, and official disclosures which culminated in the publication of a French Blue Book and a British White Paper on October 22. F. P. Walters, *A History of the League of Nations*, New York, 1952, 1960, p. 271.

[8] George Glasgow, "The Anglo-French Gaffe," *Contemporary Review*, 134 (1928), p. 645; *Survey of International Affairs, 1928*, pp. 71-72; Charles Petrie, *The Life and Letters of the Rt. Hon. Sir Austen Chamberlain*, London, 1939-40, II, 324-35. An example of such interpretations: R. P. Dutt, "The Causes of Anglo-American Differences," *Current History*, 30 (1929), pp. 195-96.

[9] Cmd. 3211, pp. 30-33.

[10] Kenneth Miller, *Socialism and Foreign Policy; Theory and Practice in Britain to 1931*, The Hague, 1967, p. 39; *Survey of International Affairs, 1928*, pp. 62-63.

[11] *Daily Herald*, 27 September 1928.

powers offended the friends of the League of Nations who insisted that in matters of such universal importance, all nations should treat each other equally and deal with each other openly. Finally, an exclusive agreement between Britain and France, especially one which worked to the disadvantage of Germany, gave rise to much press speculation that a new entente had been formed, that the two nations had allied to dominate Europe at Germany's expense, that the spirit of Locarno was no longer operative, and that the era of understanding with Germany had come to an end.[12] Thus, what was proposed as a measure to remove a deadlock in the League Preparatory Commission on Disarmament was depicted in the most sinister terms, and this criticism was to persist in London through the fall and winter of 1928.

The Disarmament Compromise gave the Germans what the British ambassador in Berlin described as a "bad shock."[13] To Schubert it seemed that, while he had carefully informed the other Locarno powers of the pending German initiative on the Rhineland, Chamberlain had negotiated with Briand behind his back for months and never mentioned the Compromise to him.[14] Moreover, in the weeks after Chamberlain's statement to Commons on July 30, London took no initiative to remove German suspicion or end the atmosphere of sinister half-secrecy which surrounded the Compromise. Chamberlain became ill, postponed the conversation he had scheduled with Sthamer for July 31, and departed on a long sea voyage to California and Canada.[15] The information which the Wilhelmstrasse received through the British embassy in Berlin was far from detailed, although it revealed the military as well as the naval provisions, and it was transmitted between two personal friends (Harold Nicolson, chargé d'affaires at the British embassy, and Freiherr Ow-Wachendorf, counselor at the German Foreign Ministry) as a result of a casual conversa-

[12] Gordon A. Craig, "The British Foreign Office from Grey to Austen Chamberlain," in Craig and Felix Gilbert (eds.), *The Diplomats, 1919-1939*, Princeton, 1953, pp. 44-46; Robert Vogel (ed.), *A Breviate of British Diplomatic Blue Books, 1919-1939*, Montreal, 1963, p. xxi.

[13] 10 May 1929, Rumbold to Cecil, Cecil papers 51099.

[14] 4 March 1929, Memorandum by Schubert, 2258/4502/120340.

[15] 31 July 1928, Sthamer to AA, 2257/4502/119612; 1 August 1928, Sthamer to Schubert, 2257/4502/110229.

tion held at a party.[16] The fullest information came from the United States Department of State; on August 11, the German ambassador in Washington was informed of the contents of a long telegram received from the British describing the Compromise.[17] Thus, by mid-August, Schubert had what he called "authentic but very confidential" information on the land disarmament agreement and had discovered the "broad outlines" of the naval agreement by "roundabout means."[18]

The actual provisions of the Compromise did not trouble Schubert. Although he delivered a sharp reprimand to Nicolson, he was privately confident that if the Anglo-French deal were not scuttled by the United States, Germany could defeat it in the Preparatory Commission on Disarmament. What concerned him most was the level of the "current intimacy between London and Paris." Apparently, it was strong enough to overcome long-standing differences between the two capitals over disarmament, to lead to a secret agreement on naval and military forces at the expense of the United States and Germany, and to cause the British to forsake the three-sided relationship of Locarno for a partnership with France.[19]

In fact, Schubert had reason for concern. Although London and Paris denied that the Compromise had abridged the Locarno relationship, Chamberlain had conceived the Compromise out of anti-German feeling, and cabinet members like Churchill had accepted it with the intent of assuring the French military predominance over Germany.[20] If the success of German policy depended on British independence from France and on London's willingness to deal evenhandedly with Paris and Berlin, then a closer Anglo-French entente would further diminish the prospects for

[16] 7 August 1928, Memorandum by Ow-Wachendorf, 2550/5138/301866-67; 26 October 1928, Memorandum by Bülow, 2550/5138/301808-809. The text in Cmd. 3211, p. 29 is abbreviated: 24 October 1928, Ow-Wachendorf to Haas, 2550/5138/301814-16.

[17] 11 August 1928, Kiep to AA, 2550/5138/301854-55; Cmd. 3211, pp. 30-32.

[18] 23 August 1928, circular letter by Schubert, 1312/2368/492412-13.

[19] 22 August 1928, Memorandum by Schubert, 2550/5138/301843-44; 23 August 1928, circular letter by Schubert, 1312/2368/492412-13.

[20] 10 March 1928, unsigned memorandum on Chamberlain-Briand conversation, AC 50/427; 7 June 1928, Hankey to Chamberlain, AC 55/235; Cab 2/5/239 (13 December 1928); Carlton, "Anglo-French Compromise," pp. 148, 161.

German success. Even without full knowledge of the exact motivations of British policy, this was perceived on the Wilhelmstrasse. Dirksen talked openly to foreign diplomats of the difficulties created for German policy by the new entente, and so did Gaus, who said that the new pro-French policy of Great Britain rendered almost hopeless the prospect for Rhineland evacuation and the attainment of other objectives of German policy.[21]

In late August, when the German cabinet approved Schubert's plan for an initiative on the Rhineland question, they also decided that Stresemann would not travel to Geneva in September to open negotiations. Müller agreed to substitute for him.[22] Stresemann's trip was canceled because he had suffered a stroke earlier in the month which had impaired his speech. And it was only with great difficulty that he obtained his doctor's permission to make a less-demanding trip to Paris in late August for the signature of the Kellogg-Briand Pact.[23] He risked his health and undertook the journey not out of deference to Briand, who asked for Stresemann's presence at the signature of the Peace Pact,[24] but as a friendly gesture toward Kellogg, whose pact, he thought, would weaken the French alliance system, give "a new strong impulse to demands for international disarmanent," and begin a new era of American participation in European politics—all of which, he believed, could work to Germany's benefit.[25] However, the chief reason for his journey was Stresemann's desire to speak with Poincaré about the evacuation of the Rhineland.[26]

Before meeting with Poincaré, Stresemann spoke with Briand. This conversation, held on August 26, displayed the damage done

[21] 28 August 1928, Schurman to State, 762.00/37.

[22] *New York Times*, 23 August 1928; 24 August 1928, Cabinet Protocol, 1698/3575/777811-12.

[23] Nachlass Koch-Weser 37/209 (23 August 1928); Gustav Stresemann, *Vermächtnis; der Nachlass in Drei Bänden*, Berlin, 1932-33, III, 514-15, 519; Gerhard Stroomann, *Aus meinem roten Notizbuch; ein Leben als Artz auf Bühlerhöhe*, Frankfurt, 1957, 1960, pp. 135-37.

[24] 3 August 1928, Hoesch to AA, 1775/3642/807100-101; 28 August 1928, Cabinet Protocol, 1698/3575/777781-82.

[25] 19 April 1928, Cabinet Protocol, 1697/3575/776777-78; 27 April 1928, Cabinet Protocol, 1697/3575/776805-808; 22 August 1928, Cabinet Protocol, 1698/3575/777781-82. Kellogg put great pressure on Stresemann to come to Paris: 13 August 1928, Kellogg to Berlin, 711.0012 Anti-War/196.

[26] Walter Zechlin, *Pressechef bei Ebert, Hindenburg und Kopf; Erlebnisse eines Pressechefs und Diplomaten*, Hannover, 1956, p. 98.

to Franco-German relations by the Disarmament Compromise. Briand was at his most evasive, and the two men had what was undoubtedly the least candid of all their discussions. In response to Stresemann's question about the entente, Briand denied that there was any secret agreement or alignment that extended further than the limitation of cruisers and submarines. He evaded Stresemann's direct question as to whether he and Chamberlain had agreed on trained reserves. When Stresemann asked him to say "frankly" what financial compensation he expected in return for evacuation, Briand shrugged his shoulders, evasively stated that a solution must and would be found, promised to discuss the matter with Müller at Geneva, and expressed his hope that Stresemann's conversation with Poincaré would go well.[27]

The Stresemann-Poincaré conversation, held on August 27, went as might be expected:[28] Stresemann presented the German thesis, the case for unconditional evacuation, and Poincaré, who regarded Stresemann as a "German nationalist" of "remarkable ingenuity" who had already drawn many more advantages from Locarno than had the French, rejected it.[29] Poincaré stated that if Berlin wanted the Rhineland evacuated, reparations must be settled; and if the Germans desired a reasonable reparation settlement, then they would have to join Paris in a European appeal to Washington for a reduction of war debts. "All of us in Europe,"

[27] Stresemann, *Vermächtnis*, III, 354-57. Briand's lack of candor with Stresemann contrasts strongly with the full explanation of French Rhineland, reparation, and war debt policy which he gave to Paul Hymans, the Belgian Foreign Minister, two days before: DDB, II, 183. Although Berthelot discussed the matter with Hoesch on September 8, it was two months before Briand frankly stated his attitude toward the Disarmament Compromise to any German: 8 September 1928, Hoesch to AA, 1336/2406/506303; 30 October 1928, Hoesch to AA, 1336/2406/506365-68.

[28] With the exception of two statements, one of which pertains to Russia and has been noted below, the record of the Stresemann-Poincaré conversation appearing in Stresemann's *Vermächtnis*, III, 357-66, is the same as the one found in the German Foreign Ministry Archives: 2544/5138/297458-71. It is Stresemann's corrected version of Paul Schmidt's original notes: 3156/7414/175495-500. Some additional important details: 29 August 1928, Memorandum by Schubert, 2257/4502/119368-80. Stresemann's correcting and editing of Schmidt's notes: 29 August 1928, Memorandum by Schubert, 2257/4502/119423-24.

[29] Konrad Adenauer, Poincaré told Paul Hymans, had warned Paris against Stresemann's "deceit" and "falsehood" and had explained that behind Stresemann's policy of Franco-German understanding there were policies which were suspect and which must be guarded against: DDB, II, 184.

Poincaré said, "are suffering to a greater or lesser extent from the situation in which we find ourselves as regards the United States." France and Germany "both have the same interests and must therefore move in the same direction." In the narrowest terms, the objective of the Franco-German rapprochement, as Poincaré saw it and described it to Stresemann, was German collaboration with France against American war debt policy.

In broad terms Poincaré viewed the understanding with Germany as a way to protect European culture from Americanization and to defend European society from Communism. France and Germany should, he had said earlier in the year, "forget the past" and "come together to work out the major European problems posed by the danger of American mammonism and Russian Bolshevism," and in June he had suggested to Breitscheid that "civilized nations" such as France and Germany unite together in a "moral alliance" against Communist agitation in Europe. Poincaré apparently did not mention the "moral alliance of civilized nations" in his conversation with Stresemann, but he did express what Stresemann termed a "boundless mania against the United States" and dwelt on the threat of Russian Communism to nations of Western Europe.[30]

Stresemann, in turn, made it clear to Poincaré that he would not pursue an anti-Russian policy.[31] He also allayed Poincaré's fears regarding German support for Alsatian autonomy, and no more was heard of the *Locarno supplémentaire*. But Stresemann made no progress toward Rhineland evacuation. To the contrary, Poincaré was convinced that he had persuaded Stresemann to delay the German initiative on the Rhineland,[32] and Stresemann left Paris believing that there was no possibility that the Rhineland could be completely evacuated in the near future. Having tested Poincaré's policy position, Stresemann suggested to Mül-

[30] 27 March 1928, Memorandum by Schubert, 1336/2406/406919-20; 23 June 1928, Memorandum by Schubert, 2544/5138/297401; 29 August 1928, Memorandum by Schubert, 2257/4502/119380. A disparaging view of schemes to turn the Locarno Triplice into an anti-American bloc can be found in A.J.P. Taylor, *The Origins of the Second World War*, New York, 1961, p. 58.

[31] This statement does not appear in the memorandum printed in Stresemann's *Vermächtnis*.

[32] This is the impression Poincaré and Briand gave Cushendun and Selby in a conversation in Paris on September 3: 2 October 1928, Selby to Chamberlain, AC 55/476.

ler on September 1 that German demands for complete evacuation be presented loosely and pragmatically at Geneva. Ready once again to accept a minor success in lieu of major victory, Stresemann suggested that while demanding complete evacuation, Müller should inform the French that Germany would welcome the evacuation of the Coblenz zone alone.[33]

Müller found much the same resistance to German claims when he met with the Allies at Geneva from September 5 to 16. In his initial conversations with Briand and Lord Cushendun, who substituted for the vacationing Chamberlain, both men tried to postpone the opening of negotiations. Briand suggested negotiations be handled later by ambassadors through normal diplomatic channels, and Cushendun seconded him, giving Chamberlain's illness as the reason for postponement. Müller refused to be denied the first objective of German policy as outlined in Schubert's *Denkschrift*, and in a conversation with Briand on September 5, he demanded immediate discussions at Geneva among all the powers interested in the Rhineland question. Briand insisted that if negotiations were to begin, France must be "offered something." His tactic, as he explained it to Cushendun and Hymans, was to entice the Germans into making financial proposals and thereby break down their demand for evacuation without compensation. Müller countered with the compromise foreseen in the Schubert *Denkschrift*: Germany would cooperate in a search for a reparation settlement, but the two sets of negotiations on evacuation and reparation must be kept separate and parallel. Briand then agreed to open formal negotiations at Geneva, but without describing the financial compensation required by France or specifying other French counterdemands.[34] Lord Cushendun reacted to Müller's brief for unconditional evacuation in the spirit of the entente. He identified himself with French policy, and did so with a bluntness never employed by Chamberlain with a German negotiator. Having previously assured Briand he wished to "maintain the entente with France," he asked Müller on September 8 not to demand he "break with the French government on

[33] 1 September 1928, record of telephone conversation, 1774/3642/807078-79.
[34] 5 September 1928, Memorandum by Schmidt, 2257/4502/119649-58; 5 September 1928, Pünder to Köpke, 1775/3642/807849-51; DDB, II, 183; 2 October 1928, Selby to Chamberlain, AC 55/476.

this issue; . . . I cannot," he said, "follow a line which is directed against the French government."[35]

After years of probings and proddings from Berlin, formal negotiations on the end of military occupation were to begin. Characteristically, the negotiations started with a well-publicized conference of foreign ministers and heads of governments and without prior agreement between the two sides on what form the results might take. An indication of how far apart Germany and the Allies were on the eve of formal Rhineland negotiations can be seen in the public exchange between Müller and Briand before the League Assembly which took place on September 7 and 10.

In his speech to the Assembly on September 7, Müller sought to refute the French thesis that sufficient guarantees of security did not yet exist to permit disarmament—and, by implication, evacuation. He applied the German thesis to the disarmament problem, and he used the same arguments which Berlin used to support its demand for prompt evacuation. Müller contended that the public expressions of confidence made by European politicians in the League of Nations, in the Locarno Treaty, and the Kellogg Pact stood in sharp contrast to the maintenance of armies and armaments. On the one hand, those politicians solemnly pledged themselves to mutual understanding and the maintenance of peace; on the other, they acted as if the guarantees of peace they signed did not exist and maintained "the barriers raised as a result of the World War." In attempting to follow the paths of both conciliation and enforcement, French policy was, Müller said, "double faced." France must choose either armament and enforcement or understanding and conciliation.

Müller's public characterization of French policy as "double faced" brought a sharp response from Briand, just as Stresemann's designation of French policy as "hypocritical" had done during the winter debate. Briand took Müller's address personally, perceiving in it "certain rather direct references to my alleged facility of speech and disinclination for action." In an address to the Assembly on September 10, he replied to Müller di-

---

[35] 8 September 1928, Memorandum by Schubert, 2257/4502/119672-73; 8 September 1928, Memorandum by Schubert, 1775/3642/807568-77; 8 September 1928, Pünder to Köpke, 1775/3642/807838-39; 8 September 1928, Cushendun to Lindsay, FO. 371/12903/122; 8 September 1928, Cushendun to Birkenhead, FO. 371/12903/143; 2 October 1928, Selby to Chamberlain, AC 55/476.

rectly—mentioning him frequently by name, pointing his finger at him, and characterizing his speech as pacifist propaganda. Although Briand voiced his usual sympathy for German impatience and his desire for understanding and conciliation, he defended France's cautious attitude toward disarmament by describing Germany's capacity to launch an *attaque brusque*.[36] His speech was a clear defense of the French thesis that sufficient guarantees of security did not exist to permit disarmament—and, by implication, evacuation. His truculent tone, more noticeable in Geneva than Paris, caused the speech to be termed thereafter in the short-hand terminology of the German Foreign Ministry as Briand's *Böse Rede*.

The next day, August 11, the first of three meetings between Müller and the representatives of the five powers represented on the Conference of Ambassadors (Britain, France, Belgium, Italy, and Japan) took place.[37] There, after Müller had given a full presentation of the German petition for unconditional evacuation, he and Briand reiterated their agreement to separate, parallel negotiations on reparation and the Rhineland. But when Briand urged the Germans to propose a financial settlement to be submitted for the approval of financial experts, Müller refused. So at the second meeting of the six powers, held on September 13,[38] Müller and Briand agreed on what amounted to a second Dawes committee. To relieve Berlin of the responsibility for formulating and proposing a feasible reparation settlement, financial experts from all the interested governments, including the United States, would meet together to generate a definitive settlement of Germany's obligations. Having agreed to discuss reparation, it was now Müller's turn to insist on compensation. If he returned to Berlin empty-

[36] Records of the Ninth Ordinary Session of the Assembly, Plenary Meetings, Text of the Debates, League of Nations, *Official Journal*, Special Supplement, No. 64, Geneva, 1928, pp. 58-59, 79-83. Ernst Geigenmüller, "Botschafter von Hoesch und die Räumungsfrage," *Historische Zeitschrift*, 200 (1965), p. 608.

[37] 11 September 1928, Memorandum by Schmidt, 1775/3642/807532-52; 12 September 1928, Pünder to Köpke, 1775/3642/807828-30; 11 September 1928, Memorandum by Cushendun, FO. 371/12903/179; DDB, II, 187.

[38] 13 September 1928, Memorandum by Schmidt, 1775/3642/807477-96; 13 September 1928, Memorandum by Schubert, 1775/3642/807797-802; 13 September 1928, Memorandum by Cushendun, FO. 371/12903/209; DDB, II, 188; 13 September 1928, record of telephone conversation, 1775/3642/807810-11.

handed, Müller warned, it would appear that the German petition for evacuation had been denied. After some hesitation and
following some prodding by Cushendun, who expressed sympathy for Müller's plight, Briand offered to make a gesture. He
would evacuate French troops from the Coblenz zone as soon as
the financial experts were appointed and Germany consented to
what Briand called "a Commission of Verification and Conciliation," a term coined to soften the impact of permanent foreign
surveillance of the Rhineland on German public opinion.

Briand's insistence on inspection of the demilitarized zone,
after indicating for months that he did not share Paul-Boncour's
ideas, was, in Hoesch's words, one of Briand's "painful sur-
prises."[39] In accordance with the Schubert *Denkschrift*, Müller
refused to agree to any compensation for the evacuation of
Coblenz, or to any permanent international inspection, without
the consent of the government. However, following the meeting
of September 13, he telegraphed the cabinet in Berlin to recommend acceptance of Briand's Commission of Verification, a measure he and other Social Democrats had long favored, provided
Coblenz was evacuated immediately, Mainz was freed soon thereafter, and the Verification Commission took a lax and lenient
form.[40]

The cabinet considered Müller's proposal on September 15. In
the absence of Müller, Stresemann, and Schubert, the other
members took a somewhat heterodox view of the priorities of
German policy. Led by Julius Curtius, Minister of Economics and
a proponent of a new reparation settlement,[41] they decided that
the formation of a committee of financial experts was of such
"decisive significance for the future of Germany" that it "must
take precedence over the evacuation question." The success of
reparation negotiations, they informed Müller, "required discreet
negotiations over the evacuation-security problem." Secondly,
with the exception of the members of Müller's own party, they

---

[39] Briand never offered Berlin any explanation of his renewed interest in
Rhineland inspection other than to say later that the idea "had sprung out
of his head at Geneva as Minerva had sprung from the head of Jupiter":
24 November 1928, Hoesch to AA, 2258/4502/120185-87.

[40] 14 September 1928, Memorandum by Müller, 2244/5138/297548-53; 14
September 1928, Memorandum by Gaus, 1775/3642/807455-57.

[41] Julius Curtius, *Sechs Jahre Minister der Deutschen Republik*, Heidelberg, 1948, pp. 93-95; Stresemann, *Vermächtnis*, III, 368.

refused to accept permanent inspection of the Rhineland. Characterizing it as a pretense, a "snooping commission" and an organ to control the construction of railroads in the Rhineland, the non-Socialists led the cabinet in imposing limits on the Commission of Verification which made compromise with Briand impossible. The jurisdiction of the Verification Commission was to terminate in 1935, be restricted to Coblenz and Mainz rather than the entire demilitarized zone, and be established only in exchange for the complete evacuation of the Rhineland and the return of the Saar. For the evacuation of Coblenz alone, as Theodore von Guérard (ZP) said, there was not to be the "slightest compensation."[42]

"The German cabinet has spoken," Müller informed Briand and the representatives of the other four Allied powers on September 16. Briand, supported by Paul Hymans, insisted that the Commission of Verification must continue its activities for the duration of the Locarno Treaty—perpetually—and he suggested that discussion of the term of the commission be continued through normal diplomatic channels. Müller agreed, stipulating that parallel, but separate, negotiations on evacuation and reparation also be conducted. Cushendun who, as Selby said, had "supported the French attitude as opposed to the German claim," concluded the meeting with a perfunctory reaffirmation of British independence: the British government had no direct interest in continuing occupation or in establishing a Commission of Verification; they reserved the right "to take proper steps in order to promote Rhineland evacuation . . . without necessarily being bound in its decision by any conditions."[43]

At the end of this third and final meeting between Germany and the Allies, the six powers issued a joint communiqué to the press in which they announced their decision 1) to open "official negotiations" on the early evacuation of the Rhineland; 2) to ap-

[42] 15 September 1928, Cabinet Protocol, 1698/3575/777838-40; 15 September 1928, Gröner to Müller, 1775/3642/807775-79; 15 September 1928, Köpke to Geneva, 2544/5138/297583-88; 15 September 1928, Memorandum by Pünder, 1775/3642/807448-51; 16 September 1928, Memorandum by Köpke, 2544/5138/297589.

[43] 16 September 1928, Memorandum by Schmidt, 1775/3642/807411-32; 16 September 1928, Pünder to Köpke, 2544/5138/297590-92; 16 September 1928, Schubert to Köpke, 2544/5138/297612-18; 2 October 1928, Selby to Chamberlain, AC 55/476; 16 September 1928, Memorandum by Cushendun, FO. 371/12904/43-46; DDB, II, 189.

point "a committee of financial experts" to propose "a complete and definite settlement of the reparation problem"; and 3) to set up a Commission of Verification and Conciliation, "the composition, mode of operation, objects, and duration" of which would "form the subject of negotiations between the governments concerned."[44]

This communiqué—thereafter referred to as the Geneva communiqué or the communiqué of September 16—represents a watershed in the history of the Locarno era. First, it indicated German success in bringing the Allies to negotiate an end to occupation and French success in winning the cooperation of the other powers in making arrangements for their financial security. Moreover, the communiqué implicitly removed from consideration certain proposals which had been made since the time of the winter debate. There would be no partial evacuation which might push the paramount question of complete evacuation into the background by putting off the demands of the Germans with what Hermann Pünder termed a "momentary success."[45] Neither would there be a partial reparation settlement involving the payment of a capital sum out of the Dawes annuities; instead a new and final payment plan would be devised. Finally, there would be no new assurances of the territorial *status quo*—no *Locarno supplémentaire*, no Eastern Locarno, and no voluntary renunciation of the Anschluss.[46]

The Geneva communiqué also reflected the impasse which had been reached in the meetings of the six powers and in German relations with the West. Neither side had won acceptance for its position regarding compensation for evacuation; neither the French nor the German thesis had triumphed. In order to open official negotiations on the Rhineland question, Müller had found it necessary to agree to negotiations designed to reach a final reparation settlement. On the other hand, Briand had pledged himself to open evacuation negotiations in exchange for separate

[44] *Documents on International Affairs, 1928,* pp. 49, 53.

[45] 18 September 1928, Memorandum by Pünder, 2545/5138/297656. Pünder was State Secretary in the Reich Chancellery.

[46] At Geneva, Auguste Zaleski, the Polish Foreign Minister, had attempted to persuade both Briand and Cushendun that Poland should be a party to any agreement on evacuation: 13 September 1928, Memorandum by Cushendun, FO. 371/12903/233. Polish efforts continued through November without success: 23 November 1928, Sargent to Erskine, FO. 371/12905/161-63.

reparation negotiations; Müller was not persuaded to propose a specific financial settlement, and Berlin was not committed to the principle of compensation. The issue which both sides regarded to be of prime importance, whether the Rhineland was to be evacuated or whether occupation was to continue until compensation was arranged, was not resolved at Geneva, and it was not mentioned in the communiqué. This disagreement and ambiguity permitted each side to interpret the Geneva discussions and the communiqué of September 16 in the manner most favorable to their position, and each did so. This conflict over what had been determined at Geneva was to plague the relations between Germany and the West for the rest of the year, and in December it was to bring the level of hostility between the two sides to a point not reached since the spring of 1927.

On September 18 Müller told the cabinet that the discussions at Geneva were "an important step forward," and the cabinet gave him its approval. He had, Müller explained, overcome Briand's attempts to avoid discussion of evacuation and opened formal negotiations on the Rhineland without admitting the dependence of evacuation on new arrangements for reparation or security. He claimed to have separated evacuation from compensation and established it before world public opinion as the paramount issue for negotiations among the Allies.

Viewed from Berlin, the assurance given by Briand at Geneva —that the evacuation and reparation negotiations would be separate and parallel—was of great importance if the freedom of the Rhineland was to be expedited rather than delayed. There was no assurance that financial experts could arrive at a final reparation settlement satisfactory to both Germany and the creditor powers, or that their efforts would not be delayed by long debate and hindered by technical problems. Once begun, evacuation negotiations could be completed more quickly than the reparation negotiations—particularly if the French were under some pressure to handle expeditiously a matter which German propaganda had long claimed to be of great urgency. Moreover, the formal separation of the three issues would permit the German government to deal separately with the Commission of Verification and attempt to restrict its jurisdiction, or even reject it completely—as Schubert and Köpke hoped to do. Finally, with evacu-

201

ation separated from reparation, the Germans were able to play the role of the injured party whose right to evacuation without compensation was being denied. As planned in August, Müller had announced his disappointment with the outcome of the Geneva conversations to the representatives of the other five powers on September 16; he repeated this for the press on September 18 and at the same time stated that the German government insisted on the right to unconditional evacuation.[47]

In France, where no political group to the Right of the Socialists considered evacuation and reparation to be separate issues, the results of the Geneva discussions were popularly regarded as a victory for the French position. After September 16 there developed in France what Hoesch termed a "half-unconscious and half-intentional illusion" that Germany would tacitly tolerate "a kind of *de facto* juncture between evacuation, reparation, and security."[48] Poincaré and the rest of the Council of Ministers to whom Briand reported insisted that complete evacuation was dependent on a new and final reparation settlement,[49] and even though the Geneva communiqué recognized no such dependency, Briand proceeded as if financial security for France was a prerequisite to evacuation. In an interview published in the *Frankfurter Zeitung* on September 19, Briand indicated that complete evacuation could begin only when the reparation problem had been settled. To soften the blow and make an evacuation-reparation nexus acceptable to Berlin, he predicted that the reparation settlement could be made in two months—an example of what one American diplomat called a combination of Briand's "natural enthusiasm and financial innocence."[50] Then, in an important speech at Chambéry on September 30, Poincaré publicly set forth France's financial claims for the first time: the reparation settlement must include sufficient funds both to cover French war debt payments to England and America and to provide France with an indemnity to pay for the reconstruction of war-devastated

<hr>

[47] 18 September 1928, Memorandum by Pünder, 2545/5138/297654-59; 18 September 1928, Cabinet Protocol, 1698/3575/777854-57; 18 September 1928, Memorandum by Schubert, 1775/3642/807339-48; 21 September 1928, Köpke to Washington, 2545/5138/297660-61; Geigenmüller, "Hoesch und die Räumungsfrage," pp. 619-20.

[48] 21 November 1928, Hoesch to AA, 2258/4502/120182-84.

[49] Michel Soulié, *La vie politique d'Edouard Herriot*, Paris, 1962, p. 298.

[50] 21 September 1928, Poole to A. Young, 462.00 R296/2380½.

northern France.[51] The priority which Poincaré and Briand gave to the revision of the Dawes plan thus separated them from the Germans. Strangely, it set them apart from the British too.

In London there was a still different view of the agreement of September 16. The British Treasury did not share Poincaré's desire for a new reparation settlement, nor did it share Briand's optimism about the promptness with which one could be devised. Neither Winston Churchill, the Chancellor of the Exchequer, nor Frederick Lieth-Ross, Deputy Controller of Finance, who advised him on reparation and war debt questions, believed the time had come to revise the Dawes plan. To begin negotiations would be, in Churchill's terms, "both futile and dangerous."[52] It would be futile because the United States was not yet ready to reduce its war debt claims and thereby permit Britain and France to reduce in turn their reparation claims to a level Germany could pay. Lieth-Ross believed the Germans could pay a maximum of 1.5 billion marks per year without transfer protection. If this annuity were then capitalized, he calculated that it would yield only 1.08 billion per year after discounts were made to the lending bankers and commissions were paid to the brokers. As this was 40 per cent of what the creditors received under the Dawes plan, the result would be, Lieth-Ross warned, a settlement which would "impoverish Germany without enriching us."[53]

Negotiations to revise the Dawes plan would be dangerous for Britain. According to the calculations of the Treasury, it was theoretically possible for Paris and Berlin to concoct a scheme that would satisfy their own requirements, but not those of London. Receipts from Germany were divided among the reparation creditors, not in proportion to the size of each creditor's debt to the United States but according to the Spa percentages agreed upon in 1920, before war debts were settled. Because France's share of each mark of reparation was more than twice as large as

[51] Cautiously, Poincaré did not explicitly promise to exchange evacuation for reparation: *Le Temps*, 1 October 1928.

[52] 20 September 1970, Memorandum by Churchill, FO. 371/12878/71-73.

[53] Moreover, Lieth-Ross calculated that reparation bonds worth 23.75 billion marks—the sum necessary to yield an annuity of 1.5 billion—could be sold only at the sacrifice of the capital demands of the German economy. After the investment needs of German business had been met, he predicted that Germany could borrow no more than 8-10 billion marks through the sale of reparation bonds: Frederick Lieth-Ross, *Money Talks; Fifty Years of International Finance*, London, 1968, pp. 104-105.

Britain's, Poincaré could accept reparations of 1.5 billion marks from Germany and still have enough to pay off French war debts while Churchill could not.[54] To provide sufficient revenue to allow the British to pay off their war debt, either the Spa percentages would have to be abandoned and reparation receipts distributed according to debt payment needs, or the reparation annuity would have to be set at 2 billion marks, a figure the Treasury did not believe Germany would accept. The British might, therefore, be placed in the position of having to reject a schedule of payments which both the Germans and French found acceptable. And if they did so, Churchill warned, they would "be denounced as the sole obstacle to the pacification of Europe."[55]

To avoid the dangers of a premature settlement, the Treasury wanted to postpone negotiations for as long as possible.[56] Lieth-Ross wished to continue the Dawes plan for two or three years until Germany was unable to pay the standard Dawes annuity and reparation payments had to be canceled or reduced. At that time the United States would find it necessary to cancel or reduce its claims; Germany's creditors would be able to do the same, and the problem of war-incurred international indebtedness would be resolved.[57] Churchill wanted to delay negotiations at least until the Rhineland question became so urgent that there developed what he called "a united European position" regarding reparations and war debts. Then, when Germany and the creditors had agreed on a reparation-war debt policy, he wanted to draw the American government into the negotiations, thereby compelling the United States to accept debt payments no larger than what the creditors could collect from Germany. If the Amer-

[54] If the German debt were fixed at 1.5 billion marks for 36 years, this would probably be satisfactory to the Germans who would find their average annuity cut to 60 per cent of the standard Dawes annuity. Bonds would be sold, delighting American bankers, who could purchase them at a discount. The French could then use their share of the sum raised to liquidate their war debts, provided Washington and London were willing to discount their claims on Paris in exchange for prepayment: 20 September 1928, Memorandum by Lieth-Ross, FO. 371/12878/75-99.

[55] 20 September 1928, Memorandum by Lieth-Ross, FO. 371/12878/75-79; 20 April 1928, Waley to Howard Smith, FO. 371/12877/1-5; 5 October 1928, Lieth-Ross to Churchill, FO. 371/12878/124; Lieth-Ross, *Money Talks*, p. 103.

[56] 20 September 1928, Memorandum by Churchill, FO. 371/12878/71-73.

[57] 9 October 1928, Wilson to State, 462.00 R296/5737; 19 October 1928, Poole to A. Young, 462.00 R296/2422½; 22 October 1928, Poole to A. Young, 462.00 R296/2423½.

icans refused, then upon them, and not on the British, would fall what Churchill called "the onus . . . for arresting European appeasement and recovery."[58] By implementing this delay tactic, the Treasury had consistently resisted revision of the Dawes plan since the time of Thoiry and continued to do so in September 1928.[59]

When Churchill discovered that Cushendun had agreed to the appointment of a committee of financial experts he was "very agitated," as Lindsay put it, and he dispatched an angry telegram to Cushendun explaining his disappointment with the conversations at Geneva. Churchill insisted that Cushendun try to postpone the date for the meeting of the experts "so that nothing can be settled for some time," and asked him to announce that the Balfour note of 1922 remained the basis of Britain's reparation-war debt policy, i.e., British debts to the United States must be completely covered.[60] The date for the convocation of the experts was not discussed at Geneva, but Cushendun did announce to the meeting of the six powers and to the press on September 16 that the British would not accept any reparation settlement which provided them with less from Europe than must be paid the United States. At the same time, he stated that Britain would not be a party to any request for a remission of war debts.[61] With this statement Cushendun indicated that London did not intend to make any financial sacrifices for the benefit of Germany and France, and he dispelled any hope that Allied claims on Germany

[58] 15 September 1928, Churchill to Cushendun, FO. 371/12904/8-9.

[59] 9 January 1928, Lieth-Ross to Sargent, FO. 371/12875/140; 22 March 1928, Memorandum on a conversation between Treasury and Foreign Office representatives, FO. 371/12876/133-35; 23 March 1928, Memorandum by Hopkins, FO. 371/12876/152-57; 26 March 1928, Sargent to Lindsay, FO. 371/12876/127-30; 11 April 1928, Hopkins to Tyrrell, FO. 371/12876/230-32; 20 September 1928, Memorandum by Lieth-Ross, FO. 371/12878/75-79; 17 September 1928, Memorandum by Gilbert, 462.00 R296/2402; 23 October 1928, Gilbert to Mellon, 462.00 R296/2425.

[60] 15 September 1928, Lindsay to Cushendun, FO. 371/12904/17; 15 September 1928, Churchill to Cushendun, FO. 371/12904/8-9. The Balfour note had originally stated that the British would demand no more of their debtors than they were obliged to pay the United States. In 1928 the Treasury reinterpreted the note to mean that the British would demand of their debtors sufficient funds to cover their payments to America.

[61] Carl M. Frasure, *British Policy on War Debts and Reparations*, Philadelphia, 1940, p. 120; J. W. Wheeler-Bennett and Hugh Latimer, *Information on the Reparation Settlement; Being the Background and the History of the Young Plan and The Hague Agreements, 1929-1930*, London, 1930, pp. 72-74.

might be reduced in the near future as a result of a reduction in European payments to the United States.

In the autumn of 1928, the Germans took a leap in the dark: they demanded the opening of formal negotiations with no knowledge of what the outcome of those deliberations would be. Haunted by the fear that the Locarno policy was a blind alley rather than a road to revision, and looking for a political success for a Great Coalition divided on almost every issue other than the restoration of Germany to equality with the victors of the war, Schubert, Stresemann, and Müller decided to claim freedom for the Rhineland. It did not prove to be a good time to accelerate the pace of German demands for concessions from the Allies. The British and French had just coordinated their disarmament policies at the expense of the United States—potentially the world's strongest naval power—and at the expense of Germany—potentially Europe's strongest military power; it would not take nearly as much arrogance and defiance to continue the coordination of their Rhineland policies and deny the German petition for unconditional evacuation. This they did. Refused his primary objective, Müller grasped at the secondary one—separate and parallel Rhineland-reparation negotiations. As a result, three issues were opened at Geneva—but with no agreement between Germany and the Allies as to the terms on which they were to be resolved. What would the new reparation settlement look like? Would it be highly favorable to Germany, as Curtius and the rest of the cabinet seemed to believe? Or, would Germany have to indemnify France and pay all that Britain, France, and the other creditors owed the United States—as Cushendun said at Geneva on September 16, and as Poincaré said at Chambéry on September 30? Would the French Army stay on the Rhine until Germany agreed to pay that sum—as Briand told the *Frankfurter Zeitung*, or would the Germans realize their hope for prompt evacuation undelayed by protracted reparation discussions? Would the French be content now that the reparation question was to be considered, or would they insist on agreement to a new payment plan before any troops were withdrawn? Would the British support the French? Would they keep their troops in Germany in pursuit of a policy which the Treasury regarded as "futile and dangerous"? Or, might they depart from the Rhine at any time—

as Cushendun suggested at the last meeting of the six powers? Having overcome long-standing differences on naval and military disarmament, could Paris and London now reconcile their widely divergent reparation policies, and would they do so again at German expense? What was the potential extent of the Anglo-French entente?

2. *The Entente and the Reparation Invoice October-November 13, 1928*

On September 28, the American government rejected the Anglo-French Naval Compromise, ending all chance that it might serve as a basis for further negotiation.[62] This did not eliminate concern on the Wilhelmstrasse, however. Still unanswered was what Gerhard Köpke termed the "very serious question" of whether the Compromise had a "general political significance" going beyond the disarmament question.[63] It was to this question that two German observers—Hans Dieckhoff, Embassy Counselor in London, and Kurt Rieth, Embassy Counselor in Paris—turned their attention.[64]

Both men agreed that the Disarmament Compromise was the top of the iceberg; beneath the waterline was an extensive and deliberate policy of cooperation which the Wilhelmstrasse termed "the newest Anglo-French Entente Cordiale."[65] London and Paris had taken similar positions on the Kellogg Pact, collaborated in the Balkans,[66] and cooperated on "every question discussed at the League," especially the Polish-Lithuanian dispute. Regarding Germany, the two governments had negotiated an exclusive agreement on disarmament, held joint military maneuvers in the

[62] Cmd. 3211, pp. 34-38.

[63] 11 October 1928, circular letter by Köpke, 2250/5183/301834-36. Köpke was Director of Division III (Western Europe).

[64] 20 September 1928, Dieckhoff to Haas, 2545/5138/297666-69; 19 October 1928, Rieth to AA, 5183/K1821/458775-84; 27 October 1928, Dieckhoff to AA, 5836/K1982/514009-30. Also Harry Kessler, *Tagebücher, 1918-1937*, Frankfurt, 1961, p. 571.

[65] 11 October 1928, Bülow to Paris, 5183/K1821/458774. Bülow was a Counselor of Legation in Division II.

[66] On August 10 the British and French governments made a joint démarche in Sofia, a move which seemed to indicate that Britain was abandoning a pro-Italian policy in the Balkans in favor of support for France and the Little Entente: *New York Times*, 25 August 1928.

Rhineland,[67] and confronted Müller with similar policies on evacuation and compensation. At Geneva Cushendun had acted not as the "honest broker" demanded by the spirit of Locarno, Dieckhoff wrote, but as the "trailblazer (*Wegebner*) for Briand and the French thesis." Neither man believed a written military agreement or a binding political alliance had been concluded, but Dieckhoff thought that military and political authorities in Paris and London maintained close contact.

Rieth and Dieckhoff differed as to how the entente operated, and how long it would endure. Rieth opined that London acted out of self-interest and supported Paris in specific cases, particularly when the two capitals could agree to sacrifice German interests to their own mutual benefit. For example, although the British were not in agreement with French Rhine policy, they found it expedient to allow the French to maintain occupation in order to make Germany ultimately responsible for the payment of England's war debt. For this reason Rieth predicted that London might in the future align with Berlin against Paris in those instances where British and German interests coincided. Dieckhoff, however, did not foresee the British joining the Germans against the French. The entente, he thought, was based not on expediency but on the political principles of Chamberlain, Cushendun, and Tyrrell. As long as these three men remained in positions of power and influence, London would continue to resist the German thesis and give support to France—even in the face of opposition from British public opinion. Dieckhoff even pessimistically predicted that the entente might well be the destruction of the Locarno Treaty itself. Given the current intimacy between London and Paris, could the British view France as the aggressor in a Franco-German conflict? Did they really intend to give military assistance to Germany after having endorsed French military superiority in the Disarmament Compromise?

Dieckhoff put forth his estimate of the entente in late October, and just as he did so, his prediction that it would prove impervious to public criticism was being tested. In England the opposition parties perceived in the Disarmament Compromise an issue which might shake the position of the Conservative government, and with a general election pending in 1929, they launched an

[67] *New York Times*, 11 August 1928.

attack on Chamberlain's foreign policy.[68] This campaign of criticism began with speeches by MacDonald and Lloyd George to their respective party conferences on October 2 and 12; it was continued and intensified in early November with the opening of Parliament for its final session prior to dissolution; and it culminated with a long and thorough criticism of the government's foreign policy by Lloyd George before the House of Commons on November 13.[69] These statements sustained the loud public outcry against the Disarmament Compromise, and criticism of Chamberlain's policy became, for the first time, a major part of the political program of the opposition parties.

This criticism had two intellectual sources: the liberal internationalism of Philip Kerr, who was more concerned with good Anglo-American relations than with French security and who advised Lloyd George on foreign policy, and the radicalism of former members of the Independent Labour Party with their commitment to open diplomacy and general disarmanent, men who decisively influenced the formation of Labour policy. MacDonald, Lloyd George, and their followers wove these two strands into a single line. Condemning the Disarmament Compromise as "the most sinister event since the war," as Lloyd George said,[70] Liberal and Labour critics charged the government with reverting to secret diplomacy, striking a bargain which jeopardized the prospect for general disarmament, attempting to reestablish military collaboration with France, and thereby recapitulating the policies which had led to the World War. Moreover, the opposition extended their critique to Chamberlain's entire policy—the alienation of the powerful United States, the disregard for Germany, and the commitment to France, the enforcer of the Treaty of Versailles. Finally, they demanded improved relations with the United States and a reversal of Britain's Ger-

[68] Philip Kerr believed that for the first time the opposition had an issue on which to attack the government with effect: 26 October 1928, Kerr to Stevenson, Kerr papers v. 245, pp. 775-76.

[69] 2 October 1928, MacDonald to Labour Party Conference, *Report of the 28th Annual Conference*, pp. 183-84, 187; 12 October 1928, Lloyd George to National Liberal Federation, Lloyd George papers G/175; Commons, debates, v. 222, c. 19-26, 79-87, 721-38, 747-48.

[70] 12 October 1928, Lloyd George to National Liberal Federation, Lloyd George papers G/175. Lloyd George took this phrase from Philip Kerr: 28 September 1928, Kerr to Lloyd George, Kerr papers v. 242, pp. 457-58.

man policy. The Germans had signed the Treaty of Locarno, joined the Kellogg Pact, and fulfilled the Treaty of Versailles by disarming and paying reparations. Therefore, Britain and France —instead of sustaining military occupation and rearming themselves with cruisers, submarines, and trained reserves—must perform their own obligations of 1919 by disarming and withdrawing from the Rhine immediately and without further compensation. Both parties thus supported the German thesis on evacuation. And in *Labour and the Nation,* a manifesto listing the tasks which "must be undertaken by a Labour Party in power," the party pledged itself to "the immediate and unconditional withdrawal of all foreign troops from the Rhineland."[71]

With Chamberlain out of the country, the defense of the Disarmament Compromise and the entente fell to Cushendun, Baldwin, William Bridgeman, First Lord of the Admiralty, and Lord Salisbury, Lord Privy Seal and Conservative leader in the House of Lords. There was, the government insisted, no "secret pact" to arm France and Britain. The negotiations were not secret because their existence had been revealed in March 1928 by the British and French delegates to the League's Disarmament Preparatory Commission; there was no "pact," only a tentative agreement that would become effective when accepted by the powers. The Compromise was now dead, and in response to repeated allegations by Hugh Dalton and others, Bridgeman denied that Britain had secret conventions with France and conducted naval staff talks with Paris.[72]

While confirming the death of the Disarmament Compromise, the Conservative government left some confusion regarding the state of Anglo-French cooperation vis-à-vis Germany. On November 6, Lord Salisbury publicly affirmed Cushendun's private statement of September 16 that the government reserved the right to withdraw British troops whether or not there was a reparation settlement, and Churchill went even further on November 8 and stated that reparation and evacuation were separate issues.[73] Baldwin and Cushendun, on the other hand, showed no inclination to reorient Britain's European policy as demanded by the opposition. The Prime Minister rejected the demand that Britain

[71] *Labour and the Nation,* London, 1928, pp. 5, 12, 48.
[72] Commons, debates, v. 222, c. 823-34, 1709; Lords, debates, v. 74, c. 61-78.
[73] Lords, debates, v. 74, c. 40; Commons, debates, v. 222, c. 218.

evacuate the Rhineland, giving French opposition as the reason. And Cushendun, in a speech at Blackpool on October 25, clumsily tried to evade the charges of a new entente; there was no new entente, he stated, because the old one had never been dissolved.[74] This provoked immediate criticism in the press, and the next day, in a speech at Albert Hall, Baldwin had to deny explicitly that the government had abandoned the position of "impartiality and conciliation" assumed at the time of Locarno.[75] He did, however, admit in another speech delivered on November 9 that within the impartiality of Locarno, France had a certain precedence, the place of "closest cooperation." Typically, he then offset this by stating that Anglo-French cooperation "does not, cannot, and shall not react to the detriment of Germany or any other power." Baldwin thus relegated Germany to the status of a junior partner in the Anglo-French entente; Locarno, he said, had "extended" Anglo-French cooperation to include Germany.[76]

Baldwin's counterbalancing of Locarno and the entente did not propitiate the government's critics like Lloyd George who was unwilling to accept his general and contradictory statements of goodwill as a substitute for a reorientation of British policy.[77] The same discontent was expressed in the German press and in the German embassy in London. Dieckhoff did not know whether Baldwin's statements were "pretty words," made under the pressure of severe criticism, or an indication of a "new departure" in British policy. He was certain, however, that if the British wished to give practical application to Baldwin's expressions of goodwill for Germany, they would soon have opportunity to do so in the Rhineland-reparation negotiations. As the *Frankfurter Zeitung* suggested, the damage done to Locarno by the Disarmament Compromise could be repaired provided the British ceased to disregard German interests, withdrew their concession on trained reserves, and insisted with the French on prompt evacuation and a moderate reparation settlement.[78]

Sir Horace Rumbold, the new British ambassador to Berlin,

[74] Commons, debates, v. 222, c. 747; London *Times*, 26 October 1928.
[75] London *Times*, 27 October 1928.
[76] *Ibid.*, 10 November 1928.
[77] Lloyd George dismissed Baldwin's speech as a "long catalogue of compliments to nations": Commons, debates, v. 222, c. 931.
[78] 10 November 1928, Dieckhoff to AA, 2258/4502/120140-41; *Frankfurter Zeitung*, 14 November 1928. Also *Vossische Zeitung*, 16 November 1928.

summarized for London the German reaction to the Disarmament Compromise in a dispatch dated October 17. The Wilhelmstrasse believed, he reported, that the Compromise indicated that Britain had abandoned Locarno, withdrawn from European affairs, and left France a free hand on the Continent. As a result, London's influence in Berlin had declined considerably. Rumbold regarded this as a matter for concern, and he suggested that London take the lead in restoring cordial Anglo-German relations. Without indicating what might be done, Rumbold mentioned that the situation might be improved "by some overt effort on our part."[79]

Rumbold's description of anti-British feeling in Berlin prompted the Foreign Office to conduct a general review of Anglo-German relations during the latter part of 1928. But this review did not lead to a change of policy. Neither Rumbold's "overt effort" nor Dieckhoff's "new departure" resulted. Instead, German criticism of the Disarmament Compromise, the entente, and Britain's Locarno policy combined with chronic anti-German feeling within the Foreign Office to stiffen resistance to Anglo-German reconciliation purchased at the price of concessions to Berlin. This resistance was expressed most fully in a long memorandum authored by Victor Perowne, a Second Secretary in London. His views received the enthusiastic endorsement of Orme Sargent, a Counselor at the Foreign Office who encouraged Perowne to expand his ideas, first expressed in late October as a long minute, into a lengthy policy paper. This memorandum, written under the influence of the recently published Crowe memorandum of 1907, was completed in December. Only the intervention of Sir Ronald Lindsay prevented its dispatch to Berlin as a guide for Britain's German policy.[80]

Perowne asserted that Berlin had misjudged British policy. The fear that Britain had abandoned the evenhandedness of Locarno was "largely visionary," a product of the "mercurial disposition of the German race." With a sense of "morbid self importance,"

[79] 17 October 1928, Rumbold to Cushendun, FO. 371/12916/318.

[80] 23 October 1928, Minute by Perowne, FO. 371/12916/297-304; 10 December 1928, Memorandum by Perowne, FO. 371/12906/223-34. Also 18 August 1928, Memorandum by Perowne, FO. 371/12903/5. The volume of *British Documents on the Origins of the War, 1898-1914*, which reproduced the Crowe memorandum, was published on August 2: *New York Times*, 2 August 1928.

which was "typical of the race as a whole," Stresemann and Müller falsely saw all agreements to which Germany was not a party as directed against Berlin. They reacted to the Disarmament Compromise as their predecessors had reacted to the Dual Entente.

Berlin, not London, was responsible for the unsatisfactory status of Anglo-German relations. The Germans, Perowne maintained, had disrupted the harmony of the Locarno Triplice with their ingratitude, their "foolish and ostrich-like intransigence," and their insatiability. They showed no "practical recognition" of "the friendly British disposition" displayed since Locarno. Instead, Berlin rejected British advice to meet the French halfway and demanded the evacuation of the Rhineland without first preparing a feasible and acceptable reparation scheme to offer in exchange. The end of military occupation would not bring the cessation of German demands and lasting and harmonious relations between Germany and the West; "the evacuation of the Rhineland," Perowne wrote, "will be only a stage, not the crown, of the 'conciliation' policy as far as Germany is concerned." In fact, Stresemann had established a "program" of goals which he was "carrying out" step by step: troop reduction, withdrawal of military control, evacuation, reduction of reparation payments, and return of the Polish Corridor.

Perowne recommended against leading the French along the road of concession to Germany. Mediation with Paris was unnecessary because Germany's "tiresome and unaccommodating disposition" and her unwillingness to follow London's "excellent advice" showed that she was "quite capable of looking after herself." Appeasement would not succeed because of Berlin's program of extravagant goals. The lessons pointed out in the Crowe memorandum twenty years earlier needed repetition today, he indicated: "Every concession made to Germany only whetted her appetite for more." Then, as now, British concessions "entirely failed to improve relations with Germany."

Many of the thoughts expressed in such vivid language by Perowne—the racist assumptions, the resentment of German criticism and independence, which was described as "ingratitude" and "intransigence," the attribution of an elaborate program to Stresemann, the futility and the dangers of Anglo-German cooperation—were shared by other members of the British foreign

213

service.[81] For example, William Seeds, the British representative on the Inter-Allied Rhineland High Commission, applied the "Perowne line" to British Rhine policy. "The evacuation of the Rhineland," he wrote in late October, "will . . . produce a remarkable effect—not, I am afraid, quite the effect which we all desire and hope for." Occupation was one of the provisions of Versailles which kept "the German" in a "chastened mood"; it reminded him of his defeat and warned him that he must "walk warily." When the Rhineland was evacuated there would be changes in the German demeanor: "The German's rebound from humility to arrogance is notorious to all who know him." And there would be changes in policy: Germany would seek to dominate Europe economically and pursue "a highly rectified Eastern frontier." Moral: active cooperation with Germany was futile, for it would not increase British influence over German policy. It would bring only "French resentment, . . . German ingratitude, and a result which cannot be foreseen, but for which we would have to bear both the responsibility and the blame."[82]

Had the time come to end occupation? Should British foreign policy be transformed? Should the French be led to unconditional evacuation in order to accommodate Germany? Just as Rhineland negotiations were to begin, the Liberal and Labour parties gave a loud and public "yes" to these questions. In the midst of the furor over the Disarmament Compromise, the Foreign Office staff replied with a private "no." What would the government do? In the absence of Chamberlain, Baldwin had parried the attacks of the opposition, avoided extreme positions, and had not committed himself on specifics. Specifics were left to each department— Rhine policy to the Foreign Office, reparation policy to the Treasury. And in October, as British Rhine policy rigidified, British reparation policy underwent a complete change. After years of opposition, the Treasury became reconciled to a prompt final settlement of reparations.

[81] Much of the tone of the Perowne memorandum was set by dispatches from Rumbold, who spoke of the Germans as a "mercurial race" with a "craving for expansion and world recognition" and who suggested that military occupation be sustained to coerce Berlin into a reparation settlement: 17 October 1928, Rumbold to Cushendun, FO. 371/12916/318; 23 October 1928, Rumbold to Cushendun, FO. 371/12905/59-60.

[82] 29 October 1928, Seeds to Cushendun, FO. 371/12905/113-14.

Between September 20 and November 13, Parker Gilbert traveled between Berlin, London, Paris, and Brussels urging all concerned to write a final reparation settlement and formulate a new payment plan.[83] As Poincaré had favored a final settlement of international indebtedness for some months, Gilbert's chief task in Paris was to persuade him not to seek further reduction of the Franco-American war debt as part of that settlement. Poincaré's design was to form a united European front against the United States and appeal to Washington to reduce its claims on Europe. This scheme, which he had proposed to Stresemann during their private conversation of August 27, was rejected by Cushendun on September 16, when he announced at Geneva that Britain would not participate.[84] Gilbert, meeting with Poincaré on September 20, completed the disillusionment and dissuasion of the French Premier, and at Chambéry on September 30, Poincaré announced that the final settlement must cover French war debts. After talking with Poincaré again on October 3, Gilbert was able to assure Andrew Mellon, Secretary of the United States Treasury, that the French Premier had no intention of reducing Germany's obligations at the expense of America, that he would make no appeal for a further reduction of the war debt, and that he would seek to collect sufficient funds from Germany to pay the full amount of the Mellon-Berenger agreement. Gilbert wrote that Poincaré was making "an honest and determined effort to meet these problems in the way that would be most acceptable to the United States government." This was "entirely reasonable," Gilbert thought.[85] Thus, by early October, Paris had accepted the

[83] Etienne Weill-Raynal, *Les réparations allemands et la France*, Paris, 1947-49, III, 410.

[84] Lieth-Ross favored a general reduction of reparations and war debts but wanted the initiative to come from Berlin, not the creditor powers: 25 September 1928, Lieth-Ross to Lindsay, FO. 371/12878/84-92. Any such proposal would have been rejected by Washington: 17 September 1928, Memorandum by A. Young, 462.00 R296/2382; 31 October 1928, Kellogg to Gilbert, 462.00 R296/2425. Calvin Coolidge, *The Talkative President; the Off the Record Press Conferences of Calvin Coolidge*, Amherst, Mass., 1964, p. 198.

[85] 4 October 1928, Gilbert to Mellon, 462.00 R296/2396. Gilbert also kept the American government informed of his activities through the American embassies in Europe: 28 September 1928, Poole to State, 462.00 R296/2383; 5 October 1928, Poole to A. Young, 462.00 R296/2389½; 5 October 1928, Wilson to State, 462.00 R296/2418; 9 October 1928, Wilson to State, 462.00 R296/2537.

Gilbert plan and posed no further problem for the Agent General. The chief obstacle to a new settlement was the long-standing opposition of the British Treasury.[86]

On October 15, Gilbert met with Churchill and other Treasury officials in London. There he achieved a major success: he persuaded them not to delay or obstruct the convocation of a committee of experts. He brought about this change by assuring Churchill that Germany could pay an annuity of 2 billion marks (the sum necessary to cover Britain's future yearly war debt payments), that she could do so without transfer protection, and until Britain's debt to the United States was discharged. Gilbert admitted that such a large annuity would be paid only if the Germans and the creditors believed it could be paid. The way to create that belief, he maintained, was to give this annuity the imprimatur of an independent committee of experts. This committee, he added, must be convened promptly (in November) and decide quickly (before Christmas); hesitation would lead to skepticism about the validity of its conclusions and about the feasibility of large annuities.[87]

Churchill offered no further resistance to the Gilbert plan even though Lieth-Ross warned him that Germany could pay no more than 600-800 million marks without transfer protection.[88] On October 17, the Chancellor of the Exchequer announced his change of policy to the cabinet. He told them that the papers previously circulated to them—position papers prepared by Lieth-Ross a month before—were no longer relevant. Churchill asked for, and received, their authorization to propose to Poincaré a reparation settlement with annuities of the size promised by Gilbert.[89] With the government's foreign policy being subjected to intense criticism because of the Disarmament Compromise, and with an electoral campaign approaching, the cabinet was unwill-

[86] The Treasury was inclined, Gilbert wrote at this time, to "play dog in the manger": 24 September 1928, Gilbert to Jay, Owen Young papers.

[87] 16 October 1928, Fischer and Hopkins to Churchill, FO. 371/12878/191-95.

[88] Lieth-Ross, *Money Talks*, p. 103. Lieth-Ross feared that if a committee of experts were convened they might, under the influence of the sanguine and optimistic Gilbert, place an unbearable burden on Germany: 22 October 1928, Poole to A. Young, 462.00 R296/2423½.

[89] Cab 23/59/47 (17 October 1928); Henry Clay, *Lord Norman*, London, 1957, pp. 267-68; P. J. Grigg, *Prejudice and Judgement*, London, 1948, pp. 208-209.

ing to adopt a position which would expose it to the charge that it was obstructing a final resolution of the aggravating reparation problem and preventing the evacuation of the Rhineland. The government could not afford to "bear the onus of 'averting European appeasement and recovery,'" as Rumbold put it.[90]

Churchill met with Poincaré and Gilbert in Paris on October 19 and seized the initiative. He proposed a settlement with annuities of 2 billion marks, and Poincaré did not dissent. He insisted that the Rhineland would have to be evacuated, and Poincaré agreed. He called for the ratification of the French war debt to England, and Poincaré consented.[91] Thus, the two men agreed on the reparation demands they would make on Germany, and thereby they extended the Anglo-French entente to the reparation issue. In July Chamberlain and Briand had agreed on disarmament; in September Briand and Cushendun had taken the same line on the Rhineland; in October Churchill and Poincaré agreed on reparation. By reconciling the last major difference between Paris and London, Churchill and Poincaré brought the entente to completion.

The Poincaré-Churchill conversation of October 19 was an important milestone in Parker Gilbert's program; all the creditors had now committed themselves to a definitive reparation settlement patterned on his design. Gilbert reported his success in a letter to Andrew Mellon four days later, assuring the Secretary of the Treasury that Churchill, like Poincaré, intended to collect sufficient reparation from Germany to meet the claims of the United States. "The British government," he wrote, "has abandoned, at least for the time being, any effort to satisfy the Balfour note by way of general cancellation or by means of concessions from America"; Churchill would approach the problem by getting "the maximum possible payments from Germany." This seemed "natural and logical" to Gilbert. It would, he admitted, leave "no room for any large percentage of reduction"; the new annuities, as he calculated them, would average between 2 and 2.5 billion marks and extend over 35 to 40 years.[92]

[90] 20 September 1928, Rumbold to Lindsay, Rumbold papers. Selby stated the obverse: by cooperating in the solution of the reparation problem, it might be possible for the cabinet to find a way out of what he termed "our existing embarrassments": 1 November 1928, Selby to Chamberlain, AC 55/478.
[91] 19 October 1928, Memorandum by Churchill, FO. 371/12878/231-32.
[92] 23 October 1928, Gilbert to Mellon, 462.00 R296/2425.

The payments Gilbert expected from the Germans were larger than the annuities of 1-1.6 billion marks paid since 1924; they approached the 2.5 billion marks paid beginning in September 1928; and they were to be made without the transfer protection afforded by the Dawes plan. He was, nevertheless, "optimistic" about German capability to pay a settlement designed for the creditor powers.[93] As one American diplomat wrote, Gilbert was "confident of Germany's ability to pay a good fat annuity for a good number of years. . . . If they [the Germans] go into negotiations at this time it must be with the expectation of paying handsomely."[94] If Gilbert were to persuade the Germans to proceed with the discussion of a final settlement, he would score a success even more remarkable than his conversion of Churchill.

On October 25, Gilbert reported to Müller, Rudolf Hilferding, Minister of Finance, and Hjalmar Schacht, President of the Reichsbank, on his conversations with Poincaré and Churchill. He informed the Germans that London and Paris intended to collect from Germany reparation sufficient to indemnify France and to cover their war debt payments to each other and to the United States; and he added his own opinion that the positions taken by Poincaré and Churchill would have to be respected by the committee of experts. He did not talk of approximate figures with the Germans, as he had with the creditors. In fact, he told them he had not discussed with the creditors the terms of the eventual settlement; he had, he stated, only spoken of procedural matters with them. He then urged the Germans to take the diplomatic initiative and call for the convocation of a committee of financial experts. Müller reportedly registered no dismay when Gilbert indicated that Germany could expect few concessions from her creditors, and the next day he and Hilferding recommended to the cabinet that the German government initiate the convocation of an experts' committee "as quickly as possible," and do so without discussing the actual amount of the settlement. There was no opposition within the cabinet, and the government's decision was announced in a press communiqué and then communicated to the five Allied powers in a short "verbal note" delivered on October 30.[95]

[93] *Ibid.*
[94] 22 October 1928, Poole to A. Young, 462.00 R296/2423½.
[95] 26 October 1928, Cabinet Protocol, 1699/3575/778226-28; Erich Eyck,

The decision taken by the Müller government on October 26 was an important one; it led in the spring of 1929 to the politically unpopular acceptance of the Young plan with its average annuity of approximately 2 billion marks for 59 years. It was also a decision which became the subject of much controversy. Müller subsequently insisted that he made the decision in October unaware that he was involving Germany in negotiations which would lead to annuities of 2 billion marks. Hilferding later told Gilbert that the conference of experts would never have taken place had the German government known beforehand the figure the Allies would demand there. Schacht, who became chief German representative on the committee of experts, claimed that the level of creditor expectations was concealed from him prior to the conference.[96] What did the Germans know, and not know, in the autumn of 1928? What prompted their involvement in a definitive reparation settlement?

In mid-September, when the cabinet accepted the Geneva communiqué with its proposed committee of experts, Müller, Hilferding, Curtius, and Schacht had reason to believe—from what Gilbert had been saying in Berlin—that the amount of the revised annuity would be limited to what American bankers believed Germany could pay in foreign currencies each year. Placing their confidence in Gilbert, they were enthusiastic about a new determination of Germany's obligations.[97] It was not until late October that the Agent General began to tell them of a less favorable settlement, one based on creditor needs. At that time Müller,

---

A History of the Weimar Republic, Cambridge, Mass., 1962-63, II, 181; Wheeler-Bennett and Latimer, *Reparation Settlement*, pp. 75-77. Müller's sanguineness: 26 October 1928, Poole to State, 462.00 R296/2433.

[96] Hilferding: 3 May 1929, Cabinet Protocol, 1701/3575/780398. On the statements of Müller and Schacht see below, pp. 269-70 and n. 95.

[97] 6 February 1928, Memorandum by Schubert, 2756/5881/430267-68; 28 February 1928, Memorandum by Schubert, 2544/5138/297349-62. Curtius and Schacht had a naïve trust in Gilbert: Josef Becker, "Heinrich Köhler, 1878-1949; Lebensbild eines badischen Politikers; mit einen dokumentarischen Anhang aus dem Nachlass," *Zeitschrift für die Geschichte des Oberrheins*, 110 (1962), p. 437; Moritz J. Bonn, *Wandering Scholar*, New York, 1948, p. 307. The Reichsbank president expected Germany to benefit greatly from a new settlement: 16 October 1928, Rumbold to Cushendun, FO. 371/12878/199-200; Hjalmar Schacht, *Account Settled*, London, 1949, pp. 18-21, and Schacht, *The End of Reparations*, New York, 1931, pp. 41-45; Earl Beck, *Verdict on Schacht; a Study in the Problem of Political Guilt*, Tallahassee, Fla., 1955, pp. 8-9; Bonn, *Wandering Scholar*, p. 307; Eyck, *Weimar Republic*, II, 175-80.

Hilferding, and Schacht did not know that the creditors had agreed to press for annuities of 2 billion marks without transfer protection; however, Gilbert's statements did provide them with the basis for an estimate in marks of creditor expectations. The German government then initiated arrangements for a committee of experts, hoping to design a committee which would not be bound by British and French claims. In their note to London and Paris of October 30, the Germans proposed that the committee be composed of "independent experts enjoying international reputation . . . and not tied by any instructions of their respective governments"; they suggested that American citizens be added to the committee and that the experts be assigned the task of proposing a "definite and complete settlement of the reparation problem." By making the experts independent, by adding Americans who had no direct claims on Germany, and by assigning the committee a comprehensive and indefinite mandate, the Germans hoped to leave the way open for an examination of Germany's capacity to pay, an examination which would, presumably, result in a favorable settlement. Schacht, although somewhat sobered by Gilbert's statements of October 25, subsequently agreed to be chief German delegate to the committee of experts, expecting to free Germany from the burdens of the Dawes plan and believing incorrectly that he would be able to reject any settlement he considered unfavorable.

The German government expected to derive additional benefits from their démarche. They hoped to further evacuation negotiations. On Schubert's recommendation, they decided that the German ambassadors in Paris and London should express dissatisfaction at the outcome of the Geneva negotiations and press for the opening of evacuation negotiations through normal channels when the experts began their discussion of reparation. To permit the Rhineland question to "fall asleep," as Curtius put it, would be to accept the French thesis that evacuation was dependent on reparation and to sacrifice the promise of September 16 to accelerate the discussion of both questions simultaneously. Moreover, by taking the diplomatic initiative, Berlin could avoid discussions on the Commission of Verification and Conciliation. Germany would not, Schubert assured the cabinet, initiate discussion of verification, and if Paris raised the issue, "negotiations would be conducted in a dilatory manner." The hope of the government, as Müller expressed it, was that "possibly French desires could be satisfied by a new system of debt and reparation agreements so that a special commission for the Rhineland could be avoided."[98]

The Germans had gone to Geneva in September with the objective of bringing the Rhineland question out of the half-darkness in which it had dwelt since Thoiry; they returned having agreed to participate in the proposal of a new and final reparation settlement. Then a situation heavy with potential difficulties developed. On September 16, Cushendun announced that British receipts had to cover out-payments to the United States. Poincaré set the same requirement on September 30 at Chambéry and added an indemnity for war damages. Both creditors thus stated their requirements for an acceptable settlement while Briand, in a newspaper interview published on September 19, indicated French intentions to continue the military occupation of Germany until that settlement was made. Churchill then reversed the Treasury's reparation policy, decided on a prompt final settlement, and agreed with Poincaré on the level at which German payments were to be set. With a final reparation settlement pending, Churchill wanted to keep the British Army on the Rhine as a way of extracting an adequate settlement from Germany although in public he disassociated the two issues.[99] And, faced with criticism of the entente, the Foreign Office found no reason to recommend a departure from Chamberlain's long-standing opposition to unilateral evacuation. Thus, although the British government cautiously withheld public support of the French position on evacuation, the two countries were in essential agreement on reparation and occupation. Unless an avenue of escape were found, the German claim to a free Rhineland would lead

[98] 26 October 1928, Cabinet Protocol, 1699/3575/778228-32; 29 September 1928, Memorandum by Schubert, 2258/4502/120090-91; 1 October 1928, Cabinet Protocol, 1698/3575/777879-81; 30 October 1928, Hoesch to AA, 1336/2406/506365-68; 30 October 1928, Cushendun to Rumbold, AC 50/467. Schacht's attitude after October 25: 1 November 1928, Rowe-Dutton to Lieth-Ross, FO. 371/12879/169-72; Bonn, *Wandering Scholar*, p. 307.

[99] "It is for them [the Germans] to say what price in prolonged national effort they will pay for the liberation of their soil . . .": 19 October 1928, Memorandum by Churchill, FO. 371/12878/231-32. Commons, debates, v. 222, c. 217-18.

them into a creditor-designed reparation settlement of annuities of 2 billion marks or more without transfer protection.

In theory, several escape routes were open. In the end, the Germans could reject any settlement which was too costly and still press for evacuation. For this reason they refused to recognize the principle of compensation, continued to demand unconditional evacuation, and insisted on separate and parallel negotiations. In the short run, an attempt could be made to reduce the cost of the settlement to Germany by a reduction of American war debt claims. Poincaré wanted the Germans to cooperate in this attempt; Lieth-Ross wanted the Germans to take the lead; Berlin showed no interest in either. Instead, the government decided in late October to pin its hopes for an acceptable settlement—a settlement reflecting what Berlin considered Germany's limited capability to pay rather than extensive needs of the creditors—on a committee of experts not bound by instructions and free to make their own proposal.

Neither Poincaré nor Churchill was ready to admit that the experts should be independent and unbound by instructions.[100] They did not want the question of German capacity reopened; they did not want their own claims disregarded; and they feared independent experts might do both. If the experts were to be unbound by governmental instructions, then their task must be limited to consideration of what Churchill called "technical aspects." Before the experts met, he thought, the creditors must all agree on the principles of the settlement, and the Germans must offer assurances that they were, as he put it, "hopeful of a successful settlement on the basis of Allied objectives."[101] With this in mind, he and Poincaré exchanged written notes outlining their claims on October 30 and November 3. On November 3 and 15, the German ambassadors in Paris and London were called in to receive these memoranda.[102]

[100] Churchill rejected a suggestion from another member of the government that the experts be unbound by instructions: Cab 23/59/48 (29 October 1928).

[101] 19 October 1928, Memorandum by Churchill, FO. 371/12878/231-32; 5 November 1928, Memorandum by Churchill, FO. 371/12879/155, 161.

[102] FO. 371/12879/46-50, 79-80. The memoranda were not actually delivered until November 14 and 19 due to German reluctance to accept them: 6 November 1928, Tyrrell to London, FO. 371/12879/144-45; 15 November 1928, unsigned memorandum, FO. 371/12879/227. The British insisted that their reparation and war debt receipts equal their payments to the United

3. *Evacuation Without Compensation and the Surge of Anti-Locarno Feeling in Germany, November 13-December 1928*

On November 3 Gustav Stresemann returned to Berlin to resume control of German foreign policy. Except for a short period in August, he had been absent from the Wilhelmstrasse since June 20. During that time, the conduct of German policy had been active but lacked direction and foresight. On September 15 the German cabinet had endorsed the idea of a final reparation settlement, apparently assuming that it would benefit Germany. Then, on October 26, knowing the general, but not the exact, requirements of the major creditors, the Müller government had somewhat nonchalantly further committed themselves. It was not until November that German reparation policy adopted the posture of resistance and complaint it was to retain thereafter. Two things contributed to this: one was Stresemann's return, which gave to German policy a tone of deliberation, realism, and even pessimism. The other was the cognizance in Berlin that the creditors expected annuities of 2 billion marks or more.

By mid-November Stresemann was fully aware of the difficulties facing German reparation policy and had decided upon the course to be taken. From the notes sent by Poincaré and Churchill, it was evident that London and Paris wanted to set the terms of the new settlement before the experts met, preclude an examination of Germany's capacity to pay, and limit the work of the experts to an investigation of how the funds required by the creditors were to be raised. And in a conversation with Stresemann on November 13, Gilbert discussed figures with a member of the German government for the first time. He mentioned annuities of 2-2.5 billion marks and asserted that such payments were within Germany's capacity. Professing unconcern about the dependence of reparation payment on German borrowing from abroad, Gilbert maintained that the new settlement would encourage further foreign investment and thereby promote the

States: 19 November 1928, Sthamer to AA, Abt. II—Besetzte Gebiete Räumung des besetzten Rheinlandes, 1 (German Foreign Ministry, Bonn). The French repeated the position taken by Poincaré at Chambéry. Rome and Brussels also prepared memoranda which they sent to the other creditors and to Berlin: Weill-Raynal, *Réparations allemandes*, III, 411-14.

prosperity necessary to make annuities of this magnitude bearable.

Stresemann was not convinced. The new settlement, he told Gilbert, must not be based on what Germany might be able to pay and transfer provided the German economy continued to receive the artificial stimulus of heavy foreign lending; the new annuities must be set at a level Germany could pay out of her own resources—1.5 billion marks. Stresemann threatened that unless the experts were allowed to examine German capacity, he would not recommend the establishment of an experts committee to the Reichstag; instead, he would wait until an economic crisis demonstrated Germany's limited capacity and evoked proposals for a more favorable settlement. Faced with an obstacle to his grand design, Gilbert equivocally stated that the experts would not be bound by the statements of Poincaré and Churchill. They would be independent and free to determine the sum of Germany's reparation obligations.[103]

Stresemann then launched a counterattack against the Poincaré-Churchill attempt to predetermine the experts' recommendation. He did so with a statement to the press on November 14, a speech to the Reichstag on November 19, and a note to the creditors dated November 23. While publicly agreeing to the convocation of a committee of experts, Stresemann insisted that the terms of the settlement not be prejudiced by the problem of inter-Allied debts or by the advance claims made by Germany's creditors. He reserved for Berlin the right to reject the report of the experts if it was not satisfactory. To be acceptable, he stated, the settlement must be within Germany's capacity to pay and transfer—without having to borrow from abroad and "without endangering the nation's standard of living." The necessary prerequisite to such a settlement was a committee of experts who were "independent of all political considerations," uninstructed by their governments, able to conduct a thorough and impartial examination of Germany's capacity, and free to base their recommendation on the results of that investigation.[104]

---

[103] Stresemann, *Vermächtnis*, III, 378-82; Eyck, *Weimar Republic*, II, 181. In 1925 Stresemann wrote that 1.75 billion marks was the maximum Germany could pay: 7 September 1925, Stresemann to Crown Prince, 3168/7318/159872.

[104] Reichstag, *Verhandlungen*, v. 423, s. 17, pp. 416-17; Stresemann, *Vermächtnis*, III, 384-86; 23 November 1928, German memorandum, FO. 371/12880/54.

Stresemann thus decided not to accept responsibility for the termination of the preparations underway for the convocation of a committee of experts. He was led to that decision by a combination of hope and despair. He hoped that independent experts would reduce the annuity to an acceptable level. And he hoped that American financiers, men who presumably had no interest in seeing the financial health of their debtor impaired, would prevent any attempt to impose annuities beyond German capacity. On the other hand, he knew that the creditors, having endorsed the search for a new reparation settlement, could be opposed only at great risk. Because of Germany's dependence on foreign credit, the West could not be defied. "We are not only militarily disarmed," he told the press, "we are financially disarmed; we have no kind of resources left." Stresemann regarded participation in expert discussions as the least disagreeable of what he termed the "conspicuously ugly" alternatives facing him. To Gilbert, Stresemann compared himself to Ibsen's Nora, continually hoping for the miracle "that must happen, but never does."[105]

One prong of Stresemann's November counteroffensive was directed against the position taken by Poincaré and Churchill on reparation; the other was directed against the position assumed by Briand and Cushendun on the Rhineland. In his Reichstag speech of November 19, Stresemann demanded the withdrawal of Allied troops independent of any financial deliberations. Germany, he stated, would not purchase evacuation with either financial compensation or a Commission of Verification enduring beyond 1935. He attempted to exploit public sentiment against occupation by suggesting that the British and French were not negotiating the Rhineland question with goodwill, and he made a direct effort to divide opinion in England. He criticized the policy of Baldwin, Cushendun, and Chamberlain by referring to those who address "friendly and sometimes cordial words . . . to Germany" and declare that they have no interest in continuing occupation, but who "so far have not put their view into practice." At the same time, he praised the opposition parties, citing the "very large foreign circles which consider the maintenance of foreign troops in German territory to be in flagrant contradiction with the course of international affairs during recent years."[106]

[105] Stresemann, *Vermächtnis*, III, 382, 384-86.
[106] Reichstag, *Verhandlungen*, v. 423, s. 17, pp. 414-15.

Because the British were not publicly committed to support the French thesis of compensation for evacuation, Stresemann had some reason to hope that London might respond to his efforts.[107]

Stresemann's two-pronged assault was indicative of the disjuncture which had characterized German policy since September and which was to continue to do so for the next six months. On the one hand, the Müller government insisted that the Rhineland must be evacuated independently of any arrangements for a reparation settlement; on the other hand, they took step after step leading to a reparation settlement without any comparable progress toward evacuation. To have renounced Germany's legal and moral right to evacuation and admitted the principle of compensation would not have hastened evacuation. Rather, it would have meant the abandonment of a propaganda point which evoked a response from French and Belgian Socialists and from the potential government parties in Britain. And at home it would have exposed Stresemann to the accusation that he was purchasing German freedom. It would have tied evacuation to long and difficult reparation negotiations and possibly led to the termination of Rhineland discussions in the event the complex financial deliberations broke down. The Germans could not renounce their claim to unconditional evacuation; at the same time they could not avoid undermining its credibility by cooperating in the convocation of the committee of experts. In the long run, this disjuncture was to permit the creditor powers to arrange for financial compensation before evacuation was granted and to deny to the Germans the parallel negotiations on which Müller had counted so heavily in September. In the short run, it was to lead Briand and Chamberlain to suggest publicly that Stresemann's claims were not to be taken seriously.

Stresemann's renewed demands for unconditional evacuation caused Briand little difficulty. The entire cabinet and all the parties in the Chamber to the Right of the Socialists supported the policy of compensation for evacuation, and when a Socialist Deputy did call for the immediate and unconditional withdrawal, Briand simply went before the Chamber on December 4 and, with customary optimism and placidity, repeated the compromise line he had adopted during the winter debate. While promising to pursue an understanding with Germany until there was "a gen-

[107] See above, p. 210.

eral liquidation of the war," he dismissed Stresemann's demand for immediate evacuation as a tactical maneuver designed to placate German public opinion, and he insisted on a reparation settlement and a Commission of Verification.[108]

Stresemann's Reichstag speech, with its pointed references to British policy, caused Austen Chamberlain considerably more trouble. Baldwin and Cushendun had not been able to end the opposition's attack on the entente with France, and when Chamberlain returned to London, he found himself repeatedly questioned in Commons regarding Britain's attitude toward the Franco-German controversy over evacuation. Did he support, he was asked on December 3, German demands for immediate evacuation or the French position linking reparation and evacuation? The Foreign Secretary replied that Germany had no legal right to complete evacuation because Germany had not yet "completely executed and discharged the whole of her reparation obligations." As a matter of policy, Chamberlain added, he would welcome early evacuation by all three powers. But, he refused to answer the direct question put to him—whether his policy linked evacuation and reparation.[109] Chamberlain's statement was welcomed by the French press and by Briand, who was able to claim British support for his rejection of unconditional evacuation when he spoke to the Chamber the next day, but it brought him nothing but criticism from the opposition at home. The attack continued in the House of Commons, where, on December 5, Chamberlain again declined to choose between the French and German positions. And on December 10, when a spokesman for Chamberlain again declined to elaborate on the position taken by the Foreign Secretary on December 3, the patience of the opposition members wore thin, and one of them accused the government of "preserving a policy of slavish subservience to France."[110] Actually, Chamberlain's public rejection of the legal basis of Germany's claim to immediate evacuation was of little practical importance. What was important was whether or not he favored early evacuation as a matter of policy. On this issue he sought to spare the govern-

[108] Chambre débats, 1928, pp. 3229-36.

[109] Commons, debates, v. 223, c. 397, 823-24. The most complete and lucid statement of the government's attitude toward Germany's claim to unconditional evacuation was made by Lord Hailsham before the House of Lords on December 10: Lords, debates, v. 72, c. 460-70.

[110] Commons, debates, v. 223, c. 1189-93, 1689-92.

ment from criticism by maintaining that they favored early evacuation, and by declining to support either the French or German position on compensation. In private, however, he was more candid and sided unequivocally with the French. He told Sthamer on December 5 that the important thing was to make progress on the practical measures which would lead to evacuation.[111] Like Briand, Chamberlain required a reparation settlement prior to evacuation.

In Germany, the statements of Chamberlain and Briand on December 3 and 4 brought to a climax much of the widespread disillusionment with the Locarno policy which had been developing since August. The Anglo-French Disarmament Compromise had given rise to much popular suspicion that Britain and France were collaborating against Germany; and Briand's *Böse Rede* of September 10 seemed to confirm that Paris was taking a new and harder line against German claims. Then, in early December it appeared that British policy had not changed as a result of the reaction against the Disarmament Compromise, that the entente continued, that it extended to the issues of evacuation and reparation, that Chamberlain had broken the contract he had made at Locarno to serve as an honest broker, and that he had formed a new front with Briand against Germany. Both men were demanding payment for evacuation—something for which the German people had been told they had already paid and now deserved as a matter of justice. Stresemann's policy, it seemed, was bankrupt; Berlin could no longer hope to be treated as an equal by the Western powers; the Locarno era had come to an end; German policy must take a new course. All these opinions appeared in the German press during the last quarter of 1928.

Disillusion with Locarno had been expressed before, but after Briand's *Böse Rede* it was expressed not only by the Hugenberg press but also by the moderate Nationalist press and the formerly pro-Locarno liberal, Catholic, and democratic papers; and it was voiced with much greater frequency and vehemence—particularly after the statements of Chamberlain and Briand in early December.[112] Alfred Hugenberg's *Berliner Lokalanzeiger* said

[111] 6 December 1928, Chamberlain to Rumbold, FO. 371/12906/25.

[112] A pessimistic view of the Locarno policy in a paper which reflected the views of the DVP: *Deutsche Allgemeine Zeitung*, 25 September 1928. A scathing attack on Chamberlain's entente policy by an independent Democratic paper: *Berliner Tagblatt*, 22 November 1928.

that Chamberlain and Briand had destroyed the last illusions of the Locarno policy. The Nationalist *Kreuzzeitung* asserted that Germany had been hoodwinked. Even the *Deutsche Allgemeine Zeitung*, a paper which supported Stresemann's own party, stated that Germany had been deceived about the political consequences that would follow from the Locarno Treaty. Gustav Stolper's *Deutsche Volkswirt* complained that Chamberlain and Briand had broken the promise of Locarno to regard Germany as an equal and were treating Stresemann like a child, to be bribed with candy and slapped for speaking up boldly. The Democratic *Frankfurter Zeitung* said that Briand must choose between the enforcement of Versailles and the conciliation of Locarno, and the *Kreuzzeitung* added that the decision must be made at the December meeting of the League Council. If not, Stresemann must break off cooperation with the West and seek support for German aims elsewhere.[113] In the Reichstag on November 19, Count Westarp (DNVP) labeled the Locarno policy a failure and called for the adoption of a new course, and Ludwig Kaas (ZP) referred to the "undeniable failure of German foreign policy" and spoke vaguely of an alteration in the "dynamics of German foreign policy" unless there were rapid improvement.[114]

Growing opposition to Stresemann's policy in the press and in the Reichstag might have been of little importance had it not been that those who were voicing the criticism were becoming more prominent and influential. On December 8, Ludwig Kaas, who had recently become publicly critical of the Locarno policy and had privately advocated in meetings with his party's leaders the removal of Stresemann from the cabinet, became chairman of the Center Party, replacing Wilhelm Marx, a man who had cooperated closely with Stresemann.[115] Earlier, the leadership of the

[113] *Berliner Lokalanzeiger*, 5 December 1928; *Kreuzzeitung*, 5 December 1928; *Deutsche Allgemeine Zeitung*, 7 December 1928; *Deutsche Volkswirt*, 7 December 1928; *Frankfurter Zeitung*, 6 December 1928; *Kreuzzeitung*, 4 December 1928.

[114] Reichstag, *Verhandlungen*, v. 423, s. 17, pp. 417-35.

[115] 4 October 1928, Memorandum by Pünder, R43 I/199/135-36 (Bundesarchiv); Josef Becker, "Joseph Wirth und die Kries des Zentrums während des IV. Kabinetts Marx (1927-1928); Darstellung und Dokuments," *Zeitschrift für die Geschichte des Oberrheins*, 109 (1961), pp. 424-29; Eyck, *Weimar Republic*, II, 170-71; Erich Matthias and Rudolf Morsey (eds.), *Das Ende der Parteien 1933*, Düsseldorf, 1960, pp. 283-87; Helmut Schorr, *Adam Stegerwald; Gewerkschaftler und Politiker der ersten deutschen Republik* . . . , Recklinghausen, 1966, pp. 128-46.

DNVP had moved to the Right; on October 20, Alfred Hugenberg was elected chairman of the party. Hugenberg and his supporters, the racists and the Pan-Germans, were militant opponents of parliamentary democracy and of the foreign policy of Gustav Stresemann, a man for whom Hugenberg had a strong personal dislike. With his election, the DNVP turned away from the policies of Cuno von Westarp and Professor Otto Hoetzsch, men who had accepted the aims and methods of Stresemann's policy, had criticized it primarily for its meager results, and had sought to silence the attacks on Hugenberg, his press, and his followers. The DNVP thus departed into what has been called the ranks of the "bitter and disaffected opposition," and this in turn prepared the way for the formation, nine months later, of the National Opposition coalition, comprising the DNVP, the Nazis, and the Stahlhelm—an organization which also became more stridently critical of Stresemann during the autumn of 1928.[116]

Thus after September 1928, both the government and the nascent National Opposition voiced disappointment with the course German relations with the West were taking. They competed with each other for the support which such statements found among the German populace, and ultimately the forces of the National Opposition were to prevail. The defenders of the policy of understanding were unable to keep up the pace set by their opponents, who claimed that Stresemann was constantly outwitted by London and Paris and that they knew how better to defend German rights. While Hugenberg was free to express German disappointment with unrestrained indignation, Stresemann accompanied his distress with calls for further patience.[117]

Within the German Foreign Ministry there was little inclination to reorient German policy in response to growing criticism. The case against a new course was put most strongly and most

[116] Volker R. Berghahn, *Der Stahlhelm; Bund der Frontsoldaten, 1918-1935*, Düsseldorf, 1966, p. 116; Karl Dietrich Bracher, *Die Auflösung der Weimarer Republik*, Stuttgart, 1957, pp. 288, 309-16; Attila Chanady, "The Disintegration of the German National Peoples' Party, 1924-1930," *Journal of Modern History*, 39 (1967), pp. 71-72, 81-84, 86, 90; Robert Garthwol, "DNVP and European Reconciliation, 1924-1928; a Study of the Conflict between Party Politics and Government Foreign Policy in Weimar Germany," unpublished doctoral dissertation, Chicago, 1968, pp. 309-18. Louis Hertzman, *DNVP; Right Wing Opposition in the Weimar Republic, 1918-1924*, Lincoln, Neb., 1963, pp. 4, 185-86; Matthias and Morsey, *Das Ende der Parteien*, pp. 544-48.
[117] Geigenmüller, "Hoesch und die Räumungsfrage," p. 620.

consistently by Leopold von Hoesch. He argued that Briand's rejection of the German thesis on September 10 and December 4 did not signify an abandonment of his policy of rapprochement with Germany and an end to the Locarno era. Briand, Hoesch maintained, was simply representing himself as the "conscientious, cautious, and tenacious guardian of French interests" in order to further the policy of understanding, and he would continue his efforts until he won the rest of France to his policy and eliminated all outstanding differences with Germany. Therein lies, Hoesch wrote, "the value of a person like Briand to us." Unlike the opponents of Stresemann's policy, Hoesch did not believe that open conflicts between Paris and Berlin indicated that the policy of understanding should be abandoned; rather, conflicts showed the need to continue the present policy. "The function of the so-called policy of understanding," Hoesch wrote, "is precisely that these unavoidable clashes, which under any other policy would lead to severe restrictions on the rebuilding of Germany, can be solved by mutual understanding and leave the road to *Freiheit und Aufstieg* open to us."[118] *Freiheit und Aufstieg* were the goals of German policy; understanding with France was the means. This was an apt, concise summary of German Locarno policy, although it was not the way Stresemann presented it in his public statements, where he usually depicted freedom from occupation as the means and understanding as the end.

Stresemann and Hoesch were the two men who best understood the methods and objectives of German policy, and the Foreign Minister agreed with the ambassador that neither should be altered, although he was discouraged at the slowness with which his efforts brought results. Stresemann refused to regard Briand's *Böse Rede* as cause for a new departure; rather he dismissed what he called Briand's "violent improvisations" as one of "the risks involved in wholly impromptu oratory."[119] Then, in his Reichstag speech of November 19, he had proffered a duplex reply to the advocates of a new course: the policy of understanding, he said, was the only one possible "in view of our complete military helplessness"; and at the same time, he presented that

[118] 11 September 1928, Hoesch to Geneva, 1775/3642/807822-26; 5 December 1928, Hoesch to Stresemann, 2258/4502/120219-22; Geigenmüller, "Hoesch und die Räumungsfrage," pp. 608-609.
[119] Stresemann, *Vermächtnis*, III, 370-71.

policy as an uncompromising defense of German interests, calling for the unconditional evacuation of the Rhineland and a reparation settlement within Germany's capacity to pay.[120] Having determined that he could do nothing other than continue the policy of understanding, Stresemann found that policy encountering new difficulties. At home, his policy was opposed; abroad Chamberlain and Briand did not take his claims seriously. With his options limited, his health failing, and his opponents more vocal, the first week of December found Stresemann discouraged and embittered, and as he traveled to Lugano for the December meeting of the League Council he made no attempt to hide his feelings from the world press.[121]

Throughout the meetings he held at Lugano with Briand and Chamberlain from December 9 to 14, Stresemann was pessimistic, despondent, and irascible.[122] He did not, however, adopt a new course and attempt to force Chamberlain and Briand to choose once and for all between the enforcement of Versailles and the pacification of Germany, as his opposition demanded. Faced with criticism at home, Stresemann dared not risk Anglo-French rejection of German claims. Rather than changing strategies, he attempted to use the opposition to his policy within Germany to tactical advantage. He mentioned Kaas's attack on the Locarno policy in particular, and he told Briand and Chamberlain that the continuation of his policy—and the tenure of the Müller cabinet—depended on immediate and unilateral concessions from the Allies. Because of what he termed the "seriousness of the existing situation and the danger of a radical revulsion in the attitude of important political factors in Germany," he most have achievements in the form of immediate and specific assurances from them.

[120] Reichstag, *Verhandlungen*, v. 423, s. 17, pp. 416-17.

[121] *New York Times*, 9 December 1928.

[122] The fullest firsthand accounts of the talks held in Lugano are to be found in the memoranda prepared by Paul Schmidt and the notes kept by Schubert: 2365/4587/184433-623. Stresemann made summary reports to the cabinet and Foreign Ministry: 21 December 1928, Cabinet Protocol, 1700/3575/779131-35; 22 December 1928, Stresemann to Western European embassies, 2258/4502/120255-62. Chamberlain's brief summaries, including his description of Stresemann's disposition, are to be found in Cab 23/59/57 (19 December 1928); 13 December 1928, Memorandum by Chamberlain, FO. 371/12906/171-72; 18 December 1928, Chamberlain to Tyrrell, AC 55/493; 19 December 1928, Chamberlain to Rumbold, AC 55/430.

Stresemann received none of the concessions for which he asked. At Lugano Briand and Chamberlain together insisted that discussion of evacuation be coupled with the progress of the negotiations on compensation. They stated that Rhineland negotiations—negotiations on evacuation and the Commission of Verification—would be opened and conducted through normal diplomatic channels when the reparation experts were appointed and began their deliberations. When the negotiations on reparation and security showed progress, the Coblenz zone would be evacuated. When the experts arrived at a settlement and agreement was reached on a Commission of Verification, then complete evacuation would take place as soon as logistic considerations permitted. In addition, Briand assured Stresemann that negotiations on the Rhineland would continue even if the deliberations of the experts came to a standstill or they failed to arrive at a settlement.[123] In an attempt to make the dependency of complete evacuation on a reparation settlement palatable to Stresemann, Briand drew a bright picture of the future. With characteristic optimism, he predicted that the experts would quickly arrive at a proposal, that they would formulate a scheme more favorable to Germany than the one implicit in the statements of Churchill and Poincaré, and that their recommendations would prevail over the demands of the creditors.

The most serious conflict at Lugano came when Briand insisted that the Commission of Verification be discussed when negotiations on evacuation were opened. Stresemann put up what he called an "uncompromising struggle," using "all kinds of arguments" to demonstrate that the commission was both unnecessary and a potential danger to Franco-German understanding. Briand replied that Stresemann was using "a smokescreen" of "false complaints" to mask considerations of German national interest. And Briand's insistence on verification was supported fully by Chamberlain, who stated that the need for a commission was substantiated by information he had received regarding the capabilities of the Reichswehr. The discussion ended with Briand promising to put his proposal in writing for the confidential inconsiderations of Stresemann and Chamberlain. Stresemann interpreted Briand's willingness to negotiate and Chamberlain's unwillingness to use

[123] 14 December 1928, Memorandum by Schmidt, 2365/4587/184621. This latter promise was made in a private Stresemann-Briand conversation in the absence of Chamberlain: 1 January 1929, Chamberlain to Rumbold, FO. 371/13615/5.

the information available to him as signs that both men were weakening. He told Schubert that the Commission of Verification was "as good as dead" provided the Germans proposed an alternative measure.

Neither Anglo-French unity on compensation, nor Briand's assurance that the reparation settlement would be both prompt and beneficent mollified Stresemann. He rejected Briand's offer to evacuate Coblenz, insisted on complete and unconditional withdrawal, and tried to eradicate the loose association of evacuation, reparation, and security which had been made on September 16 at Geneva. At Lugano Stresemann asked Briand and Chamberlain to join him in a press communiqué which omitted reference to the Geneva agreement, stated that the Locarnites recognized occupation as "the most urgent problem" to be resolved, and promised to promote evacuation as soon as possible despite differences among them over Germany's legal claims.[124] At the same time, Stresemann threatened to give to an American newspaper an interview outlining once more Germany's legal case for evacuation without compensation. Chamberlain was, he complained, being "inundated by a flood of criticism in the press and questions in Parliament," and to deny his opposition at home additional ammunition, he wanted no disclosure of the differences between Stresemann and himself in the press. "Our object," he told Schubert, "must be to keep people quiet, not start discussion." He demanded that the press communiqué mention the spirit of Locarno, the Geneva agreement, and no more; and he asked that Stresemann not give the interview to the American newspaper. When Schubert refused, Chamberlain's irritation with German ways broke through his normally formal and courteous exterior: "You are the most difficult nation in the world," he exploded; "I try to help you, and you ruin me."[125] Both issues were finally resolved by compromise. Stresemann agreed to publish his interview after the British Parliament had adjourned on December 20,[126] and a compromise communiqué,

[124] 12 December 1928, Memorandum by Schubert, 2365/4587/184505.

[125] 11 December 1928, Chamberlain to Rumbold, FO. 371/12906/33; 14 December 1928, Memorandum by Schubert, 2365/4587/184604-607; 15 December 1928, Memorandum by Schubert, 2365/4587/184640; 18 December 1928, Chamberlain to Tyrrell, AC 55/593.

[126] It appeared in the December 27 issue of the *Baltimore Sun*: Wheeler-Bennett and Latimer, *Reparation Settlement*, p. 84.

mentioning the Geneva agreement in a form acceptable to Germany, was issued to the press.[127]

While the Foreign Ministers were in Lugano, Poincaré and Hoesch were discussing the formation of the committee of experts in Paris, and on December 22, they published a protocol announcing their agreement on the composition of the committee and on the mandate to be given the experts. First, the experts were to be independent and unbound by formal instructions from their governments. This was something of a victory for the Germans, who believed that no body of uninstructed, independent experts would be willing to set a sum beyond Germany's capacity to pay. However, the victory was less than complete, for the designation "independent expert" permitted the appointment of the governors of the various national banks, men who had a large stake in defending the currency and financial stability of their countries and who maintained close contacts with their governments. Secondly, the experts were "to draw up proposals for a complete and final settlement of the reparation problem" proposals providing for "a settlement of the obligations resulting from existing treaties and agreements between Germany and the creditor powers." The Hoesch-Poincaré protocol specified neither a settlement within Germany's capacity, nor a settlement meeting the minimum requirements set by the creditors in the weeks since mid-September. The experts were appointed without the conflicting expectations of Germany and the creditors being resolved. In Washington, Charles Dawes, now Vice President of the United States, noted that the experts would "in effect . . . conduct a diplomatic negotiation, not . . . an expert research," and they would conduct their negotiations within "limitations fixed by their governments." "These limitations," he concluded, "seriously jeopardize the possibility of arriving at any results acceptable to both the Allies and to Germany."[128]

[127] 15 December 1928, Memorandum by Schubert, 2365/4587/184637-43. The texts of the various proposed communiqués: 2365/4587/184585-86, 626, 644-45.

[128] Documents on International Affairs, 1928, pp. 55-56; Survey of International Affairs, 1928, p. 135; 1929, p. 141; Wheeler-Bennett and Latimer, Reparation Settlement, pp. 78, 81; 4 December 1928, Dawes to Lamont, Lamont papers 91/10; Charles Dawes, Notes as Vice President, 1928-1929, Boston, 1935, p. 156.

PART SIX

THE FINAL REPARATION SETTLEMENT
JANUARY-JUNE 1929

1. *The Politics of Disappointment, January-April 1929*

THE members of the committee of experts representing the four principal Allied powers, Germany, and the United States were formally appointed in January 1929. The committee met for the first time on February 11. Owen D. Young was elected chairman, and what was officially named "The Committee of Experts, 1929" came to be called the "Young committee." It met in Paris at the newly constructed Hotel George V for five months and concluded its deliberations on June 7. These months were a period of heightened tension and conflict between Germany and the West. Not only was there persistent conflict among the experts at Paris over the terms of the reparation settlement, but the Locarnites themselves became more uncompromising. Briand refused even to discuss the evacuation of the Rhineland until the experts had reported. Chamberlain withstood political pressure at home and refused to use the threat of independent British evacuation to move Briand toward withdrawal from the Rhine. And Stresemann, disappointed and dejected, came to speak of his deception at the hands of Briand and Chamberlain and to talk of the failure of his Locarno policy.

At Lugano in December, Briand and Chamberlain had stated that Rhineland negotiations would begin when the financial experts began their deliberations; and when the experts were appointed in January, Stresemann attempted to initiate evacuation negotiations through normal diplomatic channels. Hoesch was called to Berlin for consultation, and on January 24, he made the démarche at the Quai d'Orsay. At Stresemann's instruction, the ambassador repeated for Briand the year-old German thesis: evacuation was a legal and political necessity; it was not dependent upon a reparation settlement; the lack of progress at Geneva and Lugano had disappointed all Germans; to alleviate this disappointment, some immediate progress toward evacuation must be made independently of the experts' negotiations.

Briand replied to Hoesch by insisting that Stresemann had misunderstood the import of the conversations at Geneva and Lugano: the committee of experts must first complete their deliberations; then the governments concerned would simultaneously discuss the experts' report and consider evacuation. The parallel

negotiations discussed at Geneva did not mean Rhineland negotiations simultaneous with the deliberations of the experts, but
negotiations at the time of the political discussions between the
governments over the acceptance of the experts' report. Although
Briand made what Hoesch called some "vague but well-inten-
tioned remarks," he offered no definite promises, and he refused
to reply to Hoesch's repeated objections that immediate progress
must take place.[1]

Briand's refusal to conduct Rhineland negotiations prior to the
report of the Young committee was at variance with what Stresemann and Müller regarded as the most encouraging and important assurance they had received at Geneva and Lugano—that
evacuation negotiations would begin with the convocation of the
committee of experts.[2] Briand may have been correct in claiming
that Stresemann had misunderstood the import of two recent
foreign ministers' conferences, in which case there is cause to
question the willingness of the Locarnites to understand each
other at their tea parties and reason to doubt the efficacy of the
Locarno diplomatic method. It is probable, however, that Briand
was saying, in effect, that hotel-room conversations had no official
standing and were not legally binding. Indeed, Briand had reason
to seek an escape from projected parallel negotiations, for there
was opposition to such discussions within the French government.

To Poincaré, the evacuation of the Rhineland in advance of the
date named in the Versailles Treaty was something to be granted
only in exchange for the payment of reparation in advance of
schedule, and he was disinclined to discuss anticipatory evacuation until arrangement was made for anticipatory reparation payment. In the summer and fall of 1928 he had favored the gradual
evacuation of the Rhineland as advance payment of reparation
was actually received by the French Treasury. His scheme, apparently modeled on the one employed by the Germans after the
Franco-Prussian war, called for evacuation in stages over a
period of years as German reparation bonds were actually sold

---

[1] 24 January 1929, Hoesch to AA, 2258/4502/120316-17.

[2] Schubert reported the promise of simultaneous negotiations to Nikolai
Krestinski, the Soviet ambassador to Berlin, as one of the major results of
the Lugano conversations: 29 December 1928, Memorandum by Schubert,
2258/4502/120271-72.

to the public and revenue was received in Paris.[3] In January 1929
Poincaré continued to be impressed with the importance of commercialization (the delivery by the German government of negotiable bonds for the amount of the reparation debt), the sale of
those bonds to the public, and the receipt of advance payment by
the French government. On January 11 he told the Chamber of
Deputies that these were the most important benefits France
would derive from the new reparation settlement.[4] And he sent
a memorandum to Briand insisting that evacuation was dependent on commercialization and rejecting the notion of any Rhineland negotiations until commercialization was assured.[5] In late
January the Quai d'Orsay adopted Poincaré's position. The actual
withdrawal of French troops, it was decided, would begin only
when the reparation question had been "settled," i.e., when the
German debt ceased to be political and became commercial.
Evacuation would be discussed with the Germans only when the
experts had actually produced a scheme which provided for the
commercialization of the German debt.[6] By the end of January, therefore, parallel negotiations had slipped away from
Stresemann.

Like Briand, Chamberlain returned from Lugano to find serious opposition to the line he had taken there. At home, his foreign
policy was subjected to continued criticism from the opposition,
and there was even dissent among Conservatives. The attack of
the opposition, which had begun in October 1928, took the form
of frequent interpellations in the House of Commons, just as it
had since early December. The critics were largely those "radicals" who contributed so much to the development of Labour
foreign policy in the 1920's—Noel and Charles Buxton, Arthur
Ponsonby, Josiah Wedgwood, J. M. Kenworthy, and Charles
Trevelyan. These men were all ex-liberals, and for the most part
they had been members of the Union for Democratic Control and
the Independent Labour Party; they were all long-time opponents

[3] 12 July 1928, Hoesch to AA, 2544/5133/297407; *New York Times*, 14 December 1928.

[4] Chambre débats, 1929, pp. 57-58.

[5] Berthelot showed this document to Hoesch: 29 January 1929, Hoesch to
Schubert, 2258/4502/120320-24.

[6] 4 January 1929, Tyrrell to Chamberlain, AC 55/497; 4 February 1929,
Tyrrell to Chamberlain, AC 55/501.

of the peace treaty and Wedgwood had even voted against Locarno because it confirmed Versailles.[7] Their attack on Chamberlain's policy was, however, no mere skirmish conducted by eccentric pacifists and Francophobes; the views they expressed were the official position of the Labour Party as set forth in *Labour and the Nation* and of the Liberal Party as outlined in the speeches of Lloyd George and various party manifestoes. The radicals were, moreover, joined in their attack by Hugh Dalton, an opponent of treaty revision, and one of the persons most responsible for the formulation of Labour foreign policy.[8] Together, they deplored what they saw as a return to the prewar policy of entente with France and a departure from the evenhanded treatment of Berlin and Paris implicit in the Locarno Treaty. They called for immediate and unconditional evacuation, protested against what they regarded as Chamberlain's unsatisfactory replies to their questions on British Rhineland policy, and suggested that it was time to either change foreign policies or change governments. To this attack on the government's German policy, they added criticism of its disarmament policy, a call for improved relations with the United States, and a demand for the resumption of diplomatic relations with the Soviet Union.[9] Wedgwood and Kenworthy in particular were inveterate questioners; Wedgwood had asked 456 one year, and Kenworthy had become known for his "constant guerrilla war from the back benches." The two of them, supported by other radicals and allied with Dalton, were more than a match for the government spokesmen.[10]

[7] Mosa Anderson, *Noel Buxton, a Life*, London, 1952, Chaps. 10-12; Catherine Cline, *Recruits to Labour; the British Labour Party, 1914-1931*, Syracuse, N. Y., 1963, pp. 69-70; J. M. Kenworthy, *Peace or War?* New York, 1927, p. 311; R. B. McCullum, *Public Opinion and the Last Peace*, London, 1944, p. 52; C. V. Wedgwood, *The Last of the Radicals; Josiah Wedgwood, MP*, London, 1951, pp. 128-30; Josiah Wedgwood, *Memoirs of a Fighting Life*, London, 1940, p. 256.

[8] Hugh Dalton, *Towards the Peace of Nations; a Study in International Politics*, London, 1928, pp. 30, 39-46; Henry R. Winkler, "The Emergence of a Labour Foreign Policy in Great Britain, 1918-1929," *Journal of Modern History*, 28 (1956), pp. 247-58.

[9] Commons, debates, v. 223, c. 2983-87, 3412-24; v. 224, c. 7, 152, 166, 1428; v. 225, c. 2298.

[10] J. M. Kenworthy, *Sailors, Statesmen and Others; an Autobiography*, London, 1933, p. 169; Josiah Wedgwood, *Fighting Life*, pp. 202-203; C. V. Wedgwood, *Last of the Radicals*, p. 139.

The attack continued until Parliament was prorogued on May 10, 1929, preparatory to the general election.

Chamberlain's vulnerability to attack could make the government's foreign policy a liability in the pending elections, and there was understandable concern among Conservative members. As early as December 1928, Chamberlain was faced with disaffection and impatience among what he termed "a large section of the best conservative opinion."[11] He received reports that even Conservatives close to the government were anxious to deprive the opposition of continued military occupation as a weapon in the electoral campaign, and that they were pressing the London *Times*, which supported the entente with France, to break with Chamberlain's policy.[12]

Faced with widespread impatience with his Rhineland policy on both sides of the House of Commons, Chamberlain's position became, as he said, "daily more difficult." He instructed Tyrrell to describe his difficulties to Briand, Berthelot, and Poincaré and to inform them that unless the French "show a really conciliatory disposition," his position might well "become impossible."[13] The implication of his statement was, of course, that if Paris wanted the Baldwin government, which had shown so much consideration for French policy, to remain in office, then the Quai d'Orsay must take some step toward evacuation. The tone of his plea reflected the approach Chamberlain had long used in Paris—the "discreet" application of pressure, done "in the way that persuades instead of the manner which estranges."[14] The French, however, proved unwilling to adapt their foreign policy to the requirements of Conservative politics; after talking to Berthelot

[11] 18 December 1928, Chamberlain to Tyrrell, AC 55/493. One dissident young Conservative backbencher was Captain Harold MacMillian who predicted that the government's foreign policy, and its failure to deal with unemployment, would bring it defeat in the election: 8 November 1928, MacMillian to Cecil, Cecil papers 51166.

[12] 4 February 1929, Tyrrell to Chamberlain, AC 55/501; 8 February 1929, Chamberlain to Tyrrell, AC 55/503; 17 April 1929, N. Henderson to Tyrrell, FO. 371/13617/24-27.

[13] 18 December 1928, Chamberlain to Tyrrell, AC 55/493. The German embassy in London was informed of the pressure on Chamberlain and the *Times* and of Chamberlain's instructions to Tyrrell: 4 February 1928, Dieckhoff to AA, 2258/4502/120326-27. Sthamer reported that the pressure on Chamberlain came from J.C.C. Davidson, chairman of the Conservative Party organization: 8 March 1929, Sthamer to AA, 2258/4502/120364.

[14] 8 February 1929, Chamberlain to Tyrrell, AC 55/503.

on January 26, Tyrrell reported that there was "no prospect" of even discussing evacuation until reparations were settled.[15] Chamberlain was thereby confirmed in the strategy he had been following: he rejected suggestions that the British Army of the Rhine be withdrawn unilaterally, prior to the arrangement of compensation for France, because separate British withdrawal would not be in Germany's interest. The French would replace the departed British soldiers with troops of their own, he thought; Paris and Brussels would be left in control of the Rhineland High Commission and be free to control the conditions of occupation without restraint from London; Britain would be excluded from subsequent Rhineland negotiations and unable to push the French toward evacuation. So Chamberlain continued to promote complete evacuation by aiding the French in securing a final reparation settlement and a permanent Commission of Verification.[16] "The object of our policy is, and must be," he wrote, "to get the French out."[17]

As long as Stresemann complied with the requests of Briand and Chamberlain to keep his public demands for evacuation to a minimum, Chamberlain could continue to meet opposition criticism in the House of Commons. He could depict Stresemann's quiescence as tacit agreement that continued British occupation was in Germany's best interest. If, however, Stresemann publicly demanded unilateral British evacuation, Chamberlain could no longer use what Sthamer called his "convenient evading argument"; he would be placed in the "extraordinarily embarrassing" position of having to admit that he maintained occupation only out of consideration for France; the British government would "be forced to show its true colors on the question of separate evacuation." And this admission, given the prevailing state of opinion in Britain, would "make a very bad impression and unfavorably influence the election," Sthamer thought.[18]

In early February Chamberlain received indications that Berlin was about to alter its attitude on separate British withdrawal. Albrecht Bernstorff, of the German embassy staff, told Walford

[15] 28 January 1929, Tyrrell to Chamberlain, AC 55/500.
[16] These were, Chamberlain wrote, "the indispensable conditions of success": 1 January 1928, Chamberlain to Rumbold, FO. 371/13615/5.
[17] 8 February 1928, Minute by Chamberlain, AC 55/432.
[18] 8 March 1929, Sthamer to AA, 2258/4502/120363-65.

Selby, Chamberlain's private secretary, that the German government would soon open a newspaper campaign calling upon the
British to evacuate the Rhineland. Rumbold thought Bernstorff
was "trying a little bit of blackmail" to encourage the British to
press the French; Chamberlain thought it a simple attempt to
split the entente. He also believed that a Wilhelmstrasse press
campaign might well force the Baldwin government to withdraw
British troops, and he took steps to preclude this. He authorized
Rumbold to tell Stresemann that separate withdrawal was not in
German interest and that his consideration for German welfare,
his desire to remain in a position to promote the evacuation of the
French Army, was "the only reason" he had decided against
separate withdrawal.[19] Chamberlain then repeated this to Stresemann personally on March 7 during the spring session of the
League Council.[20] Stresemann did not press for British withdrawal, and Chamberlain was able to return from Geneva and
inform the House of Commons, on March 18, that Stresemann,
Briand, and himself had agreed unanimously to postpone all discussion of the Rhineland until after the Young committee had
reported. Thereafter, he and Rumbold remained convinced that
Stresemann would not demand separate British withdrawal.[21]

Six weeks later, on May 30, the Conservatives were defeated at
the polls, and the Baldwin government resigned on June 4. To the
end, Chamberlain adhered to the same policy: French requirements for security and reparation must be met before German
demands for concessions. When faced with opposition at home
and the threat of electoral defeat, he made inquiries in Paris.
Finding no help there, he might have evacuated British troops
unilaterally, but he did not. He kept them on the Rhine to execute
the award made to the Allies in 1919. Behind this policy lay not
merely a blind subservience to French policy, as his critics alleged, but also a lingering deep suspicion regarding Germany.
Chamberlain told Mussolini, on April 2, that "one must not trust
too implicitly" in the improved relations between Germany and
the West. "Only the future would show whether Germany would
really accept her present position, or whether she would once

[19] 20 February 1928, Rumbold to Chamberlain, AC 55/442; 8 February
1929, Chamberlain to Rumbold, AC 55/441.

[20] 7 March 1928, Stresemann to AA, 2258/4502/120353-54.

[21] Commons, debates, v. 226, c. 1487; 18 April 1929, Minute by Chamberlain, FO. 371/13617/22; 1 May 1929, Rumbold to Sargent, FO. 371/13617/53.

again resort to arms and stake everything on the hazards of a new war. . . . Let our policy be such as to take away all provocation and all excuse for a new war, but it was necessary also, that the perils and risks of such an adventure should be so evident as to be an effective deterrent, and for this, union between Great Britain, France, and Italy was needed. Germany was still restless, still prone to suggest that her good behavior must constantly be bought by fresh concessions."[22] The Baldwin government resigned a month later, and Chamberlain left the Foreign Office as he had entered it.

When presented with an apparent opportunity to exploit Chamberlain's vulnerability, Stresemann did not demand unilateral British evacuation. By April 1929 he and Schubert had come to place little value on separate British withdrawal. They wanted the complete evacuation of all foreign troops, and they were willing to await the report of the Young committee and see if complete withdrawal would follow as Briand had promised.[23] If the experts failed to reach agreement, then Berlin would persistently demand evacuation without compensation. The new Labour government, which Schubert expected to replace the Conservatives, probably would respond to this demand.[24] So without asking for unilateral British evacuation, Stresemann did not explicitly bind himself not to ask for it, and he carefully avoided making any formal promise of compensation. He merely postponed discussion of the Rhineland until the experts succeeded or failed and the Conservatives left office.

Meanwhile, Stresemann had little confidence in what Chamberlain could or would do to promote evacuation in the short period before the elections. He was disillusioned at London's failure to adopt an independent Rhine policy. He was embittered at Chamberlain's attempts to move the French by mere cajolery. And he was especially disappointed at the Conservatives' efforts to provide themselves with what he termed an "alibi" for their unpopular Rhineland policy by public statements implying that Berlin did not desire separate British evacuation.[25]

[22] 8 April 1929, Chamberlain to R. Graham, FO. 371/13617/28.
[23] 9 April 1929, Memorandum by Schubert, 2258/4502/120385.
[24] 1 May 1929, Rumbold to Sargent, FO. 371/13617/54.
[25] London *Times*, 6 April 1929; 6 April 1929, Schubert to Sthamer, 2258/4502/120378-79; R. H. Bruce Lockhart, *Retreat from Glory*, London, 1934, p. 362.

By April 1929 the inherent difficulties of Stresemann's Locarno policy had become clear. Nothing now remained of his hopes of 1925 to free the Rhineland as a consequence of Germany's agreement to the Locarno Treaty and its membership in the League of Nations. This disappointment had been expected, and preparations had been made for it in August 1928. After the Geneva meetings in September, the Germans publicly expressed their regret at the denial of immediate and unconditional evacuation and continued to make demands for it. And following Lugano, similar statements continued to emanate from Berlin.[26] Stresemann was, no doubt, disappointed at the outcome of the Geneva and Lugano conversations, but he was prepared to be, and Berlin's lamentation had an air of contrivance about it. The Müller government conducted, as one cabinet member put it, "a policy of pouting."[27]

However, during the first third of 1929, Stresemann encountered new disappointments for which he was less well prepared. Two of the hopes to which he had clung in November 1928 evaporated. Paris delayed evacuation negotiations once again, until after the Young committee had reported. Chamberlain withstood his opposition and decided not to use British participation in occupation as a means of coercing the French into unconditional evacuation. No longer could Stresemann hope that the British would exert a moderating influence on French Rhine policy, or that foreign troops would be withdrawn in anticipation of an eventual reparation settlement, or even that evacuation would be discussed parallel to the deliberations of the Young committee. With no alternative but to accept the decisions made in London and Paris, Stresemann fell back once more on the tactic of proclaiming "the disappointment of the German people." And this in itself brought difficulties, for his disillusionment reverberated through Germany in the spring of 1929. It was taken up by those who were weary of the moderation and the com-

[26] German disappointment and demands were put forth in a resolution passed by the Reichstag on December 15 and in Hindenburg's New Year's greeting to the assembled Berlin diplomatic corps: Reichstag, *Verhandlungen*, v. 436, n. 1093, p. 12; *New York Times*, 2 January 1928. Stresemann stated both in an interview published simultaneously in the *Baltimore Sun* and in the German press on December 27. He gave a similar statement to Jules Sawerwein of *Le Matin* during the first week of January; however, Poincaré and Briand reportedly prevented its publication: 16 January 1929, Schurman to State, 462.00 R296/5658.

[27] "ein Politik des Schmollens": Nachlass Koch-Weser 37/255.

promises of the Locarno policy and of Weimar politics in general.

Beginning in January 1929, conflict among the parties within the Müller cabinet incapacitated the government and all but tore it apart.[28] This was the most severe of the many cabinet crises suffered by the Weimar Republic since 1919, and it had many of the elements which, under conditions of grave economic dislocation, brought an end to Müller's Great Coalition and to effective parliamentary government in Germany a year later. It was not resolved until April 10, and even then a stable government, based on agreement on issues, could not be formed. The resolution of April, reconstituting a *de facto* Great Coalition, amounted to little more than a truce among the parties for the specific purpose of passing the budget of the Reich and continuing the diplomatic negotiations initiated in September 1928. The cumulative effect of these events was to promote, among both the German policy-making elite and the general public, fatigue with the Weimar system which seemed to permit repeated cabinet crises which were ended only after compromises had been reached, and problems patched over, in lengthy negotiations among party Reichstag delegations.

As Stresemann saw it, the crisis of January-April 1929 was due to the inordinate power of the party delegations which withdrew, or threatened to withdraw, their representatives from the cabinet without regard for the preferences of the majority of the cabinet or the Reichstag. Thereby, the parties exerted excessive influence over the direction of public policy and protected special interests at the expense of what he called the "great and fundamental" questions of state. He was particularly disturbed at the right wing of his own party which wished to withdraw him, the Foreign Minister, from the government after six years of political responsibility in order to represent without compromise the inter-

[28] On the crisis of 1929, its significance, and Stresemann's reaction to it see Gustav Stresemann, *Vermächtnis; der Nachlass in Drei Bänden*, Berlin, 1932-33, III, 427-43; Karl D. Bracher, *Die Auflösung der Weimarer Republik*, Stuttgart, 1957, pp. 287-90; Werner Conze, "Die Krise des Parteienstaates in Deutschland, 1929/30," *Historische Zeitschrift*, 178 (1954), pp. 47ff.; Erich Eyck, *A History of the Weimar Republic*, Cambridge, Mass., 1962-63, II, 195-200; Annelise Thimme, *Gustav Stresemann; eine politische Biographie*, Hannover, 1957, pp. 120-21; Helga Timm, *Die Deutsche sozialpolitik und der Bruch der grossen Koalition im März 1930*, Düsseldorf, 1952, pp. 118-24; Henry A. Turner, Jr., *Stresemann and the Politics of the Weimar Republic*, Princeton, 1963, pp. 244-62.

ests of manufacturers and employers and to join the incipient National Opposition in a campaign of emotional nationalism. Stresemann had a cure for this—the reform of the parliamentary system to curb the power of the Reichstag delegations and the reorganization of his own party to diminish the influence of its right wing. However, he postponed the execution of his projects to attend to what he considered a more pressing problem, the Rhineland-reparation settlement.

Stresemann refused to allow the cabinet crisis of 1929 to obstruct the course of his foreign policy. He could not have the authority of the German experts on the Young committee jeopardized by the defeat of the government which had authorized their negotiations and appointed them. So he sought to avoid a showdown with the government parties, pleading with them to defer any precipitous action until the Rhineland-reparation negotiations were concluded. Moreover, if those negotiations were to succeed, he could not afford to have his party remove him from office midway through them. When it appeared that the DVP might do so, he threatened to resign his offices within the party rather than abandon his ministry and policies. He intended to remain Foreign Minister and to preserve the six-year alliance between himself and the SPD, consistent supporters of his policy, as long as was necessary to settle the issues he had raised in September 1928.

Although aware of the weaknesses of German parliamentarianism, Stresemann was inclined to attribute a large share of the responsibility for the difficulties which he and the Müller government faced to the vulnerability of his foreign policy to criticism. For this he blamed Briand and Chamberlain. In the face of growing popular impatience for results and worn down by poor health, Stresemann's periodic fits of discouragement, despair, and bitterness became increasingly deep.[29] In a letter to D'Abernon on March 30, and in an interview with Bruce Lockhart on April 13, he described his Locarno policy as a thing of the past.[30] The support he had garnered for his policy in 1925 had been dissipated by the Allies' subsequent trifling and belated concessions. He had never imagined that Germany would still suffer military

[29] On Stresemann's emotional depression see Stresemann, *Vermächtnis*, III, 520-21.

[30] Stresemann, *Vermächtnis*, III, 392-95; Lockhart, *Retreat from Glory*, pp. 359-63.

occupation so many years after Locarno. Continued occupation had ruined his hopes; it was "driving everybody back to the German Nationalists. . . . The ground here is slipping away under my feet." Matters were made worse, he complained, by Poincaré's shortsighted policy of using occupation to extract higher reparation payments. If the spirit of Locarno was to survive, Paris must not continue to use occupation as a lever against Germany. The Rhineland must be evacuated and the Saar returned to Germany at the time the experts' report was adopted. After that it would be too late. He threatened to use the same courage with which he had previously promoted the Locarno Treaty to proclaim publicly that Locarno was dead. His former hope, he would add, that Locarno would be the beginning of a new era had been the result of his having been deceived as to the intentions of Briand, and especially of Chamberlain. Thus, in four years Stresemann's tone had changed remarkably. In 1925 he had defended his Locarno policy with vigor, confidence, and optimism. He had remained hopeful through the winter debate. He was less confident in November 1928, when he compared himself to Nora and defended his policy as the only one possible in the face of Germany's financial and military vulnerability. By April 1929, his tone was one of unmitigated complaint.

There was much to complain about. Even though a truce had been declared among the warring partners of the Great Coalition on April 10, opposition to the Locarno policy was growing stronger and spreading from the DNVP to the ZP and his own party. Gone were the hopes at which he had grasped in November 1928. What remained was the chance that the Young committee, at the insistence of the American experts, would recommend a settlement based on what could be paid and transferred out of Germany's own resources—without recourse to foreign borrowing—rather than one based on the creditors' need for annuities of 2 billion marks or more. In the two weeks following April 17, this prospect disappeared also

2. *The Young Conference, February 11-April 17, 1929*

Before the Young conference began, Charles Dawes had predicted that the major task facing the experts would be the reconciliation of German estimates of their country's capacity to pay with creditor estimates of their needs. He was correct. With the opening of deliberations on February 11, German capacity and creditor needs came into immediate conflict; for two months there was no agreement; and by mid-April the conference was at the point of breakdown.[31]

During the first week of the conference, Hjalmar Schacht, President of the Reichsbank and the chief German expert on the committee, gave a masterful and detailed presentation of information on German capacity. He argued that if transfer protection was to be terminated, as Gilbert had suggested in his report of December 1927, then Germany's obligations must be limited to payments of 1 billion marks per year. No more than 2 billion marks a year could be transferred out of the country, Schacht stated, and since Germany was already making interest payments in foreign currencies of 1 billion marks per year, only 1 billion marks remained for the payment of reparation annuities. In addition, he argued that German payments could endure for no longer than thirty years, for Article 233 of the Treaty of Versailles called for the payment of the reparation debt in one generation.[32]

In reply, the creditor experts told Schacht that their governments had been assured that Germany could pay annuities of 2 billion marks or more, and Emile Moreau, Governor of the Bank of France and chief French expert, indicated that the creditors

[31] The committee of experts established no formal secretariat to keep formal minutes of the discussions taking place in the meetings: Denys P. Myers, *The Reparation Settlement, 1930*, Boston, 1930, p. 21. Fred Bate, Young's secretary, was appointed to keep a formal record of the conclusions, decisions, and recommendations taken in the plenary sessions. The texts of the most important documents formally presented to the committee and reports of its deliberations by the German experts can be found in 4050/L138/031242-4051/L138/031822-26. At Kellogg's request, Young sent periodic summary reports to the President and the Secretaries of State and Treasury: FRUS, 1929, II, 1029-65. The best sources on the committee's deliberations are the papers of Owen Young, the correspondence and diary of Thomas W. Lamont, and the papers of Stuart Crocker, an aide to Young, which include his unpublished "personal memoirs," written in Paris during the course of the conference. The best published accounts are Thomas W. Lamont, "The Final Reparations Settlement," *Foreign Affairs*, 13 (1930), pp. 336-63; Etienne Weill-Raynal, *Les réparations allemandes et la France*, Paris, 1947-49, III, 422-38. The members of the committee briefly summarized the course of their deliberations in their final report: Allied Powers, Reparation Commission, Official Documents, *Report of the Committee of Experts on Reparation, 1929*, pp. 7-10.

[32] Lamont papers 178/17 (25 February); FRUS, 1929, II, 1029-34.

could receive annuities of 2.5 billion marks simply by continuing the Dawes plan. He also made clear that the French had no intention of limiting payment to thirty years; he insisted that it extend nearly sixty years, the term of French war debts.[33]

These were at the onset the two opposing positions: 1 billion marks for thirty years versus 2 billion marks or more for sixty years. The terms of agreement would depend in large part on the position taken by those who were neither reparation debtors or creditors—the American experts, Owen D. Young and J. P. Morgan, Jr. Schacht's argument was one designed to appeal to Germany's commercial creditors, the American bankers who might fear that high reparation payments would absorb the foreign exchange necessary to pay the interest on German bonds. Would Young and Morgan be persuaded?

The function of the American experts, as viewed by the American government, was to defend the financial interests of the United States. Washington suspected that the other powers, particularly the British, would attempt to connect the reparation settlement with the war debt problem and revise both sums downward. Washington decided to permit American citizens to participate in the work of the committee; they could then informally explain to the other experts that Germany's reparation debt must be set without modification of existing inter-Allied war debt agreements.[34] This representation was to be unofficial, of course, for the American government wished to avoid all responsibility for the reparation settlement, and elaborate procedures were adopted to save Washington from officially nominating or appointing the American experts.[35]

Those appointed, Young and Morgan, did not regard themselves as defenders of American war debt policy, or as agents of the American government.[36] But, they did assume that European

[33] Crocker memoirs, pp. 14-15; Lamont papers 273/5 (12 February); Hjalmar Schacht, *The End of Reparations*, New York, 1931, pp. 55-56.

[34] 26 October 1928, A. Young to Kellogg, 462.00 R296/2959; 6 November 1928, A. Young to Poole, 462.00 R296/2423½; 2 January 1929, A. Young to Kellogg, 462.00 R296/3060.

[35] The American experts were appointed by the Reparation Commission and the German government: Lamont, "Final Settlement," p. 342.

[36] When, midway through the deliberations at Paris, Mellon tried to get Young to act in defense of American interests, Young and Morgan considered resigning from the committee of experts: 8 April 1929, Stimson to Young, FRUS, 1929, II, 1038-40; 10 April 1929, Young to Hoover, Stimson, and Mellon (draft, not sent), Young papers.

debts to the United States had been settled with the debt funding agreements of 1923-26, and they believed that creditor needs for funds to cover war debt payments were within German capacity to pay. Young told one German diplomat in 1928 that since 1924 he had looked forward to a final reparation settlement of 2 billion marks per year.[37]

As Young knew, annuities of 1 billion marks did not represent limits of German capacity; the figure represented how much foreign currency Schacht was willing to promise to transfer out of Germany each year under all possible circumstances. Schacht himself conceded that annuities of 2.5 billion marks could continue to be collected within Germany, and he admitted privately to Young and Josiah Stamp, the chief British expert, that a sum larger than 1 billion marks could be transferred provided some protection was offered against possible transfer difficulties.[38] To determine just how much Schacht was willing to offer the creditors, Young proposed partial transfer protection. He divided the annuity into two categories: part of each annuity would be unconditionally transferable; it would be paid in foreign currencies in all circumstances. The remainder would be conditionally transferable; in times of financial dislocation, Germany could call upon a Special Advisory Committee which could recommend a two-year moratorium on the transfer of this portion.[39] Young thereby hoped to overcome Schacht's reservations about committing Germany to the payment of anything larger than what could be safely transferred and to set the annuity at a level which represented German capacity to pay under conditions of economic prosperity and financial stability. He told Josiah Stamp that he wanted to raise the total annuity to 2.25 billion marks, of which 1.5 billion would be conditional and 750 million unconditional.[40] By making part of the annuity conditional, Young could meet the German desire for protection; by making part of it unconditional, he could satisfy the major objective of the French, anticipatory payment.

[37] 14 November 1938, Prittwitz to AA, Abt. II, Besetzte Gebrete, Raümung des besetze Rheingebiete, I (German Foreign Ministry, Bonn).

[38] Lamont papers 173/1 (19 February) and 178/17 (25 February); 18 February 1928, Memorandum by Stamp, 462.00 R296/2723; Crocker memoirs, p. 40.

[39] 1 March 1928, Crocker to Mrs. Young, Crocker papers; Crocker memoirs, pp. 43-46. The committee would be advisory to the proposed Bank for International Settlements which was to replace the Reparation Commission as the agency for the receipt and disbursement of the German annuity.

[40] Crocker memoirs, pp. 38-39.

With some measure of transfer protection, Germany could be expected to pay more than 1 billion marks per year, and with the prospect of anticipatory payment, the creditors hopefully would accept less than the 2.5 billion marks of the standard Dawes annuity.[41]

Even after Young divided the annuity, neither side was willing to propose reasonable figures for formal consideration. Schacht privately suggested to Young a thirty-year schedule of payment with a capital value of 28 billion marks, and in spite of the repeated efforts of the American experts, he would not raise his figures.[42] Moreau, on the other hand, continued to insist on the abolition of transfer protection and on annuities of 2.5 billion marks for 58 years. He told Young on March 18 that if the Germans did not accept a settlement of this magnitude, the French Army would stay in the Rhineland, the Dawes annuities would increase with the index of prosperity, and when Germany defaulted, the French Army could move still further into Germany.[43] The British and Italians were unwilling to associate themselves with Moreau's demands, and the creditors were unable to agree among themselves on a reasonable schedule of payments to propose to Germany. When the aggregate claims of all the creditors were totaled and presented to the committee on April 6, it was evident that they were far outside the area of debate: the annuity amounted to 2.9 billion marks if paid over 37 years and 2.67 billion if paid over 58 years. When Schacht heard these figures, he rejected them as impossible and left the room. In the ensuing discussion among the creditor experts, Lord Revelstoke, the second British expert, asked Young to prepare for the creditors a schedule of annuities which they could then present to the Germans.[44]

In preparing this schedule Young's procedure was, as he later explained, to deal first with the requirements of the creditors and then try to match German capacity to them.[45] He based his estimate of creditor needs on a set of principles worked out by the

[41] Lamont, "Final Settlement," p. 345.

[42] Lamont papers 178/1 (6, 14, 15 March); FRUS, 1929, II, 1029-34. On the calculation of capital value see Myers, *Reparation Settlement*, p. 54.

[43] 12 March 1928, Herrick to Kellogg, 462.00 R296/2730; Crocker memoirs, pp. 66-67.

[44] *Ibid.*, p. 69; Lamont papers 173/1 (6 April) and 373/6 (6 April).

[45] Crocker memoirs, p. 118.

American experts in cooperation with Parker Gilbert and his staff. According to these principles, which had been presented to the committee on March 27, France would receive an indemnity of 40 billion francs and revenue to cover her war debt payments (referred to as "outpayments"). Italy would receive an indemnity 10 per cent as large as that of France and her outpayments would be covered. Britain's future war debt payments would be covered. Belgian outpayments would be covered, and she would receive from Germany a sum to cover her "mark claims."[46] From these principles Young derived a schedule of annuities which he submitted to the creditor experts on April 8. The yearly payments began at 1.75 billion marks and remained under 2 billion for the first ten years. They averaged 2.1 billion for the first 37 years, while outpayments and indemnities were paid; then they declined during the next 21 years while Germany paid reparation only to cover creditor outpayments for the term of their debts to the United States.[47] Advantageously, this schedule covered outpayments, provided France with an indemnity, gave Germany a decade of breathing space, and placed the average annuity significantly below the standard Dawes annuity. With the average annuity set at 2.1 billion marks rather than at 2.5 billion marks, the Germans would have no reasonable cause to reject the proposal, Young told the creditors.[48]

However, before the Germans could consider Young's proposal, the creditors themselves rejected it. Then, on April 11, they agreed among themselves on an alternative 58-year schedule with a capital value of 39 billion marks and annuities beginning at 1.85 billion and averaging 2.22 billion for the first 37 years.[49] When they presented this to Schacht on April 13, his face became pale and tense, his voice trembled, he refused even to comment on it, and the meeting broke up.[50] When, at the suggestion of the creditors, the committee reconvened, Schacht sarcastically declared

[46] See above, p. 152, n. 18.

[47] Young's principles, dated March 28 and entitled "Annex 7," Young papers; FRUS, 1929, II, 1034-36; Crocker memoirs, pp. 73-77. Young's proposal, dated April 8 and entitled "Annex 9," Young papers; Lamont papers 273/6 (8 April); Crocker memoirs, pp. 91-92.

[48] Lamont papers 273/6 (9 April).

[49] Creditor proposal dated April 15 and entitled "Annex 10," Young papers; 13 April 1929, Young to Stimson, 462.00 R296/2786; Lamont papers 173/1 (11 April).

[50] Crocker memoirs, p. 105.

that the creditors had made their proposal not as independent financial experts but as four "interdependent experts," allied together in an assertion of claims made by politicians at home. The conference was in danger of ceasing to be a committee of financial experts and becoming a conference of government representatives, he asserted. So far, the committee had only seen a schedule reflecting Allied needs; the time had come, he stated, to approach the problem from the other end, from the aspect of German capacity.[51]

On April 17 Schacht made his proposal—nonvariable annuities of 1.65 billion marks for 37 years only, with a capital value of 26 billion marks. He suggested two alternative methods of payment. Under plan B, the entire annuity would have transfer protection. Under plan A, 450 million marks per year would be paid unconditionally. Schacht made the assumption of these unconditional payments dependent on the improvement of Germany's capacity to transfer. Germany's transfer capacity, he maintained, was hindered by an adverse balance of payments, caused by 1) the need to import raw materials to compensate for the loss of former German colonies, and 2) by the need to import foodstuffs, which was the result of the loss of agricultural lands in Eastern Europe and the decline in the productivity of East Prussia due to its having been "cut off from the Reich." If Germany was to make unconditional payments, he said, "she must be put into a position to create her own colonial raw material producing basis," and "appropriate measures should . . . be agreed upon with the purpose of eliminating [the] detrimental conditions" caused by the territorial settlement in Eastern Europe.[52]

Strictly speaking, Schacht did not explicitly demand the return of Germany's former colonies and Eastern territories. Rather, he called attention to the need to increase Germany's transfer capabilities by removing certain barriers separating Germany from East Prussia and her former colonies.[53] He had, however, been an enthusiastic and naïve advocate of the German case for colonial

[51] *Ibid.*, pp. 110-18; Bate's committee records (15 April), Young papers.

[52] Schacht's proposal dated April 17 and entitled "Annex 13," Young papers; Schacht, *End of Reparations*, pp. 63-71. Also Eyck, *Weimar Republic*, II, 184-86; W. W. Schmokel, *Dream of Empire; German Colonialism, 1919-1945*, New Haven, 1964, pp. 85-86.

[53] Schacht subsequently made much of this rather fine point: Schacht, *End of Reparations*, p. 73.

mandates and for the return of the Corridor and Upper Silesia long before the revision of the Dawes plan was even considered.[54] And soon after coming to Paris, he had informally told the American experts that he would leave the conference and return to Berlin unless the committee agreed immediately to recommend the return of the Polish Corridor, access by mandate to former German colonies, and the reduction of European tariff barriers to encourage German exports.[55] When he then raised the matter for the first time formally in the plenary session of April 17, he was greeted with several moments of dead silence followed by expressions of astonishment and cries of anger and indignation from Stamp, from Revelstoke, from Alberto Pirelli, the chief Italian expert, and from Emile Francqui, leader of the Belgian delegation. Moreau pounded the table and threw his ink blotter; he flatly refused to discuss plan A with its "political conditions"; and he predicted early rejection of plan B with its small annuity and full transfer protection.[56]

To save the conference, Young then suggested that if Schacht seriously desired to base the annuities on an independent economic expert's estimation of German capacity, then the committee should attempt to agree on annuities for the next five, ten, or fifteen years, a short term over which experts could make reasonable predictions.[57] When a subcommittee, chaired by Revelstoke, met to discuss the short term on April 18, Schacht flatly refused to raise the annuity above 1.65 billion marks and indicated that the time had not yet come for a final reparation settlement. Nego-

---

[54] DBFB, IA, I, 200; London *Times*, 26 March 1926; Moritz J. Bonn, *Wandering Scholar*, New York, 1948, p. 303. A summary of Schacht's attitude toward colonies: K. R. Bopp, *Hjalmar Schacht; Central Banker*, Columbia, Mo., 1939, p. 68.

[55] Young was able to persuade Schacht not to carry his demands to the full committee, apparently by assuring him that later in the conference he would seek a sympathetic hearing for them insofar as they touched on economic problems, i.e., the plight of German agriculture and the need for access to overseas raw materials and markets: Crocker's personal records, 16 and 17 February 1928; 1 March 1928, Crocker to Mrs. Young, Crocker papers; 19 April 1928, Lamont to Leffingwell, Lamont papers 178/21; Lamont papers 173/1 (16, 17, and 20 February, 18 March); Lamont, "Final Settlement," pp. 346-47. On 18 February Schacht and Stamp discussed colonies and the Corridor, as well as the Upper Silesian question: 18 February 1928, Wilson to Kellogg, 462.00 R296/2723.

[56] Crocker memoirs, pp. 117-34, 138-40.

[57] *Ibid.*, pp. 134-38.

tiations were broken off, and the subcommittee agreed to call a plenary session of the full committee for April 19, when it would report its failure to reach an agreement and propose that the deliberations of the experts be adjourned. Before the full committee could meet, however, Revelstoke died suddenly, and the final session was postponed until April 22.[58]

3. *Germany Accepts the Young Plan*
April 19-May 3, 1929

On April 17 and 18 Schacht proposed terms for a reparation settlement, imposed political conditions on them, and precipitated a breakdown of the Young conference; and he did all this without previously notifying the German government. Stresemann, Müller, and Hilferding—the three men ultimately responsible for German reparation policy—were naturally surprised by Schacht's action. They were also incensed, for Schacht had agreed to notify the cabinet prior to taking any decisive step in the deliberations at Paris. But, as Hilferding said to the cabinet on April 19, "the German experts had obviously not kept their promise, for the government was presented with the German offer as an accomplished fact." On the same occasion, Stresemann complained that Schacht had not only overstepped his authority as a financial expert, but also acted in defiance of an earlier warning from the Foreign Minister against raising territorial questions. Stresemann had informed Schacht that the colonial and Polish questions were not to be discussed at this time, were not to be raised by anyone other than the Foreign Minister through normal diplomatic channels, and were definitely not to be raised by the German experts at Paris. Stresemann found it "especially depressing" that Schacht had not notified the government in advance, for in his opinion Schacht's action could have far-reaching diplomatic, financial, and political consequences. Insistence on political conditions, Stresemann feared, would break up the conference and enable the creditors to blame that break on Germany. This would isolate Germany diplomatically, deprive the Great Coalition of an opportunity for a diplomatic success, and lead to a collapse of German credit. Foreign lenders, he predicted, would

[58] The committee's negotiations of April 17-18: Lamont papers 273/6 (18 April); the report of the German experts, 4501/L138/031749-54; 19 April 1928, Cabinet Protocol, 1701/3575/780277-79.

stop issuing new credits to Germany, and loans currently in force would be called in.

With so much at stake, the cabinet decided on April 19 to inform Schacht of their opposition to a termination of the deliberations at Paris and their objections to his personal diplomacy. Hilferding quickly wrote Schacht that his action infringed seriously on the authority of the government and notified him that the cabinet wanted to consult with the German experts prior to April 22. The German experts left Paris on April 20 and met with the cabinet in Berlin on April 21. There it was agreed that Schacht would drop his quasi-political conditions so that the April 17 schedule of payments could serve, along with the creditor proposal of April 13, as a basis for negotiation. A press communiqué was then issued reaffirming the experts' freedom of negotiation.[59]

Since the summer of 1928, Schacht's reparation policy had evolved without much consistency. He was initially highly optimistic about the revision of the Dawes plan. He apparently came to Paris hoping to secure payments lower than those acceptable to the Müller government and prepared to reject any proposals unsuitable to him.[60] When the creditor experts rejected his two suggestions—annuities of 1.65 billion marks with either full transfer protection or quasi-political conditions—he was faced with the alternatives of either breaking off the negotiations or trying to shift responsibility for the acceptance of the committee's report from himself to the politicians in Berlin.[61] Schacht showed no desire to break off negotiations, either before or after his April 20-21 trip to Berlin. Instead, he undertook discussions at Paris premised on a 2-billion-mark annuity and induced the cabinet to take responsibility for a settlement on those terms.

On April 18, after the Revelstoke subcommittee had decided to recommend the adjournment of the conference, Schacht agreed to drop his quasi-political conditions, or rather he claimed that

---

[59] 19 April 1929, Cabinet Protocol, 1701/3575/780276-90; 21 April 1929, Cabinet Protocol, 1701/3575/780291-303; Stresemann, *Vermächtnis*, III, 395-401; Eyck, *Weimar Republic*, II, 184-87.

[60] 1 November 1928, Rowe-Dutton to Lieth-Ross, FO. 371/12879/169-72.

[61] As early as March 15, Ferdinand Eberstadt told Crocker that the German experts "were trying in some way to get a report shaped up in such form that they would not have to sign it, but would make the political leaders at home sign it": Crocker memoirs, p. 61.

he had been misunderstood and denied making proposals which could be characterized as political.[62] He also made it clear, privately and publicly, that his proposal of April 17 was not to be considered an ultimatum and that he wished to continue discussions. On April 19, after adjournment had been postponed until April 22, Schacht initiated informal discussions with Pierre Quesnay, Moreau's assistant, on a ten-year schedule, after being warned by Young that annuities of approximately 2 billion marks were the only reasonable basis for discussion.[63] Then, after returning from Berlin on April 22, Schacht took an ambiguous position. Although he insisted that he could not agree to annuities above 1.65 billion marks in his capacity as a financial expert, he authorized Young to prepare a new schedule of payments—after having been told again by Young that the only schedule to which the American experts would give their approval was one with annuities of approximately 2 billion marks.[64]

Young prepared a schedule of payments which, in his opinion, would be acceptable to the American experts, meet the needs of the creditors, and be within Germany's capacity to pay and transfer. Young's schedule, dated April 25, was essentially the same as the Young plan which was finally adopted by the committee a month later. As adopted, it provided for 37 annuities which rose irregularly from 1.7 to 2.43 billion marks and averaged 2.05 billion marks. Of this, 660 million was to be paid and transferred unconditionally; the transfer and payment of the remainder were conditional. In addition, Germany would pay for nineteen years at 1.6 to 1.7 billion marks and for three years at 900 million marks. The present capital value of this schedule was 34-37 billion marks, 40 per cent higher than Schacht's offer but 7.5 per cent lower than the creditors' offer of April 13.[65]

Schacht declined to accept Young's compromise of April 25 on his own authority. The cabinet, he stated, held ultimate responsibility in matters of reparation, and he insisted that the cabinet must act on the proposal—particularly since acceptance of it

[62] 18 April 1928, Schacht to Young, Young papers.

[63] Crocker memoirs, pp. 150-52; London *Times*, 20 April 1928.

[64] 22 April 1929, Memorandum by Schacht, Young papers; Crocker memoirs, pp. 162, 164, 176-77; 30 April 1929, Lamont to Leffingwell, Lamont papers 178/23.

[65] Young's proposals dated April 25 and May 6 and entitled "Annex 17," Young papers; Lamont, "Final Settlement," pp. 347-48.

involved political judgment as well as financial expertise. On the evening of May 1 Schacht, again in Berlin, met with Müller, Stresemann, Hilferding, Curtius, and Joseph Wirth and then with other members of the cabinet.[66] Schacht admitted having tentatively accepted Young's compromise in Paris, but he insisted that he could not give final and formal assent on his own authority. His convictions, he stated, prevented him from accepting the Young compromise or any annuities exceeding 1.65 billion marks; the Young proposal was financially impossible. It was "a purely political document which would handcuff us for generations and leave us no possibility of an independent foreign policy." His recommendation as a financial expert was continuation of the Dawes plan with its advantageous transfer protection, even though it meant, he admitted, the gradual cessation of foreign loans, resulting in deprivation, hard work, and low wages for all segments of the German population.

Having divorced himself from responsibility for accepting Young's proposal, Schacht then tried to get the cabinet to take responsibility for adopting it. He stated that he would sign the Young plan in spite of his convictions; he would compromise himself intellectually "in the interest of the fatherland." He said: "I will sign and keep quiet. I will make no trouble for the government. I will, perhaps, go on a trip or something." He was not prepared, however, to sacrifice what he referred to as his "decency." If he signed, he must be directed to do so in writing by the German government. Presumably, if Schacht signed at the direction of the cabinet, he would not be subject to criticism; Reichstag opposition to the plan would be directed against the government. Not satisfied with Müller's verbal assurance that the cabinet had always protected the German experts and would continue to do so, Schacht insisted on a written statement.[67]

The Müller government was also unwilling to break off the Paris negotiations, but they too attempted to avoid direct responsibility for the acceptance of the Young compromise. Meeting on May 2, after Schacht had left Berlin, they decided to inform Schacht merely that the Young compromise should not be rejected.[68] In writing they limited their liability even further. The

[66] Wirth was Minister for Occupied Areas.
[67] 1 May 1929, Memorandum by Pünder, 1701/3575/780339-57, 58-66.
[68] 2 May 1928, Cabinet Protocol, 1701/3575/780367-74.

telegram to Paris simply stated: "The unanimous opinion of the full cabinet moves in the direction of the meeting called yesterday afternoon by the Chancellor with Ministers Hilferding, Stresemann, Curtius, and Wirth."[69] Although he had already accepted Young's figures in Paris on May 2,[70] Schacht telegraphed the cabinet on May 3, complaining that the wording of their message was "very ambiguous" and asking for a "written explanation."[71] The cabinet met that evening and, after thoroughly debating the Young plan, agreed to send Schacht the statement he demanded. Realizing that otherwise Schacht might well scuttle the Young conference and present the cabinet with another accomplished fact, they sent an immediate and unequivocal answer to Paris accepting the Young plan. Promptness was necessary; otherwise, Curtius stated, "Herr Reichsbankpräsident could make trouble." Clarity was imperative because, as another cabinet member said, "one could never be quite sure of Schacht's attitude."[72]

The decision to accept the Young plan has been called "the most controversial action in the German post-war policy of understanding."[73] It was a decision taken by the cabinet on May 3, and it was taken for a variety of reasons. Ironically, none of those reasons was based on a calculation of Germany's financial and economic capacity. In contrast to what Stresemann and other Germans had told Gilbert and creditor representatives, they privately conceded the impossibility of predicting Germany's capacity with any exactitude. They did not accept the Young compromise because they believed it was within Germany's capacity, nor did they accept it in spite of a belief it was beyond German capabilities. Instead, the Müller government saw

[69] 2 May 1929, Cabinet Protocol, 1701/3575/780373; 2 May 1928, Pünder to Müller, 4050/L138/031148.

[70] Crocker memoirs, p. 196; Schacht, *End of Reparations*, p. 78.

[71] 3 May 1929, Schacht to Cabinet, 1701/3575/780406.

[72] 3 May 1929, Cabinet Protocol, 1701/3575/780396-405.

[73] Otto Meissner, *Staatssekretär unter Ebert, Hindenburg, Hitler; der Schicksalsweg der deutschen Volkes von 1918-1945, wie ich ihn erlebte*, Hamburg, 1950, p. 176. In addition to the sources indicated below, the following analysis of German reparation policy is based on 1 May 1929, Memoranda by Pünder, 1701/3575/780339-57, 358-66; 2 May 1929, Cabinet Protocol, 1701/3575/780367-74; 3 May 1929, Cabinet Protocol, 1701/3575/780375-83; 6 May 1929, Cabinet Protocol, 1701/3575/780431-32; 21 May 1929, Cabinet Protocol, 1702/3575/780571-79; Nachlass Koch-Weser 39/37-49.

no alternative. Rejection of Young's proposal, the cabinet expected, would mean financial chaos for the Reich followed by serious economic, social, and political complications.

The expected financial difficulties were of two types. One was the long-term difficulty mentioned by Schacht on May 1. Rejection of the Young plan would mean the termination of the experts' conference and continued payment of the standard Dawes annuity; the Reich budget, already in great difficulty, would be further strained by large contributions to the standard Dawes annuity; increased taxes and the gradual restriction of foreign credit would result in economic contraction and depression within two or three years. The second difficulty was immediate: rejection of the Young plan could result in the prompt withdrawal of foreign credits from Germany. During the last two weeks in April, when it appeared that the Young conference was in danger of breaking down, the gold and foreign exchange holdings of German banks were diminished by 110 million dollars. This decrease came at a time when the country's credit was under increased strain due to the reduction of the Reichsbank's rediscount rate the previous January and because of cash deficits in the Reich budget. When added to the 100 million dollars withdrawn since the first of the year, the withdrawals of late April forced the Reichsbank to raise its discount rate from 6.5 to 7.5 per cent on April 25 in an attempt to diminish the outflow.[74] German diplomats like Schubert and financial experts like Schacht attributed the withdrawals to an "attack on the mark"—a politically inspired attempt by the French government, operating through the Bank of France, to prompt French banks to withdraw funds from Germany in order to intimidate the German experts and the German government.[75] The French denied this and attributed the gold drain to a lack of confidence on the part of foreign investors in a German government irresponsible enough to scuttle the reparation settlement.

Available evidence indicates that the following factors influ-

[74] Stresemann, *Vermächtnis*, III, 401-402; Stephen Clarke, *Central Bank Cooperation, 1924-1931*, New York, 1967, pp. 165-66; Eyck, *Weimar Republic*, II, 187.

[75] 30 April 1929, Memorandum by Schubert, 2258/4502/120397; Schacht, *End of Reparations*, pp. 88-91, and Schacht, *My First Seventy-six Years; the Autobiography of Hjalmar Schacht*, London, 1955, pp. 238-39.

enced the fluctuation of German exchange reserves in April-May 1929.[76] 1) In the late 1920's the franc was particularly strong among world currencies; during the six months following *de facto* stabilization in December 1926, the Bank of France acquired the largest foreign exchange reserves of any central bank in the world.[77] Reichsbank reserves were, on the other hand, particularly vulnerable to French pressure in April 1929. The flow of funds from the United States had been restricted since mid-1928 because available credit was taken up by the growing speculation on Wall Street. Meanwhile, French banks had substantially increased their short-term holdings in Berlin since late 1928,[78] placing Paris in a position, at politically opportune moments, to withdraw short-term credits, disrupt German finances, and attach political conditions to new loans. In 1924-26 the Americans and British played the game of financial diplomacy and attached semi-political conditions to the granting of loans and credits; in 1929-31 the French were in a position to do so.[79]

2) Emile Moreau was a resourceful and courageous financier. He was a patriotic guardian of French economic strength and political interests who cooperated closely with Poincaré in the formulation of French reparation policy. With Poincaré he had stabilized the franc without assistance from the banks of stable currencies, and he owed no debts—personal or monetary—to Schacht, Mellon, New York Federal Reserve, or to Montagu Norman, the Governor of the Bank of England. Under an agreement negotiated in August 1927, Moreau could not use his foreign exchange to raid the gold reserves of other central banks,[80] but

[76] A pioneer study of this problem: Paul Einzig, *Behind the Scenes of International Finance*, London, 1932, Chap. 6.

[77] Between December 1926 and May 1927 the foreign exchange holdings of the Bank of France grew from 50 to 770 million dollars: Andrew Boyle, *Montagu Norman; a Biography*, London, 1967, p. 227; Clarke, *Central Bank Cooperation*, p. 111; Leland Yeager, *International Monetary Relations; Theory, History and Polity*, New York, 1966, pp. 285, 287.

[78] Clarke, *Central Bank Cooperation*, pp. 148-50, 164-65.

[79] French financial diplomacy in 1931: Edward W. Bennett, *Germany and the Diplomacy of the Financial Crisis, 1931*, Cambridge, Mass., 1962, pp. 7, 248-49, 310, 315-16; Karl E. Born, *Die deutsche Bankenkrise 1931; Finanzen und Politik*, Munich, 1967, pp. 54-56, 64-65; D. S. Landes, *The Unbound Prometheus; Technical Change and Industrial Development in Western Europe from 1750 to the Present*, Cambridge, 1969, pp. 374-75.

[80] Paul Einzig, *The Fight for Financial Supremacy*, London, 1931, p. 88; and Einzig, *Montagu Norman; a Study in Financial Statesmanship*, London, 1932, pp. 89-91.

he had no reservations about transferring funds from other foreign banks to Paris by less direct means. According to his own diary, he considered, on occasion, the use of monetary transfers in order to further the political objectives of the Poincaré government.[81]

3) The evening following Schacht's quasi-political demands (April 17), Quesnay told Young's secretary that 200 million dollars, a sum equal to most of France's short-term holdings in Germany, would be withdrawn by the following noon. This threat was not carried out, however. Schacht threatened to use any reduction of Germany's gold and exchange holdings as evidence of Germany's limited capability to transfer reparation payments, and the French soon decided not to provoke an acute financial crisis in Berlin through a massive withdrawal of short-term credits.[82]

4) By April 19, the day Schacht resumed negotiations with Quesnay, Thomas Lamont, an alternate American expert and a Morgan Partner, was advising J. P. Morgan and Company in New York to increase its credits to Germany, and soon thereafter both Montagu Norman and George L. Harrison, Governor of the Federal Reserve Bank of New York, made it clear to Schacht that they would support the Reichsbank. The French had no reason to reduce their holdings after the Germans accepted the Young compromise, and the immediate crisis passed.[83]

Those who made policy in Berlin in May 1929 were convinced that they were at the mercy of their creditors, and this conviction played an important role in the cabinet's decision to accept the Young plan. Parker Gilbert told Hilferding that a breakdown at Paris would "seriously shake the German economy," and Hilferding subsequently told the cabinet that the events of late April

---

[81] Emile Moreau, *Souvenirs d'un gouverneur de la Banque de France; histoire de la stabilisation du franc (1926-1928)*, Paris, 1954. Also Boyle, *Norman*, pp. 225-27; Lester Chandler, *Benjamin Strong, Central Banker*, Washington, D.C., 1958, pp. 364-65; Clarke, *Central Bank Cooperation*, pp. 115, 164; Einzig, *Behind the Scenes*, Chap. 6, and Einzig, *Norman*, p. 88.

[82] Crocker memoirs, pp. 147-48; Schacht, *Seventy-six Years*, p. 239; 27 April 1929, Lamont to Potter, Lamont papers 179/22.

[83] 29 April 1929, Lamont to J. P. Morgan and Company, Lamont papers 178/23; Crocker memoirs, p. 209; Clarke, *Central Bank Cooperation*, p. 166. On the close association between Norman, Schacht, and New York Federal Reserve see Boyle, *Norman*, pp. 174, 223-24; Edward Francis-Williams, *A Pattern of Rulers*, London, 1965, p. 213.

had convinced him that "Germany had little to expect from a return to the policy of the Dawes plan."[84] Moreover, in a financial crisis induced by decreased credit and continued high reparation payments, Germany would receive little outside help. Those countries which had the resources to aid Germany were her direct or indirect creditors, and they would have to balance their desire to save their debtor against their resentment over Germany's obstruction of a final reparation settlement. Finally, Parker Gilbert was not likely to be of any assistance, for while foreign exchange was leaving the country during the crisis of late April, he did not suspend the transfer of reparation payment in order to protect the mark; he continued to purchase foreign currency in Berlin.

Meanwhile, Germany would suffer greatly from the financial crisis, and the country would be forced to make what Hilferding termed "colossal sacrifices."[85] It was feared that a business recession and unemployment would result from restricted credit. This would, Stresemann believed, present the Russians with an opportunity to renew their efforts to precipitate a Communist revolution in Germany; he thought it "not improbable" that the violent and bloody May Day demonstrations then in progress were an indication of what the future held for Germany at the hands of the Comintern.[86] Budgetary difficulties, unemployment, and popular disturbances would bring down the Great Coalition and necessitate, Wirth argued, "an enabling law or some other dictatorial measure"—an alternative which he considered unacceptable.[87] If Stresemann, Hilferding, and Wirth were correct—and no one in the cabinet disputed them—the German government faced financial crisis, business recession, increased unemployment, social unrest, and political dictatorship. To avoid this, the government unanimously agreed to accept the Young plan. The telegram they sent to Schacht on May 3 stated:

[84] 3 May 1929, Cabinet Protocol, 1701/3575/780399; 21 May 1929, Cabinet Protocol, 1702/3575/780573.

[85] 21 May 1929, Cabinet Protocol, 1702/3575/780573.

[86] 2 May 1929, Cabinet Protocol, 1701/3575/780370. In three days of armed conflict in Berlin beginning on May 1, 23 persons were killed, 73 wounded, and 2000 were arrested. The demonstrators, using barricades and rooftop snipers, were defeated through the use of machine guns, tear gas, and hand grenades. As a result the Communist Party's paramilitary organization, the Roter Frontkämpfer Bund, was dissolved.

[87] 1 May 1929, Memoranda by Pünder, 1701/3575/780355.

The government is convinced that the rejection of Young's proposal has as its unavoidable consequence the wreck of the conference without any assurance that the negotiations will be resumed on either a political or economic basis. If the negotiations fail, the government stands in severe economic and political danger. Therefore, [the government] unanimously believes that the acceptance of Young's proposals is unavoidable.[88]

Although the acceptance of the Young plan was based more on political considerations than on financial expertise, there is little evidence that Rhineland evacuation played any immediate role in the government's deliberations. The Rhineland was not mentioned in the cabinet's discussions. Although the ministers assumed that a reparation settlement would facilitate evacuation, the Young compromise was not accepted as the price of evacuation, and the Germans agreed to the details of compensation prior to any Allied agreement to withdraw from the Rhine. Probably, the cabinet would have had to accept Young's proposal in spite of any compensatory diplomatic gains.

The Müller government strove to avoid the consequences that would follow from a rejection of Young's schedule of payments; this does not mean they regarded the Young plan as an ideal reparation settlement, or that they intended to commit Germany to meet Young's annuities in all events for two generations. Guérard and Curtius told the cabinet that the transfer mechanism of the Dawes plan, controlled by the Agent General, a representative of the creditor powers, had given the mark no protection in late April, and the government agreed that the conditional part of the annuity must have genuine protection from transfer during times of financial difficulty. In their May 3 telegram to Schacht, they made their acceptance of Young's plan dependent on this.

The cabinet did not regard the Young plan as a lasting reparation settlement; instead they agreed that Young's schedule of payments must be revised completely when the political-economic situation changed, a circumstance which Hilferding predicted would take place within ten years.[89] Their only disagree-

---

[88] 3 May 1929, Cabinet to German Experts, 1701/3575/780405; Schacht, *End of Reparations*, pp. 77-78.
[89] 1 May 1929, Memorandum by Pünder, 1701/3575/780352.

ment was over the means by which the plan was to be revised. Guérard and Stegerwald, both Centrists, wanted to insert in the terms of the plan a clause providing for revision. Stresemann and Curtius wanted to rely on diplomatic pressure. Curtius feared that if the German experts demanded a formal revision clause, the Allies would then demand an arrangement providing for revision upward as well as downward. It was more important, he stated, to promote the practical conditions leading to downward revision. The government, he maintained, should act in the manner of Stein and Hardenberg after the Peace of Tilsit. He recalled that by means of "difficult and bitter negotiations," the two Prussian statesmen had succeeded in lowering, and finally cancelling, Prussia's payments to France. Twentieth-century German politicians, he thought, would eventually succeed in reducing the annuity to 1 billion marks.[90] The cabinet finally decided not to mention revision in the telegram of May 3; instead, they sent a separate letter to the German experts asking them to discuss revision at Paris.[91] And in the end, a clause providing for a reduction of payment was incorporated into the Young plan.

In June 1929, after the Young committee had issued its final report, the Müller government accepted the plan as a basis for negotiation with the creditors over political questions—the evacuation of the Rhineland and the return of the Saar. After those negotiations were completed in August, the government defended the plan against a Hugenberg-initiated popular referendum in November-December. Finally in March 1930, the cabinet secured the ratification of the plan by the Reichstag. Throughout this period, the unpublicized position of the government and the Foreign Ministry was that the Young plan was a temporary arrangement: the annuities had been set too high; they were never to be formally acknowledged as a final reparation settlement—"unthinkable," wrote Hoesch; the plan included provision for subsequent revision, and it was the prospect of revision which made

[90] 2 May 1929, Cabinet Protocol, 1701/3575/780371; Nachlass Koch-Weser 39/49; Julius Curtius, *Sechs Jahre Minister der Deutschen Republik*, Heidelberg, 1948, p. 95.

[91] 3 May 1929, Cabinet Protocol, 1701, 3575/880399-405; 3 May 1929, unsigned letter to Berger and Claussen, Handakten Ritter, Reparation, Schriftwechsel zwischen Reichskanzler und Reichsbankpräsident Schacht (German Foreign Ministry, Bonn).

the plan acceptable.[92] Of course, this dictum was not a prominent feature of the government's public pronouncements, and this has contributed to some misunderstanding of German reparation policy. Acceptance of the Young plan was not an error of judgment, an act of treason, or an attempt to purchase evacuation. In an emergency, it was an escape from the detrimental consequences that would follow from rejection of the plan. It was not an ideal, final, and permanent reparation settlement but a temporary resolution to be revised at an opportune time.

In Paris, Schacht gave his approval to the Young plan in conversations with the American experts on May 2-4, and on May 4 it was formally placed before the creditors.[93] The reasons for his approval, Schacht indicated later, were much the same as those which influenced the government: the breakdown of the conference would lead to a severe financial and economic crisis. The 59 annuities fixed in 1929 would never be paid. The Young plan, with its provision for subsequent revision, held out "a whole series of opportunities for an active German reparation policy"; the payments could be considered again at a time when sanctions, such as military occupation and direct controls on German finances, would no longer be available to the creditors.[94]

Schacht accepted the Young plan with much more difficulty than did the government, and beginning in early May 1929, he began to construct an account of the reparation settlement which minimized his own responsibility for the plan, an account which was subsequently published in 1931 in his book *End of Reparations.* Briefly, Schacht alleged that by deception and betrayal, his independent status as a financial expert had been taken from him. Prior to the conference, he asserted, members of the cabinet had agreed with Parker Gilbert to annuities of 2-2.2 billion marks

[92] This position, expressed by Hoesch on August 2, 1929, came to be the one used by Stresemann, Curtius, and Hilferding to justify their reparation policy within official circles: 15 August 1929, Pünder to Meissner, 2241/4498/107822ff. Also, Curtius' statement to Schuman: 31 May 1929, Schuman to State, 462.00 R296/2935.

[93] Crocker memoirs, pp. 196, 203-208; Lamont papers 173/1 (3 May) and 273/6 (4 May).

[94] Speech by Schacht to Reichsverband der deutschen Industrie in Munich: *Vossische Zeitung,* 28 June 1929; 31 May 1929, Poole to Castle, 462.00 R296/3034; Schacht, *End of Reparations,* pp. 79-80, 103, and Schacht, *Seventy-six Years,* p. 243; Bonn, *Wandering Scholar,* p. 308.

without informing him.[95] After coming to Paris, he was surprised to discover that the creditor experts were not independent but were allied together, in collusion with Parker Gilbert, and bound to the positions taken by their governments.[96] When he proposed what he claimed to be a reasonable settlement on April 17, he was "attacked from the rear" by the left-wing press in Germany which falsely characterized his proposal as "political," and the cabinet took from him his freedom to negotiate, insisting that he accept the Young compromise with its higher annuities.[97] Nevertheless,

[95] Gilbert informed Schacht, on April 26, that the German government had declared its willingness the previous autumn to accept annuities of this magnitude: Schacht, *End of Reparations*, pp. 47-48, 54, 56-58. When Schacht informed the cabinet of this on May 6, Müller, speaking for the cabinet, replied that no minister had ever had a conversation with Gilbert in which a figure of 2-2.2 billion marks was discussed. Müller should have stated that no minister had ever agreed to this figure in conversation with Gilbert. For when Schacht checked Müller's statement with Gilbert, the Agent General replied that the Chancellor's statement was "not in accordance with the facts." Gilbert cited his conversation with Stresemann on November 13 in which this figure was mentioned. He also mentioned his October 25 conversation with Müller, Hilferding, and Schacht, thereby implying that it should come as no surprise to Schacht that the reparation settlement would be expensive: 6 May 1929, Schacht to Müller, 4050/L138/031153-54; 8 May 1929, Schacht to Gilbert, 3176/7387/169815; 9 May 1929, Gilbert to Schacht, 3176/7387/169816-17; Schacht, *End of Reparations*, pp. 59-60. Schacht in turn informed Müller on May 10 that Gilbert had contradicted him: 10 May 1929, Schacht to Müller, 3176/7387/169814.

[96] Schacht's conversation with Poole: 31 May 1929, Poole to Castle, 462.00 R296/3054; Schacht, *End of Reparations*, p. 49.

[97] 6 May 1929, Schacht to Müller, 4050/L138/031153-54; Schacht, *End of Reparations*, pp. 74-75 and Schacht, *Seventy-six Years*, pp. 242-43. In spite of Schacht's complaints about his lost independence, he continued to negotiate at Paris without respect to the cabinet at Berlin. He accepted Young's proposal without honoring his promise to inform the cabinet first of the definitive terms of Young's compromise—causing Müller to complain on May 6 that the German experts were keeping the cabinet less well informed than prior to April 17: 6 May 1929, Cabinet Protocol, 1701/3575/780431-32. In response to Schacht's allegations, Hilferding and Curtius drafted a statement of reply which stated that Schacht had strongly urged a final reparation settlement upon the government in September 1928, that he had been informed of the Stresemann-Gilbert conversation of November 13, soon after it took place, and that the cabinet had intervened only when Schacht insisted that he could not take exclusive responsibility for accepting the Young compromise, and then only in response to an urgent telegram from Schacht. The telegram of May 3 was not, they stated, an order to Schacht but merely an assurance that the experts had the complete support of the cabinet in accepting the Young plan: 11 May 1929, Memorandum by Hilferding and Curtius, 1702/3575/780785-89; Stresemann, *Vermächtnis*, III, 382-84. This

Schacht was unwilling to break off the negotiations at Paris or to resign from the committee as Albert Vögler, the second German expert, did on May 17.[98] Therefore, he was faced with the prospect of accepting an agreement that would expose him to intense criticism. Unlike Stresemann and Müller, he was not accustomed to making unpopular political decisions, and he sought to escape from responsibility by viewing himself as the victim of the designs of others.[99]

Having shifted ultimate responsibility from himself to the government, Schacht was tractable and conciliatory at Paris thereafter.[100] However, after May 4, prolonged and serious opposition to the Young plan came from the creditors, who now found themselves called upon to make sacrifices under the scheme proposed by Young and accepted by Schacht. The French were asked to reduce their claim to indemnity; the British were asked to renounce their claim to funds to cover previous war debt outpayments; and the Belgians were asked to surrender their mark claim.[101] It was not until May 29 that agreement was announced, and the report was signed on June 7.[102]

---

statement, approved by the entire cabinet on June 5, was to be communicated to Schacht when the Paris negotiations were concluded: 5 June 1929, Cabinet Protocol, 1702/3575/780788-89.

[98] Vögler, the second German expert, resigned because no provision was made for revision. He believed that Germany's capacity to pay was even more limited than did Schacht and had strong reservations about Schacht's offer of 1.65 billion marks. His agreement to the Young compromise was dependent on an explicit revision clause. When it was rejected, he told Hilferding on May 14 that he could not sign the report. Hilferding persuaded him to change his mind, but a meeting with Fritz Thyssen and the Reichsverband der Deutschen Industrie ended Vögler's weeks of indecision: 21 May 1929, Cabinet Protocol, 1702/3575/780573-77.

[99] For a more sympathetic view of Schacht's behavior at the Young conference see Amos E. Simpson, *Hjalmar Schacht in Perspective*, The Hague, 1969, pp. 32-39.

[100] Crocker memoirs, pp. 292, 297-98.

[101] The final report of the Young committee did not provide a settlement of Belgium's mark claim. It did, however, recommend that the Young plan not become operative until Belgium and Germany had agreed on a settlement. After bilateral negotiations between German and Belgian representatives, a 320-million-mark settlement was reached on July 13: Klaus Pabst, *Eupen-Malmady in der belgischen Regierungs-und Parteienpolitik, 1914-1940*, Aachen, 1964, pp. 481-88; Pierre van Zuylen, *Les mains libres; politique extérieure de la belgique, 1914-1940*, Brussels, 1940, pp. 236-38.

[102] The last month of deliberations: Lamont, "Final Settlement," p. 348, Weill-Raynal, *Réparations allemandes*, III, 433-38.

4. An Analysis of the Plan

The Young plan granted to each creditor, with the exception of Great Britain, an indemnity, a sum to cover war damages.[103] In addition, each creditor, including Britain, was allotted funds to cover what were called outpayments, i.e., their war debt payments to the United States. Outpayments absorbed 74.2 per cent of what Germany was scheduled to pay; 23 per cent was for indemnity.[104] Having failed to get the United States to reduce its claims, the Allied powers succeeded in getting Germany to underwrite their debts to the United States. It was for this reason that the schedule of payments ran for 59 years, the same term as the inter-Allied debt funding agreements.

The schedule was divided into two time periods. During the first 37 years, the payments increased from 1.7 to 2.43 billion marks and covered indemnity, outpayments, and the interest and principle on the Dawes loan of 1924. During the last 22 years, when the annuities covered outpayments only, they diminished significantly and averaged just under 1.7 billion marks. One-third of each of the first 37 annuities—660 million marks—was to be paid and transferred unconditionally. This part was commercialized—made legally subject to sale to the public. Unconditional payments of this magnitude would make available for sale bonds with a face value of 12.6 billion marks which could be marketed, it was estimated, for 8-9 billion marks.[105] As the French were to receive 500 million of each unconditional annuity, they would obtain 75 to 80 per cent of the proceeds of any sale.

To make commercialization possible, the Germans sacrificed all transfer protection over one-third of the first 37 annuities and assumed a total of 59 annuities with an estimated capital value of 34-37 billion marks.[106] The first 37 Young annuities averaged 2.05

[103] In addition to the text of the Young plan, see the following analyses of the plan: J. M. Keynes, "The Report of the Young Committee," *Nation and Athenaeum*, 45 (1929), pp. 359-61; Lamont, "Final Settlement," pp. 348-56; Myers, *Reparation Settlement*, pp. 50-141; Weill-Raynal, *Réparations allemandes*, III, 438-88; Owen D. Young, University of California Charter Day Address of March 24, 1930, Young papers.

[104] The discrepancy represents direct American claims on Germany.

[105] James W. Angell, *The Recovery of Germany*, New Haven, 1929, p. 337; Lamont, "Final Settlement," p. 351.

[106] Total payments, as opposed to present capital value, were 121 billion marks: C.R.S. Harris, *Germany's Foreign Indebtedness*, London, 1935, p. 6.

billion marks. This figure was larger than the 1 to 1.67 billion mark annuities paid between 1924 and 1928, but it was 20 per cent smaller than the standard Dawes annuity (2.5 billion) Germany would have paid if the Dawes plan had remained in operation. During the first decade of the plan, the annuities were below the average figure of 2.05 billion; over the next 27 years they gradually increased to 2.4 billion at the rate of less than 1 per cent per year. The 20 per cent benefit to Germany during the first 37 years involved a greater sacrifice on the part of the creditors than casual observation might indicate. Because more than one-half of creditor reparation receipts went ultimately to the United States, a 20 per cent reduction in German payments meant a 40 per cent reduction in net receipts to the budgets of the creditors. It also represented a saving to Germany which was potentially greater than 20 per cent. Payments of 2.5 billion marks were the minimum Dawes annuity; in normal times they would have been augmented by the prosperity index, which would have, one expert predicted, raised the Dawes annuity to 3.2 billion marks within ten years. If such augmented annuities were projected over 59 years, their capital value was 38 per cent greater than the capital value of the Young plan.[107] In essence, the Young plan differed from the Dawes plan in that the Germans gave up a measure of transfer protection and agreed to pay unconditionally a sum of 660 million marks per year for 37 years in exchange for a reduction in the size of the total annuity during the first ten years. The Young plan, then, represented a significant short-term gain for Germany.

The largest annuities were to be paid from years 11 to 37, and experts expected Germany to meet these payments out of increased tax receipts concomitant with the expansion of the German economy, and without increased taxation. In case the German economy and the revenue of the Reich did not continuously expand, Germany was given certain safeguards. In the event of short-term difficulties, Berlin could, after ninety days' notice, postpone the transfer of the conditional two-thirds of the annuity for as long as two years. And under certain circumstances, the internal payment of one-half of the conditional annuity could be postponed. Although no formal provision was

---

[107] Lamont, "Final Settlement," p. 349; 18 March 1929, de Sanchez to Lamont, Young papers.

made for revision, a Special Advisory Committee, convened at the time of transfer postponement, was authorized to recommend further adjustments in the schedule of conditional payments. In recognition of the *de facto* relationship between the Young plan and the war debt funding agreements, special provision was made for a reduction of reparation payments in the event the United States reduced or renounced its war debt claims. During the first 37 years Germany would receive two-thirds of any such benefit; during the last 22 years Germany would obtain the entire benefit.

The Young plan freed Germany from foreign control. The Reparation Commission was to be abolished, and along with it the machinery by which it received revenue directly from the income of the German railroads, industry, and taxation was abrogated. To administer the receipt and disbursal of the annuities, receive the advice of a Special Advisory Committee on the postponement of the conditional part of the annuities, and aid in the commercialization of the unconditional part of the annuity, the committee recommended the establishment of a Bank for International Settlements.[108] The main security provided the creditors by the Young plan was a special tax on the revenue of German railways, the yearly revenue of which was equal to the total of the unconditional annuity. The remainder of German payments were to come from the budget of the Reich.

Inevitably, the Young annuities were primarily suited to the needs of the creditors.[109] The needs of the creditors, especially the amount needed for the outpayments, were readily predictable and calculable, and could be easily defended against reduction. On the other hand, the payment of 1-1.67 billion mark annuities during the first four Dawes years had not tested German capacity, and the experts of 1929 had available to them no more compelling evidence with which to predict German capacity to pay and transfer over sixty years than the experts of 1924 had possessed. Consequently, there was considerable margin in which German capacity could be roughly estimated and adjusted upward to meet Allied needs. Thus, in setting the sum that Germany was to pay, the creditors were favored, not only by their superior political power, but also by purely financial considerations.

[108] Henry H. Schloss, *The Bank for International Settlements; an Experiment in Central Bank Cooperation*, Amsterdam, 1958, pp. 27-101.

[109] Cf. Jacques Chastenet, *Raymond Poincaré*, Paris, 1948, pp. 281-82, and Chastenet, *Histoire de la troisième république*, Paris, 1952-63, v, 177.

In theory, the members of the committee were independent experts appointed for their technical competence to solve a complex financial problem and to make recommendations for the approval of the governments. This independence was necessitated by the unwillingness of any government to propose a final settlement and by the widely held belief that politicians created difficulties when they discussed reparation; only by taking the problem away from them and putting it in the hands of bankers could it be resolved. However, in practice the deliberations of the financial experts could not be depoliticized, and the discussions of the Young experts were a political negotiation. The issues the experts were asked to resolve were of great political significance, and their recommendations were determinate. The committee's report would, it was recognized, bind the governments involved; no nation could reject the report without uniting the rest of Europe and America against it as an obstacle to peace, understanding, and the final liquidation of the war. In contrast with the Dawes committee, the Young committee brought together creditor and debtor experts. The reconciliation of German capacity and creditor needs required not only financial expertise but also, as Lamont wrote, "an understanding of diplomatic and political expediency."[110] The result was a plan which took into account "all the political factors affecting a final settlement," as Young told the experts at the completion of their labors.[111]

The experts thus had an ambiguous status. Each had to choose between being an impartial expert or a government representative. Moreau chose the latter alternative and at one point flatly declared that he would not sign any report which was not satisfactory to the French government.[112] Young and Stamp chose the former alternative and threatened to resign when their governments sent them instructions.[113] Schacht deliberately sought instructions from the politicians, instructions which were reluctantly given.

The ambiguous status of the experts was of particular consequence for German policy. The Germans had entered into the making of a final reparation settlement hoping that independent experts would impartially examine Germany's capacity, see the

[110] Lamont, "Final Settlement," p. 343.
[111] 7 June 1929, Young to experts, Young papers.
[112] 3 May 1929, Lamont to Leffingwell, Lamont papers 179/9.
[113] On Young's threatened resignation see above, p. 252, n. 36. For Stamp's threat see below, p. 285, n. 19.

merit of the German position, reduce Germany's obligations, and agree to a schedule of payments based on what Germany could transfer without foreign borrowing. When this hope was not realized, Schubert complained of betrayal by "experts and allegedly independent persons," and Stresemann blamed Poincaré and Moreau for turning a conference of financial experts into a political negotiation.[114] Here, too, was fuel for the fire of German disappointment.

[114] 30 April 1929, Memorandum by Schubert, 2258/4502/120396-97; Stresemann, *Vermächtnis*, III, 404.

PART SEVEN

"THE FINAL LIQUIDATION OF THE WAR"
JUNE-JULY 1929

1. *A New Course for British Policy: The Second Labour Government*

On August 6, representatives of Germany and the five principal Allied powers met in Holland, at The Hague, to consider the report issued by the committee of experts on June 7. During the intervening two months the powers prepared for what is commonly called The Hague conference but was at the time grandiosely termed "The Conference for the Final Liquidation of the World War." During June and July there was a flurry of activity through normal diplomatic channels as London, Paris, and Berlin arranged for the time, place, and agenda of the conference, and as the three powers prepared—after years of postponement—to discuss a comprehensive financial and political settlement. Stresemann prepared by announcing to the Reichstag on June 24 that German acceptance of the Young plan would depend on political rewards—the complete evacuation of the Rhineland and the return of the Saar to Germany. The French arranged for their long-term financial security: the cabinet accepted the Young plan on June 19, and on July 21 the Chamber of Deputies ratified the war debt agreements with Britain and the United States. Capitalization and the receipt of prior payment continued to be a matter of concern to Poincaré and Tardieu, and they proposed to delay evacuation until assured of both. Briand, meanwhile, worked to exclude the Saar from the agenda of the conference and to win approval for his Commission of Verification. In both cases he received some support from the newly elected Labour government in England, but on two other significant questions the MacDonald cabinet declined to accommodate Paris. They did not accept the Young plan; and on July 26, shortly before the conference opened, Philip Snowden, the new Chancellor of the Exchequer, told Commons that he intended to modify it at The Hague. And they decided on a Rhineland policy different from Chamberlain's: on July 17 they agreed that under certain circumstances the British Army of the Rhine would be evacuated unilaterally. All three Locarno powers went to the conference in August with firm positions on the major issues; each power had not, however, secured the prior consent of the others. Consequently, some of the major political and financial problems of the Locarno era were to be debated, negotiated, and resolved at the conference itself; and the

Locarno era came to a close with a meeting much less harmonious than the one with which it had opened in October 1925. All three powers contributed to the combat at The Hague. The French and Germans came to no prior agreement on the disposition of the Saar and the Commission of Verification; neither did they agree beforehand on the date and conditions of evacuation. The British made new departures in policy without first consulting Paris or Berlin. As a result, the harmony of the Locarno Triplice was thoroughly disrupted.

In the British general elections, held on May 30, the Conservative Party lost 159 seats in the House of Commons while Labour gained 137, making it the largest party for the first time in history. Although Labour did not have an absolute majority, Liberal support permitted a Labour government to take office on June 5. The election did not turn on any single dramatic issue—in spite of Lloyd George's promise to alleviate unemployment with a New Deal-style public works program[1]—and the results of the polling have been attributed to the swing of the pendulum, to the uninspired campaigning of the Conservative Party candidates, and to the rebellion of the "more intelligent young voter" against "out-of-date, backward-looking leadership." Ineptly, the party in power campaigned against the opposition and went to the voters with the slogan of "Safety First"—safety from general strikes and Labour experimentation with nationalization. On the other hand, the Labour and Liberal parties presented bolder, more positive and attractive programs, capitalized on the apparent fatigue and complacency of the government, and urged the electorate not to reelect candidates of a party which had made no deliberate attempt to deal with widespread and chronic unemployment (11 per cent in 1928).[2] To counter opposition criticism of the Baldwin government, Conservative candidates could not point to a dis-

[1] R. F. Harrod, *The Life of John Maynard Keynes*, New York, 1951, p. 395; Robert Skidelsky, *Politicians and the Slump; the Labour Government of 1929-1931*, London, 1967, pp. 56-61; A.J.P. Taylor, *English History, 1914-1945*, New York, 1965, pp. 267-68.

[2] A. H. Booth, *British Hustings, 1924-1950*, London, 1958, pp. 78-80; William McElwee, *Britain's Locust Years, 1918-1940*, London, 1962, pp. 149-54; Taylor, *English History*, pp. 269-70. Foreign policy played a modest role in the electoral campaign; 56 per cent of the Labour candidates criticized Chamberlain's policy in their election addresses: E. A. Rowe, "The British General Election of 1929," unpublished B. Litt. thesis, Oxford, 1959, p. 299.

tinguished record on domestic affairs or a list of foreign successes. Chamberlain's Disarmament Compromise, his apparent unenthusiasm over general disarmament, the alienation of the United States, the entente with France at the expense of Germany, and the alleged return to prewar secret diplomatic methods were not assets on the hustings. Chamberlain's policy may, it has been suggested, have "cost the Tories many votes."[3]

Baldwin's slogan, "Safety First," was directed against the domestic program of the Labour Party, but it was in foreign affairs that the second Labour government attempted to be most innovative.[4] Labour came to office in 1929 with a preconceived set of foreign-policy attitudes and a "definite program of action."[5] In 1924 the first Labour government had abandoned E. D. Morel's negativistic anti-French and anti-Versailles policy, and at the Birmingham conference of October 1928 the party membership gave formal approval to the more moderate, realistic, and practical policy which Arthur Henderson and Hugh Dalton had formulated during the intervening years.[6] The general precepts of the Henderson-Dalton policy, as put forth in *Labour and the Nation*, have been summarized as follows: "The limitation of national armaments, the eradication of outstanding grievances, particularly in Europe, the arbitration or other pacific settlement of international disputes, and the provision of pooled security against aggression." In the implementation of this policy, the League of Nations was to play a prominent role.[7] Specific policy objectives

[3] McElwee, *Britain's Locust Years*, p. 149. Also David Carlton, "The Anglo-French Compromise on Arms Limitation, 1928," *Journal of British Studies*, 8 (1969), pp. 141-43; Gordon A. Craig, "The British Foreign Office from Grey to Austen Chamberlain," in Craig and Felix Gilbert (eds.), *The Diplomats, 1919-1939*, Princeton, 1953, pp. 43-45; Robert Vogel (ed.), *A Breviate of British Diplomatic Blue Books, 1919-1939*, Montreal, 1963, p. xxi. Chamberlain himself was reelected by a narrow margin of 43 votes; he attributed his near defeat to bad housing conditions in West Birmingham: 31 May 1929, Chamberlain to Mary Carnegie, AC 4/1/1297.

[4] Henry R. Winkler, "Arthur Henderson," in Craig and Gilbert (eds.), *The Diplomats*, p. 318.

[5] Hugh Dalton, "British Foreign Policy, 1929-31," *Political Quarterly*, 2 (1931), pp. 489-90.

[6] Richard Lyman, *The First Labor Government, 1924*, London, 1958, Chap. 10; Henry R. Winkler, "The Emergence of a Labour Foreign Policy in Great Britain, 1918-1929," *Journal of Modern History*, 28 (1956), pp. 247-52, and Winkler, "Arthur Henderson," pp. 313, 315.

[7] Winkler, "Emergence," p. 247. The precepts of Labour foreign policy: Labour Party, *Labour and the Nation*, London, 1928, pp. 14-15, 41-43. A

included the restoration of relations with Russia and the pacification and reconciliation of Germany. The latter, to be achieved by supporting German recovery and equality of treatment, entailed the end of England's special relationship with France, the immediate and unconditional evacuation of Germany, and general disarmament rather than unilateral German disarmament.[8]

Henderson, who was appointed Foreign Secretary in the Labour government, and Dalton, who became his Parliamentary Under-secretary, came to the Foreign Office determined to depart from the policies of Austen Chamberlain and to implement the principles of *Labour and the Nation*. Dalton maintained that during the period since Locarno Chamberlain had done little to prevent war, to achieve lasting peace, and to construct "the new international order." Chamberlain had consistently opposed international arbitration, done nothing to further general disarmament, offered reservations to the Kellogg Pact, shown a preference for old diplomacy, special alliances, and balance of power politics, favored France over Germany, and alienated Russia and the United States. Chamberlain, Dalton wrote, had "persistently and stupidly stifled hopeful beginnings," "blocked the work of the League in every direction," and followed a policy of "wooden unimaginative conservatism" and "defensive timidity and obstruction."[9] Henderson informed Ronald Lindsay, the Permanent Under-secretary, and the rest of the Foreign Office staff in his first meeting with them that there could be too much continuity in foreign policy, and when he and Dalton discovered residues of their predecessor's policy in the papers of the permanent staff, they circulated copies of *Labour and the Nation*, with its lengthy indictment of Chamberlain's foreign policy, through the Foreign Office; and along with the document went the instruction that future policy was to harmonize with the pronouncements therein.[10] For

discussion of them: the works of H. R. Winkler; Michael R. Gordon, *Conflict and Consensus in Labour's Foreign Policy, 1914-1965*, Stanford, 1969, p. 46; Kenneth E. Miller, *Socialism and Foreign Policy; Theory and Practice in Britain to 1931*, The Hague, 1967, pp. 195-96.

[8] Elaine Windrich, *British Labour's Foreign Policy*, Stanford, 1952, p. 74; Winkler, "Arthur Henderson," p. 324.

[9] Hugh Dalton, *Towards the Peace of Nations; a Study in International Politics*, London, 1928, pp. xi, 93, 114. Also Miller, *Socialism and Foreign Policy*, p. 194; Winkler, "Arthur Henderson," p. 317.

[10] Hugh Dalton, *Memoirs*, London, 1953-62, I, 218, 223-24; Mary A. Hamil-

all this, Henderson's innovation was realistic and responsible; it proved to be neither as abrupt nor as extreme as might be inferred from Labour's preelection attacks on Chamberlain and from what Henderson facetiously called "the Bolshevik character of the new administration."[11] His German policy was a case in point.

Henderson avoided taking extreme positions on treaty enforcement and military occupation. Prompt evacuation was necessary, he thought, to the reconciliation of Germany and the peace of Europe; he saw it as one of his primary tasks; and unlike Chamberlain, he publicly recognized that the Germans had a "right" to immediate evacuation because they had fulfilled the provisions of the Treaty of Versailles. However, Henderson did not begin his term in office with the separate withdrawal of British troops; he felt obliged to persuade the French and Belgians to evacuate the Rhine.[12] In a carefully worded passage in the Speech from the Throne, delivered on July 2, the government expressed its hope to withdraw British troops in conjunction with France and Belgium and its expectation that a reparation settlement would make collective evacuation possible.[13] Henderson refused to be swayed by Lloyd George's insistence that evacuation was long overdue and had "nothing to do with" a final reparation settlement.[14] Like-

---

ton, *Arthur Henderson*, London, 1938, p. 284. The text of Dalton's memorandum may be found in his papers in the British Library of Economic and Political Science.

[11] Dalton, *Memoirs*, I, 218. Two members of the Foreign Office staff were able to record in their memoirs that there had been more continuity than innovation during Henderson's term of office: Ivone Kirkpatric, *The Inner Circle*, London, 1953, p. 41; Walford Selby, *Diplomatic Twilight, 1930-1940*, London, 1953, pp. 133-39.

[12] Commons, debates, v. 229, c. 417; Dalton, *Memoirs*, I, 221, and Dalton, "British Foreign Policy," pp. 492-93. Also Catherine Cline, *Recruits to Labour; the British Labour Party, 1914-1931*, Syracuse, N.Y., 1963, p. 97; Winkler, "Arthur Henderson," p. 325.

[13] Commons, debates, v. 229, c. 47.

[14] Commons, debates, v. 229, c. 153. The Liberal election manifesto had criticized Chamberlain's Rhineland policy, although a strong phrase in Philip Kerr's original draft calling for immediate evacuation was deleted by Lloyd George: Kerr papers v. 111, p. 26; v. 425, p. 257; v. 445, pp. 720-21; Lloyd George papers G/12/5/19. Lloyd George raised the Rhineland issue in Parliament at the suggestion of J. L. Garvin, Editor of the *Observer*, who called continued occupation the work of "technical reactionaries" and urged Lloyd George to give moral leadership to the Labour government in the matter: 29 June 1929, Garvin to Lloyd George, Lloyd George papers G/8/5/19.

wise, he rejected the suggestion of members of his own party that he ask Berlin immediately whether Germany might prefer the unilateral withdrawal of the British Army of the Rhine.[15] Henderson's policy, as he explained it to Commons, was to go to the conference and work for collective evacuation at the "earliest moment." But he explicitly refused to commit Britain to continue occupation until the Young plan was accepted, and he reserved the right to evacuate whenever expedient.[16]

The policy of simultaneous evacuation which Henderson pronounced to Parliament was based on the assumption that it would take place promptly. He wanted all British troops out of Germany by Christmas. What he did not announce publicly was that if Paris and Brussels decided to delay evacuation beyond that date, he intended to withdraw British troops unilaterally. The cabinet approved this policy on July 24.[17] Thus, Henderson departed from Chamberlain's German policy; he was prepared, if necessary, to withdraw British forces independently of a reparation settlement and independently of the French.

Henderson's intention to withdraw British troops by December 1929 and his willingness to do so unilaterally was of great importance, for on July 17, a week before the separate withdrawal of British troops was authorized, the cabinet decided to permit Philip Snowden to seek the revision of the Young plan at the impending conference.[18] This raised a set of possibilities which might necessitate separate British withdrawal, thereby ending joint occupation, the primary visible symbol of the entente. It was quite possible that because of British opposition, the Young plan would not be adopted; the Dawes plan would remain in force; the French would not gain the financial security of a final reparation settlement and would refuse to end military occupation. Henderson would then have to break with the French and withdraw British troops separately in order to be out of Germany by December.

It was "the problem of arrears," as it was termed, which pro-

[15] Commons, debates, v. 229, c. 395; v. 230, c. 15. *Labour and the Nation* had called, simply and bluntly, for the immediate and unconditional evacuation of all foreign troops; however, the party's election manifesto made no mention of Germany at all: *Daily Herald*, 1 May 1929.

[16] Commons, debates, v. 229, c. 417-18, 497-98, 854-55.

[17] Cab 23/61/30 (24 July 1929).

[18] Cab 23/61/29 (17 July 1929).

voked Snowden to seek the revision of the Young plan. Since 1922, the British Treasury had made war debt payments to the United States of approximately £200 million more than had been collected from Germany and Britain's other European debtors. The issue at stake in 1929 was whether the British should be allowed to catch up on their "arrears" by receiving revenue from the Young annuities to close this gap. Revenue from the Young plan, when added to British war debt receipts, would cover future British payments to the United States, but it would not cover arrears. Churchill had approved British participation on the committee of experts because he expected the Germans to pay annuities of 2 billion marks, and he expected the British to receive 23 per cent of each annuity—the portion allotted to Britain at the Spa conference of July 1920. The Young experts had set the annuity at 2.05 billion marks, but they had reduced Britain's share to 20.6 per cent. In effect, they took from England the surplus over future payments that would have resulted had the Spa percentages been retained, and they divided it among the other creditors, principally Italy and France. The British experts had accepted this, and Churchill, rather than interfering with their independence and breaking up the conference, had been content to inform the House of Commons on May 9 that the British government would reserve its decision on the Young plan until it was submitted.[19] By his own admission, Churchill was "not a good Shylock": he had little grasp of technicalities; he was bored by long financial negotiations; he had given generous settlements to Britain's debtors; and he had been willing, as he told the cabinet, not to insist on the complete recovery of arrears.[20] His successor was more intransigent.

[19] Commons, debates, v. 227, c. 2310-11; Cab 23/60/21 (9 May 1929). Churchill did inform Stamp of his objections to the proposed settlement in late April, an action which evoked a threat of resignation from Stamp: Crocker memoirs, p. 182. Churchill considered breaking off negotiations if necessary and would have been happy, Stamp told Lamont, if the difficulties made by Schacht put an end to the conference: Cab 23/60/18 (24 April 1929); Lamont papers 173/1 (26 April 1929).

[20] P. J. Grigg, *Prejudice and Judgement*, London, 1948, p. 208; Frederick Lieth-Ross, *Money Talks; Fifty Years of International Finance*, London, 1968, pp. 88, 95; Cab 23/59/48 (29 October 1928); Cab 23/60/48 (24 April 1929). Crewe, who saw Churchill negotiate with the French, reported that the Chancellor "was apt to talk lightly of hundreds of thousands, and even half millions, as matters scarcely worth considering": 14 January 1925, Crewe to Chamberlain, AC 52/179.

Although a nominal socialist, Snowden had very Gladstonian notions about public finance.[21] Professing a desire to protect the British taxpayer, he saw no reason why the Treasury should not receive funds in excess of future war debt payments to cover arrears when the Young plan allotted to the other creditors a similar surplus to indemnify them for war damages. Why should the British sacrifice to benefit France and Italy when they had already reduced their war debt claims on those two countries by 42 and 18 per cent respectively and now had the largest war debt of the three countries? On April 16, during the electoral campaign, Snowden had announced to Commons his belief that the Treasury should spare the British taxpayer by collecting as much as possible from foreign governments; he had criticized the Conservatives for adhering to the Balfour note and stated that the Labour government might repudiate it. Once in office, Snowden informed the House of Commons on July 9, as Churchill had done two months earlier, that the British government was not committed to accept the recommendations of the Young experts. Then, after winning the approval of the cabinet on July 17, he went a step further. On the 26th, he announced to Commons his intention to seek a redivision of creditor receipts from Germany when the governments met at The Hague to discuss the Young plan.[22]

On the eve of The Hague conference, Henderson and Snowden were each prepared to depart from the policies of their predecessors. Each was determined to see new "principles" put into operation, and each was willing to jeopardize the entente to do it. Snowden, like Henderson, regarded the impending conference as an occasion to actually negotiate outstanding difficulties rather than an occasion to adopt previously contracted solutions. He did not secure French consent to the modification of the Young plan prior to the conference. He assumed that his statements to Commons on July 9 and 26 constituted sufficient notice to them. The two men decided on different courses for different reasons, but the effect of each decision was the same: both were set on a collision course with the French.

---

[21] Skidelsky, *Politicians and the Slump,* p. 69.

[22] Commons, debates, v. 227, c. 119-21; v. 229, c. 683-85, c. 1676-83. Henderson, Dalton, and the Foreign Office did not favor Snowden's plans for the revision of the Young plan, but Henderson, intimidated by Snowden, was

2. *Stresemann and the Return of the Saar*

During the nine months following the German démarche of September 1928, Briand had postponed Stresemann's demands for formal Rhineland negotiations with repeated predictions that the financial experts would soon submit their report, and that then the nations of Europe would negotiate "the final liquidation of the war." He first used this hyperbolic phrase on September 16 to refer to the three issues mentioned in the Geneva communiqué, and it subsequently appeared in his speech to the Chamber of Deputies on December 4 and in the joint communiqué issued following the Lugano conversations.[23] Not until mid-1929 did Stresemann show much interest in the term. On June 11, during the League Council Session at Madrid, he and Briand agreed to propose a large international conference to arrange for "the final liquidation of the war." By accepting this formula Stresemann agreed to a simultaneous settlement of three issues listed in the Geneva communiqué and tacitly renounced German claims to unconditional evacuation. Had the Young experts failed, Stresemann would have continued to demand evacuation without compensation,[24] but when they succeeded, he altered his tactic and attached political conditions to German approval of the plan.

If there was to be a final liquidation of the war, Stresemann told Briand at Madrid, The Hague conference must discuss not only the evacuation of the Rhineland but also the return of the Saar to Germany. Briand responded in his characteristic manner: he stated that he had not studied the problem, added that it would not be difficult to resolve, and asked Stresemann to come to the conference prepared to discuss the Saar and to bring the proper experts and documents with him.[25] With this exchange began the only serious discussions of the return of the Saar to Germany which took place between the Peace Conference and 1935.

---

unwilling to oppose the Chancellor in the cabinet meeting: Dalton diary (17 June 1929).

[23] *New York Times*, 17 September, 5 December, and 16 December 1928.

[24] On April 30, when it appeared that there would be no reparation settlement, Schubert told Rumbold that "the Rhineland question must be dealt with in any case." Complete anticipatory evacuation was "extraordinarily necessary for reasons of high politics": 30 April 1929, Memorandum by Schubert, 2258/4502/120396-400.

[25] 22 June 1929, Stresemann to Sthamer, 2546/5138/298737-40. Also 29 June 1929, Nicolson to Henderson, FO. 408/54/2.

To be sure, the Germans had called for the return of the Saar at Locarno, at Thoiry, at Geneva in September 1928, and at Lugano in December; but these were isolated and inconsequential probes. The Madrid conversations introduced a vigorous German campaign which resulted in formal Franco-German negotiations which continued until July 1930. Stresemann had long regarded the return of the Saar as the next issue to be pressed after the evacuation of the Rhine and the revision of the Dawes plan. However, he had postponed any initiative on the question until the Rhineland-reparation negotiations were underway; it was not until late in May 1929 that he decided to tie the Saar to the other issues and demand its return at the conference.[26]

Stresemann's campaign for the return of the Saar, conducted in conversations with the Allies in June and July, was supported by a carefully formulated argument: if there was to be a final reparation settlement which the Germans would accept and execute of their own free will, then the Saar coal mines, which had been transferred to French ownership as reparation for the destruction of French mines, must be restored to Germany. At the same time, political control of the district must be taken from the League of Nations and given to Germany. If the Saar remained under international control after the Rhineland was evacuated, all the resentment and propaganda which had previously been directed against the military occupation would, the Wilhelmstrasse threatened, come to be focused upon foreign control of the Saar. The Saar would become a "focal point of poison," a menace to the policy of understanding. The French counterargument—that the Treaty of Versailles provided for League administration of the Saar territory in order that the population of the district might have the right of self-determination, the right to express their choice of national allegiance in a plebiscite to be held in 1935—was dismissed as nothing more than a "high phrase." Because the Saar population had repeatedly demonstrated its unanimous desire for immediate reunion with Germany, continued League administration was actually a violation of the principle of self-determination. By returning the Saar immediately, without waiting for a plebiscite, the French could spare themselves the

[26] Eugen Mayer, *Skizzen aus dem Leben der Weimarer Republik; Berliner Erinnerungen*, Berlin, 1962, p. 95; Maria Zenner, *Parteien und Politik im Saargebiet unter dem Völkerbundsregime, 1920-1935*, Saarbrücken, 1966, p. 223.

embarrassment of a resounding defeat later. In exchange for the Saar, Berlin would negotiate the repurchase price of the coal mines and provide for continued French access to the raw materials and markets of the area in a spirit of goodwill and accommodation.[27]

The return of the Saar, the evacuation of the Rhineland, the approval of the Young plan—these were the goals of German policy in June 1929. Although the Young plan contained significant short-term advantages over the Dawes plan, approval of it was not an objective which the Müller government could appear to pursue avidly; no German government could seem eager to accept any reparation payment plan. Of course, no German government needed to, because the creditors could be counted on to insist on payment. Similarly, no French government could appear eager to return the Rhineland and Saar, and as a result no French government had yet committed itself to either. Briand had made no specific promises as to when evacuation would take place. Would it be after the Young plan was adopted, after it was ratified, or after the reparation debt had been capitalized? Although Poincaré had repeatedly outlined French claims to financial security, he had never publicly bound himself to evacuation in return; and as late as December 1928, Chamberlain had doubted whether Briand could in fact carry the rest of the cabinet with him for early evacuation. So, in the weeks after the Young experts reported, Stresemann's task was to gain assurance from the French government that Germany would be duly rewarded for its financial cooperation.

On June 19, while stopping in Paris on his return from Madrid, Stresemann had breakfast with Poincaré, Briand, and other members of the French Council of Ministers; and there he tested French attitudes on the Saar and the Rhineland. The day before, the French cabinet had publicly announced its decision to accept the Young plan,[28] and that afternoon Poincaré was to propose ratification of France's war debt agreements to the Foreign

---

[27] Unsigned, undated note of the Saar settlement, 2546/5138/298597-601; 26 June 1929, Sthamer to AA, 2546/5138/298705-707; 1 July 1929, Memorandum by Schubert, 2546/5138/298628-34; 5 July 1929, Schubert to Sthamer, 2546/5138/298579-80; 6 July 1929, Schubert to Hoesch, 2546/5138/298541-49; Zenner, *Parteien und Politik im Saargebiet*, p. 225.

[28] *New York Times*, 19 June 1929.

Affairs and Finance committees of the Chamber of Deputies. To secure ratification of those agreements, Poincaré wanted to be able to assure the Chamber that Germany would accept the Young plan, the source of France's income for war debt payments, and he asked Stresemann to give him that certainty. Stresemann, however, refused to commit himself. Hoesch answered for him, saying that the Germans could not accept the Young plan until it was made clear "what consequences that acceptance would bring." This hint was greeted with silence, and Stresemann left Paris resolved to make no decision on the Young plan until the results of the conference were certain.[29]

The German government could not, however, remain completely silent on the Young plan. In May the DNVP had demanded a Reichstag debate on the plan, and the cabinet had refused to hold one until after the experts had completed their report. The Nationalists persisted, and on June 15 Alfred Hugenberg announced his intention to place before the German electorate a referendum to prevent the Young plan from coming into force.[30] Then on June 20, the Reichsverband der Deutschen Industrie refused to endorse the plan until the political benefits Germany would derive in exchange were certain. Faced with such opposition, the Müller government found it necessary to seek a vote of confidence on the Young plan prior to the conference. The German cabinet accepted the Young plan on June 21 as a basis for negotiation, but made final acceptance contingent upon "the general liquidation of the war."[31] The Reichstag debate followed on June 22 and 24. The DNVP attacked the Young plan, and Stresemann defended it on June 24, not as the ideal settlement of Germany's obligations, but as an improvement over the Dawes plan and the only alternative to a financial crisis—a crisis such as that of 1923—in which Germany once again would be able to offer no defense against the reparation demands of the creditors other than the bravery of her people and their willingness to suffer privation. He also suggested that the government could not guarantee the complete execution of the plan, and that

[29] 19 June 1929, Memorandum by Hoesch, 2546/5138/298741-48.
[30] 31 May 1929, Cabinet Protocol, 1702/3575/780715-16; Gustav Stresemann, *Vermächtnis; der Nachlass in Drei Bänden*, Berlin, 1932-33, III, 407-408; *New York Times*, 16 June 1929.
[31] 21 June 1929, Cabinet Protocol, 1702/3575/780928-31; Stresemann, *Vermächtnis*, III, 408.

he himself believed that the Young annuities would be paid for less than ten years. Finally, he stated that the plan would be ratified only if there was a general liquidation of the war which, he specified, included not only the freedom of the Rhine, but the return of the Saar. The government survived motions of no confidence proposed by the Nationalists, the Nazis, and the Communists, and went to the conference at The Hague with majority support in the Reichstag.[32]

During the next few days Stresemann approached the British, Belgians, and Italians to ascertain their views on the time, place, and agenda of the conference. At the same time, he insisted that the Saar question be placed on the agenda and be discussed and settled simultaneously with the Rhineland and the Young plan.[33] The Belgians and Italians raised no objections to the discussion of the Saar (or the Rhineland),[34] but Henderson was reserved and unaccommodating when Sthamer talked to him on June 26 and 28. Although completely willing to discuss the Rhineland at The Hague, he would not commit himself to negotiate a Saar settlement. His chief concern, apparently, was that the conference not be overburdened by the introduction of too many issues that might interfere with what the British regarded as the chief task of the conference—the modification of the Young plan.[35]

Although it was now apparent to Stresemann that Germany could "scarcely expect energetic English support,"[36] he was unwilling to give up his claim to the Saar, and he continued to make formal acceptance of the Young plan contingent upon its return. He also realized that a Saar settlement would be difficult to obtain without British support, and he decided to meet British objections. In order not to overburden the conference with the details of the Saar settlement, Stresemann decided that he and

[32] Reichstag, *Verhandlungen*, v. 429, s. 94, pp. 2810-14, 2877-84; Stresemann, *Vermächtnis*, III, 408-11; Erich Eyck, *A History of the Weimar Republic*, Cambridge, Mass., 1962-63, II, 203-204.

[33] 25 June 1929, Stresemann to Sthamer, 2546/5138/298715-17.

[34] 25 June 1929, Hortsmann to AA, 2546/5138/298710-11; 25 June 1929, Neurath to AA, 2546/5138/298712-13.

[35] 26 June 1929, Sthamer to AA, 2546/5138/298705-707; 26 June 1929, Henderson to Yencken, FO. 408/53/70; 28 June 1929, Henderson to Nicolson, FO. 408/53/76. A *Times* editorial warned that introduction of the Saar question at the conference would "inordinately complicate its labours": London *Times*, 27 June 1929.

[36] 29 June 1929, Stresemann to Hoesch, 2546/5138/298652.

Briand should merely conclude "an agreement to agree": at the conference Germany and France would agree in principle and commit themselves to conclude a Saar settlement at a later date. Subsequently, experts from the two powers would settle on the repurchase price of the Saar mines, and the League Council would be empowered to decide under what sovereignty the Saar territory would be placed. The resulting settlement would be annexed to the agreement embodying the results of the conference, or put in the form of a League Council resolution.[37] In presenting this change of tactics to the cabinet on June 28, Stresemann softened the blow by depicting Rhineland evacuation as practically assured: "England was for evacuation." Theodore von Guérard alone insisted that the original equal priority of the Rhineland and Saar settlements be maintained; the cabinet approved the "agreement to agree," and the next day Hoesch and Sthamer were instructed to propose it to Paris and London.[38]

Briand—in another of his "painful reversals," as Hoesch called them—refused to begin formal Saar negotiations. The Saar, he maintained, in a conversation with Hoesch on July 1, did not belong on the agenda of the conference for, unlike the Rhineland, it had not been mentioned in the Geneva communiqué of September 16, 1928. Hoesch then reminded Briand of his many promises to liquidate the war and his Madrid suggestion that Stresemann come to the conference prepared to discuss the Saar question. Evasion now became more difficult for Briand. He became "rather upset," Hoesch noted, and replied that Stresemann "must be mistaken on this point." What he had stated, Briand maintained, was that he would be willing to discuss with Stresemann personally any studies of a Saar settlement which the Wilhelmstrasse might prepare. But he categorically denied saying these studies should be brought before the conference and made the subject of formal negotiations. He was, Hoesch reported, "very emphatic on this point" and suggested that "if such divergent interpretations of important conversations were possible, the usual free and easy conversations between himself and the Reichsminister must be abandoned in the future." Pointing out that Briand

[37] 6 July 1929, draft text for a preliminary agreement on the Saar, 2546/5138/298553-54.

[38] 28 June 1929, Cabinet Protocol, 1702/3575/780997-99; 29 June 1929, Stresemann to Hoesch, 2546/5138/298655-56; 29 June 1929, Stresemann to Sthamer, 2546/5138/298673.

"subsequently interprets conversations in a manner convenient to himself," the ambassador suggested to Stresemann, as he had in previous similar situations, that there was nothing to be gained from engaging Briand in an "insoluble conflict over exegesis."

Believing there were better ways to bring Briand to a Saar settlement, methods other "than provoking him to anger by emphasis on his Madrid remarks," Hoesch appealed to the policy of understanding. He urged Briand to pursue "a generous policy" and to continue the general liquidation of the war, of which a Saar settlement was a part. Briand replied frankly: the Council of Ministers would have nothing to do with formal negotiations on the Saar question. Several ministers would "blow up" if the issue were raised. He had "weathered many storms," and he might be able to persuade the cabinet to accept a Saar settlement after a few more tempests, but he could not do so by the time of the conference. Hoesch offered to speak to Poincaré personally about the Saar, but Briand discouraged this, saying that such a conversation would be "very disagreeable." He suggested that the job of convincing Poincaré had best be left to him.[39]

Thus, Stresemann had gone to Madrid in June to prepare for a formal discussion of the Saar at an international conference, and he had returned thinking Briand had agreed to this. Briand thought the two of them had agreed only to informal, bilateral talks such as those they frequently held in Geneva hotel rooms. He did not want countries not sharing France's direct interest in the area to discuss the matter; they might support German claims and leave France in isolation. For this reason, he insisted on the exclusion of the Saar from the official agenda of the conference. His decision was approved by the Council of Ministers in early July, announced in the Paris press on July 5, and then communicated to Hoesch.[40]

The British, too, were unwilling to see the final reparation settlement made dependent on the return of the Saar. Dalton thought the Germans should be content with the Rhineland and not "ask for a second helping with their mouths full."[41] Henderson

---

[39] 1 July 1929, Hoesch to AA, 2546/5138/289604-608; 3 July 1929, Hoesch to Stresemann, 2546/5138/289618-27.

[40] Zenner, *Parteien und Politik im Saargebiet*, p. 223; *Petit Parisien*, 5 July 1929; 6 July 1929, Hoesch to Stresemann, 2546/5138/298533-34.

[41] Dalton diary (23 July 1929).

consulted the Quai d'Orsay, and after doing so decided to support the French position. On July 5 he formally agreed to place the Rhineland on the agenda of the conference, but he declined to do the same for the Saar. The Saar was, he wrote to Sthamer, "entirely distinct" from the two principal problems with which the conference was to deal. He tacitly excluded Britain from the consideration of the Saar at the conference, although he did not exclude the possibility of informal Franco-German talks and reserved the right to state his position on the Saar after their conclusion.[42]

By the time The Hague conference began, Briand had agreed to an exchange of views on the Saar informally with Stresemann; but he had not agreed to conduct formal negotiations—or even to hold conversations between French and German experts—either during the conference or afterward. Nevertheless, on the eve of the conference Stresemann told the cabinet that Briand had been "greatly softened up" during the negotiations of June and July. For his part, Stresemann promised, he would not accept the Young plan until "complete clarity on all political questions had been reached."[43] He and Schubert still hoped that there would be some recognition or mention of these Saar conversations in the final protocol of the conference, and to permit this he hoped that the agenda would mention "the Young plan and associated political questions." The term "political questions" was broad enough to include Saar conversations within the purview of the conference, and vague enough not to offend the French.[44]

3. French Military Security: The Commission of Verification

French diplomats had alluded to a special commission of inspection for the Rhineland since 1924, but it was not until the

[42] 28 June 1919, Tyrrell to Henderson, FO. 408/43/77; 3 July 1929, British memorandum on the Saar, FO. 408/54/7; 3 July 1929, French memorandum on the Saar, FO. 408/54/8; 5 July 1929, Henderson to Sthamer, 2546/5138/298576-77. Also Henderson's statement to the House of Commons on 15 July 1929: Commons, debates, v. 230, c. 10-11.

[43] 2 August 1929, Cabinet Protocol, 1702/3575/781138; Zenner, *Parteien und Politik im Saargebiet*, pp. 233-34.

[44] 2 July 1929, Schubert to Hoesch, 2546/5138/298549; 8 July 1929, Schubert to Neurath, 2546/5138/298535-36; 13 July 1929, Schubert to Hoesch, 1631/3375/732533-42.

meeting at Geneva in September 1928 that Briand insisted on Rhineland inspection with any tenacity; it was not until the Lugano meeting in December that he showed any inclination to make specific proposals; and it was not until early 1929 that a draft agreement for the Commission of Verification proposed at Geneva was drawn up. The draft, composed at the insistence of René Massigli, was dated February 25 and delivered in Berlin and London just prior to the Geneva meeting in March.[45] The Commission of Verification, which had its inception and christening in September 1928, departed in two important respects from the scheme Briand had discussed with Stresemann and Chamberlain in December 1926. It was not to be a standing commission in permanent session, and it was not to reside in the Rhineland or anywhere else in Germany. Rather, it was to be convoked in Geneva in the event one of the Locarno powers alleged that the demilitarized status of the Rhineland had been violated. It was authorized to travel to the Rhineland without a German invitation and there originate inquests, make inquiries, take testimony from witnesses, and conduct on-site investigations. It was to be composed of one civilian representative from each Locarno power and be presided over by a voting president appointed by the League of Nations Council. Its function was to prevent any compromise of French security which might result from the delayed verification of either flagrant or nonflagrant violations of demilitarization. It was also intended to give the French means to investigate violations of such small magnitude that they might hesitate to make them into major political incidents by bringing them immediately before the League Council, violations which might otherwise be ignored until their cumulative effect jeopardized French security. After verifying the occurrence of a violation, the commission would then recommend a settlement by majority decision. This decision would be reported to the League Council and, unless one power raised objections before the Council within a specified period of time, it would be binding on all the Locarno powers.

[45] The draft, along with an explanatory note, was handed to Lindsay on February 27 and to Schubert on March 1: FO. 371/13618/129 and 2258/4502/120330-37. Massigli had earlier given Walford Selby a full description of the proposed Commission of Verification: 21 September 1928, Massigli to Selby, FO. 371/12904/137-40. Massigli's role in the formulation of the proposal: 29 January 1929, Hoesch to Schubert, 2258/4502/120322.

Chamberlain was persuaded that the French would not withdraw from the Rhine until the Commission of Verification was established, and he had favored it, as he had permanent resident inspection in 1926.[46] Hoping that the Germans would accept a British proposal more readily than a French one, he had asked his staff to prepare a verification scheme in mid-January, which he considered sending first to Briand and then to Stresemann.[47] However, when Orme Sargent dissuaded him from taking the initiative,[48] and Tyrrell recommended British support for French proposals, Chamberlain reconsidered; and in mid-February he had urged Briand to dispatch a proposal to Stresemann and himself.[49] Briand did so. Thereafter, Chamberlain continued to commend verification, and at Geneva in March he alone had wanted to discuss the text of Briand's proposal.[50]

Following Chamberlain's departure from office, Briand sought

---

[46] 16 March 1929, Chamberlain to Rumbold, Rumbold papers.

[47] The scheme Chamberlain favored was designed to meet Briand's requirements, and it was remarkably similar to that given to Selby by Massigli in September 1928. The commission was to be permanent and nonresident, but its members would be able to visit the Rhineland and make on-site inspections. However, it differed in one remarkable feature—it offered the Germans reciprocity. The commission would be empowered to investigate military activities on the French side of the frontier as well as in the demilitarized zone. Chamberlain considered giving the draft to Briand for his consideration, and Tyrrell favored this: 18 December 1928, Chamberlain to Tyrrell, AC 55/493; 19 January 1929, Tyrrell to Chamberlain, AC 53/498; undated draft convention composed by Hurst, FO. 371/13618/124-28.

[48] Sargent, a Foreign Office Counselor, persuaded Chamberlain not to dispatch the scheme to Paris. Chamberlain's action, he argued, might be discovered in Berlin; Stresemann would be convinced that Chamberlain had committed himself in advance to the French position; British influence at the Wilhelmstrasse would diminish; and Chamberlain would be placed in an embarrassing position at home. Chamberlain then considered asking Briand if the French wished him to take the initiative and propose his scheme simultaneously in Paris and Berlin: 24 January 1929, Chamberlain to Tyrrell, AC 55/499. But, on the recommendation of Sargent and Victor Wellesly, Deputy Under-secretary, he decided to take no initiative at all: 8 February 1929, Chamberlain to Tyrrell, AC 55/503; Cab 23/60/11 (13 March 1929). As Tyrrell pointed out, Chamberlain's scheme was ill conceived. On the French side of the frontier large numbers of troops were garrisoned, and what came to be called the Maginot Line was to be constructed there. This area was not demilitarized; hence there was no justification for international inspection: 11 February 1929, Tyrrell to Chamberlain, AC 55/504.

[49] 11 February 1929, Tyrrell to Chamberlain, AC 55/504; 14 February 1929, Chamberlain to Tyrrell, AC 50/486.

[50] 7 March 1929, Stresemann to AA, 2258/4502/120353-54.

to win from the Labour government the same support Chamberlain had given him. His efforts were in vain for the Foreign Office staff strongly opposed permanent inspection and was disinclined toward a temporary commission. In mid-June Henderson informed Paris that the only commission he could support was one which would terminate in 1935.[51] Only Tyrrell continued to favor permanent inspection. On June 26 he gave Hoesch the impression that he was still urging Briand's scheme in London. Hoesch, consequently, recommended to Stresemann that Berlin stay in close contact with Henderson in order to "reveal the French disguise in London" and prevent him from being "deluded by the siren songs of Paris."[52]

The German attitude toward the Commission of Verification remained what it had been prior to the French draft proposal of February 25. Berlin found permanent, special inspection of the Rhineland unacceptable. The Center Party threatened to leave the cabinet if Stresemann agreed to it. And their chairman, Ludwig Kaas, led the public attack on the commission, charging that it was one more manifestation of French designs on the Rhineland: denied an autonomous Rhineland at the Peace Conference, the French had used demilitarization and military occupation to interfere in the affairs of the area. Now, with the end of military occupation in sight, they sought to establish a special commission to provide themselves with the means for future intervention.[53]

On the Wilhelmstrasse, the Commission of Verification was seen as a French attempt to give the Rhineland a special international status and to substitute for troops of occupation another form of permanent international control. The commission, it was feared, would amount to foreign dominion; because of the composition of the commission, the German delegate would be forever outnumbered in any votes taken, and Berlin would have little

---

[51] 24 June 1929, Memorandum by Sargent, FO. 408/54/68; 31 July 1929, Memorandum by Howard Smith, FO. 371/13618/121; 13 June 1929, Henderson to Tyrrell, FO. 408/53/62; 21 June 1929, Henderson to Tyrrell, FO. 371/13618/130.

[52] 27 June 1929, Hoesch to Stresemann, 2546/5138/298683-84; 3 July 1929, Hoesch to AA, 2546/5138/298602-603; DDB, II, 202.

[53] Ludwig Kaas, "Zur völkerrechtlichen Sonderstellung der Rheinlande nach der Räumung," *Europäische Gespräche; Hamburger Monatshefte für auswärtige Politik* (May 1929), pp. 222-31. Joseph Wirth, a Centrist and Minister for Occupied Areas, rejected permanent inspection in a published exchange of letters with Kaas: *Germania*, 13 July 1929.

influence over its activities. Regarding those activities, it was impossible to tell, Schubert argued, to what misuse future French governments might put the commission. "The door would be open," Schubert wrote, "to all kinds of chicanery, especially industrial espionage." Stresemann suspected, moreover, that the French would employ the commission to "restrict the economic development of the most highly industrialized area in Europe"; he feared they would interfere with the construction of roads, airports, and railroad lines, platforms, and sidings. The German public, Schubert argued, would never tolerate the Commission of Verification, and French attempts to establish it would only negate the good impression created by the evacuation of the Rhineland. In the formula of the Wilhelmstrasse argument, the Commission of Verification was not only "dangerous" and "unacceptable" but also "superfluous." It was superfluous because machinery to handle non-flagrant violations already existed. They could be discussed through normal diplomatic channels, or if the French found this satisfactory and genuinely desired to manage violations in a conciliatory manner, they could bring the matter before the Franco-German Conciliation Commission provided for in Article 3 of the Treaty of Locarno—a commission on which they were not guaranteed a majority. And if the French desired inspection, they could institute one through the action of the League Council under Article 213 of the Treaty of Versailles.[54]

Because the Commission of Verification had been included in the Geneva communiqué, Stresemann realized that he could not refuse to discuss it at The Hague conference. He did intend, however, to limit its duration to the period prior to 1935, and to this objective he publicly committed himself in his Reichstag speech of June 24.[55] To make the commission nonpermanent was his minimum objective; his maximum goal was to eliminate it completely by proposing the use of existing alternative procedures—particularly the Locarno Conciliation Commission. Since Lugano

[54] Stresemann first characterized the Commission of Verification as "unacceptable," "superfluous," and "dangerous" at Lugano in December 1928; Gaus and Schubert used the terms, and the formula became the standard German reply to the French proposal of February 25: 21 January 1929, Memorandum by Gaus, 2258/4502/120305-308; 4 March 1929, Memorandum by Schubert, 2258/4502/120338-41; 5 July 1929, Schubert to Sthamer, 2546/5138/298578-81. Also Stresemann, *Vermächtnis*, III, 542-43.

[55] Reichstag, *Verhandlungen*, v. 425, s. 94, p. 2814.

he had, in conversations with foreign representatives, rejected the French Commission of Verification, and insisted on discussion of an alternative, although he did not present that alternative himself.[56] Berthelot, at least, responded encouragingly: in late January he told Hoesch that Briand was not enthusiastic about the commission and viewed it mainly as a way of securing public and parliamentary approval for evacuation. He added that it would provide no significant additional security for France and that he personally would not insist on it.[57] Stresemann, therefore, had reason to express his hope to the cabinet on June 28 that "the whole commission idea could be done away with."[58]

Stresemann and Schubert realized that the abolition of all special inspection for the Rhineland depended on the position adopted by England. It was of decisive importance, therefore, that Henderson not be deceived by what was called the "seductive form of the French idea," and Sthamer was instructed on June 29 to "counteract energetically" French efforts.[59] Henderson, in turn, did not commit himself to Briand's Commission of Verification, but he remained willing to accept a commission of limited duration.[60] Stresemann, therefore, expected difficulties at the conference. He would, however, as he told the cabinet on the eve of The Hague conference, initially refuse to agree to any commission of any kind. If he was not successful, his maximum concession would be, he promised the Center Party and the rest of the government, a commission with authority in the Coblenz zone until January 1930 and at Mainz until 1935.[61]

4. Financial Security for France: Ratification of the War Debt Agreements and Advance Reparation Payment

Under the Dawes plan, the payment of reparations was assured by certain semi-political controls. German railroads and industries were mortgaged; bonds were issued and held in trust by the

---

[56] 28 December 1928, Memorandum by Schubert, 2258/4502/120268-69; 28 December 1928, Rumbold to Chamberlain, AC 55/431.

[57] 29 January 1929, Hoesch to Schubert, 2258/4502/120322.

[58] 28 June 1929, Cabinet Protocol, 1702/3575/780998-99.

[59] 29 June 1929, Stresemann to Sthamer, 2546/5138/298673; 5 July 1929, Schubert to Sthamer, 2546/5138/298564-65.

[60] Commons, debates, v. 230, c. 885-88, 1267-68.

[61] 2 August 1929, Cabinet Protocol, 1702/3575/781138-40.

Reparation Commission. Commissioners were appointed for the German National Railroad and the Reichsbank, and foreigners sat on the governing boards of both. The revenues from excise taxes on alcohol, tobacco, beer, and sugar, and the income from customs, were pledged to the payment of reparations and administered by a Commissioner for Controlled Revenues. The Agent General could, and did, issue periodic reports disapproving of the monetary and fiscal policies of the German government.[62] In brief, German finances were in a state of foreign administration and receivership similar to that of countries which had encountered difficulty in meeting their obligations to European creditors during the nineteenth century.

The report of the Young experts called for the abolition of the Dawes controls, leaving only a tax on railway revenues to guarantee the payment of the unconditional annuity. The French were willing to evacuate the Rhineland largely because bonds secured by these unconditional payments could be sold to the public, providing them with advance payment and making continued occupation of less importance. There was, however, no assurance that the French Treasury would receive advance payment even if Germany accepted the Young plan, for the plan merely provided for the posting of bonds and legalized their sale. The experts could not guarantee that the bonds would actually sell. Whether or not the Young plan would succeed and produce cash depended largely on the willingness of American investors to purchase more German securities, which was by no means assured, given the weakness of German finances and the attraction of speculative domestic stocks on Wall Street.

The French were disinclined to give up the guarantee of occupation with no assurance that advance payment would actually take place—especially after hearing Stresemann's statement of June 24 that the Young plan would not last ten years.[63] For some

[62] Harold G. Moulton and Leo Pasvolsky, *War Debts and World Prosperity*, Washington, D. C., 1932, pp. 52-60.

[63] The following discussion of French attempts to link capitalization to evacuation is based on statements by Briand, Berthelot, and Massigli to German, British, and Belgian diplomats: 29 June 1929, Hoesch to AA, 2546/5138/298643-46; 1 July 1929, Hoesch to AA, 2546/5138/298618-27; 3 July 1929, Hoesch to Stresemann, 2546/5138/298532-33; 3 July 1929, Tyrrell to Lindsay, FO. 371/13618/236-38; 15 July 1929, Lindsay to Tyrrell, FO. 371/13618/50; 26 July 1929, Tyrrell to Henderson, FO. 408/54/35; DDB, II, 200, 202.

time Poincaré had insisted that evacuation be postponed until reparation bonds had actually been sold to the public, and André Tardieu, who had become Minister of the Interior in November 1928, expressed similar views in June-July 1929. Neither man was willing to agree to evacuation merely in exchange for German acceptance and ratification of the Young plan. French plans, as Massigli explained them to one British diplomat in early July, were to begin the evacuation of the Mainz zone only after a portion of the reparation bonds had been sold to American investors. London rejected this, refusing to make the Germans pay (in terms of prolonged occupation) for something beyond their control—the possible disinclination of American investors to purchase more foreign securities.

Aware of British and German resistance, Briand hesitated to impose upon Berlin capitalization as a prerequisite to evacuation. He told Hoesch in early July that the Council of Ministers had decided that occupation would be terminated once the Young plan was "put into effect" (*mise en oeuvre*). To the ambassador he interpreted this somewhat ambiguous phrase to mean ratification of the Young plan by all powers, Reichstag passage of the legislation necessary to implement the plan, and the actual beginning of payment. He specifically eliminated capitalization as a condition for evacuation. In the Chamber of Deputies, however, Briand was less specific. When Leon Blum demanded that the government pledge itself to evacuate the Rhineland as soon as the Young plan was adopted, Briand replied on July 16 that evacuation would take place only when the Young plan had been ratified by all powers, and when "it will be really applied" (*il sera réellement appliqué*).[64] By the time of The Hague conference, the French had not won the assent of the other powers to prior capitalization, and their failure was covered over with brief, vague phrases.

Formal assent was not necessary, for a *de facto* connection between evacuation and capitalization could be arranged without the agreement of the Locarnites, and it was. To allow time to test German goodwill and the marketability of the reparation bonds before occupation was ended, it was decided to set the date for evacuation well into the future. Briand informed Hoesch "very

---

[64] Chambre débats, 1929, pp. 2562, 2582; Edouard Bonnefous, *Histoire politique de la troisième république*, Paris, 1956-62, IV, 354-55; Etienne Weill-Raynal, *Les réparations allemandes et la France*, Paris, 1947-49, III, 505-506.

secretly" on July 1 that a date had been set for the completion of evacuation. However, he refused to disclose the date, and he asked that Stresemann not make a serious issue of it at the conference. Subsequent events were to prove that other members of the cabinet had not given up their concern about capitalization, and that Briand went to The Hague in August venturing to extend occupation for more than a year thereafter.

The commercialization and capitalization of the German reparation debt was not the only prerequisite to the financial security Poincaré desired; it was also necessary that France's war debt agreements with the United States and Great Britain be ratified.[65] Ratification of both by the National Assembly was desirable as the *finale* to Poincaré's three-year effort to rationalize French public finances. It was imperative that the Mellon-Berenger agreement be ratified prior to August 1 if France was to avoid paying what amounted to a 400-million-dollar penalty.[66] And ratification without reservations—reservations stating that the debt agreement would be honored only if the Young plan went into effect—was necessary if the United States Senate was to ratify the plan in turn. To meet this deadline and these conditions, Poincaré apparently hoped initially to begin The Hague conference in early July, secure adoption of the Young plan, bring the plan before the National Assembly in late July, and then, with France's reparation income assured, attain ratification of French war agreements before August 1. He told Stresemann at their breakfast meeting of June 19 that the conference should begin on July 5. Stresemann had earlier that same day agreed with Briand to August 5 and objected to Poincaré's earlier date.[67] The German Foreign Minister presumably wanted sufficient time to prepare the other powers for a discussion of the Saar and was concerned

[65] For the considerations which led Poincaré to propose ratification of the Mellon-Berenger and Caillaux-Churchill Debt Funding Agreements and his successful efforts to achieve their ratification, see Bonnefous, *Troisième république*, IV, 348-63; Jacques Chastenet, *Raymond Poincaré*, Paris, 1948, pp. 282-83, and Chastenet, *Histoire de la troisième république*, Paris, 1952-63, V, 178-80; Pierre Miquel, *Poincaré*, Paris, 1961, p. 598; Michel Soulié, *La vie politique d'Edouard Herriot*, Paris, 1962, pp. 319-21; Weill-Raynal, *Réparations allemandes*, III, 489-92.

[66] See above, p. 160, n. 39.

[67] 19 June 1929, Memorandum by Hoesch, 2546/5138/298741-48; 22 June 1929, Stresemann to Sthamer, 2546/5138/298733-34.

only that the conference be completed by September 1 so that Germany could begin to pay the smaller Young annuities on that date. He and Poincaré compromised on July 15, a date which Stresemann welcomed. It was early enough to assure the adoption of the Young plan by September 1, and late enough to make the French negotiate against a deadline of August 1. "It was desirable," he told the cabinet, "that this pressure be utilized."[68] The necessity of having the Young plan accepted quickly could make the French more tractable on political questions.

Poincaré was faced with what Hoesch termed a "really horribly embarrassing situation."[69] If the conference convened in mid-July, the French would possibly be at the mercy of stalling, perpetrated by Stresemann to gain his political demands or by Snowden to revise the Young plan. The only way to avoid being placed at this tactical disadvantage was to secure the ratification of the debt agreements before the conference began. This involved overcoming public opposition to the debt agreements, which seemed to add financial sacrifice to the cost of lives and property sacrificed during the war, and add it at the very time when Germany's obligations were being reduced. It included overcoming hostility toward the United States which was at the time raising tariff barriers against French exports. And it meant the near-impossible task of overcoming growing parliamentary opposition to ratification before all the other governments accepted the Young plan with its coverage of French outpayments. Louis Barthou, French Minister of Justice, even predicted that Poincaré's government would fall if it asked for ratification of the debts before the Young plan had been adopted.[70] The opposition Right might vote against ratification, particularly if there were no assurance of payment from Germany. The opposition Left, including the Radical Socialists, who had left the government in November 1928, might vote against ratification in order to defeat Poincaré. Even if Poincaré succeeded in getting the debt funding agreements ratified prior to the adoption of the Young plan, he was still faced with difficulties. The conference might fail to adopt the plan; he would then either have to repudiate a ratified treaty, or find himself obliged to pay the United States in spite of what

[68] 21 June 1929, Cabinet Protocol, 1702/3575/780928-29.
[69] 27 June 1929, Hoesch to Stresemann, 2546/5138/298684.
[70] 19 June 1929, Memorandum by Hoesch, 2546/5138/298744.

he knew to be Germany's uncertain ability to pay the Dawes annuities. In spite of all these risks, Poincaré finally decided to seek ratification of the Mellon-Berenger agreement prior to the adoption of the Young plan. He would take his chances with the Chamber rather than either be at a disadvantage when he faced Snowden and Stresemann, or pay a penalty to the United States. So on July 1, Briand asked Berlin to postpone the conference until early August.[71]

Poincaré had been preparing for ratification of the debt agreements since June 19. On that afternoon he began the defense of his reparation-war debt policy before the combined Foreign Affairs and Finance committees of the Chamber of Deputies. His technical speeches, which continued almost every afternoon for two weeks, were full of dates and statistics and devoid of literary grace and rhetorical elegance. They exhausted the subject matter, Poincaré himself, and his audience. In spite of his effort, he had difficulty overcoming the widespread fear that France might once again be victimized by her former enemy and her recent allies. Popular resentment against American war debt policy remained high, and Stresemann's Reichstag statement of June 24, suggesting that the Young plan would not last ten years, aggravated suspicion that France was to be deceived. The desire to escape from having to accept long-term debt payments by August 1 with no assurance that they would be covered with income from reparation, reached a high point on June 27. That night Henri Franklin-Boullion charged, in an emotional speech to the Chamber, that France was being forced to consider the Mellon-Berenger agreement "with a knife at her throat." The Chamber, swept by what a member of the American embassy staff called "an emotional outburst of resentment and feeling of impotence," passed a resolution asking the government to seek postponement of the penalty date until December 31.[72] The request, which Poincaré declared to be futile, was made apologetically by Paul Claudel, the French ambassador to Washington, and denied regretfully by Henry Stimson, the American Secretary of State.[73] On July 11, with the August 1 deadline approaching, the Chamber of Deputies

[71] 1 July 1929, Hoesch to AA, 2546/5138/298620.

[72] *New York Times*, 28 June 1929; 1 July 1929, Armour to State, 800.51 W89 France/584.

[73] 28 June 1929, Memorandum by Castle, 851.51/1558; 29 June 1929, Memorandum by Stimson, 851.51/1555.

began full debate on the British and American debt agreements. Even then they had to be defended against amendments providing that they not be ratified at all and that they be ratified only after the ratification of the Young plan. On July 17 Poincaré succumbed to a prostate ailment. Briand, Barthou, and Henri Chéron, who had become Minister of Finance in November 1928, carried on; and on July 21, the Chamber ratified the debt agreements with a margin of eight votes. The Right, although hostile to ratification, voted for it in order to support the government of Poincaré; the Left voted against the agreements, which had been negotiated by the *Cartel des Gauches* in 1926, in order to vote against Poincaré. After a brilliant speech by Briand, the Senate ratified the agreements on July 26.[74] The next day Poincaré resigned, never to return to office. On July 31, the day he entered the hospital for surgery, Aristide Briand received a vote of confidence for what was to be his eleventh and final ministry.

It was not immediately clear what effect the resignation of Poincaré would have on Briand's foreign policy. Briand tried to use the occasion to expand the base of support for his policy by incorporating the Radical Socialists into his new cabinet. However, they refused to enter the government unless given the Ministry of Interior, which Tardieu would not renounce. So Briand retained Poincaré's personnel and went to The Hague, leaving behind a cabinet which included Tardieu, Barthou, and André Maginot. In the period just prior to his resignation, Poincaré had kept these, the nationalists and the Germanophobes, in line behind a policy of evacuation in return for anticipatory payment. As part of this exchange Poincaré had favored no additional compensation; he never supported the Commission of Verification. And he was interested in no greater concessions: when the return of the Saar was discussed, Briand found that Poincaré ceased to be a shield against the Right and became the spokesman for a hostile cabinet.[75] The Premier thus both promoted and restricted Briand's foreign policy. With Poincaré no longer available to protect him, it was possible that Briand would have to be more cautious. On the other hand, it was conceivable that Briand would feel free from restraint because of Poincaré's resignation; his

[74] Chambre débats, 1929, pp. 2554, 2562. Senat débats, 1929, pp. 966-72.
[75] 3 July 1929, Hoesch to Stresemann, 2546/5138/289604-608.

opponents had, after all, lost a leader. It was also possible that Briand's policy would not change. Perhaps Briand and Poincaré did not differ significantly in their policies. Perhaps Briand had only used Poincaré's hesitancy as an excuse for his own doubts about Franco-German understanding. It could be, as Berthelot once put it, that Briand was a man who said "Yes, but," while Poincaré was a man who said "No, however."[76] The conference at The Hague would tell.

[76] 6 March 1928, Memorandum by Schubert, 2544/5138/297367.

PART EIGHT

THE FIRST HAGUE CONFERENCE
AUGUST 1929

1. The Break in the Entente, August 6-11

ON THE first day of The Hague conference, Berthelot philosophically remarked to Schubert that "every conference had to have its crisis." Schubert replied: "Right, but the crisis should not come so early."[1] What was unusual about The Hague conference was that its crisis began so soon and lasted so long. It began on the afternoon of August 6, only five hours after the conference had officially opened, and it was not resolved until August 28, three days before adjournment. Ironically, it was not military occupation or the level of German reparation payments—the two issues that had divided Germany from the other Locarno powers for eighteen months—that stalemated the conference for three weeks and repeatedly brought negotiations to the point of breakdown. Rather, it was a conflict among Germany's creditors over the distribution of reparation payments. The major disputants were not Stresemann, Briand, and Henderson, but Snowden on one side and the finance ministers of the other creditor powers, led by Henri Chéron of France, on the other. Consequently, while the London conference with its display of Anglo-French unity and German cooperation had opened the way to the Locarno era, The Hague conference, rife with open conflict between the three powers, closed the era.

The dispute between the creditors began on August 6 when Snowden rejected the Young plan, charging that it called upon the British to make sacrifices in excess of those to be made by the other creditors, and insisted on three changes in it. His primary demand was that Britain's total reparation receipts be increased. To permit this, he asked not that German payments be enlarged but that the receipts be redistributed among the creditors. He wanted the Spa percentages restored, which would increase Britain's share of the annuity by an average of £2.4 million (48 million marks) and permit some adjustment of arrears. Secondly, Snowden wanted the Spa percentages applied to the unconditional portion of the annuity, which would enlarge Britain's share of it from £900,000 to £6 million. He doubted that Germany would pay the full annuity regularly; the conditional portion,

[1] 6 August 1929, Memorandum by Schubert, 2240/4498/107321-23.

309

which comprised over 90 per cent of Britain's receipts, would be postponed, and once postponed, never recovered. Therefore, he demanded an increase in Britain's share of the unconditional portion, which he compared to a high-grade bond, and a corresponding decrease in Britain's share of the conditional portion, which he compared to common stock in "a perhaps not very sound concern." Lastly, Snowden objected to the provision made in the Young plan for payment in kind. The plan provided for the continuation of payment in kind for another ten years and allowed the recipients to reexport the commodity. Snowden protested this because German payments in coal would depress the market for British coal first in France and Italy, and then through reexport, in countries which were not even parties to the Young plan.[2]

The economic value of Snowden's demands was slight. The £2.4 million per year represented 2 per cent of Germany's reparation bill and was less than one-half of 1 per cent of the annual English budget. However, as Snowden saw it, he was not merely defending a trifling sum at The Hague. His policy was at stake. He intended to end what he called Churchill's practice of "quixotic generosity"; no longer were war debt and reparation settlements to be made by calling on the British Treasury, "the milch cow of Europe," to make the necessary financial concessions. Snowden, a nominal socialist, was fighting to reduce public expenditure and to protect the British taxpayer. A former pacifist and a nominal internationalist, he was, by his own admission, struggling to reassert "the rights and the influence of Great Britain in international diplomacy." Referring to the policy of Baldwin, Chamberlain, and Churchill, he said: "England's foreign policy in the past few years has been so weak that the time has now come for England to resume her place in international relations to which her position in the world entitles her. Other nations have been taking advantage of her weakness, and the moment has

---

[2] Snowden's position: Commons, debates, v. 229, c. 683-85 (9 July 1929), and v. 230, c. 1676-86 (26 July 1929); Philip Snowden, *An Autobiography*, London, 1934, II, 783-85. Also Colin Cross, *Philip Snowden*, London, 1966, p. 236; J. W. Wheeler-Bennett and Hugh Latimer, *Information on the Reparation Settlement; Being the Background and the History of the Young Plan and The Hague Agreements, 1929-1930*, London, 1930, pp. 108-112. The text of Snowden's speech of August 6: Snowden, *Autobiography*, II, 789-91.

come to change all that."[3] Snowden came to The Hague determined to depart from his predecessors, to implement new principles, and set British policy on a new course. This was to be accomplished through the restoration of the Spa percentages and the redistribution of the reparation annuity among the creditors.

Snowden had not discussed his demands with the other creditors prior to the conference; he had merely announced his intentions to the House of Commons on July 26. In the absence of a preconference agreement to modify the Young plan, the other creditors insisted that the conference was an occasion to adopt and implement the Young plan. The experts' report, they correctly pointed out, stated that the Young plan must be accepted or rejected without modification, and on August 7 they refused Snowden's demands of the previous day. The conference was divided into financial and political commissions to deliberate the Young plan and Rhineland evacuation, and at the first meeting of the Financial Commission, held on August 8, Snowden refused to discuss any of the other business of the conference, i.e., the procedures necessary to put the Young plan into operation, until distribution had been modified.[4] A long stalemate began.

For a man who wanted to conduct complex negotiations at an international conference, Snowden was, as Dalton wrote, neither a skilled nor a patient negotiator. He was not merely discourteous; he gave expression to the biting sarcasm and vituperative invective which had long characterized his discourse in cabinet and Parliament.[5] By August 10, he was, by his own admission, impatient with Henri Chéron's unyielding opposition; and to a speech by the French Minister of Finance, once more rejecting Snowden's demand for modification, Snowden replied extempo-

---

[3] Snowden's statement on his principles: *New York Times*, 18 August 1929; Snowden, *Autobiography*, II, 826. For criticism of him by other Labourites see Hugh Dalton, "British Foreign Policy, 1929-31," *Political Quarterly*, 2 (1931), pp. 493-94 and Dalton, *Memoirs*, London, 1953-62, I, 235; Kenneth E. Miller, *Socialism and Foreign Policy; Theory and Practice in Britain to 1931*, The Hague, 1967, p. 206. On Snowden's appreciation of the irony of his situation see P. J. Grigg, *Prejudice and Judgement*, London, 1948, p. 229.

[4] Snowden, *Autobiography*, II, 788-96.

[5] Cross, *Snowden*, pp. 217, 238; Dalton, "British Foreign Policy," p. 494; Denys P. Myers, *The Reparation Settlement, 1930*, Boston, 1930, p. 25; Harold Nicolson, *King George the Fifth; His Life and Reign*, London, 1952, pp. 146-47; Robert Skidelsky, *Politicians and the Slump; the Labour Government of 1929-1931*, London, 1967, p. 67.

raneously, characterizing Chéron's argument as "grotesque and ridiculous" and threatening to leave the conference.[6]

With this statement, the Anglo-French dispute became personal. Chéron was little better suited to negotiate redistribution than was Snowden. The chief of the press department of the German Foreign Ministry described him as a "fat, excitable man, anxiously concerned about his position."[7] He took the terms "grotesque" and "ridiculous," which received great attention in the Paris press, to apply to himself personally. His anger was aroused, and his representatives came to Snowden and demanded an explanation. On the morning of August 11, in a private meeting, Snowden offered an apology; Chéron accepted it; the two men exchanged courtesies; and some atmosphere of good humor was restored to the conference.[8] This spared the conference from immediate breakdown but brought the two sides no closer to agreement. Neither Snowden nor Chéron was willing to yield. In fact, a battery of threats was leveled at Snowden. He did not flinch.

In 1929, the Bank of England, like the Reichsbank, was vulnerable to the pressure of French financial diplomacy. Following the stabilization of the franc in December 1926, the Bank of France had acquired large sterling reserves held on deposit in London. If these deposits were converted to gold in London and the gold shipped to Paris, the dollar-gold reserves of the Bank of England would be diminished and British credit would be squeezed. Moreau thus held what has been called "a vise-like grip on the London money market."[9] Even without making direct gold purchases in London, Moreau could conduct financial diplomacy by indirect and untractable methods: he could increase the flow of gold from London by maintaining a discount rate higher than that of London; he could encourage French banks to sell sterling;

[6] Snowden, *Autobiography*, II, 796-98; 10 August 1928, Financial Commission, stenographic notes, 2241/4498/107505-45.

[7] Walter Zechlin, *Pressechef bei Ebert, Hindenburg, und Kopf; Erlebnisse eines Pressechefs und Diplomaten*, Hannover, 1956, p. 82.

[8] 11 August 1929, unsigned note, 2241/4498/107588; Snowden, *Autobiography*, II, 798-99, 803. In the official minutes of the conference the words "grotesque" and "ridiculous" were changed to "wholly inaccurate": David Carlton, *MacDonald versus Henderson; the Foreign Policy of the Second Labour Government*, London, 1970, p. 43.

[9] Andrew Boyle, *Montagu Norman; a Biography*, London, 1967, pp. 189, 223-24, 227, 238.

he could even sell it himself through agents. Whether Moreau did or did not sell sterling for political reasons cannot be established with exactitude; but in early July 1929, with Snowden's demand for Young plan revision, gold began to drain from London to Paris; and by August 5, the day before The Hague conference began, Norman was telling the Treasury that Britain might well be forced off the gold standard.[10]

Less than a week later, the Bank of France threatened to make Norman's nightmare come true. About August 10, Quesnay came to Lieth-Ross at The Hague and stated that unless Snowden withdrew his objections and accepted the Young plan, all the sterling held by the Bank of France in London (£240 million) would be converted to gold and transferred to Paris. Lieth-Ross regarded this as a "political bluff"; the French, he reasoned, had no interest in seeing the collapse of the pound. He abruptly dismissed Quesnay along with Pirelli and Franqui, who had accompanied him— the "blackmail party" as he called it. As in April, Quesnay did not carry out his threat, and no massive withdrawals from London took place. However, the steady and rapid drain begun in July continued, unabated by Lieth-Ross's indignation and bravado. By August 16, British gold reserves had fallen below the established minimum normal requirement. In all, London lost to Paris gold reserves valued at £26.6 million (129 million dollars) between July and October, and on the eve of the Wall Street crash, English reserves stood at a low point for the 1920's.[11]

Even the threat of intervention and repudiation by his government did not move Snowden. The cabinet and the House of Commons had approved Snowden's plans for the Young plan modification, and he made this known to the other delegations at The Hague on August 8. But, he did not tell them that he was bound by the cabinet to consult London before taking any action that might lead to a breakdown of negotiations.[12] Snowden was not free to scuttle the conference if his demands were not met; MacDonald was free to intervene, and he could be expected to do

[10] Stephen Clarke, *Central Bank Cooperation, 1924-1931*, New York, 1967, pp. 32, 166-67; Henry Clay, *Lord Norman*, London, 1957, p. 252; Paul Einzig, *Behind the Scenes of International Finance*, London, 1932, Chap. 6, p. 52; Skidelsky, *Politicians and the Slump*, p. 116.

[11] *New York Times*, 17 August 1929; Clarke, *Central Bank Cooperation*, pp. 150, 166; Einzig, *Behind the Scenes*, pp. 49-50.

[12] Cab 23/61/29 (17 July 1929); Snowden, *Autobiography*, II, 785, 795.

so. The Prime Minister had a strong interest in foreign affairs; he was an experienced negotiator of reparation settlements; he did not like Snowden; he did not favor the Chancellor's Young plan policy; and he did not intend, he indicated to Dawes and Lamont on July 31, to have the British government block ratification of the plan.[13]

The possibility of intervention came about when Parker Gilbert, J. P. Morgan, Jr., and Thomas Lamont, all of whom were in England at the time, came to the conclusion that The Hague conference could be saved only through MacDonald's efforts. On August 9, Moreau and Quesnay, who were in daily telephone contact with the Americans, informed them that the conference was within days of a breakdown. Lamont passed this information on to MacDonald, who was vacationing in Scotland. At MacDonald's invitation, Lamont and Morgan drove to Edinburgh where they met with the Prime Minister and Montagu Norman on August 10.[14] Norman and the Americans pictured for MacDonald the consequences of a breakdown in negotiations: Germany would collapse financially; the French would withdraw their deposits from London; England might well be forced off the gold standard. Norman and the others urged the Prime Minister to go to The Hague and restrain Snowden. MacDonald then dispatched a telegram warning Snowden of the dangers of a breakdown or adjournment, reminding him that he was bound to consult the cabinet prior to taking any precipitate action, and suggesting that he—MacDonald—come to The Hague, or that someone come from The Hague to London for that consultation.[15] The telegram was sent to the Treasury Office in London, where an inexperienced clerk, unable to find a copy of the correct code, called The Hague on the telephone and read it in English. The telephone lines at The Hague were tapped, and the possibility that MacDonald's message might become known provided Snowden with the opportunity to refuse to invite MacDonald to The Hague and

[13] Charles Dawes, *Journal as Ambassador to Great Britain*, New York, 1939, p. 44.

[14] Lamont papers 173/1 and 180/30 (9 August); 12 August 1929, Lamont to Young, Lamont papers 180/31.

[15] Lamont papers 173/1 (10 August); 10 August 1929, Sthamer to AA, 2241/4498/107552; Dalton, *Memoirs*, I, 235-36; Snowden, *Autobiography*, II, 799.

also to escape from control. Snowden wired MacDonald immediately:

> The consequences of any leakage of this message may be disastrous. So far my main task has been to convince the foreign delegations that I am not bluffing and have been speaking with the full authority of His Majesty's Government and with the complete approval of the country at large. . . . I very much fear that my task of reconciling the Young Plan with British interests has become almost impossible. The only chance seems to me immediate issue by you of a statement that I have the fullest support both of yourself and of every member of the Government in the position which I have taken up and which I intend to maintain.[16]

MacDonald "caved in," as Dalton put it: he replied the same day assuring Snowden that he had the support of the Prime Minister and the whole country.[17]

As a result of MacDonald's abortive intervention, Snowden and the other creditors, who came to be called the "sacrificing powers," were brought no nearer agreement. If anything, the resolve of each side was stiffened. MacDonald's first telegram did become known to the other delegations; they now knew that the British government was divided, that Snowden was not free to break up the conference, and that he might concede to them if his bluff were called.[18] On the other hand, Snowden had demonstrated to MacDonald that he would not tolerate interference, and he remained determined to show the sacrificing powers that London supported him and that he would not retreat.[19] Thus, as the second week of the conference began on August 12, both sides remained equally intractable. And as the minister-delegates had reached no agreement by making formal statements in meetings of the Financial Commission, it was decided to substitute informal discussions among lower level officials.

[16] *Ibid.*, 800-801.

[17] Dalton, *Memoirs*, I, 236; Snowden, *Autobiography*, II, 801.

[18] 13 August 1929, Sthamer to AA, 2241/4498/107703; 13 August 1929, Memorandum by Schubert, 2241/4498/107683, 686-87; Carlton, *MacDonald versus Henderson*, pp. 44-45.

[19] Against the wishes of Henri Jaspar of Belgium, the chairman of the conference, Snowden released the text of MacDonald's second telegram to the press on August 10: Snowden, *Autobiography*, II, 801-802; *New York Times*, 12 August 1929.

With no assurance that the finance ministers would adopt the Young plan, Briand was unwilling to conduct serious negotiations on the evacuation of the Rhineland—either in formal meetings of the Political Commission or in informal conversations with Stresemann. On August 8, in the first session of the Political Commission, he carefully made evacuation dependent on permanent financial security for France. He did advance one step, however. The Rhineland would be evacuated, he promised, when there was a reparation settlement "which can be put into force at once." No French minister had ever made this promise formally. Poincaré had always insisted that a financial settlement must precede evacuation, but he had never explicitly stated that evacuation would necessarily follow. And Briand's assurances had heretofore been private and informal. Briand stated that since he had promised evacuation there was no need for further discussion; and he refused to discuss specific dates for evacuation in the Political Commission until the Financial Commission had accepted the Young plan.[20] Thus, the parallel negotiations, which Briand had promised in September 1928 and then postponed until after the Young committee had reported, did not take place at The Hague.

Henderson regarded the end of military occupation as a more urgent matter. It was, he told the Political Commission, more necessary than a reparation settlement to "bringing about that general appeasement which we so ardently desire."[21] On August 9 he told Briand privately that the entire British Army of the Rhine would be evacuated between September 15 and Christmas. He admitted that there was a long-standing Anglo-French agreement to evacuate simultaneously, but he did not agree to postpone British withdrawal until the French were ready; instead, he urged Briand to evacuate along with the British. Coerced, Briand agreed to begin the evacuation of Coblenz on September 15, but he refused to name a terminal date for French occupation.[22]

Henderson thus departed from the practices of Austen Chamberlain. He came to an international conference without having agreed with Paris on how to handle German demands. At The

[20] 8 August 1929, Political Commission, stenographic notes, 2240/4498/107364-75; 8 August 1929, Memorandum by Schmidt, 2240/4498/107347-51.
[21] 8 August 1929, Political Commission, stenographic notes, 2240/4498/107362; Mary Agnes Hamilton, *Arthur Henderson*, London, 1938, p. 316.
[22] 9 August 1929, Henderson to Lindsay, FO. 371/13619/197.

Hague he exerted British leadership in Anglo-French relations. By August 9 he and Snowden had put an end to the most significant element of the Anglo-French entente—British deference. If Paris declined to accept the reversals of roles and refused to follow London's lead, the entente would come to an end.

The extent to which Henderson was willing to strain the entente is clear from the conversation he had with Stresemann on August 9, an hour after he spoke with Briand. Stresemann told the British socialist that he and the Social Democrats would have to resign if The Hague conference did not yield a decision on evacuation, and Müller's cabinet would be replaced by a government of the radical Right. In reply, Henderson promised to withdraw from the Rhineland by Christmas even if no reparation agreement was reached at the conference. He did not consider himself bound by Chamberlain's private assurances to Briand, for he professed to have no information relating to the Rhineland-reparation nexus other than the Geneva communiqué of September 1928.[23]

Briand initially withheld from Stresemann the promise made to Henderson to begin evacuation on September 15.[24] Instead, he told the German Foreign Minister on August 10 that the evacuation of the Coblenz zone would begin soon after the National Assembly ratified the Young plan, in late October he thought, and be completed quickly. He refused, however, to give any date for the evacuation of the Mainz zone. When Stresemann pressed him, stating that he could not return to Berlin without the date on which all foreign troops would be off German soil, Briand became vague and evasive with his Locarno partner of four years. He indicated that logistical problems would prolong the withdrawal of the large numbers of French troops in the Mainz zone, and he promised to discuss a terminal date for evacuation with his military experts when they arrived at The Hague the following week (August 11-17).[25] Briand procrastinated because he could not risk having Paris discover that he had agreed to end occupation by a definite date without being assured of financial

[23] 9 August 1929, Memorandum by Schmidt, 1313/2368/493078-81.

[24] In fact, Briand subsequently tried, without success, to get the British to delay their evacuation: 11 August 1929, Phipps to Sargent, FO. 371/13619/195-96.

[25] 10 August 1929, Memorandum by Schmidt, 1338/2406/507693-97; 10 August 1929, DD to AA, 2241/4498/107586-87.

security. Might he not be recalled from The Hague as he had been from Cannes? Subsequent events suggest that he was willing to extend military occupation long after the ratification of the Young plan in order to have time to capitalize the German reparation debt and to build fortifications along France's borders. Like most French politicians, Briand was unwilling to abandon military occupation before providing for financial and military security.

Stresemann saw no reason why occupation should be prolonged because of the intransigence of Snowden and other conditions beyond Berlin's control. And that evening at a press conference he restated his demand for evacuation regardless of the outcome of the financial negotiations, pointed out the disagreement between England and France on this matter, and predicted that Henderson would stand firm against Briand.[26]

The first week of The Hague conference produced political alignments unusual for the Locarno era. Briand found himself alone and facing the united opposition of Stresemann and Henderson, and Snowden separated himself from the representatives of the other Locarno powers and alienated the French. The nationalist press in Paris even talked of the end of the Entente Cordiale.[27] The second week of the conference was to bring Snowden no closer to agreement with the sacrificing powers, and the gap separating Briand from Stresemann and Henderson was to widen further. By August 19, Stresemann was threatening not to sign the Young plan and to end the policy of understanding with France, and on the same day Henderson was to declare that the British Army of the Rhine would be withdrawn from Germany unconditionally and unilaterally.

2. The Locarno Powers Divided, August 13-21

The foreign ministers, like the finance ministers, decided that their differences were too great to be dealt with in large formal meetings, and after August 12 the Political Commission did not meet for three weeks. Instead, representatives of the four Rhineland powers (Britain, France, Belgium, and Germany) met to discuss evacuation and the Commission of Verification. On

[26] Gustav Stresemann, *Vermächtnis; der Nachlass in Drei Bänden*, Berlin, 1932-33, III, 548.

[27] *L'Echo de Paris*, 11 August 1929.

August 13 Henderson opened the first of these meetings by stating that Ramsay MacDonald wanted to announce to the League Assembly in September that evacuation was underway. Therefore, the evacuation of British troops would begin by September 15 and be completed by Christmas. Paul Hymans, the Belgian Foreign Minister, added that Belgian troops could also be withdrawn by the end of December. In an attempt to preserve the unity of the occupying powers, Briand then announced a concession and proposed a compromise. He was prepared to begin evacuation before the Young plan was ratified; the French Army of the Rhine would leave Coblenz along with the British and Belgian troops between September and December. The evacuation of the third zone would then begin after the Young plan had been ratified and gone into effect in late October. Then Briand proposed that the three powers, having begun their withdrawal together, should end it simultaneously. Although he declined to name an end date for French occupation, he admitted that evacuation might take a long time, and he asked that some English and Belgian troops remain in the Mainz zone until all French troops had left. Henderson and Hymans rejected Briand's proposal for a common Rhine policy; instead, they granted Briand three or four days to consult his military experts and inform the Rhineland powers of the end date for French evacuation.[28] Stresemann, meanwhile, did not aid Briand in his efforts to reconcile the policies of the occupying powers. Once more he informed the press of the differences between the Allies, and he disclosed Henderson's intention to withdraw British troops no matter what the outcome of the conference.[29]

August 13, the day Briand promised to name an end date for occupation, was a day of optimism at The Hague. Snowden had apologized to Chéron the day before, MacDonald's first telegram was common knowledge among the delegations, and Briand and Berthelot expected Snowden to give way under further pressure from London.[30] However, during the next three days there was to be no further intervention from London, no weakening of Snowden's resolve, and no agreement between him and the sacri-

[28] 13 August 1929, Memorandum by Schmidt, 1632/3375/733066-73 and FO. 408/54/47; 14 August 1929, DD to AA, 2241/4498/107760-61; DDB, II, 210.

[29] Stresemann, *Vermächtnis*, III, 552-53.

[30] See above, p. 315, n. 18.

ficing powers. Consequently, Briand could not give the Rhineland powers a terminal date for occupation.

Snowden was not swayed. MacDonald and the Foreign Office staff remained anxious about the situation at The Hague, and the Prime Minister urged Thomas Lamont, the ablest conciliator among the Americans, to go to the conference. Snowden, however, let Lamont know that he would not be welcome, and on August 14 MacDonald concluded that he would have to allow Snowden full powers of negotiation and decision.[31] Henderson disapproved of Snowden's intransigence but was unable to influence him. When he tried to sway Snowden by threatening to leave the conference, Snowden called his bluff, and Henderson remained—frustrated. Henderson's personality and office put him at a great disadvantage: he could not transgress his code of personal loyalty and thwart his cabinet colleague, nor could he defy the tradition that the Treasury, not the Foreign Office, controlled war debt and reparation policy.[32] Meanwhile, Snowden had the support of William Graham, the third cabinet member at The Hague, and the enthusiastic endorsement of outraged taxpayers, and fervent patriots at home.[33] Convinced he was defending high principles, Snowden refused to negotiate; he did not approach the others; he expected his opponents to come to him, and when they did, he insulted them.[34] Thus, a Chancellor of the Exchequer had taken over control of Britain's European policy and sharply altered its direction from the course set by Chamberlain five years before. On the evening of August 14, after an ultimatum from Snowden, the sacrificing powers submitted to him a written statement of their position. Snowden found it unacceptable.[35]

To Briand, it now seemed that Snowden would remain obstinate to the end, and that the conference would produce no agreement. Meeting with Stresemann on August 16, he refused to name a terminal date for occupation, gave difficulties with his military experts as the reason, and promised a definite date on August 19. Stresemann, convinced that Briand was only using his generals

[31] Lamont papers 173/1 (8, 11, 13 and 14 August); 14 August 1929, MacDonald to Lamont, Lamont papers 180/31; Carlton, *MacDonald versus Henderson*, p. 54; Dawes, *Journal as Ambassador*, pp. 50, 53, 54.
[32] Grigg, *Prejudice and Judgement*, pp. 228-29; Cross, *Snowden*, pp. 238-39; Dalton, "British Foreign Policy," p. 494.
[33] Cross, *Snowden*, pp. 239-40.   [34] Dalton, *Memoirs*, I, 235-36.
[35] Snowden, *Autobiography*, II, 803-808.

as a pretext for not committing himself, asked him to name an approximate date, and suggested April 1, 1930. Briand refused.[36]

Although the conference continued, no significant progress toward agreement was made by August 19, and Snowden himself now considered a breakdown in negotiations a real possibility for the first time.[37] Briand, equally uncertain as to the outcome of the financial negotiations, told Stresemann in private conversation on August 19 that, contrary to his promise of August 16, he was unable to name a date for the termination of occupation. He and his military experts could not agree on a date, he stated, and he had asked a member of the General Staff to come from Paris to resolve their differences. Perturbed at these delays, Stresemann became insistent. He threatened to deny Briand the attainment of financial security, stating that the ratification of the Young plan was in jeopardy. When Briand stated that publication of the date proposed by his military advisers would arouse the German public, Stresemann replied that the German public would be more angered if a date were not given immediately. He asked Briand to give him an approximate date "personally and confidentially."

Briand surrendered. For the first time, he discussed specific terminal dates for occupation with Stresemann. His military experts had initially suggested an evacuation period of eighteen months (April 1, 1931). At Briand's insistence, they had reduced the period first to fifteen months (January 1, 1931) and then to six months. However, the six-month period would begin only with the end of winter, which Briand dated as March 31. Thus, the evacuation of Mainz would not be complete until September 30, 1930, provided the Young plan was ratified, of course. Briand added that he personally believed occupation would be ended by mid-July 1930, with the exception of the Trier to Landau sector of the Franco-German border, which would remain occupied until the end of October.[38] These dates were strictly confidential. Stresemann did not mention them to the other members of the German delegation, and Briand did not repeat them at the meeting of the Rhineland powers which took place later the same day.

[36] 16 August 1929, Memorandum by Schmidt, 2241/4468/107868-70; 17 August 1929, DD to AA, 2241/4498/107908.

[37] Snowden, *Autobiography*, II, 809-10.

[38] 19 August 1929, Memorandum by Schmidt, 2241/4498/107983-89; 20 August 1929, DD to AA, 2241/4498/108048-50.

There, he continued to maintain that the French public would object if the end of evacuation were announced before the Financial Commission reached agreement on the Young plan.[39]

Stresemann rejected the dates named by Briand in their private conversation of August 19. That same day, following the meeting of the Rhineland powers, he sent a personal letter to Briand—an uncommon action. In it he described the "shattering impression" the October date would make on the German public, appealed to their personal relationship and their joint pursuit of the policy of understanding, and urged Briand to shorten the evacuation period to April 1. Unless Briand did so, Stresemann would not, he threatened, submit the results of the conference to the German cabinet; he would not sign the Young plan; and he would not continue the policy of Franco-German understanding.[40]

The reasons Briand gave to Stresemann for the one-year lapse between the conference and the end of occupation were those of military logistics. He stated, in the first place, that new barracks had to be built in France to receive the army of occupation; old ones had to be renovated; quarters had to be found for commissioned and noncommissioned officers. If evacuation were hurried, if the Army of the Rhine were returned before places were prepared for each unit, personnel might be shuffled, established units broken up, and the cadres, so vital to France's reserve army, would be weakened. Secondly, no troops could be moved during the winter months, which Briand specified as December 1 to March 31. The reason for this, he explained, was the experience of the previous winter when 350 troops had died from influenza after their officers had forced them to parade and maneuver in zero-degree weather. As a result, Paul Painlevé, the Minister of War, was compelled to promise the Chamber that in the future large-scale, wintertime troop movements would be avoided. At The Hague Briand pointed to Painlevé's promise and the lack of barracks as the reasons the evacuation of the 50,000 French troops in the Mainz zone could not begin for six months (March 31) and not be completed until six months later.[41]

[39] 19 August 1929, Memorandum by Schmidt, 2241/4498/107997.

[40] Stresemann, *Vermächtnis*, III, 555-57; Eugen Mayer, *Skizzen aus dem Leben der Weimarer Republik; Berliner Erinnerungen*, Berlin, 1962, p. 92.

[41] 8 August 1929, Memorandum by Schmidt, 2240/4498/107347-51; 15 August 1929, Memorandum by Schubert, 2241/4498/107787-91; 16 August 1929,

Stresemann's own military expert informed him that there were sufficient barracks already available in France and that, with proper planning, it was logistically possible to withdraw all French forces and their supplies in two or three weeks.[42] He and Schubert therefore rejected Briand's explanation. In Stresemann's opinion, Briand was "advancing . . . absurd arguments" and relying on "finessing tactics."[43] Emulating Snowden, Schubert described Briand's statements as "laughable" and "grotesque." It would be understandable, he told one French delegate, if Briand delayed the completion of evacuation out of consideration for his political opposition in France, but to attribute the delay to military logistics was to use what Schubert regarded as a transparently shabby pretext.[44]

Stresemann insisted on promptness, both in deciding on the date and in carrying out the evacuation process. And his insistence, along with his rejection of Briand's logistical argument, was put by Schubert to Berthelot on August 13 and to Louis Loucheur, a French delegate at The Hague, on August 21. He and Stresemann were disturbed, Schubert said, at the way the Rhineland negotiations were "creeping along." If Briand used pretexts and delays, if he haggled over the details of evacuation, if it seemed to the German people that evacuation was an ill-willed compromise arrived at after long and painful negotiation, then ratification of the Young plan would be jeopardized and there would be a "severe and disastrous break" in the policy of under-

Memorandum by Schmidt, 2241/4498/107863-70; 16 August 1929, Memorandum by Schubert, 2241/4498/107983-89. Also 21 August 1929, Memorandum by Schmidt, 2241/4498/108113. The furor over the casualties of 1928-29: 18 and 19 March 1929, Herrick to State, 851.00/1009; 6 April 1929, Heingartner to State, 862.00/2458; Jean Raymond Tournaux, *Sons of France; Pétain and de Gaulle*, New York, 1964, pp. 65-67.

[42] 8 August 1929, Schubert to Köpke, 1631/3375/733006; 18 August 1929, Memorandum by Geyer, 2241/4498/107950-53; 26 August 1929, Geyer to DD, 2242/4498/108278; 27 August 1929, Memorandum by Geyer, 2242/4498/108317.

[43] Stresemann, *Vermächtnis*, III, 568. Stresemann's use of the word "finesse" in this context leaves no doubt that he meant the term to denote duplicity, an attempt to conceal one's intended course of action from one's opponent in order to gain the advantages offered by dissimulation. It is, therefore, probable that he had a similar meaning in mind when he used the word in his *Kronprinzen-Brief*: 7 September 1925, Stresemann to Crown Prince, 3168/7318/159875.

[44] 20 August 1929, Memorandum by Schubert, 2241/4498/108039; 21 August 1929, Memorandum by Schubert, 2241/4498/108100-102.

standing. Only prompt evacuation would convince the German people that France had made a real concession; only if the Rhineland problem were settled in an "elegant manner" could evacuation "be used as an argument for the goals of the Franco-German understanding"; only a beneficent gesture could convince the Germans "that the French had behaved themselves and could be relied upon."[45] From his own statements, and those made by Schubert at his instruction, it is evident that Stresemann was convinced, despite almost four years of periodic, confidential conversations, that Briand was deceiving him. What was at stake, as he saw it, was whether or not Briand and the French could be trusted. If not, he would, as he threatened in his personal letter of August 19, end his efforts at Franco-German understanding.

Did military logistics make the postponement and the prolongation of evacuation imperative? It did not in the British case. In October 1928, General William Thwaites, Commander of the British Army of the Rhine, and the staff of the War Office in London had made plans for a six-month evacuation period and maintained that winter was not suited to troop movements. But, Austen Chamberlain and Laming Worthington-Evans, Secretary of State for War, insisted that political considerations take precedence over military ones and demanded a three-month period. Thwaites consented in March 1929, and when later instructed by London to do so, he immediately drafted orders for evacuation.

Why did the French behave differently? Could not French troops be transported in the winter, as British and Belgian troops were to be? Couldn't they be moved in less than six months? (In spite of its size, the French Army of the Rhine eventually evacuated Coblenz between September and November 1929, and withdrew from Mainz in six weeks during May-June 1930.) Could not Briand have overruled the army as the British government did? Why did he appease his own military at the expense of the policy of understanding and the entente? It is difficult to define French Rhine policy at The Hague—Briand's motivations and his relations with his military—without access to the files of the French Army and Foreign Ministry. However, from the evidence available, it seems that the logistical reasons offered by Briand to Stresemann were of little importance in determining the pace of

[45] 13 August 1929, Memorandum by Schubert, 2241/4498/107681-86; 21 August 1929, Memorandum by Schubert, 2241/4498/108098-103.

evacuation; Loucheur admitted as much to Stresemann in Briand's presence near the end of the conference.[46] Briand was probably moved by other considerations: if the end of evacuation was delayed a year or more after The Hague conference, both the sale of reparation bonds and the construction of the frontier fortifications, which were to be called the Maginot Line, could be begun in the meantime. Thereby a politically unpleasant contingency could be avoided: the Briand government could not be charged with withdrawing the Army of the Rhine before arranging for advance reparation payment and before beginning the preparation of French defenses.

If the French Army left the Rhine promptly, the Briand government would sacrifice the *couverture* afforded by military occupation before it was replaced by other measures. In August 1929 French military capability was essentially what it had been in 1927: the army was being reduced in size and reorganized, and construction work had not yet been started on the Maginot Line. The year 1928 had been spent studying the technical problems of fortification; it was not until January 1929 that Painlevé had brought the War Ministry's plans before the Council of Ministers; and at the time of The Hague conference, the National Assembly had not approved the project.[47] Without fortifications, could the covering troops be asked to protect France from an *attaque brusque* without controlling the Rhine River?

The opposition to early evacuation was led by General Henri Mordacq, the man who had written the occupation clauses of the Treaty of Versailles. Mordacq had served in the Army of the Rhine until 1926, and there his notions about the incorrigibly aggressive and militaristic disposition of what he called "the German mentality" were reinforced through years of personal observation.[48] He concluded that the Germans not only were capable of launching an *attaque brusque* but intended to do so. And he feared the consequences of a French foreign policy which

[46] Julius Curtius, *Sechs Jahre Minister der Deutschen Republik*, Heidelberg, 1948, p. 90.

[47] Paul-Emile Tournoux, *Haut commandement, gouvernement et défense des frontières du nord et de l'est, 1919-1939*, Paris, 1960, pp. 128-30, 133-35, and Tournoux, "Les origines de la ligne Maginot," *Revue d'histoire de la deuxième guerre mondiale*, 9 (1959), p. 13.

[48] J.-J. Henri Mordacq, *La mentalité allemande; cinq ans de commandement sur le Rhin*, Paris, 1926, pp. 275-76.

he thought assumed German sincerity, was directed only at Franco-German understanding, and was conducted by politicians without his knowledge of German military capability and bellicosity.[49] In October 1928, shortly after Briand and Poincaré had made public their willingness to discuss early evacuation, Mordacq formed an organization which he called The National Committee Against the Evacuation of the Rhineland and the Abandonment of the Saar.[50] At the same time, he published a pamphlet entitled *L'évacuation de la Rhénanie?*, the main points of which received wide circulation just prior to The Hague conference in an article in the *Revue des deux mondes*. In these works he argued against early evacuation in terms similar to those put forth by Foch, in 1926-27: because the French Army was in the midst of reorganization and work on the fortification of the frontier had not yet begun, the occupation of the Rhineland was France's only safeguard against German aggression. To withdraw the Army of the Rhine would be a "crime of high treason" against France and against Poland, which would be "literally surrendered" to Germany. It would be an invitation to the immediate repeal of the Versailles Treaty and lead, sooner or later, to another European war. However, if occupation were continued for six more years, there would be time to train a new, strong, and confident French Army and to construct fortifications on the eastern frontier. For these reasons, Mordacq concluded, evacuation must continue at least until 1935.[51]

Mordacq's views were supported by Foch until his death in March 1929, by Clemenceau who discussed Mordacq's manuscript with the author before it was published, and by Alexandre Millerand, former President of the Republic, who spoke against evacuation before the Senate on July 24, 1929.[52] However, most members of the French policy-making elite accepted the notion of evacuation in exchange for financial compensation; indeed, it was against what he called "a conspiracy of silence" that Mordacq

---

[49] Mordacq, *L'évacuation de la Rhénanie?*, Paris, 1928, pp. 5, 18, 23-24.

[50] Mordacq, *Clemenceau au soir de sa vie, 1920-1929*, Paris, 1933, II, 202.

[51] Mordacq, "L'évacuation anticipée de la Rhénanie," *Revue des deux mondes*, 51 (1929), pp. 768-69, 775, and Mordacq, *L'évacuation de la Rhénanie?*, pp. 6, 19-20, 24.

[52] *L'Echo de Paris*, 1 March 1929; Mordacq, *Clemenceau*, pp. 150-51; Chambre débats, 1929, pp. 918-20.

launched his campaign.[53] Although Briand had no desire to continue occupation to its full term, he did act as if he expected
trouble from his military were he to schedule the complete withdrawal of French troops before the Chamber approved construction of the fortifications. At The Hague he told Stresemann that
the strip of German territory along the French border from Trier
to Landau would be evacuated last in order to allow time for the
preparation of the Maginot Line. One-sixth of the Army of the
Rhine, 10,000 men, would remain in this area several months after
the rest of the Rhineland was evacuated.[54]

By postponing and then prolonging evacuation, it was possible
to assure French financial security too. Advance reparation payment—through the public sale (capitalization) of a portion of the
German reparation debt—was the chief benefit the French would
derive from the Young plan. If Briand returned from The Hague
having agreed to withdraw French troops by a certain date, but
with no promise that advance payment would begin by a specified time, he would be vulnerable to criticism at home. Might not
Tardieu state that Briand had surrendered occupation with no
assurance of capitalization? At The Hague Briand could not simply insist that the bond sale precede or accompany evacuation—
neither the British, Belgians, nor Germans would agree—but he
could postpone the completion of evacuation for one year, during
which the first installment of reparation bonds could be sold and
their marketability established. The importance of capitalization
was not far from Briand's mind at The Hague.[55] But, instead of
telling Stresemann that evacuation was to be postponed until German reparation bonds had proved salable, he spoke of immutable
logistical considerations which would protract the evacuation
process until September-October 1930.

In the end, the postponement of evacuation into the summer of
1930 was to prove advantageous to France. In December 1929,
the Maginot Line project was at last brought before the Chamber,

[53] Mordacq, "L'évacuation anticipée," p. 761.
[54] 10 August 1929, Memorandum by Schmidt, 1338/2406/507693-97; 11 August 1928, DD to AA, 2241/4498/107586; 8 August 1929, Memorandum by
Schmidt, 2240/4498/107347-51.
[55] Briand attempted to win from Stresemann a promise to promote the
sale of reparation bonds on the German market: 10 August 1929, Memorandum by Schmidt, 1338/2406/507693-97.

and the first credits were passed to begin construction of the fortifications.[56] And although Snowden's long holdout precluded arrangements for capitalization at The Hague in August, a second Hague conference was held in January 1930 where Tardieu and Chéron secured the cooperation of the Germans, and the first installment of the bonds was then sold in June 1930.

The events of August 19—Briand's private admission to Stresemann that the Rhineland was a year from freedom and Stresemann's threat to end the policy of understanding—brought relations between the two of them to a low point. On that same day the breach between Briand and Henderson opened even wider. Following Briand's refusal to disclose an end date to the Rhineland powers, Henderson initiated formal arrangements with Stresemann to withdraw the British Army of the Rhine independently of France. As a result, the entente was apparently severed; Franco-German understanding was near an end; France was isolated. Even the extraordinarily patient Aristide Briand found it difficult to accept this situation with his usual casual jest. On August 21 he responded with a vehement attack on the British and threatened to leave the conference.

Henderson was led to unilateral withdrawal by a conviction that the French were doubly responsible for the stalemated conference. Chéron and the representatives of the other sacrificing powers offered inadequate proposals to Snowden; Briand formally refused to name a date for the completion of evacuation, and informally he talked of the summer of 1930. To Henderson's mind, Paris was preventing a reparation settlement and using the resulting disagreement to delay a Rhineland settlement.[57] Believing that it was logistically possible to withdraw the entire French Army by Christmas, he had first asked Briand to evacuate along with the British.[58] When Briand refused and then declined to announce an end date at the August 19 meeting of the Rhineland powers, Henderson asked Stresemann and Wirth to meet with

[56] Chambre débats, 1929, pp. 4774-75; Tournoux, *Haut commandement*, pp. 135-37.
[57] 16 August 1929, Memorandum by Schmidt, 2241/4498/107877-80.
[58] Eric Phipps, the British ambassador to Vienna and the second British representative on the Political Commission, told Schubert that it was technically possible to terminate all occupation by Christmas: 15 August 1929, Memorandum by Schubert, 2241/4498/107769-73.

him privately. There he asked the two Germans if they wanted Britain to withdraw in the event the conference failed and the French troops remained on the Rhine. Stresemann said yes, and he and Henderson negotiated a separate Anglo-German agreement. Henderson agreed to withdraw all British troops by December 31, 1929, and Stresemann agreed to settle certain unpaid claims to indemnification which had been filed by the Germans against the British forces of occupation.[59] Henderson's decision to leave France alone in the Rhineland strained the entente beyond the point to which Snowden had stretched it, but London was prepared to accept this.[60]

With Henderson and Stresemann aligned against him, and with the Locarno powers divided, Briand was in a difficult position. To save himself from complete isolation when the Rhineland powers met again, he had to negotiate a similar Franco-German agreement on evacuation. To arrange one, he asked Stresemann for a private interview. Stresemann flatly refused—an act without precedent in the history of the Locarno Triplice. Briand then publicly announced that he and Stresemann would meet. Outmaneuvered, Stresemann could not refuse to confer with Briand, and the conversation, one of the most acrimonious the two men ever held, took place on August 21.[61]

Briand began by asking Stresemann to renounce all German damage claims on the French Army of the Rhine not settled by the time evacuation was completed. Stresemann asked when that might be. Briand replied that he had nothing to add to his statement of August 19. Stresemann reiterated his inability to understand why French troops could not be moved during the winter, and to encourage Briand to hasten evacuation, he offered to renounce all claims not settled by April 1, 1930.[62] Briand objected: it was logistically impossible to complete evacuation by that time.

Having failed to agree, or even to move each other, the two men exchanged threats. Stresemann stated that if evacuation were postponed and protracted, Franco-German understanding would

[59] 19 August 1929, Memorandum by Schubert, 2241/4498/107975; 19 August 1929, Memorandum by Schmidt, 2241/4498/108007-08; 20 August 1929, DD to AA, 2241/4498/108051-52.

[60] 22 August 1929, Lindsay to Smith, FO. 371/13619/254.

[61] 21 August 1929, DD to AA, 2241/4498/108156.

[62] This policy had been approved by the entire German delegation earlier in the day: 22 August 1929, DD to AA, 2241/4498/108167.

be seriously endangered, and German public opinion would desert France for England. Briand, in turn, displayed his emotional distress at the rupture of France's entente with England and understanding with Germany. Snowden, Briand charged, was operating in collusion with Lloyd George who, he said, "had often shown bad spirit"; the two men were plotting to "blow up the conference," and "torpedo the Young plan." All the difficulties at The Hague originated with England, Briand maintained. Henderson, too, was trying to create "dissension on the continent" by deceitfully placating Germany in the Rhineland negotiations. An Anglo-German alignment against France was a mistake, Briand warned; a mistake from which Germany would suffer serious consequences. If he agreed to evacuate French troops by April, he would fall from office, Briand warned. A right-wing government would be formed in Paris; and with England no longer on the Rhine, this government would be free to pursue a tough Rhine policy.[63]

In two weeks of personal diplomacy at The Hague, Briand found Stresemann less conciliatory and patient than formerly, and he found Henderson less cooperative than Chamberlain. Unable to win their assent to delayed evacuation and to prevent a separate Anglo-German Rhineland agreement, Briand went to the meeting of the Rhineland powers, which followed his conversation with Stresemann, in isolation.

The August 21 meeting of the Rhineland powers showed the relations among the Locarno Triplice to be in full disarray. The meeting, called to debate the Commission of Verification, was about to adjourn—due to Stresemann's unwillingness to discuss the matter—when the German Foreign Minister interrupted with an announcement: he intended to settle indemnity claims against

[63] 21 August 1929, Memorandum by Schmidt, 2241/4498/108111-20. The same day Jules Sauerwein, a French journalist with close relations with the Quai d'Orsay, told Hans Redlhammer, ministerial director of Refrat D of the German Foreign Ministry, that the French delegation suspected an Anglo-German plot against France. The French, he said, not only distrusted Stresemann but had an "extraordinary mania against England." The English, according to the French, were playing "their old game of setting the continental powers against each other in order to make a good deal for themselves": 21 August 1929, Memorandum by Redlhammer, 2241/4498/108086-89. For another similar French reaction to independent British evacuation see Paul Tirard, *La France sur le Rhin; douze années d'occupation rhénane*, Paris, 1930, p. 421.

the armies of Britain and Belgium if they evacuated by December 31, 1929, and to do the same for the French provided they withdrew all their forces by April 1, 1930. Resentful of having an early evacuation date forced upon him, Briand threatened not to evacuate Coblenz as promised and to "leave the conference at once" if Stresemann made his statement public. Supported vigorously by Henderson, Stresemann replied that Briand had never given a terminal date, while Henderson and Hymans had, and if the Germans were to settle the claims question, they would have to fix one themselves. Briand replied that he had in fact given Stresemann a date. Wirth asked Briand to announce it to all those present. French troops, Briand replied, would leave the Rhineland within six months of the end of winter. Henderson rejected Briand's position: British troops would be evacuated and even transported across the English Channel during the winter; he did not expect, he added, that they would be done any harm. Then he adjourned the meeting until August 23, when the Rhineland powers would consider the Commission of Verification.[64]

3. *The End of Control over the Demilitarized Zone*

French policy regarding the institution of permanent, civilian inspection of the Rhineland remained uncertain and hesitant to the end. At The Hague conference, spokesmen for French policy still did not speak with one voice, nor did individual Frenchmen speak with consistency. At the August 9 meeting of the Political Commission, Briand, supported by Hymans, insisted on the establishment of a permanent Commission of Verification and made some effort to win the agreement of the other powers.[65] Then on August 10 he finally communicated to them formally the text of the proposal he had sent unofficially to London and Berlin in February-March.[66] Briand spoke of verification as if it were essential to France's long-term security. He admitted that international inspection of the demilitarized zone was not necessary as long as Stresemann was German Foreign Minister, but France, he stated, must prepare against the day when a government of the

[64] 21 August 1929, Memorandum by Schmidt, 1313/2368/493140-47 and FO. 371/13619/320-25.

[65] 9 August 1929, British delegation to Lindsay, FO. 371/13604/100-106.

[66] 30 August 1929, Henderson to Lindsay, FO. 408/54/53. For a description of the Commission of Verification as proposed by Briand see VII above.

"rightist circles" came to power, one which might use the Reichswehr von Seeckt had formed.[67] By contrast, Berthelot thought the
Commission of Verification would add nothing to the security of
France and relegated it to the status of the nonessential. The commission itself and the form it took were not important, he suggested; it was useful to Briand, he told Schubert on August 13,
mainly as a way of "keeping up appearances" and "bringing something home" from The Hague.[68]

Henderson was not opposed to the notion of verification and
conciliation, particularly if the commission could be deprived of
its power to conduct on-site investigations without German consent. However, Briand's Commission of Verification, providing
for inspections by majority vote, was of little interest to him, and
he told Stresemann so on August 9. The British took this position
in spite of the warnings of Harold Nicolson, First-secretary at
Berlin, who predicted that as soon as the troops of occupation
were withdrawn, the German Army would violate the demilitarization clauses and begin to construct a secret system of fortifications to protect the Ruhr from a French attack. Then with
German industry safe, he continued, "we may well find the whole
attitude of the German government changing and be faced not
with the stubborn and shifty obstruction of the past, but by an
aggressive and almost menacing determination to revise the
treaty." To this Sargent replied by listing the disadvantages and
limitations of Briand's commission, by emphasizing the ingenuity
of the Reichswehr and the incompetence of the German government, and by resigning himself to the disappearance of the demilitarized zone. "It looks as though the ex-Allies will have to
acquiesce in both the disarmament and demilitarization clauses
of the treaty being gradually whittled away, unless indeed within
the next few years some way can be found to reconcile the German nation to permanent continuance of those treaty restrictions.
The prospects of such a change of heart are not of the brightest,
but they are really all that we have to rely on." Henderson, for his
part did not want the appeasing effect of evacuation to be jeopardized by the imposition of Rhineland inspection. He did not
consider Cushendun's approval of the Geneva communiqué to be
binding on himself and the Labour government; the need for

[67] 8 August 1929, Memorandum by Schmidt, 2240/4498/107347-51.
[68] 13 August 1929, Memorandum by Schubert, 2241/4498/107687-88.

Briand's commission, he maintained, would have to be demonstrated anew at The Hague.[69]

With Henderson and Stresemann both opposed to permanent, on-site, international inspection of the Rhineland, Briand retreated.[70] The Commission of Verification had appeared suddenly at Geneva in September 1928—"sprung from his head as Minerva from the brow of Jupiter," as he himself put it. At The Hague it disappeared just as abruptly.[71] When the question of inspection was referred to a committee of legal experts on August 9, Henderson and Stresemann insisted that the lawyers be authorized to determine whether there actually was a gap in the existing treaty structure and whether a new institution of inspection, such as the Commission of Verification, was needed. Stresemann expected the discussions of the legal experts to advance the German position, and his expectations were realized. When the experts met, beginning on August 13, Fredrich Gaus prevented Henri Fromageot, the French legal expert, from opening the discussions with an explication of Briand's proposal, as the French jurist had intended to do. Instead, the German persuaded the other experts to consider the question of whether or not the commission was a legal necessity.[72] It was at this time that Briand abandoned once and for all the idea of a special institution. In 1928 he had transformed Paul-Boncour's idea of a commission resident in the Rhineland at all times into a nonresident Commission of Verification; now at The Hague, he authorized Fromageot to give up the idea of creating a new commission, and instructed him to agree to refer disputes over the demilitarized zone to the Franco-German and Belgo-German Conciliation Commissions provided for

[69] 9 August 1929, Memorandum by Schmidt, 1313/2368/293078-79; 9 August 1929, Memorandum by Schubert, 2241/4498/107441-43; 10 August 1929, DD to AA, 2241/4498/107503-504. 7 August 1929, Nicolson to Sargent, FO. 371/13619/176-82; 20 August 1929, Sargent to Nicolson, FO. 371/13619/186-91. 12 August 1929, Memorandum by Schmidt, 2241/4498/107643; 15 August 1929, Memorandum by Hurst, 2241/4498/107829-31.

[70] Stresemann's position on Rhineland inspection: Stresemann, *Vermächtnis*, III, 548-49. The attitude of the rest of the German delegation at The Hague: Mayer, *Skizzen*, p. 91.

[71] Briand's abandonment of on-site inspection may have been abetted by the promise of the German government, made on August 4 to the Conference of Ambassadors, not to extend the railway system in the demilitarized zone for military purposes: *Survey of International Affairs, 1929*, p. 187.

[72] Stresemann, *Vermächtnis*, III, 547; 10 August 1929, DD to AA, 2241/4498/107503-504; 13 August 1929, DD to AA, 2241/4498/107699.

in Article 3 of the Locarno Treaty. The legal experts adopted this formula on August 17 and 19, and on August 21 Briand announced to the Rhineland powers that he was prepared to accept their recommendation.[73]

Even though Briand renounced his plans for a new institution of inspection, Stresemann obstructed further progress. He refused to conclude any settlement of the verification question while Briand delayed setting an acceptable end date for occupation. He first ordered Gaus to cancel the meeting of the legal experts scheduled for August 20, and he then refused to discuss the problem at the August 21 meeting of the Rhineland powers.[74] On August 24, when the Rhineland powers met solely to consider the form of verification, Stresemann withheld his approval even though he was satisfied with the concessions the French had made. Although Briand had by this time shortened the evacuation period to June 30, Stresemann held out for April 30 and refused to agree to any commission until Briand had made "a completely satisfactory statement on the end of evacuation."[75] It was not until August 28, after Briand had stood fast for June 30, 1930, that Stresemann formally consented to refer disputes over the observance of Rhineland demilitarization to the Locarno Conciliation Commissions. The agreement was embodied in a joint note dated August 30.[76]

4. The Modification of the Young Plan, August 16-31

The unwillingness of Britain and the sacrificing powers to arrive at a reparation settlement confronted Stresemann with a serious dilemma. On the one hand, if the creditors did not agree among themselves and adopt the Young plan, either with or without the modifications demanded by Snowden, two consequences, both detrimental to Germany, would follow. French troops would remain in the Mainz zone, and the Dawes plan would remain in

[73] 17 August 1929, DD to AA, 2241/4498/107923; 19 August 1929, draft agreement of the jurists, 2241/4498/108046; 21 August 1929, Memorandum by Schmidt, 1313/2368/493140-41.

[74] 20 August 1929, DD to AA, 2241/4498/108052; 21 August 1929, Memorandum by Schmidt, 1313/2368/493440-41 and FO. 371/13619/319-20.

[75] 21 August 1929, DD to AA, 2241/4498/108174; 22 August 1929, DD to AA, 2242/4498/108249-50; 24 August 1929, DD to AA, 2242/4498/108264.

[76] *International Agreement on the Evacuation of the Rhineland Territory, The Hague, August 30, 1929*, Cmd. 3417, London, 1929.

force. Rather than beginning to pay the Young annuities on September 1, 1929, as the experts had planned, Germany would continue to pay the standard Dawes annuity which, over the following eighteen months, provided for payments 28 per cent greater than those of the Young plan. To meet these payments, German taxes would have to be increased, a measure which would undoubtedly bring down the precarious Great Coalition.

On the other hand, as long as the creditors searched for agreement, the threat that they would come to terms with each other at Germany's expense and settle their differences by raising German payments hung over Stresemann's head. From the French point of view, it seemed reasonable that Germany should contribute to the satisfaction of Snowden's demands. The concession made by the British experts on the Young committee had been made in order to arrive at a payment schedule acceptable to Schacht, and it was unfair to ask the French subsequently to make up what Britain had sacrificed for Germany's benefit.[77] Berthelot told Schubert on August 13 that all the powers, including Germany, would have to make sacrifices if a financial settlement were to be reached. And he was echoed the next day by Henderson who jokingly told Hilferding that the evacuation of the Rhineland had become dependent on the German Finance Minister.[78] These suggestions were made in spite of Stresemann's earlier warnings, in public and in private, against any attempt to increase German payments through an "allied alignment directed against Germany." Not unexpectedly, then, the idea of German sacrifice was vigorously rejected on August 13 and 14: Schubert told Berthelot and Eric Phipps of the British delegation that Germany could make no sacrifices beyond the Young plan, and Stresemann once more warned the creditors against coming to terms behind Germany's back.[79] However, Stresemann did little during the first two weeks of the conference to expedite a financial settlement. German representatives were not included in the negotiations which took place after the meetings of the Financial Commission were adjourned on August 10, and by intervening on the side of either

[77] *New York Times*, 26 August 1929.
[78] 13 August 1929, Memorandum by Schubert, 2241/4498/107683-84; 15 August 1929, Memorandum by Schubert, 2241/4498/107769-73.
[79] Stresemann, *Vermächtnis*, III, 549-50; 11 August 1929, DD to AA, 2241/4498/107587; 13 August 1929, Memorandum by Schubert, 2241/4498/107683-84; 14 August 1929, Memorandum by Schubert, 2241/4498/107769-73.

Snowden or Chéron, Stresemann would have alienated one or the other of the occupying powers.

By the end of the second week of the conference, however, Stresemann was moved to action. Seeing no financial solution in sight, he feared the conference would terminate without putting an end to either military occupation or the Dawes plan. To prevent this, he decided to suggest a meeting of the six powers which had signed the Geneva communiqué (England, France, Belgium, Italy, Japan, and Germany) and to propose to them a provisional settlement: 1) The Young plan would be put into operation as of September 1, 1929, no matter what the outcome of The Hague conference; the Dawes controls on German finances would be lifted; Germany would be permitted to pay the smaller Young annuities. 2) The six powers would also declare in writing to continue negotiations, at another location if necessary, until agreement was reached.[80] On August 16, the day it appeared that Snowden's ultimatum would bring the conference to the point of breakdown, Stresemann proposed a meeting of the six powers to Briand and to Henderson.[81]

As it turned out, Stresemann's plans resulted in failure. By August 22 the German delegation had become involved in the financial negotiations with Snowden but had been denied the alternative of paying the Young annuities until the plan was ratified by all the powers concerned.

Briand, as chief of the French delegation, at first rejected the idea of a six-power meeting to prepare for the breakup of the conference. When Stresemann suggested it to him on August 16, the French Foreign Minister urged him instead privately to influence Snowden to agree with the sacrificing powers.[82] Stresemann met with Snowden the next day but could not move him.[83] Then, on August 19, Briand changed his mind and consented to a six-power discussion.[84] The 19th was a day of pessimism at The Hague, and Briand, believing that Snowden would continue to

[80] 19 August 1929, unsigned memorandum, "Ideas and Suggestions for the Continuation of the Conference," 2241/4498/107955-67; Erich Eyck, *A History of the Weimar Republic*, Cambridge, Mass., 1962-63, II, 206.

[81] Snowden, *Autobiography*, II, 802-803.

[82] 16 August 1929, Memorandum by Schmidt, 2241/4498/107863-70; 17 August 1929, DD to AA, 2241/4498/107908; 16 August 1929, Memorandum by Schmidt, 2241/4498/107879-80.

[83] 17 August 1929, Memorandum by Schmidt, 1313/2368/483120-23; 17 August 1929, DD to AA, 2241/4498/107922.

[84] 19 August 1929, Memorandum by Schmidt, 2241/4498/107983-89.

hold out, sought to involve Germany in the financial discussions in order to bridge the gap between Snowden and the sacrificing powers by means of an increase in German payments. French intentions became clear on August 21 when, in response to Schubert's vehement protests against Briand's dilatory handling of the Rhineland question, Loucheur stated that Briand would shorten the period of occupation if Berlin cooperated on reparations. "We must," he said, "all try together to bring Snowden to reason; then everything would be much easier." The French, he stated, were ready to sacrifice; the Germans must sacrifice too.[85]

Snowden, too, was discouraged by August 19. Where he had rejected Stresemann's plans for the collapse of the conference two days earlier because he was still hopeful of a settlement on his own terms, he now consented to a meeting of the six powers. In a conversation with Curtius and Hilferding, he appeared eager to have the German delegation declare to the entire conference Germany's inability to pay the Dawes annuities after September 1.[86] Snowden calculated, it seems, that if the alternative of returning to the Dawes plan were taken from them, Briand and Chéron would be compelled to come to terms with him.

Stresemann, of course, had proposed the meeting of the six powers for reasons very different from those which prompted Briand to accept. While Briand wanted Germany to join the sacrificing powers, Stresemann wanted to protect the Reich against further financial sacrifice and preclude the continued payment of the Dawes annuity. Snowden gave him some reason to hope that London would permit Germany to pay the Young annuities even if the conference failed. And Briand seemed agreeable also. At 3:15 P.M. on August 21, when Stresemann privately suggested to him that the Young annuities begin on September 1, Briand did not explicitly consent, but neither did he raise any objections.[87]

The six powers met at 6:30 P.M. on August 21 and again on the

---

[85] 21 August 1929, Memorandum by Schubert, 2241/4498/108099, 102-103. On the same day Jules Sauerwein promised Hans Redlhammer that he would write an article propounding the military feasibility of evacuation in three months: 21 August 1929, Memorandum by Redlhammer, 2241/4498/108087-88.

[86] 20 August 1929, DD to AA, 2241/4498/108047-48.

[87] 21 August 1929, Memorandum by Schmidt, 2241/4498/108111-12; 22 August 1929, DD to AA, 2241/4498/108168. Loucheur, however, told Hilferding that the French delegation was unwilling to consider Stresemann's plan for a provisional settlement: 21 August 1929, DD to AA, 2241/4498/108155-56.

morning of August 22.[88] Stresemann announced that Germany could no longer pay the standard Dawes annuity, charged the creditors with bringing the conference to the point of a breakdown, and called for a provisional settlement. His request was denied. Contrary to his hopes, both Briand and Snowden refused to permit Germany to pay the Young annuity until the plan was ratified.

Briand was in no mood to conciliate Stresemann. At the meeting of the Rhineland powers which had just concluded at 5:30, Wirth had forced him to reveal September 1, 1930, as the date for evacuation; Stresemann had attempted to force Briand to accept April 1, and Henderson had rebuked him for not conceding. So at the meeting of the six powers, Briand used all the acidity at his command to tell Stresemann that there were only two alternatives—the Dawes plan and the Young plan; the combination of the two—payments under the Young plan as Stresemann desired, and distributions under the Spa percentages as Snowden desired—was, he exclaimed, "very much a bastard." He refused to prepare for the breakup of the conference, and he demanded that the creditors adopt the Young plan at The Hague. Otherwise, he warned, "the moral prestige" of the participants would suffer and conference diplomacy would be discredited.

Snowden, too, opposed Stresemann's provisional settlement and insisted that the standard Dawes annuity be paid until the Young plan was ratified. He and Briand had met privately for the first time on August 20 and, impressed by Snowden's tenacity, Briand offered him a compromise. Although he refused to alter the distribution percentages specified in the Young plan because the French public would interpret this as a defeat, Briand did offer to compensate the British for 50 per cent of their losses from the rescission of the Spa percentages; and he suggested that Snowden might get the other 50 per cent from the Italians.[89] Snowden considered this a significant gesture; his mood turned from pessimism to optimism once again, and at the meeting of the six powers, Stresemann found him unwilling to prepare for the end of the conference.

[88] 21 August 1929, Memorandum by Schmidt, 2241/4498/108130-39; 22 August 1929, Memorandum by Schmidt, 2241/4498/108175-81; 22 August 1929, DD to AA, 2241/4498/108197-99.

[89] Snowden, *Autobiography*, II, 811-12.

When the meeting of the six ministers disbanded on August 22, several things were evident. Stresemann had received no assurance that Germany could pay the Young annuities beginning on September 1, and no provision was made for the breakup of the conference. Instead, the sacrificing powers were to continue their efforts to accommodate Snowden and reach a settlement at The Hague. Moreover, the efforts at settlement would be made against a rapidly approaching deadline, for both Henderson and Snowden announced that they were tired of what they regarded as the halfhearted efforts of the sacrificing powers and that they intended to leave the conference in two days. "The Foreign Secretary of the British Empire," Henderson said with a pomposity worthy of Curzon or Chamberlain, "is a very busy man." Franco-German relations, he indicated, were only one of his concerns; he would soon have to depart for the meeting of the League Assembly at Geneva.[90] Finally, Germany would now join the sacrificing powers in their efforts to reach a financial settlement, although what contribution she would make, if any, had not been determined.

The representatives of the sacrificing creditors, now joined by Hilferding and Curtius, met during the afternoon and evening of August 22. Hilferding again made the German case for a provisional settlement. The others rejected it and insisted that Germany contribute to the satisfaction of Snowden's demands. The sacrificing creditors proposed to offer Snowden £1.8 million of the £2.4 million he demanded. They were prepared to contribute £1.44 million, and they asked the Germans to make up the difference—£360,000 (7.4 million marks). Hilferding refused. Then, at midnight on August 22, the sacrificing creditors offered Snowden £1.44 million, 60 per cent of his demands, and on August 23 Snowden rejected their proposal and demanded 100 per cent of his requirements. Twice again, on August 24 and 25, the sacrificing powers tried to persuade the Germans to increase their payments and join them in an offer to Snowden. Twice more Hilferding and Curtius refused. The creditors then deliberated alone, and at eight o'clock on the morning of August 26 they formally submitted in writing their offer of August 22. At 2:00 P.M.

[90] 22 August 1929, Memorandum by Schmidt, 2241/4498/108178-79.

Snowden replied with a seven-line note rejecting the offer as "altogether inadequate."[91]

For three weeks Snowden and the other creditors had negotiated without success. The conference was stalemated on an issue supposedly decided in June by the Young experts, and it had not yet considered the two major tasks assigned to it—arrangements for the evacuation of the Rhineland and the implementation of the Young plan. The tenth anniversary session of the League of Nations Assembly was scheduled to begin at Geneva within days, and this was an occasion which the League-minded delegates at The Hague did not want to miss. A long, acrimonious conference was about to terminate, or at least adjourn, having accomplished nothing. Then, on August 26, with this prospect in view, the other creditors announced that they could improve on the offer made to Snowden earlier that day. Encouraged by this, and under renewed pressure from the cabinet in London, Snowden let it be known, for the first time, that he would be satisfied with less than 100 per cent of his original demands.[92] Now there was reason to expect agreement, and with this hope in view, the pressure on the Germans to facilitate the settlement became intense.

The pressure came from both sides. Briand made the terms of the Rhineland settlement more attractive, thus raising Germany's stake in the adoption of the Young plan. Since August 23, the day after Hilferding and Curtius had joined the other creditors, Briand had told the Rhineland powers that evacuation might be completed by June 30, 1930; Stresemann held out for April 1, and only three months separated the two of them.[93] Snowden was more obvious. On August 26, he told Breitscheid that the conference could not succeed unless the German delegation contributed

[91] 23 August 1929, DD to AA, 2242/4498/108248-49; 24 August 1929, Memorandum by Michaelis, 1632/3375/733204-13; 24 August 1929, DD to AA, 2242/4498/108265; 26 August 1929, DD to AA, 2242/4498/108281-82; Snowden, *Autobiography*, II, 812-14; Etienne Weill-Raynal, *Les réparations allemandes et la France*, Paris, 1947-49, III, 501-503.

[92] Snowden, *Autobiography*, II, 815-17; Carlton, *MacDonald versus Henderson*, p. 47.

[93] 23 August 1929, DD to AA, 2242/4498/108249-50; 30 August 1929, Henderson to Lindsay, FO. 408/54/53. Briand shortened the period after Stresemann's personal letter of August 19 and following a personal plea from Henderson on August 22: 24 August 1929, British Delegation to FO., FO. 371/13619/269-75. Thereafter Henderson continued to press Briand to end evacuation by May 31: 25 August 1929, Henderson to Briand, FO. 371/13619/300-301.

to its success. He was unwilling to make any demands on Germany himself; he denied that he had any desire to raise German payments above the Young plan; and he depicted himself as the protector of German interests against the designs of the other creditors. But, if the Germans first agreed with the sacrificing creditors, and if the two parties then collectively made a satisfactory offer to Britain, he would accept it, he stated.[94]

With time running out at The Hague, there was a flurry of preparations for the end of the conference. Briand proposed that the six powers convene "to end a situation from which there appears to be no way out,"[95] and a meeting was scheduled for August 27 at 5:00 P.M. That noon Henderson tried, and failed, to get the Rhineland powers to make a written report to the Political Commission. Briand insisted on an evacuation end date of June 30 and refused to sign any agreement on the evacuation of Mainz unless the Young plan were adopted.[96] Stresemann refused to accept Briand's June 30 date, and at 4:30 he tried, without success, to win Briand to an earlier date and to pledge himself to evacuation, even though the conference disbanded without a financial agreement.[97]

The six powers met at 5:00 P.M., while outside the building members of the press burned copies of the Young plan. The leaders of the five delegations, including Stresemann, urged Snowden to accept the offer of August 26. Snowden rejected their plea in what one German called "a schoolmasterly and almost insulting manner." The meeting recessed at 8:30, and the German delegation withdrew, confident that no decision would be reached that evening. The four other creditors then met separately, and at midnight on August 27-28, they reached agreement with Snowden in Germany's absence.[98]

[94] 26 August 1929, DD to AA, 2242/4498/108282-83. Also 23 August 1929, DD to AA, 2242/4498/108248-49. Snowden subsequently denied suggesting that Germany make any sacrifices beyond the Young plan: Snowden, *Autobiography*, II, 824.

[95] Stresemann, *Vermächtnis*, III, 560.

[96] 27 August 1929, Memorandum by Schubert, 2242/4498/108312; 27 August 1929, DD to AA, 2547/5138/299442-43; 27 August 1927, draft report of the Political Commission, 2242/4498/108326-28; 30 August 1929, Henderson to Lindsay, FO. 408/54/53.

[97] 27 August 1929, notes for a conversation with Briand, 2242/4498/108310-11; 27 August 1929, DD to AA, 2242/4498/108321.

[98] 28 August 1929, DD to AA, 2547/5138/299443-44; Snowden, *Autobiography*, II, 818-22.

The sacrificing powers offered, and Snowden accepted, £1.8 million of the £2.4 million he had originally demanded. This was an increase of £360,000 (7.4 million marks) over the offer of August 26, and it represented 75 per cent of Snowden's original demand. Most of the adjustment in Britain's total receipts would come from 37 yearly £1.44 million payments from France, Belgium, and Italy. In addition, the English share of Germany's unconditional payments was increased from £900,000 to £4.8 million per year, in part by adjusting the schedule of annuities. The flat 37-year, 660-million-mark unconditonal annuity was raised to 700 million marks during the first years and was decreased correspondingly for the remaining years. Germany's average unconditional payment remained nearly the same. Finally, to protect the British coal industry from German payment in kind, the Italian delegation promised that the Italian national railways would purchase one million tons of coal a year from Britain at the going market price.[99]

Although Snowden's demands were met without increasing Germany's yearly payments, certain changes in the plan were made which required German approval—most notably the altered schedule of unconditional payments. However, Stresemann and the German delegation decided to withhold their consent pending Briand's agreement to a satisfactory end date for occupation. Summoned by the creditors at 1:00 A.M. on August 28, the Germans refused to approve the settlement the sacrificing powers had just reached with Snowden. The six powers met later that same day, and after a heated discussion, Stresemann still refused to agree to the settlement of the previous evening.[100] The struggle between the Germans and the creditors continued until 2:00 A.M. on August 29, with Stresemann demanding that occupation end on April 1, 1930, and Briand stubbornly holding out for June 30. Fatigued and defeated, Stresemann gave in, and later that morning, the Political Commission formally approved a report calling for the completion of evacuation by June 30.[101] At noon the Ger-

---

[99] Myers, *Reparation Settlement*, pp. 116-17; Harold G. Moulton and Leo Pasvolsky, *War Debts and World Prosperity*, Washington, D. C., 1932, pp. 204-207; Weill-Raynal, *Réparations allemandes*, III, 510-17.

[100] 28 August 1929, DD to AA, 2242/4498/108343-50.

[101] 29 August 1929, Memorandum by Pünder, 2242/4498/108353-55; 30 August 1929, Henderson to Lindsay, FO. 371/54/53; Carlton, *MacDonald versus Henderson*, pp. 52-53. Curtius has left a dramatic account of the early

man delegation met with the German Young experts and, over Schacht's protest and threat of resignation, decided to make the financial sacrifices required by the creditors.[102] On August 30 Stresemann, Briand, Henderson, and Hymans exchanged notes providing for the complete evacuation of the Rhineland.[103] And the next day, the final protocol of the first Hague conference, approving the modified Young plan and providing for a second session to deal with its implementation, was signed.[104]

5. *The Settlement of 1929*

The day The Hague Protocol was signed, the British Army of the Rhine was given final orders to withdraw from Germany. Two weeks were allotted to arrange for trains and river barges, and evacuation began on September 14, the date set by Henderson. It was completed within the 90 days allotted by him, and on December 13 the last of over 6,000 British troops, most of whom had been quartered in and around Wiesbaden, departed from Germany. Meanwhile the Coblenz zone, which was occupied by the French and Belgians, was evacuated by November 30, 1929, two months before the date scheduled by the Treaty of Versailles. On November 17 the headquarters of the Inter-Allied Rhineland High Commission was moved from Coblenz to Wiesbaden in the Mainz zone, which continued to be occupied by French troops. The evacuation of this zone began on May 20, 1930, three days after the Young plan went into effect, and on June 30, the flags of the three occupying powers were lowered from the headquarters

---

morning meeting of August 29: Curtius, *Sechs Jahre*, pp. 89-90. Also Zechlin, *Pressechef*, p. 84.

[102] Schacht looked forward to the breakdown and complete revision of the Young plan in two years. Any measure which increased Germany's burdens prior to that time was, therefore, to Germany's disadvantage. Characteristically, after making much difficulty, he backed down and promised to withhold his decision on The Hague-modified Young plan until a later date. Thus he was temporarily diverted from his unsteady course away from the agreement he had signed in June: 29 August 1929, DD to AA, 2242/4498/108351-53. Also 28 August 1929, Schacht to Stresemann, 1632/3375/733301-303; 28 August 1929, unsigned memorandum, 2242/4498/108330-32; Hjalmar Schacht, *The End of Reparations*, New York, 1931, pp. 100, 103-107; Eyck, *Weimar Republic*, II, 208.

[103] Cmd. 3417.

[104] *Protocol with Annexes Approved at the Plenary Session of The Hague Conference, August 31, 1929*, Cmd. 3392, London, 1929.

of the High Commission, and the last French soldiers departed from Mainz.[105]

Once the armies of the Allies were withdrawn from Germany, what assurance was there that they would not be replaced by German forces? Promises had been made at Locarno, but in the years that followed no measures were taken to assure that they would be kept. No Commission of Verification was established to discover violations and report them to the League Council, thereby preventing the Germans from breaking their promise and prompting the British to honor theirs. Instead, Briand and Stresemann signed a written statement at The Hague agreeing to refer disputes over the presence of military forces and installations in the Rhineland to an existent institution—the Conciliation Commissions named in Article 3 of the Treaty of Locarno.[106]

The operations of the Locarno Conciliation Commissions were less disadvantageous to Germany than Briand's Commission of Verification would have been. The commissions—one for Franco-German disputes and one for Belgo-German disputes—were composed of two Germans, two Frenchmen (or Belgians), and three neutrals; the ex-Allied powers would have no automatic majority on them as they would have had on the Commission of Verification. Moreover, the Locarno commissions were not explicitly authorized to conduct independent investigations in the Rhineland or to report directly to the League Council. Their mandate was to recommend solutions to the parties involved, and their recommendation was merely advisory and not binding. The parties had one month to accept or reject it before the matter could be brought before the League Council.[107] All this would benefit Germany and work to the disadvantage of France and Belgium in a dispute over remilitarization.

The procedures for the verification of demilitarization agreed upon at The Hague added nothing new to French security. Paris had possessed the right to bring violations of demilitarization before the Franco-German Conciliation Commission since the day

---

[105] Hamilton, *Henderson*, p. 334; Paul Tirard, "En Rhénanie—les derniers jours de l'occupation," *Revue des deux mondes*, 59 (1930), pp. 559-81, and Tirard, *France sur le Rhin*, pp. 425-45.

[106] Cmd. 3417.

[107] F. S. Northedge, *The Troubled Giant; Britain among the Great Powers, 1916-39*, New York, 1967, p. 266; W. E. Rappard, *The Quest for Peace since the World War*, Cambridge, Mass., 1940, p. 164.

the Locarno Treaties were ratified. This right, never denied, was merely stated in clear, written form on August 31 in order to conceal the denial of Briand's announced intention to achieve rights of permanent, on-site inspection. Thereby Stresemann merely made what one German official at The Hague called "a purely formal concession devoid of any material significance."[108] Of Briand's original plan, "only a shadow of a shadow survived," as Curtius later told the Reichstag Committee on Foreign Affairs.[109]

Briand was not alone in seeing his objectives frustrated, for Stresemann did not win the return of the Saar. Although informal Franco-German conversations were conducted at The Hague, the Saar question was not placed on the official agenda of the conference; it was not recognized as one of the concerns of the Political Commission; and agreement on the final protocol was not made dependent on satisfactory Saar negotiations.[110] In speaking with the Germans at The Hague, Briand and Berthelot showed no inclination to permit any serious discussions of the Saar during the conference, and Stresemann had to be content to exchange notes with Briand stating that Saar discussions had been initiated and would be continued after the conference.[111] The notes were exchanged on August 30. And on November 21, 1929, French and German experts opened discussions in Paris.

The Paris negotiations were without result. Indeed, the two sides never agreed on the basis for negotiations. The Germans looked forward to the prompt return of the Saar to German sovereignty without the plebiscite scheduled for 1935 in exchange for

[108] Mayer, *Skizzen*, p. 91. Mayer was a Politische Refrat in the Ministry for Occupied Areas.

[109] 29 November 1929, Curtius to Reichstag Foreign Affairs Committee, Bavarian State Archives, MA 103191.

[110] On August 10 Stresemann handed Briand a written note on the Saar, one clause of which stated that unless the Franco-German conversations came to a satisfactory conclusion at The Hague, Germany had the right to refer the problem to the Political Commission of the conference. Briand recognized this as an attempt to make the success of the conference dependent on a Saar settlement, and he refused to accept the note unless the clause was deleted. Stresemann did so: 11 August 1929, DD to AA, 2241/4498/107784-85; 14 August 1929, Schubert to Köpke, 2241/4498/107762-64. The various texts of the note, original and revised: 2241/4498/107554-55; 2241/4498/107579-81; 1631/3375/733013-16.

[111] 21 August 1929, Memorandum by Schmidt, 2241/4498/108119; Maria Zenner, *Parteien und Politik im Saargebiet unter dem Völkerbundsregime, 1920-1935*, Saarbrücken, 1966, p. 224.

a cash payment. The French meanwhile wanted special access to the coal and markets of the area long after its return to Germany. When the French demanded joint Franco-German exploitation of the Saar mines, Berlin decided that the price of early political reunion was too high. Because the French were unwilling to accept what appeared to be revision of the Treaty of Versailles and the Germans were unwilling to accept what looked like a shadow of the Ruhr policy, the Paris negotiations ended without agreement on July 7, 1930.[112]

The Young plan, the major topic of negotiation at The Hague, did not actually go into effect until almost nine months after the conference. Because the conference of August 1929 was largely taken up with efforts to make it acceptable to Snowden, a second Hague conference was held in January 1930 to determine the technical procedures for the implementation of the new payment plan. The German and French parliaments then ratified the Young plan in March; the ratifications of all powers were deposited in Paris on May 9; and on May 17, 1930, the plan went into effect.

The revised and final reparation settlement, which had been two and a half years in the making, lasted little more than a year. In 1931 Europe met with an international financial crisis, and in June of that year President Hoover proposed a one-year moratorium on war debt and reparation payments. Germany's creditors agreed in July, and thereafter little payment was made on these debts.[113] The Special Advisory Committee provided for in the Young plan met in December and recommended the "adjustment" of all intergovernmental war debts. At the end of the moratorium year the creditors met the Germans at Lausanne, and on July 2, 1932, the creditors agreed to write off 90 per cent of the reparation debt, provided the United States made a similar concession to them. Although the Americans refused to accept it, the Lausanne formula—general cancellation of war-incurred inter-

[112] *Ibid.*, pp. 222-50.

[113] Under the terms of the moratorium, the unconditional annuity for the year 1931-32 was to be paid but reloaned to the German National Railroad Company for the use of the German government: J. W. Wheeler-Bennett and Hugh Latimer, *The Wreck of Reparations; Being the Political Background of the Lausanne Agreement, 1932*, New York, 1933, pp. 65-66.

governmental indebtedness—stood as the final resolution of the war debt-reparation question.[114]

It is surprising that the end of reparations did not come sooner. The standard Dawes annuity represented 3.4 per cent of Germany's estimated national income and 12.4 per cent of the total cost of government. Each year reparations took from Germany's national savings a sum which otherwise might have been reinvested and promoted economic growth.[115] Given Germany's unfavorable balance of payments on account of goods and services, reparation payments amounting to 3 per cent of the German national income would have had an early deflationary effect on the economy. They did not because the outflow of capital was more than offset by the inflow of loans.[116] Beginning in 1926 large-scale American lending to Germany had permitted extensive investment without saving and large foreign capital payments without a favorable visible balance of trade.[117] Depleted capital was replaced; commodities were imported from abroad; reparation was paid regularly; and all this was done without inconveniencing the German consumer with a lower standard of living, and without disturbing the manufacturers of the creditor powers with the 40-50 per cent increase in German exports that would have been necessary to pay the standard Dawes annuity without foreign borrowing.[118]

This pleasant situation changed in June 1928 when a speculative boom began on Wall Street. Rapidly appreciating American securities cut into the market for German bonds, and there was

[114] Wheeler-Bennett and Latimer, *Wreck of Reparations*; Weill-Raynal, *Réparations allemandes*, III, 611-711.

[115] Leland B. Yaeger, *International Monetary Relations; Theory, History and Polity*, New York, 1966, p. 273; J. M. Keynes, "The Dawes Scheme and the German Loan," *Nation and Athenaeum* (4 October 1924), pp. 7-9.

[116] Between 1924 and 1931 Germany borrowed from abroad 18.2 billion marks and paid in reparation 10.3 billion marks: C.R.S. Harris, *Germany's Foreign Indebtedness*, London, 1935, pp. 9-10. Also Weill-Raynal, *Réparations allemandes*, III, 768-99, 890-91.

[117] Joseph Brandes, *Herbert Hoover and Economic Diplomacy; Department of Commerce Policy, 1921-1928*, Pittsburgh, 1962, p. 196; Clarke, *Central Bank Cooperation*, p. 108. Only in 1926 did Germany have a favorable visible balance: Moulton and Pasvolsky, *War Debts and World Prosperity*, pp. 284-85, 306.

[118] Harris, *Germany's Foreign Indebtedness*, pp. 10-13; J. M. Keynes, "The Progress of Reparations," *Nation and Athenaeum* (16 July 1927), p. 506.

a sharp decline in new foreign issues in New York. Both German capital imports and investment in new plant peaked in 1928, indicating a downturn in entrepreneurial anticipations by 1929.[119] If American loans and German business expansion were to be the basis of the new and final reparation settlement, then the Young plan was undermined before the experts met at Paris to formulate it. In April 1929, during their deliberations, other German economic indicators peaked (wage rates and cost of living indexes); the three years of German prosperity, which had begun the spring following Locarno, came to an end; and, statistically at least, the Great Depression began.[120] Then with the Wall Street crash of October 1929, seven months before the plan came into effect, Germany's export position was damaged and foreign loans were further diminished. An industrial and agricultural recession followed; there was a discernible trend toward chronic (rather than seasonal) unemployment during the first quarter of 1930; the transfer problem, previously obscured by the import of dollars, became apparent.[121] With the complete financial collapse of 1931, the transfer situation became acute, and the result was the collapse of the financial arrangements of the Locarno era—the end of the system of debts and reparations constructed since 1924. Only Germany's loans from abroad survived the general cancellation of 1932; they were defaulted in 1934.

This then was the settlement of 1929—a short-lived schedule of reparation payments which was technically final rather than provisional, the withdrawal of Allied troops from Germany without the substitution of international observation of the demilitarized zone, and the exclusion of the question of an early Saar settlement from the agenda of the European great powers. This settlement, along with the security treaties of 1925, Germany's admission to the League, and the German disarmament settle-

---

[119] Clarke, *Central Bank Cooperation*, p. 24; David S. Landes, *The Unbound Prometheus; Technical Change and Industrial Development in Western Europe from 1750 to the Present*, Cambridge, 1969, pp. 371-72; J. T. Madden, *America's Experience as a Creditor Nation*, New York, 1937, pp. 68-69.

[120] Gerhard Bry, *Wages in Germany, 1871-1945*, Princeton, 1960, pp. 167, 171, 409, 423, 475, 497.

[121] Karl D. Bracher, *Die Auflösung der Weimarer Republik*, Stuttgart, 1957, pp. 291-92; Bry, *Wages in Germany*, pp. 399-400; Helga Timm, *Die Deutsche sozialpolitik und der Bruch der grossen Koalition im März 1930*, Düsseldorf, 1952, pp. 107-12.

ment of 1926-27, comprised the legacy of Stresemann, Briand, Chamberlain, and Henderson. The settlement of 1929 was the final achievement of the men of Locarno, for almost simultaneously with The Hague agreement many of them left the scene, a reaction against their efforts began, and the era of Locarno came to a close.

PART NINE

CONCLUSION

1. *The End of an Era*

OF THE Locarno Big Three, Austen Chamberlain was the first to leave office, resigning with the rest of the Baldwin government in June 1929. On October 3, two months after the end of The Hague conference, Stresemann died. Briand's government fell on October 22, and although he continued as Foreign Minister until January 1932, he lost control over the direction of policy to André Tardieu and Pierre Laval, the two ambitious younger men who held the position of Premier. The top permanent officials did not long outlast the foreign ministers. Schubert left the Wilhelmstrasse in June 1930 to become ambassador to Rome; and in London, Ronald Lindsay was replaced as Permanent Undersecretary early the same year by Robert Vansittart, a man with little affection for the Germans. Berthelot alone remained—until March 1933. At the ambassadorial level, the two men most closely associated with the policies of the Locarno era were D'Abernon and Hoesch. D'Abernon, who had pleaded the German case more effectively than any non-German of the time, had left Berlin in 1926. Hoesch, with his clear insights into the limitations and the potentialities of the policy of understanding and his close personal relations with Berthelot, was transferred to London in 1932. Thus, most of the men who had made both the security pact of 1925 and the settlement of 1929 left their positions as The Hague settlement was being completed. Perhaps the timing of their departure was fortunate, for as they left a reaction developed against the settlement they had formed.

The reaction against the settlement of 1929 began as soon as the terms of the Young plan became apparent. Months before the plan was adopted at The Hague, elements of the political opposition in both England and Germany had rejected it. Snowden denounced it in mid-April, and in August he strained to the breaking point the entente on which Chamberlain based his Locarno policy. In Germany the National Opposition conducted a well-organized and fanatical campaign against the Young plan —a campaign with objectives far more radical than those of Snowden. They demanded the complete rejection of the plan and the termination of all reparation payments. Thereby, they hoped to discredit Stresemann's foreign policy, to disgrace the Socialist-led Great Coalition government, and to rally the various right-wing organizations radically opposed to the Republic in a movement that would reach those voters disdainful of the Weimar system.

The leadership in the German anti-Young plan campaign was assumed by Alfred Hugenberg, the chairman of the DNVP. While the experts were still meeting in Paris, he initiated a systematic propaganda campaign against the plan in his newspapers. After the experts issued their report, the DNVP announced, on June 15, that it planned to conduct "an offensive against the Paris Tribute Plan" and to call for a referendum of the German electorate in order to prevent the Young plan from coming into force.[1] To conduct the offensive a committee was formed, composed of Hugenberg and the leaders of the other National Opposition groups—Hitler of the Nazis, Franz Seldte of the Stahlhelm, Heinrich Class of the Pan-Germans, and Fritz Thyssen of the Reichsverband der Deutschen Industrie.[2] This group, which was called the National Committee for the German Referendum, first met in Berlin on July 9, and in September they published the text of a referendum to be submitted to the German electorate. The Law Against the Enslavement of the German People, called the Freedom Law for short, unilaterally repudiated the war-guilt clause of the Treaty of Versailles, demanded the immediate and unconditional evacuation of the Rhineland, called for the abolition of all foreign controls over Germany, rejected the Young plan, and stated that any member of the government who signed it would be prosecuted for treason.[3]

Although only 14 per cent of the German electorate voted for the Freedom Law when it came before them in December 1929, the campaign for its passage had important consequences.[4] It united the various factions of the National Opposition coalition in a campaign against Stresemann's foreign policy. And within that coalition the Nazi Party was enriched, strengthened, and

[1] *New York Times*, 16 June 1929.

[2] Attila Chanady, "The Disintegration of the German National Peoples' Party 1924-1930," *Journal of Modern History*, 39 (1967), p. 84.

[3] The text of the Freedom Law: Denys P. Myers, *The Reparation Settlement, 1930*, Boston, 1930, pp. 37-38. Hugenberg and the Freedom Law campaign: Erich Matthias and Rudolf Morsey (eds.), *Das Ende der Parteien 1933*, Düsseldorf, 1963, pp. 548-49.

[4] Alfred Milatz, *Wähler und Wählen in der Weimarer Republik*, Bonn, 1965, pp. 124-25.

popularized while the DNVP was weakened when twelve deputies withdrew from it following a split within the ranks of the party over the Freedom Law.[5] Moreover, the campaign brought the attack on the settlement of 1929 before the German people where that attack found a nascent response, channeled vague hostilities into a rejection of the policy of understanding and the Weimar system, and popularized right-wing radicalism. Eventually the National Opposition, with its demands for a more aggressive foreign policy, a more dynamic domestic policy, and a stronger executive authority, forced the defenders of Locarno and the Republic onto the defensive.[6] The Hague settlement, which Stresemann had intended as a measure to strengthen the Republic and its foreign policy against their opponents, proved to be the first stage of a crisis which brought an end to both.

Within a year after the Freedom Law referendum, those responsible for the formation of German policy decided that there was more to be gained by abandoning the policy of understanding than by continuing it. With the death of Stresemann, the policy had lost its author and ablest defender. In December Schacht repudiated The Hague-modified Young plan, and three months later he resigned as president of the Reichsbank.[7] Müller's Great Coalition government, united only by its willingess to conduct Stresemann's foreign policy, fell in March 1930, and Heinrich Brüning who succeeded Müller, and Curtius who followed Stresemann, made little effort to popularize the Franco-German rapprochement.[8] During the Reichstag election campaign of June-September, all the major parties deferred to popular anti-French feeling and demanded further revision of Versailles. And under the impact of the Depression, the parties of the National Opposition with their radical opposition to the Young plan, their outspoken criticism of the policy of understand-

[5] Alan Bullock, *Hitler; a Study in Tyranny*, London, 1952, pp. 141, 144-51; Karl D. Bracher, *Die Auflösung der Weimarer Republik*, Stuttgart, 1957, pp. 109-10 and Bracher, *The German Dictatorship; the Origins, Structure, and Effects of National Socialism*, New York, 1970, pp. 160-62, 167; Chanady, "German National Peoples' Party," pp. 86-87.

[6] Bracher, *Die Auflösung*, pp. 290-91.

[7] Erich Eyck, *A History of the Weimar Republic*, Cambridge, Mass., 1962-63, II, 208, 236-38.

[8] Bracher, *Die Auflösung*, pp. 296-303, 345-47; Julius Curtius, *Sechs Jahre Minister der Deutschen Republik*, Heidelberg, 1948, p. 136; Eyck *Weimar Republic*, II, 262-64.

ing, and their condemnation of the whole Weimar system, returned 26 per cent of the Reichstag deputies.[9]

Brüning laid the responsibility for the disastrous results of the
elections of September 1930 at the door of the Western powers
who had not, he thought, lifted the burdens of Versailles quickly
enough during the Locarno era. Curtius was quickly instructed
to avoid the use of the term "policy of understanding" in the
future. In mid-October Brüning publicly hinted at a moratorium
on reparation payments, and by December he had decided to
press for the revision of the Young plan. Then, the policy of
understanding came to an end in March 1931 when Curtius announced the Austro-German Customs Union without first consulting the other members of the Locarno Triplice. While Stresemann
had carefully and patiently prepared his opponents for steps of
such importance, Curtius and Brüning tried to defy French objections and pursue a policy of treaty revision independent of the
Allies rather than in concert with them.[10] Thus, in Germany the
benefits of the settlement of 1929 did not protect it from the attacks of the National Opposition, and in the face of popular
response to those attacks, Stresemann's successors departed on a
new course.

In France there was no organized revolt against the settlement
of 1929, but there were anxious doubts about the security of
French reparation receipts. This concern for financial security,
by no means a new anxiety, fed on circumstances present during
the autumn of 1929. The occupation of Germany, which was regarded in Paris as a means of assuring payment (even though it
had not proved effective prior to 1924), was soon to come to an
end. The regulatory machinery of the Agent General and the
Reparation Commission, which was authorized to declare Germany in default through a vote of the creditor powers, would be
disbanded with the expiration of the Dawes plan. Stresemann,
who had paid the Dawes annuities, died, and the National Opposition launched an attack on all reparation payment. "What

[9] Bracher, *Die Auflösung*, pp. 364-70, 645; Bullock, *Hitler*, pp. 159-60; Eyck,
Weimar Republic II, 275-77.

[10] Edward W. Bennett, *Germany and the Diplomacy of the Financial Crisis,
1931*, Cambridge, Mass., 1962, pp. 12, 20-21, 33; Eyck, *Weimar Republic*,
II, 288-89; Jürgen Gehl, *Austria, Germany and the Anschluss, 1931-1938*, London, 1963, p. 7.

would happen," Briand asked Hoesch, "if Herr Hugenberg came to power and simply renounced the Young plan?"[11] The twofold problem, now ten years old, remained: how was willful German default to be prevented, and how would sanctions be imposed once it occurred?

Only limited means would be available. One was preventative: when the unconditional portion of the annuities was sold to the public, the creditor powers would receive advance payment, and the German government would hesitate to default on the conditional portion for fear of ruining the nation's foreign credit. The second was retributive: under Article 430 of the Treaty of Versailles, the French were permitted to reoccupy the Rhineland in the event of German noncompliance.[12] In the weeks after The Hague conference, Briand and Tardieu, who became Premier on November 2, 1929, sought to assure that these safeguards and sanctions would be readily available to the creditor powers.

The public sale of reparation bonds, with the prospect of advance payment, was the chief advantage which the French received from the settlement of 1929, and Briand and Tardieu sought to see this advantage realized before the existing guarantee of payment, military occupation, came to an end. In August at The Hague, Briand had not made evacuation dependent on the public sale of reparation bonds, but he had held out for an eight-month delay between the end of the conference and the conclusion of occupation. Tardieu made his concern obvious and told the Chamber of Deputies on November 5, that all the necessary arrangements for advance payment must be made before the evacuation of Mainz began.[13] Then at the second Hague conference (January 3-20, 1930), he and Chéron sought to assure the marketability of the bonds by asking the Germans to negotiate no new long-term foreign loans before the first portion of the reparation bonds was sold, or before March 31, 1931, whichever came first. Curtius agreed, and 300 million dollars' (1.2 billion marks') worth of bonds were sold in New York in June 1930, the month

[11] 21 October 1929, Hoesch to AA, 2244/4498/109751.

[12] The imposition of such drastic sanctions was, however, an unlikely eventuality; more probably the French would ask the League Council to authorize some lesser form of sanction under Article 11.

[13] Chambre débats, 1929, pp. 3064-65; Etienne Weill-Raynal, Les réparations allemandes et la France, Paris, 1947-49, III, 558-59.

the Rhineland was evacuated. The world financial crisis prevented subsequent sales.[14]

On the matter of sanctions—also raised and settled at the second Hague conference—Tardieu wished to reserve for France and the other creditors the possibility of reoccupying the Rhineland in the event of willful default. To facilitate the application of this or lesser sanctions, he wished to preserve the default declaring functions of the moribund Reparation Commission by conferring them upon the Advisory Committee of the Bank for International Settlements. The Germans, on the other hand, contended that with the implementation of the Young plan, Germany's reparation indebtedness should become truly nonpolitical: rather than being treated as an obligation rising out of the Treaty of Versailles, it should be treated as any ordinary international commercial debt, with the creditors exercising no special political sanctions over Germany.[15] Curtius prevailed at the second Hague conference, and he and Tardieu agreed that the default determining functions of the Reparation Commission would come to an end; no longer would Germany be obliged to accept, without recourse, sanctions resulting from a decision of the creditors alone. In the future, alleged default would be referred to the International Court of Justice at The Hague, and unless, and until, the Court ruled against Germany, France would not be free to impose political or economic sanctions. Thus Tardieu, who had authored Article 430 ten years before, finally accepted what Poincaré and Briand had long since come to believe—that once the Rhineland was evacuated, it could not be reoccupied.[16] The real guarantee of German payment remained what it had been since 1924; the Germans' desire to protect their foreign credit.

Even before The Hague settlement was implemented in May-June 1930, Tardieu demonstrated the limits of French confidence in German willingness to honor the settlement of 1929. Soon afterward two events—the German elections of September 1930 and

---

[14] *Agreements Concluded at The Hague Conference, January 1930*, Cmd. 3484, London, 1930, #6; Harold G. Moulton and Leo Pasvolsky, *War Debts and World Prosperity*, Washington, D. C., 1932, p. 214; Weill-Raynal, *Réparations allemandes*, III, 559-61, 597-98.

[15] Carl E. Shepard, Germany and The Hague Conference, unpublished doctoral dissertation, Indiana University, 1964, p. 149.

[16] Cmd. 3484; Eyck, *Weimar Republic*, II, 234-35; Weill-Raynal, *Réparations allemandes*, III, 566-70.

the Austro-German Customs Union project of March 1931—
seemed to warrant Tardieu's suspicious caution and transformed
chronic French reservations regarding the policy of understanding into a near rejection of Briand's Locarno policy. Tardieu responded to the Reichstag elections with a public speech
expressing dismay at their outcome, complaining of German ingratitude for the early evacuation of the Rhineland, and
suggesting that in the future France would pursue a more independent foreign policy.[17] The announcement of the Customs
Union had a similar effect in Paris. Hoesch reported that as far as
the French public was concerned, a new stage of Franco-German
relations was about to begin—the old one, begun in the spring of
1924, having come to an end.[18] Briand considered changing his
German policy,[19] but had no chance to do so. Not only did the
Customs Union project bring him into political disrepute, but he
suffered a sharp decline in physical strength and stamina. Although he remained in office until January 1932, he was completely overshadowed by Pierre Laval, who had become Premier
in January 1931.[20] The supplantation of Briand and the rejection
of his policies completed the immediate reaction against cooperation among the Locarno powers which had begun in April 1929
with Snowden's attack on Churchill. Although the goal of an understanding between Germany and the West was periodically
renewed and survived to 1939, the Locarno era attempts to attain
that goal had come to an end, and the men who had operated the
Locarno system were gone. What did they leave to their
successors?

2. *The Legacy of 1929*

The Hague conference of August 1929 was referred to at the
time as "The Conference for the Final Liquidation of the World

[17] Pierre Renouvin, *War and Aftermath, 1914-1929*, New York, 1968, p. 248;
Eyck, *Weimar Republic*, II, 303.

[18] Gehl, *Austria, Germany and the Anschluss*, p. 7.

[19] Alexis Saint Léger Léger, *Briand*, New York, 1943, pp. 15-16. Also Walter
E. Edge, *A Jerseyman's Journal; Fifty Years of American Business and Politics*,
Princeton, 1948, p. 194; William E. Scott, *Alliance Against Hitler; the Origins
of the Franco-Soviet Pact*, Durham, N. C., 1962, p. 10.

[20] Laval, like Tardieu, intervened directly into French foreign politics;
both men took from Briand the function of chief negotiator at international
conferences—something Poincaré had not done: Bennett, *Diplomacy of the
Financial Crisis*, p. 108; Scott, *Alliance Against Hitler*, pp. 22, 34.

War." Although its agenda was certainly not the general settlement repeatedly suggested by Berthelot, it was an attempt to settle at one time many of the issues affecting the relations between Germany, on the one hand, and Britain, France, Belgium, and Italy on the other. It was the first and last such attempt made between the wars; it was as close as Europe came to a second peace conference. As such, the settlement of 1929 is a good point from which to review the accomplishments of Stresemann, Briand, and Chamberlain. None of the three realized the long-range objectives they had earlier set for themselves: Briand did not make Europe safe for France; Stresemann did not win French acceptance for German revisionism; Chamberlain's entente did not give the French the assurance and security necessary to make them comfortable with a stronger Germany.[21] Each man did, however, have more immediate policy objectives as well, and a look at the terms under which they tried to liquidate the war may illuminate those objectives and the skill with which they were pursued.

In negotiating the settlement of 1929, Briand and Poincaré gained for France something of great potential value—a reparation settlement which was adequate, definitive, and relatively secure. Financial experts from six countries had testified to the feasibility of the plan. Payment was apparently secure against willful default and unilateral repudiation: the German cabinet, Reichstag, and President had accepted the plan over vociferous radical opposition. And, more importantly, a significant portion of the risk of holding the reparation debt was to be shifted from the treasuries of the creditors to private investors. With such "financial security," it was thought no longer necessary to assure payment by means of controls over German finances, by the reservation of certain state revenues for payment purposes, and by military occupation.

Because the Young annuities were soon canceled with only a fraction of the total obligation fulfilled, it might appear at first glance that the French were subsequently deprived of any benefit from the settlement of 1929 while the Germans retained their

[21] Stresemann and Briand, A.J.P. Taylor has written, "were disappointed; both were in sight of failure when they died": *Origins of the Second World War*, New York, 1961, p. 60. Also Arnold Wolfers, *Britain and France between Two Wars; Conflicting Strategies of Peace since Versailles*, New York, 1940, p. 65.

gain—freedom from military occupation. However, when general cancellation took place in 1932, the French lost nothing of what Poincaré and Briand had bargained for in the first instance— reparation coverage for French war debt outpayments. What was lost was the indemnity provided for in the Young plan, a sum equal to one-third of the cost of reconstructing the country's war devastated area.

Because Briand and Poincaré believed that military occupation must end in 1935, all they renounced at The Hague was the right to occupy the Palatinate for five more years. Even this full term occupation was of use to France primarily as tender for financial security; it diminished in value from year to year, until in 1935 it would be worth nothing. Briand and Poincaré knew this, and they bargained it off for a definitive reparation settlement while it still had some value. The end of occupation did not diminish French financial security, for occupation did not in itself assure the regular payment of reparation; it had not done so prior to 1924. Payment had been assured by American loans, the operations of the Reparation Commission, and the awareness in Berlin that default would ruin German credit.

Nor did early evacuation diminish the long-term military security of France. Knowing that occupation was only temporary, Briand and Poincaré looked to the Maginot Line for long-term security, and both supported the construction of it. Thus, when the French Army of the Rhine was withdrawn, it was replaced by a line of fortifications constructed behind the borders of France and not by a Commission of Verification to prevent the gradual remilitarization of the Rhineland. After 1930, France's strategic frontier was the Rhine only in theory; in reality it was the border; and in 1936 reality overcame theory.

With French frontiers guaranteed by Britain and now to be fortified, with Germany in effect disarmed, and with a final reparation settlement adopted, Briand and Poincaré liquidated military occupation—the last remaining measure of treaty enforcement over which Paris had direct and singular control. They withdrew French troops without insisting on additional measures of political security. They did not insist on on-site inspection of the Rhineland, nor did they make an Eastern Locarno or voluntary German renunciation of the Anschluss conditions of evacuation. They apparently regarded the political, as well as the financial and military security of France as having been maximized; little could be added by five more years of occupation.

The desire for financial security, the transient contribution of occupation to military security, and the diminishing value of evacuation as tender all influenced French policy. But it is not certain that the deliberate conciliation of Germany was a consideration which swayed Briand and Poincaré. If this was of major importance to them in 1929, might they not have considered the return of the Saar more seriously, and might Briand not have negotiated the end date for evacuation with more generosity and candor?

What did the Germans gain and lose from the settlement of 1929? When compared with the Dawes plan, the Young plan offered some disadvantages and some advantages. The Germans gave up a measure of transfer protection, and in exchange they received a reduction in payment—particularly during the first ten years, and Stresemann and Curtius were primarily concerned with the short run. Acceptance of the plan was desirable, and necessary (given German dependence on foreign capital) even if the end of occupation had not been offered in exchange.

What benefits would complete evacuation confer upon Germany? In the event of war, Western Germany would no longer be immediately and directly accessible to the French Army; instead, the Reichswehr would have access to the Rhine bridges and be able to contest with the armies of France for control of the Rhine territory. As complete evacuation was due to take place in 1935 anyway, the premature removal of this strategic disability would be of real value only in the unlikely eventuality of a Franco-German war within the next five years. Secondly, French governments would be denied the opportunity to foster separatism among the Rhenish population and possibly detach the area from Germany. The value of this, too, was lessened by the past failure of such attempts. Finally, occupation was instituted in 1919 as a facility to enforce compliance with the Treaty of Versailles. However, after the Ruhr invasion none of the Allies showed any willingness to use military power for treaty enforcement, and after Locarno they were disinclined to delay the evacuation of any given zone. In this regard, early evacuation deprived the French of little that had not already been informally renounced. It ratified decisions made earlier, and therein lay its contribution to German security.

Evacuation, of course, lifted the inconveniences of military occupation from the population of the Rhineland,[22] although the burdens of occupation were by no means as great as they had been before the regime of occupation had been eased as a result of the Locarno Treaty.[23] Although Paul Tirard no doubt exaggerated the "benefits" of occupation,[24] it is true that rather than demanding early evacuation, local officials in the Rhineland at times bravely announced to Berlin that they were willing to sustain occupation for its full term, if necessary; an announcement which was perhaps due in part to the vested interest of some Rhenish tradesmen in maintaining a 70,000-man, year-round "army of tourists in uniform" and to the annual subventions given by the Reich to the local governments of the occupied territories to compensate them for the difficulties of occupation. Moreover, occupation imposed no special economic hardship on the German taxpayer for, since the implementation of the Dawes plan, the cost of maintaining the armies of occupation had been paid for by the creditors out of their reparation receipts.

Within Germany occupation was most resented because it was a symbol of Allied military victory and of German defeat. The Tricolor flew at Mainz, and a French general occupied the palace once used by Napoleon as his headquarters. This was a constant reminder of French supremacy, past and present; to many Germans occupation represented, the British consul at Mainz wrote, "the insolent crow of the vainglorious Gallic cock."[25] Occupation was a reminder of the disaster of 1918; it was a highly visible indication of the limitations of German sovereignty imposed by the peace of 1919; and as long as it continued, the distinction between

[22] For a discussion of the "burdens" of occupation see Carl Schmid, "Zehn Jahre fremder Besatzung am Rhein," in Hermann Oncken, *et al., Zehn Jahre deutsche Geschichte, 1918-1928*, Berlin, 1928, pp. 129-32.

[23] The conditions of occupation are not within the scope of this study. The yearly reports issued by Berlin and London: *Bericht des Reichskommissars für die besetzten rheinischen Gebiete*, Reichskanzlei, Besetzte Rheingebiete (Bundesarchiv); *Annual Report of the British Department of the Inter-allied Rhineland High Commission* (Foreign Office Records).

[24] Paul Tirard, *La France sur le Rhin; douze années d'occupation rhénane*, Paris, 1930, pp. 312-24.

[25] 27 June 1927, Magowan to Chamberlain, FO. 371/12143/45.

victor and vanquished remained, in spite of Allied willingness to submit to negotiation the questions of security, disarmament, and reparation. Evacuation, on the other hand, was a symbol of recovery from defeat, of respect regained, and of the restoration of Germany to a position of full equality among the great powers. As such, its desirability was assumed, and not debated; throughout the German body politic, the freedom of the Rhineland was accepted as Germany's primary national goal with little question or dissent. For Stresemann's constituency it became the touchstone of the success of his foreign policy; it represented what he termed the "positive advantages" to be gained through the deliberate cultivation of Allied goodwill. As long as the Allies withheld early evacuation, Stresemann was without a major tangible accomplishment to display in return for his signature on the Locarno Treaties, and he was vulnerable to the criticism of having pursued an unproductive policy. With evacuation he attained the objective which he had made his primary goal for more than four years.

With the settlement of 1929, Stresemann realized all the demands he had made at the Locarno conference in October 1925—except the return of the Saar—and he saw in it the end of one phase of his policy and the beginning of another. Stresemann did not state what the future means and ends of German policy would be, and death intervened before he indicated how he would conduct the affairs of Germany freed from the restraints imposed by the need to accommodate the occupying powers.[26] However, the course of his Locarno policy indicates that, had Stresemann remained at the Wilhelmstrasse, he would not have been quiescent or deferential. Since coming to office in 1923, he had not declined to seize the initiative; since July 1928 his policy had become increasingly assertive; since April 1929 he had become disillusioned with the cooperation among the Locarnites; and at The Hague conference he had demonstrated a new German independence from France by arranging with Henderson for unilateral British withdrawal and the hastening of French evacuation. After the settlement of 1929, Stresemann would, no doubt, have found new issues to raise. He may well have tried to complete the settlement of 1929 by persistently claiming the return of

[26] Gustav Stresemann, *Vermächtnis; der Nachlass in Drei Bänden*, Berlin, 1932-33, III, 563, 568.

the Saar. At Geneva he undoubtedly would have demanded that either the Allies disarm to the German level, or that the Germans be allowed to rearm; and he would have continued his active support of the German minority in Eastern Europe. He would probably have seized the opportunity of the deepening financial crisis of 1929-31 to work for further reduction of reparation, and no doubt he would have been more adroit than Curtius and Brüning. Finally, Stresemann had postponed any initiative on the revision of the territorial settlement in Eastern Europe until the Rhineland was evacuated; after 1929 this one barrier to treaty revision would no longer restrain him. The most important benefit of the settlement of 1929 was, then, a greater degree of diplomatic freedom in which German revisionism could operate. Stresemann had always argued that occupation was a barrier to Franco-German understanding and to lasting peace in Europe, and he stated that evacuation would promote both. What he publicized less was the notion that occupation was a barrier to revision as well. Freedom from occupation could be an important step toward revision of Versailles and independence from France rather than a step toward cooperation. As Hindenburg, with his proclivity for military terminology, said, the settlement of 1929 could be "a staging area" for the "next assault on the Treaty of Versailles."[27]

One European power could regard the settlement of 1929 as an unqualified success. At The Hague the British suffered no defeats and made no sacrifices. Instead, Snowden took back, at the expense of former ally and former enemy alike, the concessions made by the British experts on the Young committee. Moreover, the evacuation of the Rhineland and the continuation of the existing regime in the Saar both accorded with the lines of policy set out by Henderson before the conference. Most importantly, the final liquidation of the war could free London from constant attention to Franco-German problems. Arthur Henderson, the ex-trade-union secretary, put it as well as Lord Curzon might have done when he impatiently told Briand and Stresemann at The Hague that "the Foreign Secretary of the British Empire, is a very busy man."[28] When the settlement was reached, the British could, and did, depart from The Hague pleased.

These were the conditions which the framers of The Hague

---

[27] 5 September 1929, Köpke to Geneva, 2242/4498/108495.
[28] 22 August 1929, Memorandum Schmidt, 2241/4498/108178.

settlement left to their successors. The settlement of 1929 came at the end of their efforts. It was their final achievement but not their only one. For a full evaluation of their accomplishments the almost five years' personal and political relationships known as the Locarno era must be considered.

3. *The Locarno Era*

The Locarno era opened with the negotiation of a Western European mutual security pact. In the succeeding months, the withdrawal of Allied armies from Germany began, and Germany became a member of the Council of the League of Nations, symbolizing the restoration of the Reich to the status of a great power and the return of Germany to the Concert of Europe. In 1926-27 a disarmament settlement was concluded: the Allies affirmed that Germany—without a conscript army, a navy, an air force, or heavy artillery—was effectively disarmed, and the Inter-Allied Military Control Commission was withdrawn. In 1929 a final determination of German reparation obligations was made; military occupation was terminated; the controls imposed by the Dawes plan on German finances were lifted; and the claims held by the Reparation Commission on certain sources of revenue within Germany were largely removed. In the absence of direct controls—occupation, the Military Control Commission, the Reparation Commission—the ex-Allies no longer had at hand means to prevent the remilitarization of the Rhineland, the rearmament of Germany, or the repudiation of reparation; they could only react and punish transgressions once they had taken place. By implication the Germans were expected to conform to the Treaty of Versailles without prior restraint.

These new arrangements did not prove long lasting. By 1931 reparations were no longer being paid. In October 1933 Germany withdrew from the League of Nations, rejecting the notion of negotiation in concert. In March 1935 the disarmament settlement of 1926-27 was overturned when Hitler announced German rearmament. The next year, he remilitarized the Rhineland and the security pact of 1925 collapsed. By 1936 the arrangements made during the Locarno era were no more.

It is sometimes maintained that the edifice of peace designed

366

at Locarno, at Geneva, and at The Hague was in itself soundly constructed, but that it was battered down from the outside after it was completed. According to this view, great opportunities were offered, and taken, during the Locarno era. The reparation problem, which had kept wartime resentments alive during the early 1920's, was depoliticized and set aside by the Dawes plan. The British assumed some responsibility for Continental affairs, and the problem of French military security was laid away at Locarno. The foreign ministers of Germany, France, and England could, and did, talk with each other calmly and reasonably. Through their efforts, the conflict which had existed between Germany and the West during the World War and its aftermath ended, and a new era of goodwill, reconciliation, and hope dawned. Then, extraneous events intervened to destroy both the opportunities and the achievements of the Locarno era. Stresemann, a younger man than Konrad Adenauer, died prematurely in October 1929. And the same month a financial crash introduced a period of economic dislocation which aggravated all the problems that had not seemed so urgent during the prosperity of the late 1920's. The Nazi electoral victory of September 1930 forced moderates like Curtius and Brüning to pursue a more actively revisionist foreign policy in a vain attempt to popularize once more parliamentary government in Germany. Finally, Briand was defeated in the presidential elections of May 1931, and the French people thereby indicated in turn their own repudiation of the policy of understanding. The death process begun in October 1929 was complete; the Locarno era was at an end.

This somewhat exterior view has been modified at times to account more fully for some of the events of the Locarno era itself. According to this modified view, the Locarno-Hague edifice had structural weaknesses which caused it to collapse when subjected to stress. The structure of peace was weak because it was unfinished, and it was unfinished because the builders found their efforts obstructed. Opponents at home, usually die-hard nationalists, hampered the efforts of Stresemann and Briand, either by establishing limits beyond which the two men could not go, or by delaying their progress so that the belated results of their efforts had little lasting impact on public opinion. The best intentions of

Stresemann and Briand were thwarted; their hopes were not realized.[29]

Effective opposition to the Locarno policy within Germany has frequently been attributed to the DNVP, and observers of German politics have even spoken of Stresemann's "surrender to the nationalists" and the damage this did to the success of his policy.[30] While it is true that the DNVP withdrew from the Luther government in October 1925 and voted against the Locarno Treaty in the Reichstag, the party did accept Locarno, German membership in the League, and the policy of understanding with France in order to return to government in January 1927. Thereafter, the leadership of the party supported Stresemann's policy in spite of criticism of it in the Hugenberg press and by some right-wing DNVP Deputies.[31] It was not until July 1929, when Hugenberg joined Hitler and Seldte in sponsorship of the Freedom Law, that there was any highly organized opposition to Stresemann's policy, and that opposition then split the DNVP while not preventing the government, the Reichstag, and the President from accepting the Young plan.

Stresemann could agree with much of the occasional criticism levied at the Locarno policy prior to the Freedom Law. Nationalists charged that the Locarno policy was barren of practical results; since Thoiry, they stated, German foreign policy had been stalemated. Of this Stresemann was aware, and it strongly influenced the decision taken in August 1928 to demand formal negotiations on the Rhineland. What Stresemann accepted much less

[29] On nationalist resistance as an obstacle to conciliation in both countries see Martin Göhring, "Stresemann, Mench, Staatsmann, Europäer," in Joseph Scheidel (ed.), *Gustav Stresemann: Festschrift zur Wiedererrichtung des Stresemann-Ehrenmals in Mainz am 16 Oktober 1960*, Mainz, 1960, pp. 37-38; Felix E. Hirsch, "Stresemann in Historical Perspective," *Review of Politics*, 15 (1953), p. 272. The notion that the settlement of 1929 came too late: Johann Bernstorff, *Memoirs of Count Bernstorff*, New York, 1936, p. 335; William McElwee, *Britain's Locust Years, 1918-1940*, London, 1962, pp. 160-61; Annelise Thimme, *Gustav Stresemann; eine politische Biographie zur Geschichte der Weimarer Republik*, Hannover, 1957, p. 116.

[30] J. W. Wheeler-Bennett, *Wooden Titan; Hindenburg in Twenty Years of German History, 1914-1934*, New York, 1936, p. 317.

[31] Wilhelm Marx, *Der Nachlass des Reichskanzlers Wilhelm Marx*, Cologne, 1968, I, 462; Robert Garthwol, "DNVP and European Reconciliation, 1924-1928; a Study of the Conflict between Party Politics and Government Foreign Policy in Weimar Germany," unpublished doctoral dissertation, Chicago, 1968, pp. 309-12, 318.

readily, if at all, was the notion, frequently expressed in the Nationalist press after September 1928, that the Locarno Triplice should be abandoned in favor of a new alignment—although he did, when his patience was exhausted and his disappointment deepest, threaten to terminate the policy of understanding with France. Far from regarding it as an obstacle, Stresemann tried to use DNVP criticism to his advantage: as early as Locarno and as late as The Hague, he insisted that concessions must be made to him to strengthen him against his political opponents who otherwise might come to power upon his resignation.

It has also been suggested that Stresemann found himself restricted by German relations with Russia, and that he found his progress retarded by those in the foreign service and army who valued Russo-German cooperation as a means of restoring Germany to a position from which concessions could be wrested from the Western powers, and who feared that the Locarno Treaty would damage the development of that cooperation. However, the Easterners could not stop Stresemann from concluding the Rhineland Pact, joining the League, and pursuing a policy aimed at winning the cooperation of the West for evacuation, the revision of the Dawes plan, the return of the Saar, the protection of German minorities, and the revision of Germany's eastern frontiers.

In his effort to win agreement and support in the West, the Russian connection was of no real disadvantage or advantage to Stresemann. Briand once mentioned Russo-German military collaboration and tried to get Stresemann to accept permanent inspection of the Rhineland as a way of calming French politicians who were concerned about it. And Poincaré expressed concern over possible secret clauses in the Treaty of Berlin and asked Stresemann to join with him in a united front of civilized nations against Bolshevism, but neither the Berlin Treaty nor Stresemann's cool attitude toward a united front led Poincaré to deviate from his position on evacuation and financial security. Germany's Russian connection was of real concern mainly to Austen Chamberlain; sometimes it led him to cultivate better relations with Germany and sometimes not: in 1926 the Berlin Treaty led Chamberlain away from efforts to reduce the size of the occupying forces, but a year later he urged troop reduction on Briand, contending that the Western powers were struggling with Russia for the soul of Germany.

In France, the opposition to Briand's policy, which allegedly retarded his efforts at the appeasement of Germany, has been attributed to Poincaré. As Premier of France during much of the Locarno era, Poincaré was in a position to obstruct Briand's policy, and given his record up to 1923, it might be expected that he would do so. However, the "new Poincaré" who returned to office in 1926 was willing to concede evacuation in order to obtain financial security. Rather than obstructing a businesslike settlement with Germany, he actively promoted it. With his prestige and reputation for fiscal responsibility, he was able to win the approval of the Parliament and the public for a new and smaller reparation settlement. His acceptance of evacuation made it tolerable to militarists and nationalists who trusted him more than they did Briand. His presence on the Council of Ministers protected Briand against the "hard liners" and the irreconcilables. It is unlikely that the settlement of 1929 could have taken place without him.

Both Stresemann and Briand encountered criticism, but not effective opposition, from the Left. French Socialists advocated unconditional withdrawal, but their view was not taken seriously by the National Union government. Left-wing criticism of Stresemann's policy was limited to radical pacifists (and Communists), and they were few in number and slight in influence. The numerous moderate pacifists of the early 1920's went along with the Locarno policy, and as a result, the German peace movement atrophied during the second half of the decade.[32]

The most effective hindrance to Briand's policy, and to Stresemann's, came from their armies. French generals delayed the reduction of troop strength promised at Locarno and forced the postponement of early evacuation. Meanwhile, the Reichswehr gave them occasion to do so by tardy compliance with the disarmament requirements of the Conference of Ambassadors. When faced with such obstructions, neither Stresemann nor Briand confronted their military in the name of Franco-German understanding, thereby risking defeat and resignation. The reward for their patience and accommodation was belated success.

---

[32] Istvan Deak, *Weimar Germany's Left Wing Intellectuals; a Political History of the Weltbühne and its Circle*, Berkeley, 1968, p. 117.

Germany was declared disarmed almost three years after the Allies declared her in default. The troop reduction promised in 1925 was carried out in 1927. The Rhineland was evacuated in June 1930 rather than September 1927, the date mentioned at Thoiry. In the end both armies accepted Locarno and the disarmament and Rhineland settlements negotiated by Stresemann and Briand without defiance.[33]

Effective interference in the work of the Locarnites was limited: the opposition which was offered was accommodated in the short run, overcome in the long run, and only occasionally produced significant internal political tension. For the most part, Stresemann and Briand, and Chamberlain too, firmly controlled foreign policy. They were not at odds with their constituencies, and they found few serious restrictions placed upon their efforts by their parties, their parliaments, and their public. Their long terms in office testify to this. They did at times state to each other that their cabinets, or parliaments, or public opinion forbade this measure or demanded that concession, but when they did so, they made such claims to support policies which they themselves favored. Stresemann stated that the German people demanded the return of the Saar; yet, when they did not get it there were few repercussions. Briand stated that the French public and parliament required the Commission of Verification; yet, he gave up the idea and suffered no loss of support. Both men led opinion more than they followed it. They were politicians and orators of the first order; both had at their disposal large funds to purchase press support; and both had good relations with the press. Stresemann, Briand, and Chamberlain were sensitive to public and press opinion, but they did not regard it as immutable or confining, and when they followed it, they did not do so against their better judgment. Many considerations influenced the relations among the Locarno Triplice—considerations of military and political strategy, personal estimates, and even racist notions about how foreigners behaved; public opinion was but one of many factors. Yet, in spite of this latitude, the Locarnites did not succeed in making arrangements which proved adequate during the years that followed. Why not? After all, they were given the

---

[33] See for example, the evaluation of Seeckt's policies in Michael Salewski, *Entwaffnung und Militärkontrolle in Deutschland, 1919-1927*, Munich, 1966, pp. 344-45.

greatest opportunities of any politicians between the wars, were they not? Were not the late 1920's the choicest years that were eaten by the locust?

The notion that Locarno was an era of missed opportunities has had some currency.[34] The Locarnites themselves were instrumental in creating it beginning in 1925. In the rhetoric they employed to popularize their policies, they spoke of the security pact as only a beginning from which much more would follow. They frequently referred to the cooperation and goodwill which existed among them, which would, they stated, lead to further progress. They talked of a future which held understanding, and even lasting peace between Germany and the West. Later, when results did not come quickly, there was talk of disappointment, betrayal, and of Locarno being an end rather than a beginning. Subsequently, it became tempting to look back on the Locarno era, and seeing that there had been a relaxation of tensions during these years, to wish the détente had become a diplomatic revolution. This did not happen; natural enemies did not become natural allies. In 1918, the First World War had concluded with an armistice; the statesman's task was to transform that armistice into a peace. This the men of Locarno could not do.

Although certain questions regarding security, disarmament, demilitarization, and reparation were resolved, or partially

[34] Two of the most eloquent statements of the widely expressed notion that the Locarno era was an age of missed opportunities and unfulfilled hopes are found in Raymond Aron, *The Century of Total War*, Boston, 1955, pp. 96-97, and F. P. Walters, *A History of the League of Nations*, London, 1952, 1960, pp. 346-47. The notion became official dogma in 1961 when French and German teachers of history resolved to interpret the Locarno era as years of relaxation and hope: Heinrich Bodensieck, "Weimarer Republik und deutsch-französische Beziehungen," *Geschichte in Wissenschaft und Unterricht*, 13 (1962), p. 370. The major opportunity missed, it has been frequently asserted, was the opportunity to make concessions to Germany and thereby popularize among the German people statesmen pledged to republican government and a restrained and peaceful foreign policy: Bernstorff, *Memoirs, passism*; Hirsch, "Stresemann in Historical Perspective," p. 373; William S. Halperin, *Germany Tried Democracy*, New York, 1946, p. 341; Ludwig Zimmermann, *Deutsche Aussenpolitik in der Ära der Weimarer Republik*, Göttingen, 1958, pp. 472-74. These notions have been criticized by those who argue that stricter treaty enforcement during the 1920's would have deprived Hitler of advantages in the 1930's: Eric C. Kollman, "Reinterpreting Modern German History, the Weimar Republic," *Journal of Central European Affairs*, 21 (1962), p. 439; Eyck, *Weimar Republic*, II, 244.

resolved, between 1924 and 1929, fundamental rivalries and antagonisms persisted through the Locarno era. The objectives of German, French, and British policy did not change after 1925, they remained much what they had been. Stresemann, Briand, and Chamberlain came to no agreement about the place of Germany in Europe, and not having settled this question, the Locarno powers did not cease to threaten each other. The potential for a diplomatic revolution and the opportunity for transforming the armistice into a peace were more apparent than real—not only because diplomatic revolutions are difficult to conduct in an age of democratic diplomacy, but also because none of the policy makers was inclined to conduct a revolution against the old order of policy objectives.

Briand was concerned, as French statesmen had been since the war, with assurances against future German duplicity, defiance, and attack. If the Rhineland was to be cleared of Allied troops, he insisted on arrangements to assure France that Germany would continue to pay reparation although no longer compelled to do so by occupation. Even after the Reichstag accepted the Dawes plan, he remained concerned about what he and Poincaré called "financial security." To be sure, the form of assurance sought was changed. Security was no longer viewed in terms of productive pledges, as had been the case in 1922-23; now it was seen in terms of prior payment. The means of attaining it also changed. The invasion of German territory was no longer either necessary or desirable; now the denial of early evacuation proved to be sufficient coercion. The objective did not change. If anything, it became more ambitious—a German commitment to pay for sixty years and payment in advance.

Briand remained concerned about the possibility of renewed German aggression, even after the Reichstag had ratified the Treaty of Locarno. He was especially anxious about what would happen once France gave up the strategic advantages derived from military occupation. For three years, he declined to terminate occupation prior to the construction of the Maginot Line, thereby indicating a reluctance to leave France vulnerable, even for an interval. At the same time, he refused to terminate occupation without an arrangement to protect France from the gradual remilitarization of the Rhineland. Eventually, he agreed to withdraw French troops before the fortifications were constructed and without gaining his Commission of Verification, but this did not mean that his fears of invasion or remilitarization had lessened. It meant that he and Poincaré were not prepared to miss the opportunity for financial security in order to compensate for the army's delay in beginning the fortification of the border. And it meant that fear alone provided no legal justification for continued occupation; the Treaty of Versailles did not mention permanent on-site Rhineland inspection as one of France's rights. Here, there was in Briand's policy a legalism of the kind usually associated with Poincaré. As the price of evacuation, he required reparation, something specified as being due France in the Treaty of Verailles; but he did not persist in demanding the Commission of Verification, which could not be justified by the letter of the treaty and which required voluntary acceptance by Germany.

In demanding what was legally due to France, Briand turned his back on the alternative policy of the magnanimous gesture. In the end, he was no more prepared than was Poincaré to sacrifice the treaty rights of France in order to procure German goodwill. He rejected Stresemann's suggestions that the Rhineland be evacuated in regard for "political psychology," in recognition of Germany's right to evacuation without material compensation, and in return for such intangibles as the creation of an atmosphere of goodwill which would prevent renewed German aggression. Briand insisted on new guarantees. Even after the reparation settlement was assured at The Hague, his response to the German plea for a generous gesture was to make half a gesture, to split the difference between March 31 and August 31 and withdraw French troops by June 30. Briand may have been casual and informal, but he was not inclined toward generosity or softheartedness. He said this best himself: after Thoiry he mentioned to the press the rumor that he had sold the towers of Notre Dame to the Germans. "I am perhaps a little naïve," he joked, "but not to that extent."[35]

The objectives of German policy were not altered as a result of the Locarno Treaty either; Stresemann's signature on the Treaty of Locarno did not mean that he accepted the Treaty of Versailles. He still expected that much of the territory lost by Germany in Eastern Europe would be regained. He knew of and

[35] Quoted in Stresemann, *Vermächtnis*, III, 79.

approved of the secret and illegal rearmament and recognized its contribution to the defensive capabilities of the German Army.[36] However, his attitude toward the payment of reparations is not so widely understood. Ostensibly, Stresemann was prepared to accommodate the creditors. At his urging, Germany accepted the Dawes plan, paid reparation on schedule, and finally agreed to the Young plan while Nationalists and Nazis charged him with selling the German people into slavery to foreign collectors. Why did Stresemann fulfill the reparation clauses of the treaty and associate himself with an unpopular policy? No German statesman paid reparation eagerly; Stresemann paid the Dawes annuities because unilateral cancellation would have meant, at the least, the collapse of the German economy. The Dawes plan, he knew, was not a permanent settlement, and most of his efforts as Foreign Minister in the years after Locarno were directed at trying to get the troops of the creditor powers out of the Rhineland. Then he would be able to bargain for a revision of the Dawes plan and achieve a favorable reparation settlement without having the strangle hold of occupation on Germany's throat. Although the Young plan was not the favorable settlement for which Stresemann had hoped, he urged its acceptance. He was disappointed that Germany's right to evacuation without compensation was not recognized, at having to accept the Young plan prior to evacuation, at not being able to negotiate the final settlement free from the noose of occupation, and at having to postpone still longer the reparation settlement he wanted. He accepted this disappointment because he was convinced that rejection of the Young plan would lead to financial crisis, economic contraction, and political revolution.

While it is clear that Stresemann regarded the reparation agreements of the Locarno era as temporary, it is less easy to indicate the reservations he may have had about the security arrangements. It might be assumed that he had no hesitations about his decision to renounce aggression against France either by invasion or by remilitarizing the Rhineland, but his attitude about the military security of Western Europe was less simple than this. He was highly sensitive about the abridgment of German sovereignty

[36] Gaines Post, Jr., "German Foreign Policy and Military Planning; the Polish Question, 1924-1929," unpublished doctoral dissertation, Stanford, 1969, pp. 228-29.

over the Rhineland: he regarded the end of occupation as the most important goal of German policy, and he stubbornly opposed Briand's pleas for a Committee of Verification to maintain the demilitarized status of the Rhineland in perpetuity. Stresemann, of course, did not operate by means of Hitler-like surprise moves; he negotiated patiently and did not engage in unilateral repudiations. However, from what we know of his attitudes and policies, it seems unlikely that he would regard permanent restrictions on military activities carried out on one's own soil as consistent with the sovereignty of a great power.

There were, then, a number of points at which French financial and military security, and German pride and revisionism remained incompatible throughout the post-Locarno period. This incompatibility perpetuated suspicions, limited the opportunity for understanding, and diminished the prospects for Franco-German rapprochement. And during the Locarno era, those incompatibilities assumed a crucial importance. One reason was that no other power intervened to reduce the incompatibility or mediate the conflict. The Locarno era was bound on one side by Chamberlain's decision to support Stresemann's security proposal in 1925 and on the other by Hoover's declaration of a moratorium on international payments in 1931. In the intervening period Washington and London took little initiative in European affairs and did little to arrange a European settlement based on Franco-German rapprochement. As a result, the initiative was left largely to Paris and Berlin.

In contrast to American involvement on the European continent after the Second World War, the affairs of Europe were of little official concern to the United States government during the Locarno era. Washington had declined to guarantee the peace settlement of 1919, had withdrawn all American troops from the Rhineland by 1923, and took no part in the security arrangements of 1925. The Rhineland Pact, as Stresemann proposed it in January 1925, called for the United States to act as "trustee" of the nonaggression treaty. The most Coolidge did for Locarno, however, was to give the pact his public blessing in July and let it be known, through the British ambassador in Washington, that continued American loans to Europe depended on the conclusion of the treaty. American policy, he told Congress just after Locarno was signed, was to have "European countries settle their own political problems without involving this country."[37] Not being a party to the Locarno system, the Americans did not participate in the many foreign ministers' conferences which followed. Kellogg even transformed Briand's proposed bilateral neutrality agreement into a universal renunciation of war, and thereby avoided entanglement in the European security system. To be sure, Coolidge and Kellogg continued to promote naval disarmament as Hughes had done; they called the Geneva Naval Conference of 1927, sometimes called the Coolidge Conference, with disastrous results. However, this one example of American initiative during the Locarno era did not touch on Continental affairs; only England, among the Locarno powers, was directly affected.

Only American war debt policy directly and decisively influenced the relations between Germany and the West during the Locarno era, and here American policy showed little originality. Between 1923 and 1926, Washington concluded war debt funding agreements with America's major debtors (Britain, Italy, and France), and in the process greatly reduced its claims on them.[38] But, during much of the Locarno era the United States government defended those agreements against suggestions that war debts be further reduced or cancelled, or that the United States collect its due directly from Berlin rather than from Germany's European creditors. Because the American government refused to play any official role in the reparation negotiations of the Locarno era, or even formally to appoint the experts who sat on the Young committee, it was primarily by means of American intermediaries, having no official connection with the United States government, that American interests in the reparation question were represented. Parker Gilbert and Owen Young did not regard themselves as representatives of American interests, even less as agents of the American government; nevertheless, out of sympathy for the desire of the creditor powers to collect enough from Germany to pay the United States, they arranged a reparation settlement designed primarily to allow Germany's creditors

[37] Quoted in Dexter Perkins, "The Department of State and American Public Opinion," in Gordon A. Craig and Felix Gilbert (eds.), *The Diplomats, 1919-1939*, Princeton, 1953, p. 294.

[38] The French debt was reduced by 50 per cent, the British by 20 per cent, and the Italian by 75 per cent: Moulton and Pasvolsky, *War Debts and World Prosperity*, p. 101.

to pay their American debts. The tactics by which American war debt policy was conducted during the Locarno era were remarkably adroit. The objectives, however, were frequently expressed by Coolidge and Mellon by the reiteration of long-established positions, and this gave to American financial diplomacy an image of unoriginality, unresponsiveness, and inflexibility. To Europeans it appeared that American insistence on payment necessitated reparation, and thereby required continued enforcement (by means of military occupation) until other guarantees could be arranged. America was the power, French diplomats told the Germans, which in the last analysis was responsible for occupation, the barrier to understanding. The United States, it seemed, was the obstacle to the final liquidation of the war.

The abdication of the leadership which the United States had exercised during the war and the peace conference was accompanied by an era of passivity in British policy. Locarno did not mark the beginning of active English participation in the affairs of Western Europe as much as it marked the limits and the extremity of British involvement in European affairs. After 1925 the British took little initiative in the further adjustment of Franco-German differences. Preoccupied with China, Russia, and the naval rivalry with the United States, Chamberlain was content to entrust Briand, and to a lesser extent Stresemann, with the determination of how differences between them would be resolved. With regard to Europe, Britain occupied what Chamberlain called "a semi-detached position."[39]

In theory the Locarno Treaty placed London in a position to mediate between France and Germany and so shape the European settlement; theoretically Chamberlain was the honest broker of the Locarno era.[40] In fact Chamberlain "loved France like a woman," and admired Briand while he found the Germans "the most difficult people in the world." He suspected that Berlin had in mind a plan for unending treaty revision, felt that the Germans could not be appeased, and accused Stresemann of ingratitude. All this influenced Chamberlain's policy. He was at times willing to punish the Germans for negotiating agreements with Russia (just as at other times he was willing to try to attract Stresemann

[39] Austen Chamberlain, "Great Britain as a European Power," *International Affairs*, 9 (1930), p. 188.
[40] W. J. Newman, *The Balance of Power in the Interwar Years, 1919-1939*, New York, 1968, pp. 92-97.

away from Moscow with concessions), and above all he was willing to give Briand a large measure of public support and to limit his pressure on Paris to quiet and private warnings and pleadings. The manifest expression of Chamberlain's support for Briand was his resolve to keep British troops on the Rhine until the French acquired what they desired from Germany, even though there was considerable sentiment in England favoring unilateral and unconditional withdrawal. It was not until the Labour Party came to power in June 1929 that the British undertook an independent Rhineland policy; then Henderson accompanied his insistence upon prompt French evacuation with the threat of unilateral British withdrawal.

Britain and the United States, the two powers which had helped to establish the basic conditions of Franco-German relations by their participation in the war and in the making of the peace, left the two Continental powers to negotiate their own final settlement during the late 1920's. This made resolution of the German problem exceedingly difficult. It has been maintained that the problem could have been resolved either by more severity or more kindness, either by stricter enforcement or more concessions. Neither method would have worked, as Ludwig Dehio has pointed out, without the participation in Continental affairs of some power greater than Germany and France.[41] In the absence of America and Britain, the leaders of France and Germany were led to believe that their two states, and the Rhineland which separated them, were the center of the world. France had emerged from the war victorious, her mission vindicated, and Germany did not regard 1918 as a final verdict on her drive for European hegemony. Neither had yet suffered the convincing defeats of 1940 and 1945, and they were not yet "frightened into friendship," as A.J.P. Taylor has put it, by the prospect of American and Russian domination of Europe.[42] Both sides still felt they had much to gain, or lose, in the contest with each other; illusions of power survived on both sides of the Rhine.

Consequently, the history of Locarno diplomacy is largely the story of the conflict of the opposing policies of Stresemann and

[41] Ludwig Dehio, *Germany and World Politics in the Twentieth Century*, New York, 1959, p. 22.
[42] Taylor, *The Origins of the Second World War*, pp. 60-61.

Briand. The signing of the Locarno Treaties was followed by the belated evacuation of Cologne, by Germany's admission to the League, and by a series of foreign ministers' conferences at Geneva and elsewhere, but not by the expeditious achievement of the *Rückwirkung* of Locarno. Both Stresemann and Briand chose to accommodate their own military rather than each other. Stresemann allowed German disarmament to be delayed; Briand allowed the French Army of the Rhine to be maintained without reduction. Locarno was not soon followed by the complete evacuation of the Rhineland, as Stresemann hoped, or by German financial assistance to France, as Briand hoped. And when it was discovered that the two men had discussed such notions at Thoiry in September 1926, they made little attempt to pursue their objectives in the face of difficulties and opposition. Instead, Thoiry was followed by a series of vehement denials and by personal hostility and estrangement.

The Military Control Commission was withdrawn in January 1927 and replaced by military experts residing in Berlin, some of whom continued to conduct inspections. It was withdrawn after minimum concessions from Germany, and the Allies responded by stalemating what Stresemann wanted most—evacuation. More than a year of "German ingratitude" led Chamberlain to defer to France on German affairs, and long-standing hostilities and suspicions led Briand and Poincaré to defer in turn to the French military. Finding the road to revision obstructed, alarms of encirclement were sounded in Berlin in mid-1927, and the emergence of what appeared to be an Anglo-French entente compelled the Germans to look into the face of the realities of the Locarno era: although the persistence of a special relationship between France and England within the Locarno Triplice might be humiliating and disconcerting, it was preferable to other alternatives. Nothing was to be gained from leaving the Western powers for Russia or from dividing Paris from London. A France alone, hostile and unrestrained by the British, would be less, not more, willing to appease the Germans.

With few military resources, with little assistance forthcoming from Russia, the only option open to Berlin was to propagandize the Western powers: occupation was an injustice; evacuation was the way to peace. The campaign for a free Rhineland, however, resulted in counterdemands. Although there was to be no Eastern

Locarno, no *Locarno supplémentaire,* and no voluntary renunciation of the Anschluss, Paris demanded financial security—a revised and final reparation settlement—and military security—a Commission of Verification. Anticipatory evacuation was acceptable in principle and would be exchanged for compensation, but military occupation would not be abandoned in pursuit of German goodwill.

Stresemann had long regarded the revision of the Dawes plan as desirable, but he did not intend to press for it while Germany's creditors had at their disposal the leverage of military occupation. To negotiate evacuation and reparation simultaneously would only enable the French to delay evacuation while the German reparation bill was reckoned. However, things did not work out as he intended, and in the end he waited for two months, after announcing German acceptance of the Young plan, while the French postponed even the discussion of evacuation. How did the sequence of his objectives come to be reversed?

In August 1928, Berlin decided to press for the evacuation of the Rhineland, and if necessary, to engage in parallel reparation negotiations—provided the Germans were not made responsible for devising the financial arrangements. In September, in the absence of Stresemann, the cabinet agreed to participate in the formulation of a final reparation settlement with the creditors. It was not until November that it became evident that the reparation invoice would be larger than the Germans expected: Poincaré and Churchill set the amount of the reparation settlement without consulting the Germans, just as Chamberlain and Briand had agreed on military and naval armaments three months before. Knowing that the creditors expected to divide 2 billion marks between them, but hoping that independent experts—particularly Americans—would lower the sum to what could be paid out of Germany's own resources, Stresemann defended the projected final settlement before the Reichstag. In this way, a series of decisions, taken over three months, committed Germany to a final reparation settlement, and by implication, to the French thesis of compensation for evacuation. The commitment was made with little willingness: Stresemann complained bitterly about the amount of the creditors' demands; he attacked what he regarded as British collusion with the French to deny the Germans their right to evacuation without compensation; he continued to insist that in exchange for the freedom of the Rhineland, no more could be demanded of Germany than what had already been performed—disarmament and payments under the Dawes plan. In Paris meanwhile, the independent experts—including the Americans—agreed (over Schacht's objections) to meet the requirements of Churchill and Poincaré, and the annuity was not reduced to the level anticipated by Stresemann. In April-May 1929, when at long last the German government considered the final reparation settlement seriously for the first time, Stresemann and the rest of the cabinet accepted a scheme which had been determined by their creditors, immediate and once removed. They accepted the Young plan not as the price of evacuation, and not because they believed Germany could meet its obligations, but in order to avoid a financial crisis.

The change of government, and of policy, in England only introduced more discord into the Locarno Triplice. The French were threatened by Snowden's attack on the Young plan and by Henderson's outright rejection of French Rhineland policy. Yet, there was little basis for closer Anglo-German cooperation. Stresemann had no interest in siding with the English over the redistribution of reparations, for Snowden was less, not more, generous than Churchill had been. Although Henderson was unwilling to support the French in the use of the Rhineland as a pledge for reparation, by the time he came to office it was too late to alter fundamentally the settlement of 1929, and his willingness to treat France and Germany as equals had had little practical effect.

To the end Briand tenaciously defended French treaty rights in a manner worthy of Poincaré. Although he gave in on the Commission of Verification, he preserved from diminution France's rights to reparation and to exploit the Saar mines until 1935. And even after Germany had accepted the Young plan, Briand would not bargain with Stresemann over the end date for evacuation. For domestic political reasons, Briand insisted on August 31; he withstood pressure from Stresemann and Henderson to move the date up to March 31; then he and Stresemann agreed on June 30 without explaining their reasons to each other. Never did the two men discuss French Rhineland policy candidly. Consequently, a month before his death, Stresemann was writing to his friends accusing Briand of duplicity and finessing.

In 1925 Austen Chamberlain expressed what was for many the hope of Locarno—that another Armageddon could be avoided by calming French nerves, by bringing Germany into the Concert of European Powers, and by adjusting the relations between Germany and the West through negotiation and with a minimum of coercion. The central hope of the Locarno era was that three men, meeting privately and talking candidly, could order the relations of their countries with little conflict and effect a lasting rapprochement. It has been implied, at times, that these hopes were realized and that the Locarno dream came true. Stresemann, Briand, and Chamberlain have been depicted as men who got along together exceptionally well, who sat down together, and through the exercise of generosity, or at least understanding, came to amicable agreements on a wide variety of significant issues, and eventually came to a meeting of minds on the two most pressing issues of the day—military occupation and reparation. During the Locarno era, it is believed, disputes were settled, and they were settled by means of personal diplomacy in an atmosphere pervaded by goodwill.

Yet, in truth, the hopes on which the spirit of Locarno lived from 1925 to 1929 were only partially fulfilled. Four years of effort, though eventually productive of accomplishment, did not bring the three-power harmony aspired to in 1925: the Rhineland and reparation questions were resolved without the open confrontation which had earlier characterized the relations between the three powers, but French nerves were not calmed, and the German impulse toward *Freiheit, Aufstieg, und Wiedermacht* did not abate. Germany, England, and France were to come to Armageddon again, and the events of the decade of the 1930's led them there, but the difficulty of a rapprochement through goodwill when objectives differ was evident long before. It was visible in the disharmony and the absence of candor with which the final Rhineland-reparation negotiations were conducted.

The Locarno era expected much of its statesmen when it demanded that Germany and the West be reconciled and that political negotiations be conducted with a minimum of threat, conflict, and confrontation. To have met this demand, the problems considered for settlement during the Locarno era would not merely have had to be resolved, but solved fully, elegantly, and with a great show of goodwill. The men of Locarno recognized the popular appeal of elegant solutions, and the shrewdest among them—Stresemann, Schubert, and Berthelot—at times tried to turn this demand to advantage. The elegant solution, it was argued, could be achieved only if the other side made the necessary "magnanimous gesture" or "generous concession."[43] As proposed by Berlin, France would evacuate the Rhineland, perhaps return the Saar, and rectify other limitations on German sovereignty. At the same time, Paris would overlook matters of detail, minor instances of German noncompliance with the Treary of Versailles, and not haggle for various substitute guarantees of financial compensation. In return France would receive from Berlin a rich reward of intangibles: the forces of reason and peace within Germany would be strengthened; the German people and their leaders would abandon resentments and aggressive sentiments against the West; a new "political psychology" would come into being. There was in the Thoiry conversation something of the magnanimous gesture, and it was certainly reflected in Stresemann's pleas for evacuation without compensation in 1928-29.

The magnanimous gesture was never made. Thoiry came to nothing, and there was no evacuation without compensation. From Locarno to The Hague, French concessions came after a period of tough bargaining, with some ill will, and only after the Germans had put up tangible *quid pro quo*—*de facto* disarmament in 1925-26 and a long-term schedule of reparation payments in 1929.[44] The Locarno era was an age of grudging concessions and agreements inspired by no principle higher than *do ut des*. The men of Locarno accepted this inelegance, for it suited the character of their statesmanship. Stresemann, Briand, Chamberlain, and Henderson all had a highly developed sense of what was possible, and how in practice it could be attained. If they had illusions or grand designs, they did not share the same ones.

What the Locarnites did hold in common was a preference for a certain procedure which might be called the Locarno diplo-

---

[43] On the magnanimous gesture in Locarno diplomacy see René Albrecht-Carrié, *France, Europe and the Two World Wars*, Geneva, 1960, pp. 170, 178.

[44] The evacuation of Cologne and the withdrawal of military control have at times been interpreted as examples of French generosity or leniency under the influence of the spirit of Locarno: Hans W. Gatzke, *Stresemann and the Rearmament of Germany*, Baltimore, 1954, pp. 46, 65; Thimme, *Gustav Stresemann*, p. 111.

matic method. They held periodic, informal foreign ministers' conferences at which they consulted each other prior to taking action. There was a consensus among them that the differences among European nations should be worked out as were the differences among factions of a parliamentary party—patiently, quietly, away from public view, by means of compromises arranged in hotel rooms. There was among them a brotherhood of foreign ministers; they frequently appealed to each other for this or that concession; otherwise, they and their government would fall from power. Each member of the Locarno Triplice hoped for agreement with the others, and to gain this, they were willing to protect each other from political defeat by avoiding embarrassing unilateral action. To the extent that they conformed to the practice of prior consultation, the men of Locarno were "good Europeans." To be a good European during the Locarno era did not mean that one was willing to diminish the sovereignty of one's nation state; it meant that one did not take unilateral action. One went to Geneva four times a year and there consulted with the other members of the Council of Europe and attempted to act in concert with them.

The procedures of the Locarno diplomatic method were usually, but not always, followed. Prior consultation is a practice which benefits a *status quo* power; Briand, therefore, generally followed the procedure, although he departed from it when dealing with evacuation dates at The Hague, and it enabled him to conduct a tough defense of French treaty rights. Stresemann played by the rules, although he at times considered abandoning them, for defiance offered little prospect for success. In return for his loyalty he reaped some benefits but paid the price in fatigue, disappointment, and despair. Chamberlain kept the code; he consulted first, but he sometimes consulted his two partners separately rather than in concert. The most flagrant violation came with Snowden's demand for the revision of the Young plan.

Even when it was used, the Locarno diplomatic method did not always contribute to the harmonious adjustment of relations. Informal and private meetings of two or three foreign ministers should contribute to clarification and agreement, but in fact the history of the meetings was in large part a history of misunderstanding. The Locarnites disagreed as to what had been decided

385

at Locarno in 1925, at Thoiry in 1926, at Geneva in September 1928, at Lugano in December, and at Madrid in June 1929.[45] They subsequently argued over their different interpretations, sometimes bitterly, and sometimes in public. Briand threatened to discontinue the meetings, and Stresemann responded with public charges of "hypocrisy" and private accusations of duplicity and "finessing." All this casts some doubt on how much Stresemann and Briand were willing to understand each other and on the efficacy of the Locarnite meetings. Above all, the persistent strain among members of the Locarno Triplice indicates the incompatibility of the policy objectives of Stresemann, Briand, and Chamberlain. Agreement as to procedure did not alter the basic incompatibility of French, English, and German policy, and this limited the prospect for the realization of the exaggerated hopes of 1925.

It was believed at the time, and has been maintained since, that the Locarno diplomatic method resolved the problems which the pre-Locarno era only aggravated. Simply put: what was accomplished during the Locarno era was accomplished by meetings of the Big Three. This is not entirely true. The major achievement of the period, the settlement of 1929, was not something which can be attributed simply to personal diplomacy conducted in an atmosphere of goodwill. The Young plan, the condition of German freedom from military occupation, was determined by finance ministers and a committee of financial experts over whom Stresemann, Briand, Chamberlain, and Henderson had less than full control. When at last the foreign ministers came to discuss evacuation at The Hague, their deliberations were less than candid and short of amicable. Little goodwill accompanied the conclusion of negotiations; the finance ministers haggled over a few marks of reparation; the foreign ministers argued over a few months of occupation. Years of hope and effort culminated in an agreement which was minimal and grudging on all sides, and which none embraced with enthusiasm. By the end of the Locarno era, there was little more consensus than there had been at the beginning. Europe's Locarno honeymoon did not last throughout the decade, only to come to an end with the events which followed the death of Stresemann and the Wall Street crash. Relations were strained long before October 1929.

[45] See my "The Conduct of Locarno Diplomacy," *Review of Politics*, 34 (1972).

386

From his years of discussions with Briand, Stresemann became aware that the spirit of Locarno was not facilitating agreement between the two of them. For tactical reasons, he began to threaten Briand and Chamberlain with the possible demise of Locarno shortly after proposing the treaty, but it was not until late 1928 that he realized the seriousness of the event he had been forecasting. Perhaps he came to realize that the game was nearer the end than the beginning, and that he had not, and would not, achieve the goals he had earlier set for German policy. In November 1928, when it became apparent that the reparation settlement would be more expensive than he expected, he sentimentally compared himself to Ibsen's Nora, always hoping for a change for the better, and always being disappointed. In the spring of 1929, Stresemann's despair deepened further: while the financial experts carefully scheduled German obligations far into the future, Briand continued to postpone the long-promised discussion of the end of occupation and did so with no effective resistance from Chamberlain. Stresemann had clearly failed in his effort to end occupation simply in return for a German signature on the Locarno Treaty, and he began to describe his policy and his career as things of the past. He spoke bitterly of what he characterized as the shortsighted French policy of prolonging occupation in order to extract larger reparation payments. This policy, he stated, had led sections of the German electorate to repudiate the Locarno policy. And he threatened to join them. He would publicly proclaim that he had been deceived as to the intentions of Briand, and even more as to those of Chamberlain; Locarno, which had once held the promise of being the beginning of a new era, was dead.

It is not so easy to ascertain whether Briand was equally aware of the decline of the spirit of Locarno and equally discouraged by it. What is apparent is that as the years passed, Briand placed less confidence in "atmosphere," "goodwill," and verbal promises from Stresemann. Where Briand was willing to evacuate Cologne in order to encourage the Germans toward further disarmament in 1925, later he would not withdraw the French Army of the Rhine on Stresemann's assurance that Germany would continue to pay reparations in the future as had been done since 1924. Instead, he demanded that there be a new and final settlement of the reparation bill—a settlement which would allow the French to collect reparation in advance of the scheduled rate of payment. Paris showed little confidence that the evacuation of Cologne and Mainz would lead the Germans to further fulfillment.

One reason Briand insisted on binding guarantees rather than verbal assurances was that he realized that Stresemann would not always be around to honor the promises. In February 1928, Briand reminded Stresemann that neither of them was immortal and that one day a member of the right wing of the German Nationalist Party might become German Foreign Minister. Then, what good would trust placed in Stresemann do France? After Stresemann had his stroke in the summer of 1928, Briand was tactful enough not to remind him of his mortality, but at each of their meetings, as Stresemann appeared to be growing increasingly weak, the transitory nature of their relationship, and of the Franco-German rapprochement that rested on it, could not have been far from Briand's mind. In addition, Briand did not always find the methods of Locarno diplomacy suited to the requirements of French policy. At the informal meetings Briand often found the pressure of German revisionism to be so strong that he could not deal with it in the casual style most natural to him. He found it necessary to delay discussion, to claim that Stresemann had misinterpreted previous discussions, to threaten to discontinue the summit conferences, and even to resort to concealing his intentions.

Briand, like Stresemann and Chamberlain, was a victim of the fundamental disjunction of the Locarno era. On the one hand, the three men were goodwilled and well intentioned; they hoped to come to a lasting peace by negotiating compromise settlements. They concurred that men of reason, conversing periodically and informally, could promote such settlements. Such common predispositions facilitated communication, and the three even came to feel a certain personal affection for each other. On the other hand, each man accepted without question the competitive nation state system into which he had been born in the nineteenth century, and each took upon himself the task of defending against the others the interests of his nation as they had been defined during the decade of conflict which had preceded Locarno. Having done so, their hopes, their camaraderie, and their good intentions could not efface the antagonism which existed between Germany and the West between the wars.

Bibliography

I. *Government Documents—Unpublished*

7. Deutsche Botschaft in London
   Geheim   K2090
8. Referat Deutschland
   Reichstagswahlen, Mai 1928   L1722
9. Handakten
   Dirksen
   Geheimsachen   L689
   Locarno   5462
   Polen, Rheinlandräumung   5462
   Gaus
   Aufzeichnungen Staatssekretär von Schubert   3689
   Köpke   5138
   Chronologische Aufzeichnungen von Köpke,
       Staatssekretär, Reichsminister
   Material über den Zusammenhang zwischen
       Rheinlandräumung, Reparation, und interalliierten
       Schulden
   Raümung und Reparation
   Rheinlandräumung
   Vorbereitung zur Regierungskonferenz im Haag
   Konferenz im Haag 1929 betreffend Rheinlandräumung:
       Politische Kommission
   Konferenz im Haag 1929 über Youngplan: Finanzielle
       Kommission
   Material zur Regierungskonferenz im Haag 1929 über
       Youngplan und Reparationsaktionen
   Regierungskonferenz im Haag 1929 über Youngplan und
       Reparationsaktionen
   Englisch-französische Marineabkommen

Records of the German Foreign Ministry (not filmed, Bonn)
   Abteilung II—Besetzte Gebiete
       Räumung des besetzten Rheinlandes
       Handakten Friedberg
   Handakten Ritter
       Reparation
           Schriftwechsel zwischen Reichskanzler und
               Reichsbankpräsident Schacht
           Verhandlungen in Genf

Mobilisierung der Eisenbahn-Obligationen
Thoiry; Eisenbahn-Obligationen

Bavarian State Archives, Munich

State Archives, Coblenz

GREAT BRITAIN (Public Record Office)
Minutes of the Cabinet (Cab 23)
Minutes of the Committee of Imperial Defense (Cab 2)
Records of the Foreign Office: General Correspondence,
Confidential Print, and Archives of Conferences

UNITED STATES

Decimal files of the Department of State (National Archives)

II. *Government Publications*

Allied Powers. Reparation Commission. Official Documents. *Reports of the Agent General for Reparation Payments*. Berlin, 1925-30.

Belgium. Ministère des affairs étrangères. *Documents diplomatiques belges, 1920-1940*. Brussels, 1964-66.

France. Assemblée nationale. *Journal officiel. Débats parlementaires. Chambre des députés.*

————. Assemblée nationale. *Journal officiel. Débats parlementaires. Sénat.*

Germany. Auswärtiges Amt. *Akten zur deutschen auswärtigen Politik, 1918-1945*. Bonn, 1949—.

Germany. Reichskanzlei. *Akten der Reichskanzlei; Weimarer Republik*. Boppard, 1968—.

————. Reichstag. *Verhandlungen des Reichstags.*

Germany (Deutsche Demokratische Republik). Ministerium für auswärtige Angelegenheiten. *Locarno-Konferenz 1925; eine Dokumentensammlung*. Berlin, 1962.

Great Britain. Foreign Office. *Documents on British Foreign Policy, 1919-1939*. London, 1946—.

————. Papers by Command.

Statement on behalf of His Majesty's Government by the Rt. Hon. Austen Chamberlain, M. P., to the Council of the

394

League of Nations, Geneva, March 12, 1935. Cmd. 2368 (1925).

Collective Note of the Allied Powers Presented to the German Government on June 4, 1925, in Regard to the Fulfillment of the Obligations of the Treaty of Versailles with Regard to Disarmanent. Cmd. 2429 (1925).

Papers Respecting the Proposals for a Pact of Security Made by the German Government on February 9, 1925. Cmd. 2435 (1925).

Reply of the German Government to the Note Handed to Herr Stresemann by the French Ambassador at Berlin on June 16, 1925, Respecting the Proposals for a Pact of Security. Cmd. 2468 (1925).

Correspondence between the Ambassadors' Conference and the German Ambassador at Paris Respecting German Disarmament, Evacuation of Cologne Zone and Modifications in the Rhineland Régime, Paris, October-November, 1925. Cmd. 2527 (1925).

Papers Regarding the Limitation of Naval Armaments. Cmd. 3211 (1928).

Protocol with Annexes Approved at the Plenary Session of The Hague Conference, August 31, 1929. Cmd. 3392 (1929).

International Agreement on the Evacuation of the Rhineland Territory, The Hague, August 30, 1929. Cmd. 3417 (1929).

Agreements Concluded at The Hague Conference, January 1930. Cmd. 3484 (1930).

————. *Parliamentary Debates. House of Commons.*

————. *Parliamentary Debates. House of Lords.*

United States. Department of State. *Papers Relating to the Foreign Relations of the United States.* Washington.

III. *Private Papers—Unpublished*

Arthur (Lord) Balfour (British Museum)

Robert (Lord) Cecil (British Museum)

Austen Chamberlain (University of Birmingham)

Stuart Crocker (Library of Congress)

Edgar (Lord) D'Abernon (British Museum)

Hugh Dalton (British Library of Political and Economic Science)

Paul Hymans (Belgian Royal Archives)
Philip Kerr (Scottish Record Office)
Erich Koch-Weser (Federal Archives, Coblenz)
Thomas Lamont (Baker Library, Harvard)
David Lloyd George (Beaverbrook Library)
Gilbert Murray (Bodleian Library)
Horace Rumbold (Oxford)
James Edward (Lord) Salisbury (Hatfield House)
Max von Stockhausen (Federal Archives, Coblenz)
Gustav Stresemann (National Archives)
Owen D. Young (Van Hornesville, New York)

IV. *Contemporary Points of View*

Angell, James W. *The Recovery of Germany.* New Haven, 1929.

Chamberlain, Austen. "Great Britain as a European Power," *International Affairs,* 9 (1930), pp. 180-88.

———. *Peace in Our Time; Addresses on Europe and the Empire.* London, 1928.

Dalton, Hugh. "British Foreign Policy, 1929-31," *Political Quarterly,* 2 (1931), pp. 485-505.

———. *Towards the Peace of Nations; a Study in International Politics.* London, 1928.

Debeney, Marie-Eugène. "Armée nationale ou armée de métier?", *Revue des deux mondes* (15 September 1929), pp. 241-76.

———. *Le Réarmement allemand.* Paris, 1933.

———. *Sur la sécureté militaire de la France.* Paris, 1930.

Anon. (Frederick Eccard). "L'irrédentisme allemand et l'Alsace-Lorraine," *Revue hebdomadaire* (11 June 1927), pp. 121-60.

Anon. (Ferdinand Foch). "Un crime de lèse-patrie; l'évacuation anticipée," *Revue de France* (1 November 1926), pp. 5-11.

Hoetzsch, Otto. *Germany's Domestic and Foreign Policies.* New Haven, 1929.

Kaas, Ludwig. "Zur völkerrechtlichen Sonderstellung der Rheinlande nach der Räumung," *Europäische Gespräche: Hamburger Monatshefte für auswärtige Politik* (May 1929), pp. 222-31.

Keynes, J. M. "The Dawes Scheme and the German Loan," *Nation and Athenaeum* (4 October 1924), pp. 7-9.

———. "The Experts' Reports," *Nation and Athenaeum* (12 and 19 April 1924), pp. 40-41, 76-77.

———. "The German Transfer Problem" (with criticism and discussion), *Economic Journal,* 39 (1929), pp. 1-7, 172-82, 388-408.

———. "The Progress of Reparations," *Nation and Athenaeum* (16 July 1927), pp. 505-506.

———. "The Report of the Young Committee," *Nation and Athenaeum* (15 June 1929), pp. 359-61.

Koch-Weser, Erich. *Deutschlands Aussenpolitik in der Nachkriegszeit, 1919-1929.* Berlin, 1929.

Lamont, Thomas W. "The Final Reparations Settlement," *Foreign Affairs,* 8 (1930), pp. 336-63.

Mordacq, J.-J. Henri. "L'évacuation anticipée de la Rhénanie," *Revue des deux mondes* (15 June 1929), pp. 761-75.

———. *L'évacuation de la Rhénanie?* Paris, 1928.

———. *La mentalité allemande; cinq ans de commandement sur le Rhin.* Paris, 1926.

Moulton, Harold G. *The Reparation Plan.* New York, 1924.

——— and Leo Pasvolsky. *War Debts and World Prosperity.* Washington, D.C., 1932.

———. *World War Debt Settlements.* New York, 1926.

Myers, Denys P. *The Reparation Settlement, 1930.* Boston, 1930.

Oncken, Hermann, Hermann Müller *et al. Zehn Jahre deutsche Geschichte, 1918-1928.* Berlin, 1928.

d'Ormesson, Wladimir. *La Confiance en l'Allemagne?* Paris, 1928.

Royal Institute of International Affairs. *Survey of International Affairs.* London, 1920/23—.

Salter, Arthur. *Recovery; the Second Effort.* London, 1932.

Schacht, Hjalmar. *Das Ende der Reparationen.* Oldenburg, 1931. (Trans. *The End of Reparations.* New York, 1931.)

Schnee, Heinrich *et al. Zehn Jahre Versailles.* Berlin, 1929-30.

Seeckt, Hans von. *Gedanken eines Soldaten.* Berlin, 1929.

Tardieu, André. *The Truth About the Treaty.* Indianapolis, 1921.

Tirard, Paul. *La France sur le Rhin; douze années d'occupation rhénane.* Paris, 1930.

Wachendorf-Berlin, Karl. *Zehn Jahre Fremdherrschaft am deutschen Rhein; eine Geschichte der Rheinlandbesetzung von 1918-1928.* Berlin, 1928.

Wheeler-Bennett, J. W. and Hugh Latimer. *Information on the Reparation Settlement; Being the Background and the History of the Young Plan and The Hague Agreements 1929-1930.* London, 1930.

Wheeler-Bennett, J. W. *The Wreck of Reparations; Being the Political Background of the Laussane Agreement, 1932.* New York, 1933.

Williams, Benjamin H. *Economic Foreign Policy of the United States.* New York, 1929.

Wolff, Richard (ed.), *Unser Recht auf Räumung; Stimmen führender Politiker und Kundgebungen der deutschen Öffentlichkeit zur Rheinlandräumung.* Berlin, 1927.

V. Published Papers, Diaries, Memoirs, and Biographical Works

Becker, Josef. "Heinrich Köhler, 1878-1949; Lebensbild eines badischen Politikers; mit einem dokumentarischen Anhang aus dem Nachlass," *Zeitschrift für die Geschichte des Oberrheins,* 110 (1962), pp. 417-90.

Bonn, Moritz J. *Wandering Scholar.* New York, 1948.

Bourget, Pierre. *Un certain Philippe Pétain.* Paris, 1966.

Boyle, Andrew. *Montagu Norman; a Biography.* London, 1967.

Bréal, August. *Philippe Berthelot.* Paris, 1937.

Bugnet, Charles. *Foch Speaks.* New York, 1929.

Chamberlain, Austen. *Down the Years.* London, 1935.

Chandler, Lester V. *Benjamin Strong, Central Banker.* Washington, D.C., 1958.

Chastenet, Jacques. *Raymond Poincaré.* Paris, 1948.

Clay, Henry. *Lord Norman.* London, 1957.

Cross, Colin. *Philip Snowden.* London, 1966.

Curtius, Julius. *Sechs Jahre Minister der Deutschen Republik.* Heidelberg, 1948.

———. *Die Young-Plan; Entstellung und Wahrheit.* Stuttgart, 1950.

D'Abernon, (Lord) Edgar. *An Ambassador of Peace; Pages from the Diary of Viscount D'Abernon.* 3 vols. London, 1929-30.

———. *Portraits and Appreciations.* London, 1931.

Dalton, Hugh. *Memoirs.* 3 vols. London, 1953-62.

Dawes, Charles G. *Journal as Ambassador to Great Britain.* New York, 1939.

———. *Notes as Vice President, 1928-1929.* Boston, 1935.

Dirksen, Herbert von. *Moscow, Tokyo, London; Twenty Years of German Foreign Policy.* Norman, Okla., 1952.

Dorpalen, Andreas. *Hindenburg and the Weimar Republic.* Princeton, 1964.

Eden, Anthony. *Facing the Dictators; the Memoirs of Anthony Eden, Earl of Avon.* Boston, 1962.

Einzig, Paul. *Montagu Norman; a Study in Financial Statesmanship.* London, 1932.

Francis-Williams, Edward. *A Pattern of Rulers.* London, 1965.

Geigenmüller, Ernst. *Briand; Tragik des grossen Europäers.* Bonn, 1959.

Gessler, Otto. *Reichswehrpolitik in der Weimarer Zeit.* Stuttgart, 1958.

Goerlitz, Walter. *Stresemann.* Heidelberg, 1947.

Gooch, G. P. *Under Six Reigns.* London, 1958.

Grigg, Percy James. *Prejudice and Judgement.* London, 1948.

Hamilton, Mary Agnes. *Arthur Henderson.* London, 1938.

————. *Remembering My Good Friends.* London, 1944.

Herriot, Edouard. *Jadis.* 2 vols. Paris, 1952.

Heuss, Theodor. *Erinnerungen, 1905-1933.* Tübingen, 1963.

Hirsch, Felix. *Gustav Stresemann; Patriot und Europäer.* Göttingen, 1964.

Hymans, Paul. *Mémoires.* 2 vols. Brussels, 1958.

Jones, John Henry. *Josiah Stamp, Public Servant; the Life of the First Baron Stamp of Shortlands.* London, 1964.

Kelen, Emery. *Peace in Their Time; Men Who Led Us in and out of War, 1914-1945.* New York, 1963.

Köhler, Heinrich. *Lebenserinnerungen des Politikers und Staatsmannes, 1878-1949.* Stuttgart, 1964.

Laroche, Jules. *Au Quai d'Orsay avec Briand et Poincaré, 1913-1926.* Paris, 1957.

Léger, Alexis Saint Léger. *Briand.* New York, 1943.

Leith-Ross, Frederick. *Money Talks; Fifty Years of International Finance.* London, 1968.

Liddell Hart, Basil. *The Memoirs of Captain Liddell Hart.* 2 vols. London, 1965-66.

Lockhart, R. H. Bruce. *Friends, Foes, and Foreigners.* London, 1957.

————. *Retreat from Glory.* New York, 1934.

Ludwig, Emile. *Nine Sketched from Life.* New York, 1934.

Luther, Hans. *Politik ohne Parti; Erinnerungen.* Stuttgart, 1960.

McMillan, Harold. *Winds of Change, 1914-1939.* New York, 1966.

Marx, Wilhelm. *Der Nachlass des Reichskanzlers Wilhelm Marx.* 4 vols. Cologne, 1968.

Mayer, Eugen. *Skizzen aus dem Leben der Weimarer Republik; Berliner Erinnerungen.* Berlin, 1962.

Meier-Welcker, Hans. *Seeckt.* Frankfurt, 1967.

Meissner, Otto. *Staatssekretär unter Ebert, Hindenburg, Hitler; der Schicksalsweg der deutschen Volkes von 1918-1945, wie ich ihn erlebte.* Hamburg, 1950.

Middlemas, Keith and John Barnes. *Baldwin; a Biography.* London, 1969.

Miquel, Pierre. *Poincaré.* Paris, 1961.

Mordacq, Jean-Jules Henri. *Clemenceau au soir de sa vie, 1920-1929.* 2 vols. Paris, 1933.

Moreau, Emile. *Souvenirs d'un gouverneur de la Banque de France; histoire de la stabilisation du franc (1926-1928).* Paris, 1954.

Nadolny, Rudolf. *Mein Beitrag.* Wiesbaden, 1955.

Nicolson, Harold. *King George the Fifth; His Life and Reign.* London, 1952.

de Pretti de la Rocca, Emmanuel. "Briand et Poincaré (Souvenirs)," *Revue de Paris,* 43 année, 4 (1936), pp. 767-88.

Petrie, Charles. *The Life and Letters of the Rt. Hon. Sir Austen Chamberlain.* 2 vols. London, 1939-40.

Prittwitz und Gaffron, Friedrich Wilhelm von. *Zwischen Petersburg und Washington; ein Diplomatenleben.* Munich, 1952.

Rabenau, Friedrich. *Seeckt; aus seinem Leben, 1918-1936.* Leipzig, 1940.

Recouly, Raymond. *Foch; My Conversations with the Marshal.* New York, 1929.

Rheinbaden, Werner Freiherr von. *Viermal Deutschland; aus dem Erleben eines Seemannes, Diplomaten, Politikers, 1895-1954.* Berlin, 1954.

Riesser, Hans. *Von Versailles zur UNO; aus den Erinnerungen eines Diplomaten.* Bonn, 1962.

Ruge, Wolfgang. *Stresemann; ein Lebensbild.* Berlin, 1965.

Ryan, Stephen. *Pétain the Soldier.* South Brunswick, N.J., 1969.

Salter, Arthur. *Memoirs of a Public Servant.* London, 1961.

――――. *Personality in Politics; Studies of Contemporary Statesmen.* London, 1942.

Schacht, Hjalmar. *Account Settled.* London, 1949.

――――. *My First Seventy-six Years; the Autobiography of Hjalmar Schacht.* London, 1955.

400

Scheidel, Joseph (ed.). *Gustav Stresemann; Festschrift zur Wieder-errichtung des Stresemann-Ehrenmals in Mainz am 16. Oktober 1960.* Mainz, 1960.

Schmidt, Paul. *Statist auf Diplomatischer Bühne 1923-45; Erlebnisse des Chefdolmetschers im auswärtigen Amt mit den Staatsmännern Europas.* Bonn, 1949.

Schorr, Helmut. *Adam Stegerwald; Gewerkschaftler und Politiker der ersten deutschen Republik; ein Beitrag zur Geschichte der christlich-sozialen Bewegung in Deutschland.* Recklinghausen, 1966.

Schreiber, Georg. *Zwischen Demokratie und Diktatur; Persönliche Erinnerungen an die Politik und Kultur des Reiches (1919 bis 1944).* Münster, 1949.

Selby, Walford. *Diplomatic Twilight, 1930-1940.* London, 1953.

Sforza, Carlo. *Makers of Modern Europe; Portraits and Personal Impressions and Recollections.* Indianapolis, 1930.

Snowden, Philip. *An Autobiography.* 2 vols. London, 1934.

Soulié, Michel. *La vie politique d'Edouard Herriot.* Paris, 1962.

Stern-Rubarth, Edgar. *Three Men Tried . . . Austen Chamberlain, Stresemann, Briand and their Fight for a New Europe; a Personal Memoir.* London, 1939.

Stockhausen, Max von. *Sechs Jahre Reichskanzlei; von Rapallo bis Locarno; Erinnerungen und Tagebuchnotizen, 1922-1927.* Bonn, 1954.

Stresemann, Gustav. *Vermächtnis; der Nachlass in Drei Bänden.* 3 vols. Berlin, 1932-33.

Stroomann, Gerhard. *Aus meinem roten Notizbuch; ein Leben als Artz auf Bühlerhöhe.* Frankfurt, 1957, 1960.

Suarez, Georges. *Briand; sa vie—son oeuvre avec son journal et de nombreux documents inédits.* 6 vols. Paris, 1938-52.

Tabouis, Geneviève. *They Called Me Cassandra.* New York, 1942.

————. *Vingt ans de "suspense" diplomatique.* Paris, 1958.

Temperley, A. C. *The Whispering Gallery of Europe.* London, 1938.

Thimme, Annelise. *Gustav Stresemann; eine politische Biographie zur Geschichte der Weimarer Republik.* Hannover, 1957.

————. "Gustav Stresemann; Legende und Wirklichkeit," *Historische Zeitschrift,* 181 (1956), pp. 287-338.

van Zuylen, Pierre. *Les mains libres; politique extérieure de la belgique, 1914-40.* Brussels, 1950.

Vallentin-Luchaire, Antonina. *Stresemann.* New York, 1931.

Weygand, Maxime. *Mémoires.* 3 vols. Paris, 1950-57.

Zechlin, Walter. *Pressechef bei Ebert, Hindenburg, und Kopf; Erlebnisse eines Pressechefs und Diplomaten.* Hannover, 1956.

Ziebura, Gilbert. *Leon Blum; Theorie und Praxis einer sozialistischen Politik.* Berlin, 1963—.

VI. *Histories, Treatises, and Special Studies*

Albrecht-Carrié, René. *France, Europe and the Two World Wars.* Geneva, 1960.

Bariéty, Jacques. "Der Versuch einer europäischen Befriedung; von Locarno bis Thoiry," in *Locarno und die Weltpolitik, 1924-1932,* pp. 32-44. Helmut Rössler and Erwin Hölzle (eds.). Göttingen, 1969.

Beck, Reinhart. *Die Geschichte der Weimarer Republik im Spiegel der sowjetzonalen Geschichtsschreibung.* Bonn, 1965.

Bennett, Edward W. *Germany and the Diplomacy of the Financial Crisis, 1931.* Cambridge, Mass., 1962.

Binion, Rudolph. *Defeated Leaders; the Political Fate of Caillaux, Jouvenel, and Tardieu.* New York, 1960.

Bodensieck, Heinrich. "Weimarer Republik und deutschfranzösische Beziehungen," *Geschichte im Wissenschaft und Unterricht,* 13 (1962), pp. 368-70.

Bonnefous, Edouard. *Histoire politique de la troisième république.* 5 vols. Paris, 1956-62.

Bracher, Karl Dietrich. *Die Auflösung der Weimarer Republik; eine Studie zum Problem des Machtverfalls in der Demokratie.* (2nd ed.), Stuttgart, 1957.

————, Wolfgang Sauer, and Gerhard Schulz. *Die nationalsozialistische Machtergreifung; Studien zur Errichtung des totalitären Herrschaftssystems in Deutschland, 1933/34.* Cologne, 1960.

Brandes, Joseph. *Herbert Hoover and Economic Diplomacy; Department of Commerce Policy, 1921-1928.* Pittsburgh, 1962.

Bretton, Henry L. *Stresemann and the Revision of Versailles; a Fight for Reason.* Stanford, 1953.

Breuning, Eleanor. "Germany between East and West, 1921-1926." Unpublished D. Phil. thesis, Oxford, 1966.

Brunschwig, Henri. "Die historischen Generationen in Frankreich und Deutschland," *Vierteljahreshefte für Zeitgeschichte,* 2 (1954), pp. 373-85.

Bry, Gerhard. *Wages in Germany, 1871-1945.* Princeton, 1960.

Campbell, Fenton. "Czechoslovak-German Relations during the Weimar Republic, 1918-1933." Unpublished doctoral dissertation, Yale, 1967.

Carlton, David. "The Anglo-French Compromise on Arms Limitation, 1928," *Journal of British Studies,* 8 (1969), pp. 141-62.

——. "Great Britain and the League Council Crisis of 1926," *Historical Journal,* 11 (1968), pp. 354-64.

——. *MacDonald versus Henderson; the Foreign Policy of the Second Labour Government.* London, 1970.

Carr, E. H. *A History of Soviet Russia.* 7 vols. London, 1950—.

Carsten, F. L. *The Reichswehr and Politics, 1918-1933.* Oxford, 1966.

——. "The Reichswehr and the Red Army, 1920-33," *Survey,* 44/45 (1962), pp. 114-32.

Challener, Richard D. *French Theory of the Nation in Arms, 1866-1939.* New York, 1955.

Chanady, Attila. "The Disintegration of the German National Peoples' Party, 1924-1930," *Journal of Modern History,* 39 (1967), pp. 65-91.

Chastenet, Jacques. *Histoire de la troisième république.* 7 vols. Paris, 1952-63.

Clarke, Stephen V. O. *Central Bank Cooperation, 1924-1931.* New York, 1967.

Cline, Catherine. *Recruits to Labour; the British Labour Party, 1914-1931.* Syracuse, N.Y., 1963.

Connell, John (pseud.). *The "Office"; a Study of British Foreign Policy and its Makers, 1919-1951.* London, 1958.

Conze, Werner. "Die Krise des Parteienstaates in Deutschland, 1929/30," *Historische Zeitschrift,* 178 (1954), pp. 47-83.

Cormier, Thomas W. "German Foreign Policy, 1923-1926; the Illusion of Western versus Eastern Orientation." Unpublished doctoral dissertation, American University, 1968.

Craig, Gordon A. *From Bismarck to Adenauer; Aspects of German Statecraft.* New York, 1958, 1965.

—— and Felix Gilbert (eds.). *The Diplomats, 1919-1939.* Princeton, 1953.

Druc, Henech. *Die Stellung der deutschen Tagespresse und Wirtschaftswissenschaft zum Youngplan.* Basel, 1947.

Duroselle, Jean-Baptiste. *Histoire diplomatique de 1919 à nos jours.* Paris, 1962.

Dyck, Harvey L. "German-Soviet Relations and the Anglo-Soviet Break, 1927," *Slavic Review,* 25 (1966), pp. 67-83.

———. *Weimar Germany and Soviet Russia, 1926-1933; a Study in Diplomatic Instability.* London, 1966.

Einzig, Paul. *Behind the Scenes of International Finance.* London, 1932.

———. *The Fight for Financial Supremacy.* London, 1931.

Ellis, Lewis Ethan. *Frank B. Kellogg and American Foreign Relations, 1925-1929.* New Brunswick, N.J., 1961.

Erdmann, Karl D. *Adenauer in der Rheinlandpolitik nach dem ersten Weltkreig.* Stuttgart, 1966.

Eschenburg, Theodor. *Die improvisierte Demokratie; gesammelte Aufsätze sur Weimarer Republik.* Munich, 1963.

Eyck, Erich. *A History of the Weimar Republic.* 2 vols. Cambridge, Mass., 1962-63.

Feis, Herbert. *The Diplomacy of the Dollar; First Era, 1919-1932.* Baltimore, 1950.

Ferrell, Robert H. *American Diplomacy in the Great Depression; Hoover-Stimson Foreign Policy, 1929-1933.* New Haven, 1957.

———. *Peace in their Time; the Origins of the Kellogg-Briand Pact.* New Haven, 1952.

Fink, Carole K. "The Weimar Republic as the Defender of Minorities, 1919-1933; a Study of Germany's Minorities Diplomacy and the League of Nations System for the International Protection of Minorities." Unpublished doctoral dissertation, Yale, 1968.

Fischer, Wolfram. *Die wirtschaftspolitische Situation der Weimarer Republik.* Hannover, 1960.

Fohlen, Claude. *La France de l'entre-deux-guerres, 1917-1939.* Paris, 1966.

Fox, John P. "Britain and the Inter-Allied Military Commission of Control, 1925-26," *Journal of Contemporary History,* 4 (1969), pp. 143-64.

Frasure, Carl M. *British Policy on War Debts and Reparations.* Philadelphia, 1940.

Garthwol, Robert. "DNVP and European Reconciliation, 1924-

1928; a Study of the Conflict between Party Politics and Government Foreign Policy in Weimar Germany." Unpublished doctoral dissertation, Chicago, 1968.

Gasiorowski, Zygmunt. "Stresemann and Poland after Locarno," *Journal of Central European Affairs*, 18 (1958), pp. 292-317.

Gatzke, Hans W. "Gustav Stresemann; a Bibliographical Article," *Journal of Modern History*, 36 (1964), pp. 1-13.

————. *Stresemann and the Rearmament of Germany*. Baltimore, 1954.

————. "The Stresemann Papers," *Journal of Modern History*, 26 (1954), pp. 49-59.

Geigenmüller, Ernst. "Botschafter von Hoesch und die Räumungsfrage," *Historische Zeitschrift*, 200 (1965), pp. 606-20.

Gibson, Irving M. (pseud.). "Maginot and Liddell Hart; the Doctrine of Defense," in *Makers of Modern Strategy; Military Thought from Machiavelli to Hitler*, pp. 365-87. E. M. Earle (ed.). Princeton, 1943.

————. "The Maginot Line," *Journal of Modern History*, 17 (1945), pp. 130-46.

Gilbert, Martin. *The Roots of Appeasement*. London, 1966.

Göhring, Martin. *Bismarcks Erben, 1890-1945; Deutschlands Weg von Wilhelm II bis Adolf Hitler*. Wiesbaden, 1959.

Goguel-Nyegaard, François. *La politique des parties sous la IIIe république*. Paris, 1958.

Gordon, Michael R. *Conflict and Consensus in Labour's Foreign Policy, 1914-1965*. Stanford, 1969.

Gottwald, Robert. *Die deutsch-amerikanischen Beziehungen in der Ära Stresemann*. Berlin, 1965.

Grün, George A. "Locarno; Idea and Reality," *International Affairs*, 31 (1955), pp. 477-85.

Guillebaud, C. W. *The Economic Recovery of Germany; from 1933 to the Incorporation of Austria in March 1938*. London, 1939.

Harris, C.R.S. *Germany's Foreign Indebtedness*. London, 1935.

Harvey, Donald J. "French Concepts of Military Strategy, 1919-1939." Unpublished doctoral dissertation, Columbia, 1953.

Hirsch, Felix. "Stresemann and Adenauer; Two Great Leaders of German Democracy in Times of Crisis," in *Studies in Diplomatic History and Historiography in Honor of G. P. Gooch*, pp. 266-80. A. O. Sarkissian (ed.). London, 1961.

405

Höltje, Christian. *Die Weimarer Republik und das Ostlocarno-Problem, 1919-1934; Revision oder Guarantie der deutschen Ostgrenze von 1919.* Würtzburg, 1958.

Holborn, Hajo. *A History of Modern Germany, 1840-1945.* New York, 1969.

Horkenbach, Cuno (ed.). *Das Deutsche Reich von 1918 bis heute.* Berlin, 1930.

Johnson, Douglas. "Austen Chamberlain and the Locarno Agreements," *University of Birmingham Historical Journal,* 8 (1961), pp. 62-81.

Jordan, W. N. *Great Britain, France, and the German Problem, 1919-1939.* London, 1943.

Kimmich, Christoph. *The Free City; Danzig and German Foreign Policy, 1919-1934.* New Haven, 1968.

King, Jere C. *Foch versus Clemenceau; France and German Dismemberment, 1918-1919.* Cambridge, Mass., 1960.

Kochan, Lionel. *The Struggle for Germany, 1914-1945.* Edinburgh, 1963.

Korbel, Josef. *Poland between East and West: Soviet and German Diplomacy toward Poland, 1919-1933.* Princeton, 1963.

Knauss, Bernhard. "Politik ohne Waffen; Dargestellt an der Diplomatie Stresemanns," *Zeitschrift für Politik,* 10 (1963), pp. 249-56.

Kraehe, Enno. "Motives behind the Maginot Line," *Military Affairs,* 8 (1944), pp. 109-22.

Landes, David S. *The Unbound Prometheus; Technological Change and Industrial Development in Western Europe from 1750 to the Present.* Cambridge, 1969.

Lipgens, Walter. "Europäische Einigungsidee 1923-1930 und Briands Europaplan im Urteil der deutschen Akten," *Historische Zeitschrift,* 203 (1966), pp. 46-89, 316-63.

Lüke, Rolf. *Von der Stabilisierung zur Krise.* Zurich, 1958.

McElwee, William. *Britain's Locust Years, 1918-1940.* London, 1962.

Madden, J. T. *America's Experience as a Creditor Nation.* New York, 1937.

Marks, Sally. "Reparations Reconsidered; a Reminder," *Central European History,* 2 (1969), pp. 356-65.

Matthias, Erich and Rudolf Morsey (eds.). *Das Ende der Parteien 1933.* Düsseldorf, 1963.

Mayer, Arno J. *Politics and Diplomacy of Peacemaking; Contain-*

ment and Counter-Revolution at Versailles, 1918-1919. New York, 1967.

Medlicott, W. N. *Contemporary England, 1914-1964*. New York, 1967.

Milatz, Alfred. *Wähler und Wählen in der Weimarer Republik*. Bonn, 1965.

Miller, Kenneth E. *Socialism and Foreign Policy; Theory and Practice in Britain to 1931*. The Hague, 1967.

Morsey, Rudolf. *Die deutsche Zentrumspartei, 1917-1923*. Düsseldorf, 1966.

Mowat, Charles L. *Britain between the Wars, 1918-1940*. Chicago, 1955.

———— (ed.). *The Shifting Balance of World Powers, 1898-1945*. Vol. xii of *The New Cambridge Modern History*. Cambridge, 1957——.

Nelson, Harold I. *Land and Power; British and Allied Policy on Germany's Frontiers, 1916-1919*. London, 1963.

Newman, William J. *The Balance of Power in the Interwar Years, 1919-1939*. New York, 1968.

Northedge, F. S. *The Troubled Giant; Britain among the Great Powers, 1916-39*. New York, 1967.

d'Ormesson, Wladimir. *France*. London, 1939.

Pabst, Klaus. *Eupen-Malmedy in der belgischen Regierungs-und Parteienpolitik, 1914-1940*. Aachen, 1964.

Post, Gaines Jr. "German Foreign Policy and Military Planning; the Polish Question, 1924-1929." Unpublished doctoral dissertation, Stanford, 1969.

Quinn, Parle Elizabeth. "The Nationalist Socialist Attack on the Foreign Policies of the German Republic, 1919-1933." Unpublished doctoral dissertation, Stanford, 1948.

Rappard, W. E. *The Quest for Peace since the World War*. Cambridge, Mass., 1940.

Raymond, John (ed.). *The Baldwin Age*. London, 1960.

Renouvin, Pierre. "Les buts de guerre du gouvernement français (1914-1918)," *Revue historique* (1966), pp. 1-38.

————. *War and Aftermath, 1914-1929*. New York, 1968.

Rhodes, Benjamin D. "Reassessing 'Uncle Shylock'; the United States and the French War Debt, 1917-1929," *Journal of American History*, 55 (1969), pp. 787-803.

Rosenbaum, Kurt. *Community of Fate; German-Soviet Diplomatic Relations, 1922-1928*. Syracuse, N.Y., 1965.

Roskill, Stephen. *Naval Policy Between the Wars.* London, 1968—.

Rowe, E. A. "The British General Election of 1929." Unpublished B. Litt. thesis, Oxford, 1959.

Salewski, Michael. *Entwaffnung und Militärkontrolle in Deutschland, 1919-1927.* Munich, 1966.

Schinkel, Harald. *Entstehung und Zerfall der Regierung Luther.* Berlin, 1959.

Shepard, Carl E. "Germany and The Hague Conferences, 1929-30." Unpublished doctoral dissertation, Indiana University, 1964.

Schmidt, Royal J. *Versailles and the Ruhr; Seedbed of World War II.* The Hague, 1968.

Skidelsky, Robert. *Politicians and the Slump; the Labour Government of 1929-1931.* London, 1967.

Spenz, Jürgen. *Die diplomatische Vorgeschichte des Beitritts Deutschlands zum Völkerbund, 1924-1926; ein Beitrag zur Aussenpolitik der Weimarer Republik.* Göttingen, 1966.

Stambrook, F. G. " 'Das Kind'—Lord D'Abernon and the Origins of the Locarno Pact," *Central European History,* 1 (1968), pp. 233-63.

Stampfer, Friedrich. *Die Vierzehn Jahre der ersten Deutschen Republik.* Karlsbad, 1936.

Stern, Fritz. "Adenauer and a Crisis in Weimar Democracy," *Political Science Quarterly,* 73 (1958), pp. 1-27.

Stolper, Gustav. *The German Economy, 1870 to the Present.* New York, 1967.

Sturmer, Michael. *Koalition und Opposition in der Weimarer Republik, 1924-1928.* Düsseldorf, 1967.

Suval, Stanley. "The Anschluss Problem in the Stresemann Era (1923-1929)." Unpublished doctoral dissertation, University of North Carolina, 1964.

Taylor, A.J.P. *English History, 1914-1945.* New York, 1965.

———. *The Origins of the Second World War.* New York, 1961.

Thayer, Philip. "Locarno and Its Aftermath; a Study of the Foreign Policy of Aristide Briand and Gustav Stresemann, 1925-1928." Unpublished doctoral dissertation, University of North Carolina, 1956.

Thompson, Joe Allen. "British Convervatives and Collective Security, 1918-1928." Unpublished doctoral dissertation, Stanford, 1966.

Timm, Helga. *Die deutsche Sozialpolitik und der Bruch der grossen Koalition im März 1930*. Düsseldorf, 1952.

Tournoux, Paul-Emile. *Haut commandement, gouvernement et défense des frontières du nord et de l'est, 1919-1939*. Paris, 1960.

————. "Les origins de la ligne Maginot," *Revue d'histoire de la deuxième guerre mondiale*, 9 (1959), pp. 3-14.

Turner, Henry A. Jr. "Eine Rede Stresemanns über seine Locarnopolitik," *Vierteljahreshefte für Zeitgeschichte*, 19 (1967), pp. 412-36.

————. *Stresemann and the Politics of the Weimar Republic*. Princeton, 1963.

Ulam, Adam. *Expansion and Coexistence; the History of Soviet Foreign Policy, 1917-67*. New York, 1968.

Vietsch, Eberhard. *Arnold Rechberg und das Problem der politischen West-orientierung Deutschlands nach dem 1. Weltkrieg*. Coblenz, 1958.

Walters, Francis P. *A History of the League of Nations*. New York, 1960.

Wandycz, Piotr. *France and her Eastern Allies, 1919-1925; French-Czechoslovak-Polish Relations from the Paris Peace Conference to Locarno*. Minneapolis, 1962.

Watt, D. C. *Personalities and Policies; Studies in the Formation of British Foreign Policy in the Twentieth Century*. London, 1965.

Weill-Raynal, Etienne. *Les réparations allemandes et la France*. 3 vols. Paris, 1947-49.

Winkler, Henry. "The Emergence of a Labour Foreign Policy in Great Britain, 1918-1929," *Journal of Modern History*, 28 (1956), pp. 247-58.

Wolfe, Martin. *The French Franc between the Wars, 1919-1939*. New York, 1951.

Wolfers, Arnold. *Britain and France between Two Wars; Conflicting Strategies of Peace since Versailles*. New York, 1940.

Zenner, Maria. *Parteien und Politik im Saargebiet unter dem Völkerbundsregime, 1920-1935*. Saarbrücken, 1966.

Zimmermann, Ludwig. *Deutsche Aussenpolitik in der Ära der Weimarer Republik*. Göttingen, 1958.

————. *Studien zur Geschichte der Weimarer Republik*. Erlangen, 1956.

INDEX